The Beauty of Sport: a cross-disciplinary inquiry

BENJAMIN LOWE
Governors State University

PRENTICE-HALL, INC., Englewood Cliffs, New Jersey 07632

Library of Congress Cataloging in Publication Data

LOWE, BENJAMIN.
 The beauty of sport.

 Bibliography: p.
 1. Sports–Philosophy. 2. Sports in art.
3. Physical education and training—Philosophy.
I. Title.
GV706.L59   796'.01   76-28308
ISBN 0-13-066589-4

10 9 8 7 6 5 4 3 2 1

PRENTICE-HALL INTERNATIONAL, INC., *London*
PRENTICE-HALL OF AUSTRALIA PTY. LIMITED, *Sydney*
PRENTICE-HALL OF CANADA, LTD., *Toronto*
PRENTICE-HALL OF INDIA PRIVATE LIMITED, *New Delhi*
PRENTICE-HALL OF JAPAN, INC., *Tokyo*
PRENTICE-HALL OF SOUTHEAST ASIA PTE. LTD., *Singapore*
WHITEHALL BOOKS LIMITED, *Wellington, New Zealand*

To the unknown athlete

Contents

Foreword

Dr. Benjamin Lowe has written in a most timely manner and by well documented methods about the beauty of sport. He has accomplished well what he has set out to do: to point out "major avenues of inquiry" and to "place an emphasis on the questions that should be asked rather than the answers."

The writings provide a wealth of well selected, documentary evidence and background information in the inclusion of newly found and freshly used examples of statements, incidents, and art objects.

The author had his own purposes in writing the book. Those purposes grew out of his own well founded commitment to and his full information about the beauty of sport. A study of the materials presented can be thorough, meandering, or selective, but it will bring the knowledge and understanding which are frequently sought by participants, leaders, and spectators of modern sport.

The presentation is never contentious or argumentative. The author does not defend his points or positions but presents them and elaborates upon them. The reader may take issue with some of the ideas, but as a thinker about beauty and about sport and the beauty of sport, the reader finds encouragement to pursue thinking—to develop his own thoughts and standards for values and aesthetics rather than to attack the ideas of the author.

Interested, and idea-seeking readers will find material for thought, ideas which challenge, examples which illustrate, and questions which stimulate discussion. Individual questions or group discussions may be encouraged and challenged by the discussion and data. Even the disagreement of the reader or those who might be brought into class discussion groups will not destroy the value of the book's exposition but will, on the other hand, enhance its value.

Each person who directs sport for others or who participates may have some individual objectives and interpretations. As sport itself has so many manifestations, so many reasons for being, and so many millions of participants, the interpretations of the Beauty of Sport are innumerable. The presentations of this volume promote interpretation and encourage and allow for variations of thought and positive practices in the Beauty of Sport.

LEONA HOLBROOK

Preface

Social change moves very slowly. Nowhere is this more noticeable than in the change in social values. Yet, one of the trends to emerge out of the past "revolutionary" decade is reflected in the Department of State Bureau of Education and Cultural Affairs' demand for a new perspective on sport. The Bureau recommends that educators involved with sport on any level should begin to focus major attention on "the aesthetics of movement," concomitantly reducing the emphasis on competitive demands associated with victory and defeat.

This is not to say that competition *per se* is to be de-emphasized; rather it suggests that new values, values associated with beauty, should be attached to competition. *Excellence and beauty are closely related in sports, and excellence derives out of high-level competition regardless of who wins or who loses.*

Although it is only in the last ten years or so that educators and coaches have begun to study the aesthetic elements of sport through a new vision of body action, the German poet Schiller was counseling this perspective as long ago as the late eighteenth century, particularly in regard to the play of children, from which all sport grows. De Coubertin, the founder of the Modern Olympics, wrote an ode to the Olympic ideal in sport which states in the opening line:

O Sport, you are Beauty.

Such an accolade places sport on the level of one of man's greatest values —we all revere beauty, no matter what culture we come from.

The study of the beauty of sport must be based on knowledge drawn from a number of disciplines—anthropology, psychology, history, and sociology, among others. Sport is a social event, and it seems most likely that the social sciences will provide the most adequate sources for cross-disciplinary analysis. Yet, when we speak of beauty, whether it be "beauty as value" or "beauty as aesthetic response," we are obliged to inquire into the arts. The arts, too, are social events, but most typically, educated inquiry into the arts has been founded on the humanities, philosophy, liberal arts, creativity, and the like. Thus we come to a major difficulty in the presentation of this book, for no single person is educated sufficiently to deal adequately with a comprehensive cross-disciplinary approach to the beauty of sport. The best that can be hoped for is a pointing out of major avenues of inquiry with an emphasis placed on the kinds of questions that should be asked rather than on the provision of answers. If one accepts the basic premise that sport is an art form and the athlete is an artist, then sport can be interpreted in aesthetic terms. Two questions must be asked in respect to sport creating beauty: (1) Is the kinesthetic sense of coordination, skill, and success in the self (ego) the real interpretation of sports activity as beauty?—or (2) Is the visual observation of the coordination, skill, and success of the athlete, the other (alter), the real interpretation of the beauty of sport? The kinesthetic sense of "action as beauty" can be called the "subjective aesthetic," whereas observed pleasing and admired performance can be labeled "objective aesthetic." The difference is significant, and the two are unlikely to be experienced concordantly.

The introspective nature of the subjective sport-aesthetic can be closely related with what R. Tait McKenzie designated "the joy of effort." This feeling of the joy of effort can come at that supreme moment when the self reacts to the sport situation with a totality of muscular strength, control, achievement in absolute inner recognition. It cannot be measured, for it is too spontaneous. That moment can be relived in diluted fashion in the flush of post-activity exhilaration—which can, but need not be associated with victory over others. Personal success over one's previous "bests" will elicit the sensation. Everybody is capable of feeling it—champions or nonchampions, league or sandlot athletes, shot-putters or frisbee-tossers—if they have the commitment to excel in sport activity for its own sake. The rewards attendant on the personal feeling of the beauty of sport can be shared only in the telling.

Concepts such as a gracefulness, harmony, effortlessness, control, flow, power, rhythm, and many more serve man in his acceptability of perceived physical performance, and where these concepts find most application to the arts—most notably dance and the performing arts—they take on added force in the new vision brought to sports activity.

The question thus is raised: Can the aesthetics of sport be subject to scientific study? The answer to this question will indicate ultimately if there are laws attaching to the beauty of sport.

The definition of sport as "self-induced stress" has never been fully explored, and is worth a deeper treatise. Here, it is sufficient to say that by defining sport as self-induced stress, equivalent to what Kupfer (1975) means by "structured stress," all problems of distinguishing athletes (the behavioral component of sport) from each other by quasi-economic and quasi-moral grounds disappear. Questions centering on a discussion of "amateur-professional" distinctions become illogical and cannot be taken seriously by the student of sport sciences. An athlete performs either for social reward (pecuniary or prestigious) or for self-expression. In the latter instance he is an artist by intention; in the social-reward instance the athlete is acclaimed an artist by others. Interpreting sport as self-induced stress allows for both groups, the social reward and the self-expressive, to seek excellence. Different motivational forces distinguish the two groups from each other. Put into the perspective of the Olympic Games, where top-level performance is witnessed every four years, one athlete may be there for the social prestige that success will bring, one for the self-satisfaction. Nobody will be able to tell the difference. However, the one who seeks social prestige through success will be concerned about that difference, the other will not think about it. The psychology of the self excites serious discussion of the role of the athlete as artist. Taking for granted the relationship between sport and art spells the need for closer inquiry to which *The Beauty of Sport* addresses itself. Although there is inherent in many sports a conscious striving for perfection in the presentation of a communicable emotional state, it is probably in the simplicity of drawing a one-to-one relationship from the above that the sport-art paradigm appears so easily stated.

A literal point of departure is to take the representation of sport in art-forms, be these paintings, sculpture, ceramics, or whatever, and thence to pose traditional questions of style, form, line, color, texture, and the like to the art-work. Secondarily, the importance of "true" representation of sport form in the art-work comes into consideration.

A major limitation in tracing sources for the sport-art relationship lies in the fact that sport must be recognized as "natural" activity in the art-work, and not require interpretation. However, modern trends in painting and sculpture have moved away from "natural" representation, thus further limiting the scope of available evidence for study. *The Beauty of Sports* begins by providing source material for validation of the sport-art relationship, referring to representational art (painting and sculpture) as a starting point for subsequent theoretical questioning of the contribution of art to the understanding of aesthetics. This questioning is done completely within the frame of reference of sport and its root form in play.

The pursuit of the sport-art relationship by reference to painting and sculpture draws out the subtle differences that the two art-forms offer in their contribution to this study. An attempt is made to present the material in a way such that the nature of artistic understanding, taste, and appreciation remains open to personal interpretation, although still allowing that there are basic artistic tenets of form, color, line, and texture which can be viewed as constants.

The latter half of the book deals with the problem of interpretation of the aesthetics of sport. This is done from several perspectives: (1) addressing the problem as an issue moving from the purely philosophical to the psychological, which is done by restating the question in behavioral terms; (2) taking what many would agree is a sport with an injected aesthetic component, namely gymnastics, and querying the procedure for the satisfaction or realization of "aesthetics" as a given; (3) theorizing about modes of inquiry for empirical investigation into the aesthetics of sport; and (4) providing examples of empirical inquiry to demonstrate avenues that can be pursued. These final chapters show that the question is still only in the asking stage, that the definition of the problem remains a critical issue of inquiry, but that initial steps are being taken for our better understanding.

The study of the beauty of sport presents a challenge to accepted canons of aesthetics. What is applicable to one sport in aesthetic criteria may be only remotely relevant to another sport, and may be totally unrelated to any of the arts. Only the permutation of concepts will provide the ultimate answer. "Speed" and "precision" may appear unrelated as aesthetic criteria, but aficionados of hydroplane racing and motor racing will swear to the harmony of these two concepts for a successful result. Hence, the words of Ernst Jokl are heeded (Whiting and Masterson, 1974):

> This then is what may be said about the relevance of the scientific analytical as against the artistic-allegorical approach to phenomena such as those which confront us when we reflect upon sport. Both approaches are of value even though they yield different insights. The scientific analytical procedure uncovers factual elements whose synthesis may eventually unveil facts of an order higher than that from which it is made up. The artistic allegory clarifies meanings, and values, experiences, none of them amenable to measurement. (p. 26, *Readings in the Aesthetics of Sports*)

Coming to this discussion of the beauty of sport, a sense of frustration can be felt. What can be learned? How is sport perceived as beautiful? All of us know what we mean when we exclaim "Beautiful!" Those of us involved in sport certainly know what we mean—but then, how do we educate others?

One approach being developed by some sport educators is to offer a course on "The Aesthetics of Sport." Such a course employs film analysis, discussion of artistic content of paintings, sculpture, and sports photojournalism. Readings of research papers are introduced for seminar discussion, and, from the pragmatic standpoint, students are encouraged to do projects of artistic application based on sport action. Papers are written critically appraising available literature and presenting new concepts. The frontiers of knowledge delimiting inquiry in the beauty of sport are easily found, for so little is yet known. Ultimately, the student has much to educate the teacher, and in the final analysis, all can claim that they are seeing sport in a new light, with a new vision for the better understanding and appreciation of sport.

BENJAMIN LOWE

Acknowledgments

The presentation of this book could not have been accomplished without professional guidance, friendship and assistance (nonexclusive categories).

For the original guidance I am indebted to Frances Z. Cumbee, Gerald S. Kenyon, James Dennis, Robert E. Gard, and Leonard A. Larson, all of whom guided me in my first inquiries into the beauty of sport while I was a student at the University of Wisconsin. More recently, I have obtained great support from Leona Holbrook who has kindly consented to prepare the Foreword for *The Beauty of Sport,* and I sincerely thank her and Roy Cogdell for the professional encouragement shown to me.

Throughout the past ten years I have received much friendship and encouragement from Bruce and Nancy Anderson, Joe and Marge Walsh, Roger and Teresa Harrold, Art and Jane Howard, Frank Szucs, Wes White, Don Masterson, John Jackson, Colin Kelly, Jim Duthie, Pat Bird, Wilma "Billy" Wright, Maurice Yaffé, Pru Fleming, Dick Borkowski, Norm Eburne, Fred Roethlisberger, Paul Molé, John Cheffers, Guy Lewis, and from many more of my professional friends and acquaintances who have shown direct support in one way or another toward the completion of this book.

For direct assistance I am indebted to Betty Metcalf who not only typed the manuscript but checked and cross-checked references in my behalf to ensure a good manuscript. I must also thank Walter Welch and Teru Uyeyama whose personal concern has helped to make a fine production.

Finally, I must thank my wife, Donna, and my three children, Matthew, Chandler, and Amanda-Claire, for the love and patience they have shown throughout the writing of this book.

The Natural Beauty of the Athlete

1

INTRODUCTION

Who has not witnessed or experienced the beauty of sport in any of its many forms? Even while asserting that sport is beautiful, we might still ask ourselves, how is it beautiful? To feel sure that there is beauty in sport yet to entertain at the same time a self-questioning attitude toward that certainty reflects healthy thinking.

There are people who see no beauty in sport, who would quote perhaps the fact that so much of the media present other aspects of sport, such as violence. In any given group of people, one can expect to find 7 or 8 percent who express no interest whatsoever in sport, and only another 18 percent who are slightly interested in sport. The overriding majority of people, 70 percent or better, have at least a casual interest in sport; a large proportion of them could be expected to appreciate sport from an aesthetic perspective. Those who would agree that sport is beautiful may differ in their own aesthetic interpretations, and this could be reasonably expected. This diversity of opinion, judgment, and experience would adequately reflect the many facets of the beauty of sport.

This chapter explores what beauty has meant to man in relation to his athletic pursuits and in relation to interaction with his natural surroundings. What is meant by the ideal form of the body appears to have historic

1

relationship with the physical appearance of the athlete; artists have reproduced the typical athletic build when demonstrating ideal human form (see Plates 1 and 2). Out of man's recognition of human form as being the epitome of natural beauty came the sense of proportion, which was applied to many forms of artistic pursuit and explanation of the physical environment. Man's awareness of the beauty of nature is his natural reaction to his surroundings.

THE BEAUTY OF NATURE

Probably man has "always" been conscious of a personal (physiological or psychological) reaction to form and color in his natural environment. Anthropologists tell us that primitive man wove much of the fabric of nature into his folklore and mythology, testifying to the power of personal human impact that the beauty of nature had for him. The origins of the Olympic Games when traced prior to their first recording in 776 B.C. reveal a reverent association between primitive athletic contest and elements of nature employed for their symbolic expression. It is common knowledge that the Greeks employed the olive branch for crowning Olympic victors, and it is widely held that the apple bough was used for this purpose prior to using the olive. Furthermore, the setting for that most important of early religious festivals was and remains today a site of commanding natural beauty.

Primitive man and early civilizations were most likely highly responsive to the beauty of nature, but because such beauty could not be accounted for, it took on symbolic meaning. The dawning of the day, epitomized in the radiant expression of the rising sun, became mythologized in the god Phoebus, who drove a golden chariot drawn by four horses. It goes without saying that the four-horse chariot, as a means of transport, had to have been invented prior to its appearance in mythology, and the social status of one who owned such a rig had to be without doubt. The symbolic transference to the sun is thus clarified.

That the beauty of nature remains inexplicable today rests on the authority of Dobzhansky (1965) who states:

> Let it be clear at the outset that the beauty of nature refers to human feelings about certain natural objects, not to these objects themselves. It is man who is enthralled by the grandeur of a snow-clad mountain range. . . . As nearly as we are able to make it out the biological function of all this glory of form and color is pragmatic. . . . The real and unsolved problem is why these displays seem so superb to man. (p. 226)

We ascribe a consciousness of beauty to those things that we are culturally indoctrinated to recognize as beautiful. This socialization process begins with our earliest consciousness of the world about us; "pretty flower," as first taught to us by our mothers, is probably our introduction to learning that nature is beautiful. Beauty in nature has cross-cultural validity, and may even be circumscribed by universal laws. Differing cultures focus qualities of beauty on different natural forms and events according to their respective cultural needs and heritages. Whereas a radiant sunset may be universally appraised as beautiful, the grandeur of mountains or the fury of the sea may be culturally specific in their beauty according to the perspective of mountain folk or coastal people. By extension, we might presuppose that skiing is a comparatively more beautiful sport for people with greater sensitivity for mountains, whereas surfing is more beautiful to people with a greater proclivity for the coast. Such presupposition, even as a unidimensional and simplistic metaphor, gives a flavor of an extant relationship between sport and the beauty of nature. To examine that relationship more closely, it becomes necessary to view the image in which man has held the body as a feature of nature. Most often he has ascribed to the body characteristics by which to measure the rest of nature. The body is a hallmark, a basic standard, yet paradoxically it is subject to interpretations predicated upon abstract or cognitive ideas associated with the superlative.

THE BODY AS NATURAL BEAUTY

The appreciation of the body as an object of beauty has its roots in antiquity, but the analysis of the beauty of nature as a definitive mode of inquiry is traced to Baumgarten and the German poets and philosophers of the late eighteenth century. Kant improved on the original premise of Baumgarten by recommending that we think of natural beauty *as if* it were the product of some interested design—the designer being identified with God. The division of the study of aesthetics into the analysis of beauty in nature and beauty in art has great usefulness for the aesthetics of sport. Distinguishing between the two, Hegel judged that: "the work of art is of higher rank than any product of Nature." He suggests that the distinction rests on the fact that a work of art has derived from the mind of man and is therefore imbued with spiritual essence which nature lacks.

Since Baumgarten's definitive efforts to account for beauty in natural form, we have progressed very little beyond "knowing what we like" or agreeing to share some common perceptions of what is "beautiful." This has substantive meaning for any empirical deductions that we might wish to draw later.

Originally the term "aesthetics," as the Greeks defined it, meant anything that had to do with perception by the senses. Yet, within this definition, the reference for measuring aesthetic quality was the human form. Hamilton (1942) stressed this in her description of the Greek attitude toward the arts:

> The sculptor watched the athletes contending in the games, and he felt that nothing he could imagine would be more beautiful than those strong young bodies, so he made his statue of Apollo. Greek artists and poets realized how splendid man could be, straight and swift and strong. He was the fulfillment of their search for beauty. All the art and all the thought of Greece centered on human beings. (p. 16)

This fact indicates that by the first millennium Before Christ, society had reached the level of organization that allowed development of the arts on a grand scale. More pertinent to our inquiry, however, is the reverence that society had long since developed for such a specialized feature of Nature, *man himself*. The artistic adulation of the human form, the implicit recognition of its excellence by artists in their work, could not have taken place prior to the development of a value system elevating the body to the point of deification. Such deification of the human form was a logical consequence for a society embracing pantheism as its spiritual mode of religious expression.

The Body in Classical Greek Society

The study of the beauty of nature from an epistemological perspective is a relatively recent development in the history of man. Yet, the Greeks of Ancient Hellas were strongly of the opinion that the body symbolized the epitome of natural beauty.

The Greeks did not have a word for beauty; thus the inference that they were sensitive to it in the way we understand the concept of beauty today rests on sources from Greek cultural heritage. Using Plato and Aristotle as his primary references in his thesis exploring the "golden age of the body," Fairs (1970) states:

> The high ethical and aesthetic value assigned to the body, particularly to the body of the youthful athlete, was an extraordinary happening in the cultural history of the body. (p. 13)

For the Greeks, the pursuit of physical excellence (the embodiment of which we find in sculpture and vase-painting) was the avenue to a balanced and harmonious personality. The body, perceived as the source of all good and happiness, was the key to spiritual salvation. The more beautiful the body, the better the man or woman in pantheistic terms. It is not surprising then that Olympian Zeus and his attendant gods were conceived as superlative examples of man, surpassing the average Greek in such qualities as strength, beauty, courage, wisdom, and athletic ability. Why else would Olympic victors, the epitome of mortal man, be chosen by sculptors as the model by which they expressed their reverence for the supernatural?

It was widely believed by the Greeks that the Olympian gods would protect and bestow favor upon those who developed their bodies according to canons of organic vigor and graceful physical movement. "The beauty most highly revered was the nude body of the perfectly muscled, youthful athlete," states Fairs (1970), and focusing on the era of Periclean society, he adds that the aesthetic idealization of the flawless physique of the naked athlete was grounded in the political and religious structure of society. Thus, the beauty of the body was a social ideal. To be sure, a completely different value structure from the one we have inherited operated for the Greeks. In political terms, the citizen-soldier, aristocratic of birth and schooled in the gymnasium, was admired for his physical efficiency and athletic bearing, the aesthetic ideal of the Greeks stemming from the assigned superior status of the bodily beauty and graceful form of this citizen-soldier-athlete. In religious terms, the idealization of Olympian deities modeled on the personification of the superior athlete led the Greeks to seek communion with them through reverence of their own physical development. As far as they were concerned they resembled the gods, and the gods guarded and guided their development accordingly. To the gods was ascribed the possession of superior health, beauty, and athletic skill, and the citizen-soldier felt that by attempting to approximate their athletic prowess he could gain their favor for his own health, beauty, and skill. The gods represented perfection, of course, so man always had an objective to achieve.

The Greek Sense of Proportion

The concept of perfection in beauty has never been commensurably clear to man, but that has not stopped him in his efforts to achieve it. The "perfect" form of a Venus de Milo is perfect only in our present-day acceptance of the sense of proportion bequeathed to us by the Greeks. It is because we agree with the Greeks on what constitutes perfection in the human form that we can so readily speak of "the Golden Age" of Greece; in that recognition, we are saying that the sense of proportion felt by the Greeks (and demonstrated in their art) parallels what we today recognize as good proportion. But what is "the sense of proportion"?

The Greeks were sufficiently inquisitive of nature to want to estimate and explain the universe according to rational laws and principles. For this purpose they developed an intense interest in mathematics. The Platonic philosophy of education insisted that mathematics was necessary as a basis for many other branches of study. Not least, it was believed, mathematics could aid in the better understanding of the beauty of nature and art. Thus, one of the most significant discoveries in mathematics was the Pythagorean theory of proportion of commensurable quantities. Clark (1959) tells us that the aesthetic sensitivity of the Greeks was fashioned by a belief in measurable proportion. Applying the aesthetic standard of measurable proportion to the development of the human body meant that each part of the body had a measurable relationship with other parts of the body. Fairs (1970) states:

> The purpose of the aesthetic standard of measurable proportion was the development of bodily grace and symmetry. (p. 23)

The model for the perfectly proportioned body, as noted above, was that of the soldier-athlete, whose muscular body fashioned for military and athletic action was inspiration for Greek artists. The functional characteristic of this superbly proportioned physical beauty is suggested by an underlying capacity for action, which will be most efficient because it is mechanically well-structured. Expounding further on the relationship of physical proportion to beauty of form, Fairs elaborates on the idealized proportion of body to mind, which was held germane to fifth-century B.C. Greek philosophy:

> The desire for proportion and harmony in physical development was without doubt the root of the idealization of the pentathlete in the Greek athletic philosophy. . . . The perfectly proportioned body was the beautiful body and for the Greeks the beautiful body was the good body. This fusion of aesthetics and ethics in the fifth century mentality is found in the aesthetic-ethical ideal of *kalos kagathos*—beauty-and-goodness—a concept which "was used to denote the sum-total of all ideal perfections of mind and body." . . . Fifth century B.C. ideals of good and evil, of beauty and ugliness—in short, the ideals they aimed at in life—were the product of, and in turn contributed to, a well-defined personality type—the ideal of man as a unified being.
>
> In addition to *kalos kagathos,* for example, such moral virtues as *arete,* the ideal of all-around excellence, and *sophrosyne,* the ideal of self-restraint, discipline, and moderation, necessitated a Golden Mean or "nothing in excess" philosophy of life. The master-key to the good life and its attainment in the Golden Mean life-philosophy was a healthy, beautiful body. (p. 15)

The "sense of proportion" for the Greeks, then, embodied a total cultural way of life, the physical aspect being but one part.

The question of whether the Classical Greeks perceived in sport the elements of beauty that this text explores is of passing interest. What is certain is that contests of physical strength and skill were believed to reinvigorate and renew in youthfulness those who participated. By so doing, the citizen-athlete activated powers ascribed to the gods, and he even imparted, by inspiration, some of his benefits to the departed members of his family (funeral games). The life ideal of the Classical Greek was also served by athletic pursuit. Since the underlying philosophy of this life ideal embraced a sensitivity to the beauty of nature, of which man represented the epitome, the games reflected the love of perfection that such beauty represented in body and mind. It is recorded that the intense desire of the Greeks to approach the ideal of a well-rounded man directed them to establish gymnastics and athletics as a central part of their system of education.

SYMMETRY AND ASYMMETRY

The search for a better understanding of "unity" has plagued philosophers since Aristotle. As a concept of intrinsic significance, unity has been equated with beauty and, at times, has served to "explain" beauty. Santayana, author of *The Sense of Beauty,* took this one step further by attempting to account for unity in terms of "symmetry." Interpreting this facet of Santayana's thinking, Roberts (1975) states:

> Because it provides unity of both a spatially immediate and a temporally recurring kind, the concept of symmetry leads Santayana to think that unity must be the underlying essence and virtue of form; the unified manner in which the elements of an object are combined constitutes the character of the form. (p. 94)

To say that an object has symmetry is to show that the object, when bisected, has two equal parts which are the mirror image of each other. Asymmetry means that any bisecting of a given object will not result in two mutually reflective parts. This can best be illustrated by the following diagram.

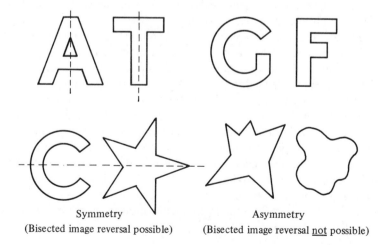

Symmetry
(Bisected image reversal possible)

Asymmetry
(Bisected image reversal not possible)

If a line is drawn horizontally through the frontal plane of the human body (through the tip of the nose and the navel), two equal parts, each mirroring the other, will demonstrate the essential symmetry of the human body. Now put that same human body into a lateral position, with a running action, and the form now becomes asymmetrical.

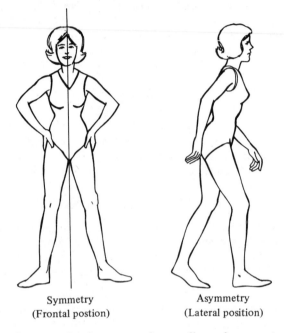

Symmetry
(Frontal postion)

Asymmetry
(Lateral position)

The student of sport who has an understanding of symmetry and asymmetry can comprehend that the nature of the asymmetry of the human form in action is intrinsically related to the basic symmetry of man. The element of subliminal (cortical) carry-over cannot be underestimated by the student in his efforts to discern beauty in sport.

To draw the link between our recognition of symmetry with our comprehension of the "symmetry" of man in asymmetrical movement, we may refer again to the sculptures of Classical Greece. The ideal of classical form has been acknowledged in such sculptures as the *Doryphorus,* and it is in reference to this example that Kenneth Clark (1959) says: "The human body has been used as the basis of a marvelously adjusted composition, carried through with such consistency [where] the movement of the leg destroys the old stiff symmetry of exact correspondence [and] a new symmetry has to be created by a balance of axes." Clark states further that such sculptures have "rhythms of movement" within them, but it takes a practiced eye and some background in art and movement to detect them. The rhythms of movement implicit in such sculpture must also satisfy the canon of proportion devised by Polyclitus (see *The Greek Sense of Proportion*), but for our purpose, they become translatable in real terms for our better grasp of asymmetrical sports movement.

A sculpture by R. Tait McKenzie, *The Plunger* is an admirable exercise in symmetry. As Christopher Hussey (1929) points out, *"The Plunger* [has] the perfect balance and symmetry [to] counteract the explosive intensity of the attitude, so that the general effect is one of repose."* The repose that Hussey intimates is another way of saying "psychological symmetry," an effect of aesthetic response (or judgment) to our perception of an athlete poised. In the poised athlete, we detect the center of gravity of the body held slightly forward of its natural position by tensed muscular control. Our major clue to this judgment lies in the line of the feet and toes, telling us that symmetrically there is an equal weight distribution either side of a line drawn from the center of gravity to the point of contact of the toes. Hence, *The Plunger* provides us with two lessons on symmetry: (1) the visual frontal plane which, when bisected, gives the mirror image indicative of pure symmetry, and (2) the perceived lateral plane which, although presenting an asymmetrical visual configuration, when bisected for mechanical analysis, presents a schematic symmetry based on weight distribution about the center of gravity. In the specific case of *The Plunger,* however, there are added lessons of aesthetic impact to be learned from the representation of tensed muscle. Impressions of tensed muscle, whether in art or in sport, provide the student with significant evidence for him to make aesthetic judgments on such qualities as poise, grace, harmony, and the like. It is the opinion of Lawther (1951) that:

> Beauty in balance-movements seems greater in asymmetrical forms (in gymnastics) in which the parts divided by the center of balance are quite different—so different that the balance problem challenges the attention. (p. 293)

This value judgment made by Lawther may be shared by many students, but there may be as many others who disagree with this view. Eysenck (1968) has demonstrated empirically that any given population is about equally divided between those expressing a preference for symmetrical pattern and those preferring asymmetrical patterns. Symmetry and asymmetry of form are recognizable by all people, and individual taste is the sole criterion for personal preference.

Whereas the symmetry of the standing human body in the frontal plane is perhaps easy to see and understand, there is a symmetry of motion in running (which is established by the repetitive actions of alternate legs and arms) which is more difficult to comprehend. Putting the image pictorially, we can refer to the compressed image given by the process of telephotography in motion films. The runner thus viewed, as in some sequences of *Tokyo Olympiad,* the film made by Ichikawa, may appear to be moving not forward, but as if he were running on the spot. The sense of this symmetry is brought out in the comments of Smith (1955) writing of the running style of Lovelock, the 1936 Olympic 1500-meter champion:

> To those who had the privilege of watching him, there was sheer wizardry in his running; something almost superhuman in the perfect co-ordination of his every movement, the apparent absence of strain, and the lyrical flow of his style and rhythm. Here, indeed, was poetry in motion. (p. 49)

The phrase to focus on here is "perfect coordination." It is this which is seen in the telescoped image of a runner or a cyclist filmed coming toward the viewer. The spatial element in the spatiotemporal conception of the activity is interfered with, and disregarding the comical and superficial "puppet-on-a-string" effect, the time element is all that remains for our perceptual grasp. Now, since the telescopic image "flattens" the picture (takes out much that is acknowledged perspectively), we are given the opportunity to see it as kinetic art. This perceptional exercise brings us closer to seeing symmetrical movement in purer mirror-image terms, and hence is a refined transitional exercise instructive in the analysis and appreciation of sport action of asymmetrical quality. Put another way, the better we understand symmetrical sports activity, the better we will be able to transfer that understanding to asymmetrical sports action. Indeed, there is instruction here for the student of the mechanical analysis of sport (kinesiology) as well as for those inquiring into sport as beauty. Equally, texts on kinesiology can be instructive for aesthetic inquiry, particularly where efficiency of motion is interpreted as approximating perfect form.

THE PHYSICAL IDEAL OF THE BODY

Undoubtedly, the concept of the "ideal" form is culturally variable. This is no less true for the concept of physical beauty held by any culture in the history of man (see Plates 1 and 2). In sixth-century Classical Greece (500–600 B.C.) the physical ideal was one which characterized strength, and the typical athlete of the period was more representative of a boxer or a wrestler. Statues dating from this period show an emphasis on development of the trunk muscles of the body rather than of the limbs. However, a change of emphasis took place in the fifth century (400–500 B.C.), when the athlete commonly represented in statues and on vase paintings was more youthful in appearance, still strong-looking, but having an all-round development and more graceful bearing. The trend toward this latter ideal is usually attributed to the work of Polyclitus, Phidias, and Myron. Myron, particularly, is reputed to have made the study of athletic motion his major concern. His study of *Discobolus* is indicative of this direction of interest. Polyclitus, on the other hand, introduced an ideal concept of posture in studies of the resting athlete, the weight of the body taken on one leg to give the lively impression of perfect poise. His *Doryphorus,* in its perfect proportion, appears to be on the point of taking a step forward. The statue gives the impression of power but not muscular overdevelopment. Thus, the *Doryphorus* represents more typically the all-round athlete than the specialist. The union of strength and beauty is the hallmark of ideal man in fifth-century Greece. Impressions of strength are tempered to reduce coarseness, and beauty is sustained because softness is eschewed. The Classical Greeks blended music with gymnastics in their educational philosophies and this combination becomes evident in the rhythmic poise of the *Doryphorus* of Polyclitus.

The Ideal Body of the Athlete

"The athlete is a man apart," states Paul Weiss (1969). He continues: "The beauty and grace of his body, his coordination, responsiveness, alertness, efficiency, his devotion and accomplishements, his splendid unity with his equipment, all geared to produce a result at the limits of bodily possibility, set him over against the rest of men." In describing the athletic build of tennis star Clark Graebner, McPhee (1970) draws attention to "the firmly structured muscles of his legs [which] stand out in symmetrical perfection." These examples reinforce our own thoughts and observations about ideal human physique.

The body of the athlete is finely muscled. This statement applies to each of the somatotype groups but is perhaps most appropriate in the mesomorph, the somatotype most typically descriptive of athletes. The curves of musculature, the physical definitions of muscle toned as evidence of exertion and use, present those aspects of the aesthetic form of the body which we take for granted as part of our cultural heritage. Culturally, we recognize and admire good musculature in its contribution to the beauty of the body, as we understand it, yet we balk at the overdevelopment of muscle since we perceive muscle bulk as being at the expense of good form. (Body-builders will dispute the generality of this statement, and their comments would be welcome.)

If we acknowledge that the body is beauty in natural form, and that the athlete epitomizes good body form because he puts it into classical patterns of action when he competes, we can infer that beauty in sport is more basically the beauty of nature than of art. Beauty in sport is mostly gratuitous, with any sense of grace, harmony, or other quality being conferred on behavior not necessarily seeking such description. Beauty in sport can be said to be natural in character, and Weiss (1969) agrees with this when he says that the athlete does not set out to create beauty. Elliott (1974) in Whiting and Masterson's *Readings in Aesthetics of Sport* also agrees: "There is no reason why in striving for victory in sport human beings should create or give rise to beauty, any more than that Nature should be beautiful, and we feel very much the same wonder and gratitude in both cases." The athlete, as representative of the "best" human physique, brings his natural beauty to the sport domain. It is the acceptance of this feature of nature, the athlete as ideal form, based on the equal acceptance that there is beauty in nature, which tends to make it axiomatic that sport is beautiful in natural terms. Further exploration of the notion of the ideal body of the athlete should test this axiom.

It has been suggested that the best of Greek sculpture was based on the concept of the ideal athletic form. By inference, Gardiner (1930) expresses the belief that the "intimate connection between athletics and art had a strong influence on athletics." Whereas we might judge the inference to be *post hoc* and choose to disagree with Gardiner that art influenced athletes to improve their techniques in Ancient Greece, we can draw a more substantive athletics-artist relationship from modern times to serve our purpose. *The Sprinter,* a sculpture completed in 1902 by R. Tait McKenzie, was modeled on the crouch start pose for sprinting invented by Charles Sherrill in 1888 (Hussey, 1929). In the forward-leaning pose of *The Sprinter,* we see the way in which the weight of the body is poised over the hands, illustrating that art instructs athletics. Pictures of Jesse Owens starting in the semifinals and finals of the 100-yard dash, as filmed by Leni Riefenstahl in *Olympia, 1936,* show close resemblance to the pose of *The Sprinter.*

In *The Sprinter,* R. Tait McKenzie attempted to illustrate the ideal average form of an athlete. His approach to obtaining the ideal was purely scientific, but the end result proved to be remarkably artistic. The commentary by Christopher Hussey (1929) on how McKenzie arrived at his ideal is noteworthy for its historical significance:

> The measurements of seventy-four of the fastest American sprinters had recently been collected and compiled by Dr. Paul C. Phillips of Amherst College. McKenzie himself was practising anthropometry at McGill, and Dr. Sargent as early as 1887 had published the results of his investigations on the "Physical Proportions of the Typical Man" and "Physical Characteristics of the Athlete" (Scribner's Magazine). Living, like the sculpture of ancient Greece, among well-formed youths, whether lightly clad for exercise or stripped in the changing rooms, would have made an artist of a man far less gifted with imagination than Tait McKenzie. Nevertheless, the first attempts at *The Sprinter* were mechanical failures. Not till the third beginning did he gain sufficient experience of the placing and construction of armatures to make the figure support its own weight.

The question of what type of figure is best suited to sprinting had been debated, and the wide differences in physique of successful sprinters made the problem of the ideal apparently insoluble. Some were giants and some were unusually short. Of Dr. Phillips' seventy-four individuals, none was without an authentic record of 10-⅖ secs. or under for the 100 yards, or 23 secs. or less for the 220 yards. Among them were such well-known athletes in their day as Baker, Wendell, Sherrill, Long, Duffey, Molson and Morros. Their average age was 21 years, average height 5 ft. 8-¾ in., about an inch taller than the average man, and average weight 145 lbs., just 6 lbs. over the average student of the same age. The lengths of the shin and thigh were average.

On the other hand, the extremes of the scale were far apart. The shortest sprinter was only 5 ft. 3 ins., the tallest 6 ft. 1 in. About twenty-four of the seventy-four fell below 5 ft. 8-¾ in., while the largest group clustered between 5 ft. 9 in. and 5 ft. 11 in. Length of limbs varied in proportion.

The girth dimensions proved both chest and abdomen to exceed the normal, and the circumference of upper arms, forearms, thighs, and calves to be still higher above normal. Yet the knees and wrists fell below normal. Thus virtually all the girths of muscle are above the average in a sprinter, and all those of bone below it. Curiously enough, while the neck is above the average in thickness, the head is considerably smaller in circumference, being normal for a man of only 5 ft. 6 in. in height. The indications here are of a brachycephalic, thick-necked type.

Strength tests showed a notable development of lungs, back and legs.

Thus the characteristics of the sprinter were shown to be no abnormal development of limbs or mysterious relation of parts, but to consist in a body framework, taller but higher than the normal, narrow hips, high insteps and short feet. The frame is clothed with a muscular system above normal size and strength.

The statue shows such a man, small boned, lithe, of the race-horse type. The pose of the body brings out the muscles of the back taut as bow-strings, and the arms and· shins can be seen stretched and alert as they await the crack of the pistol. The eyes are fixed on the goal.

The pose is as interesting athletically as the figure, since it represents the most efficient variation of a position with many possible variants. The hands are on the scratch line, grasping the corks; the left foot six inches behind the line, the right twenty-eight inches and almost directly behind the left. The right knee is bent at right angles. The runner has dug holes for his toes, and has taken up this position on the word "Get set" from the starter, his weight being taken by his hands and left leg. (pp. 12–13)

As one method of demonstrating man's concept of the ideal body form, *The Sprinter* serves as a remarkable model for instruction. It is difficult to accept (conceptually) that it represents an "ideal" for it succeeds so dynamically as an art-work representing a man poised for athletic action. Indeed, the mental exercise associated with accepting the sculpture as an "ideal" tends to oblige us into some detraction of its innate quality.

More pertinent to the purpose of inquiry into the aesthetics of sport is the scientific nature of the approach that McKenzie took. Through his dedication to science he came to explore his artistic potential, the results of which earned him further acclaim. *The Sprinter* was shown in major exhibitions of art, both in America and in Europe, thus giving McKenzie the confidence of knowing that not only was his work representative of his first love, sport, but that his artistic talent was unchallenged. This experience provided him with the impetus to do further studies. Shortly after completing *The Sprinter,* McKenzie was commissioned by the Society of Directors of Physical Education in Colleges to model a statue of the ideal all-round athlete. Again, McKenzie took the scientific approach, this time for the dimensions of *The Athlete.* Charts of the heights, weights, and other measurements of students aged sixteen to twenty-five had been kept by Dr. Dudley Sargent for about forty years. On the basis of these charts, a previous sculptor named Henry Kitson had executed two sculptures. Mc-Kenzie took these as models, and using further measurements that Dr. Paul Phillips had collected on sprinters, plus his own measurements of skaters, he was able to fashion what for him represented the ideal athlete. It is the viewpoint of Christopher Hussey (1929), McKenzie's biographer, that *The Sprinter* and *The Athlete* come close to being the best modern equivalent of the ideals of artists in antiquity. Hussey cites the grace and simplicity of the sculptures which, he says, have precedent only in Classical Greece and Renaissance Italy. He says of McKenzie: "Beauty for him, as for the ancients, is the beauty of the perfect body."

For historical veracity and a full elaboration of the origins and artistic interpretation of *The Athlete* we turn again to Hussey. He is quoted here at length, for what he says is not just his interpretation but rather a factual account of the thinking behind the sculpture as the biographer heard it directly from McKenzie:

> In pursuance of this precedent the measurements for *The Athlete* were obtained by a double test. From four hundred men who had excelled in all forms of sport, from rowing to jumping, and had been subjected to the Inter-collegiate Strength Test Competition, the average was taken of the fifty strongest men, as revealed by the latter test over a period of five years. It is unnecessary to particularize the tests made in the competition, further than to say that they are made scientifically by means of an instrument known as the dynamometer. By means of this double test, any undue specialization of development caused by rowing or gymnastics was counteracted by including the measurements of football players, jumpers, and runners.

The following out of these measurements gave a surprising result. Instead of a stout, heavily muscled, thick-boned type of figure, the proportions and girths proved much more light and graceful than might have been expected. The torso is evenly proportioned to the legs, neither unduly long nor short, and although the shoulders are exceedingly strong and the chest broad, the whole effect is one of lightness and grace. *The Athlete* is a light and slender youth compared to the *Doryphorus,* but stouter and more heavily built, with a larger head and longer torso, than the *Apoxyomenos.* He stands between the two extremes. The waist is not too small, and agility and speed are expressed by the well-turned leg and thigh, and pliant torso springing gracefully from a narrow pelvis well muscled and easily set on the thighs. With a height of 5 ft. 9 in., he carries a weight of nearly 159 pounds. The girth of neck, knee, and calf are the same, with that of the upper arm an inch and a half less. The girth of the thigh is half an inch less than that of the head. His expanded chest is 40 in., the girth of his waist 30 in. The girth of his hips is almost the same as that of his unexpanded chest, while the breadth of his waist barely exceeds the length of his foot. A distinct divergence from the classic canon is the span of the extended arms, which measures two inches more than the man's total height instead of being the same.

The Athlete is about to try the strength of his right forearm by the oval spring dynamometer. Starting with the instrument in his left hand, his feet firmly and evenly planted, he has brought his left arm across his body, placed the dynamometer securely in his right hand, bringing the body forward and to the right till his weight is borne on the right foot. The statuette shows him in the act of taking away his left hand, while he gazes intently on the instrument, concentrating his mind on the test he is about to take. Next moment he will swing round to his left and exert his utmost force to send up the indicator on the dial that registers the strength of his grip.

The occasion chosen for representation is only an excuse for a more graceful arrangement of line than could be got by a conventional standing position. It is naturally a balanced pose, so that the form is harmonious. Incidentally it is a good example of the serpentine "line of beauty" beloved of Hogarth and, on his authority, of Michelangelo. A moment of comparative inaction was chosen purposely in preference to one of intense effort, in order that the form should be balanced, the graceful flow of undulating lines be uninterrupted by contracted muscles, and potential strength be suggested rather than actual exertion displayed. But although the scientist in McKenzie gives these entirely rational explanations of his work's divergences from the merely diagrammatic, it is impossible not to see in them also the born sculptor's (possibly unconscious) instinct for beauty of form and line. (pp. 18–20)

It is the considered opinion of Hussey that McKenzie never achieved a finer work of art than *The Athlete.* Hussey quotes an authority on Greek sculpture, Professor Percy Gardner, as drawing a fine parallel between the quality of *The Athlete* and the best of sculptures produced by the Greeks. The question we might fairly ask is: How much was the artistic sensibility (and sensitivity) of McKenzie influenced by what he knew of Greek sculpture? Certainly he was not naive of their presence for, as a part of his anatomy lectures, he had used examples of sculptures from antiquity to illustrate the points he was making to his students of physical education and medicine.

In a more recent context, Robert Riger, the photographer, has stated how he first became attracted to sport as a subject for his camera.

> I was trained as an artist and as a draftsman I discovered the beauty of movement in the human figure and the endless variety of its form in changing light. As I began to sketch athletes, I began to photograph them to study and analyze various men involved in sports I knew little about. . . . Since I approached my subjects directly and honestly, I found the photographs were strong, pure expressions of man in sport. (p. 18)

The sports photographs of Riger are typical of the good sports photographer (as illustrated by many of the Plates in this text). Documentary evidence of Mickey Mantle, the former baseball superstar, should reveal what Koppett (1967) says of the physical image of that particular modern athletic hero.

> Physically, he combined the most glamorous attributes of a classic hero—Herculean strength (those 500-foot homers), incredible speed (he could get down to first base in 3.1 seconds), good looks, youth, unprecedented versatility (there had never before been a switch-hitter with such power), and unlimited potential. If ever a "perfect" player was in the making, Mantle was the one—and it's hard to exaggerate how stimulating he was to the fan's imagination. (p. 282)

In 1956 Mickey Mantle won baseball's "triple crown"—batting title (.353), home runs (52), and R.B.I. (130). The beauty of his athletic performance appears to have matched his physical beauty.

Before leaving the discussion of the ideal body of the athlete we should consider an item from *The Journal of Popular Culture*. It is noteworthy, for example, that the physiques of Superman, Batman, their proteges and others, are typically athletic. Of course, this is as much a feature of the physical demands placed on them, the superlative powers they exhibit, and the fact that they are timeless figures of a technological mythos. They are recognized for what they are in the fantasy world of ideal value aspiration. But if we heed the commentary of the modern anthropologist Arens (1975), we are invited to view the American football player as representing an exaggeration of the male physique. He states: "Consider the extent to which football gear accents the male physique. The donning of the required items results in an enlarged head and shoulders and a narrowed waist, with the lower torso poured into skintight pants." Arens would have us believe, by extension, that the deployment of accident-prevention gear sublimates the football player to the rank of Olympian god. This hardly seems acceptable to us today, and even for the Classical Greeks it is unlikely that such trappings would have served their purposes for deification of their athletic victors.

THE BEAUTY OF THE BODY IN SPORTS ACTION

Hohler (1974) in Whiting and Masterson's *Readings in the Aesthetics of Sport* describes the beauty of human motion as one of the assumptions of the self-realization of man. This thought is akin to the precept that the body of man is beautiful, a precept of tested hereditary strength since we know that the citizens of Classical Greece more than two thousand years ago held much the same opinion. Man may be permitted his cult of the body beautiful so long as he restrains his self-image to being no more aesthetic in potential than, say, that of any other living form in nature. Indeed, we can all look at a horse, a dog, a starfish, a tree, and many other manifestations of natural form and claim a sense of beauty from them. Within this category of observations the human form is viewed as beautiful. Allied to this acceptance of innate beauty in the human form is the discussion of "symmetry" and "asymmetry," the central tenets of which have application in discerning beauty in the action of racehorses or racing cars. The human form in action passes spontaneously through both symmetrical and asymmetrical configurations.

There are specific conditions under which the perception of the body, both in repose and while in movement in sport and dance, is appreciated for its intrinsic beauty. These conditions are contingent upon prior learning and the acquisition of sensitivity to form, rhythm, balance, tension, poise, variation, and mood. (Mood is more applicable to dance appreciation than to sport appreciation from an aesthetic standpoint, but this does not deprive the sport enthusiast from defining his own sense of aesthetic mood for the sport he participates in or watches.)

The Aristotelian definitions of nature and art recommend that sport be determined as the beauty of nature, since in nature, the principle of motion comes from within. In art, on the other hand, the principle of motion comes from forces external to the object (in this case, man). In his *De rebus naturalibus,* Aristotle says: "Nature is the cause of motion in natural things, not only in the body itself in which it is (immanent motion) but also on another external body (transeunt motion.)" Even when we may take the example of pole-vaulting, with the newly developed fiber glass pole which imparts extra lift, the principle holds true, because the athlete initially puts the energy into the inanimate pole at the time of planting it in the pit. The same is true of the sky-diver who, by going to a height of 10,000 feet, imbues himself with the power of gravitational force.

A major development in physical education today extols the need for man to sharpen his sensitivity to beauty of movement so that he can perpetuate and extend it to others through the cultural medium of education. Through the beauty of movement man communicates values both of beauty and of movement. By the analysis of the media of movement, a better understanding of man, his culture, his ideas, and his values can be grasped. Drama, dance, and sport represent the media of movement which serve this stated purpose of communication for better understanding. The challenge issued by MacKenzie (1969) speaks directly to the role of sport as such a medium. He states: "Few think of sport as a medium for the expression of beauty [and] it may be that those involved in teaching sports have been insensitive or tend to minimize its importance." He concurs that the beauty of sport is found in the fleeting moment describing the movement, that the beauty of the movement is a real-time phenomenon that is frequently too fast and too subtle to grasp, unless it has been recorded on film and can be replayed in slow motion. Since the body is the substance for the artistic expression in movement, the beauty of movement comes in the "perfect physical control which makes the body master of space and time." Much the same sentiment is registered by Toynbee (1961) in his appraisal of the way artists might view sport. His thesis is that sport is a viable subject for the painter or sculptor by virtue of the components of design which can be found in the action of most athletes:

> Qualities which are demanded of all athletes are sense of balance and timing and control of the mind and body in rapid movement. [Sports] demand of their exponents a sense of positional play, or one might say of pattern and design in movement, flowing and continuous, though often interrupted and changed, but still basically creative and alive. . . . It is clear that in them [sports] all—especially where real skill is displayed —these elements of balance, controlled movement, and interrelated and interdependent patterns of action exist . . . as some of the qualities of design which are searched for by an artist. (pp. 305–6)

Echoing Toynbee, Willard Manus quotes a *Sports Illustrated* commentary on basketball as "a fluid rhythm with the underlying mathematical symmetry of a fugue by Johann Sebastian Bach. What to the spectator may seem merely hectic anarchy is designed to be a smoothly integrated pattern demanding dexterity, endurance, fine timing, and continuous split second appraisal of percentages and alternatives." Most typically, whenever basketball is likened to one of the arts, commentators speak of the balletic quality of the sport (see Plate 30). These observations usually focus on the action around the boards, since a hard-running court drive would be difficult to translate into balletic movement. In citing the drive in basketball, attention is given to the force of the game, a very different component in the space-time framework from that describing action under the boards. The two forms of action can be separated but it is meaningless to do so in any full appraisal of the sport of basketball—or of any other sport, for that matter. This point is elaborated by Kupfer (1975), who speaks of an intrinsic beauty deriving from the opposition between teams:

> *Temporally extended opposition* is the significant aesthetic addition competition provides. The aesthetic objects such opposition offers range in scope and duration. We delight in a movement, play, rally or drive, a sub-unit of the game such as inning, hole (golf), or quarters, as well as a game, series of games or an entire season. The game itself no doubt is the most typical as well as accessible object of appreciation. . . . The game is the wider dramatic context for momentary movement: the body moves to the rhythm and tempo of a whole. (p. 88)

The philosophic perspective of time and space, as presented by Slusher (1967), is that, in sport, they are meaningless without due consideration of force. The view is presented that:

> The man of sport is not simply in space and propelled by force but simultaneously aware and concerned with time, [and] with goal orientation: he uses the matrix of time, force, and space to *order* his world. (p. 15)

This appears to be satisfactory as a unidimensional idea, but if we test what he says against two different time frames within a game (or a series, or a season) the fabric of his statement begins to look weak. To apply his comment to the first five minutes of a game when teams are concentrating on identifying the strengths and weaknesses of each other strategically, and then to apply it to the closing five minutes of that same game in a tied (or winning game) situation is to draw immediate attention to the fragility of the "time, force and space" paradigm set down by Slusher. Just to extend the precept of *order,* if the athlete is winning or if he is losing in the last five minutes of the game, he will in each case have very different opinions on the *"order* of his world." This example may appear to be an unnecessary equivocation, which the philosopher has the right to challenge, but the point remains that the translation from philosophic language (symbolism) to behavioral language is a dire communications problem typical of the discussion of the beauty of sport.

The Athlete's Perspective

The beauty of sports action is probably best recognized and understood by athletes. More specifically, the beauty of any particular sport is probably acknowledged more fundamentally by athletes of that sport. It may well be true that the beauty in a sport is sport-specific, the highest appreciation of which is privy only to the athletes. There is also the viewpoint that the individual who is liberally educated and who has acquired the skills of artistic appreciation has the necessary sensibilities for full appreciation of the beauty of sport. Putting it another way, Keenan (1975) states:

> Lack of artistic appreciation for the athletic contest may also be attributed to lack of knowledge of aesthetic qualities. Both player and spectator must possess some understanding of aesthetic qualities to judge a contest's artistic form . . . only the skilled recognize the extreme difficulty and fully appreciate the artistry of another's performance. (p. 41)

The perfect combination, it would appear, is for the athlete to have aesthetic education, a refined appreciation for the arts, and artistic form. Jay Wright, a poet and playwright who formerly played minor league baseball, wrote in *Sports Illustrated,* in 1969:

> I sit in the stands, a wise ex-ball player, pointing out to friends the cabalistic purity of the diamond's dimensions, the number of players, balls, strikes; [and] what I make of the game . . . is an art, one that is completely enclosed in its own esthetic. (p. 33)

A similar sentiment is expressed by Bill Russell, who said of basketball:

> To me, one of the most beautiful things to see is a group of men coordinating their efforts toward a common goal—alternately subordinating and asserting themselves to achieve real teamwork in action. . . . Often, in my mind's eye, I stood off and watched that effort. I found it beautiful to watch. (p. 18)

Russell spoke these words while he was a player-coach, at that point of transition in his life when he felt himself growing out of the participatory athletic role. He would never have had time for this kind of reflection in the height of his playing days.

The distinction having been made between what is beauty in nature and how it differs from beauty in art, we can turn to the views of other supreme athletes for their feelings on the beauty of their own athletic performance. To take Roger Bannister as a prime example, it is fair to interpret his perspective of the beauty of sport as being more properly the beauty of nature than of art. In two instances in *The First Four-minute Mile* he reinforces this judgment: "I was running now, and a fresh rhythm entered my body. No longer conscious of my movement, I discovered a new unity with nature . . . a new source of power and beauty," and, "Sport changed from being a jumbled striving of individual athletes and teams to a new unity with a beauty that is evident in man's highest endeavor."

"Aesthetic movement in sport is not simply skilled movement," writes Aspin (1974) in Whiting and Masterson's *Readings in the Aesthetics of Sport,* "it has, as well as that, certain qualities of excellence that are *distinctly* appraised, such as, say: flowing movement over a full range; perfect balance and poise; symmetrical movement with good line (where the latter is often curving, as in the flight of an implement used in sport)." Arnold Palmer is reputed to have said: "What other people may find in poetry or art museums, I find in the flight of a good drive—the white ball sailing up into that blue sky, growing smaller and smaller, then suddenly reaching its apex, curving, falling and finally dropping to the turf to roll some more, just the way I planned it." Palmer would be either flattered or embarrassed to be told that he had just expressed himself very poetically in that simple description of the flight of the ball. These words, reflecting the inner personal perspective of the beauty of sport as seen by one particular athlete, endorses the recommendation that more athletes should be consulted for their perceptions.

This judgment is expressed in similar terms by Elliott (1974): "A full treatment of the aesthetics of sport would involve close examination of each sport individually—yacht-racing, for instance, has a beauty which is peculiar to it, and this could well be the case with every sport." Elliott implies, of course, that the athletes of the given sports would be consulted, thus he is in agreement with the precept offered here that much of the aesthetics of sport can be explained by reference to criteria that are *sport-specific*. The judgment that a wrestler sees more that is beautiful in wrestling than would a tennis player, and vice versa, is a tenet that can be tested by reference to appropriate groups.

Why Superstars Look Beautiful in Action

It has been said by John Lawther (1951) that great athletes have good form because they save energy. By this he means that the extra skill of the superstar makes his motions more effective, without needless motion. The superstar saves energy by the sound mechanics of his form which is utilized for endurance or for the more forceful expression of his skill. This is why both distance running and sprinting can be called beautiful in spite of the very different techniques of leg action. Greek artists knew this and depicted it on the vases (*amphorae*) that they illustrated with athletic scenes. Extending on this thought, Maheu (1962) attributes those qualities distinguishing superstars to what he calls "style":

> Style—the expression of individuality which always reveals itself—occurs in both sport and art at the highest pitch of perfection. (p. 9)

Style, for Maheu, is a superlative, not merely a descriptor differentiating two techniques of delivery or performance. Certainly, superstars are differentiated (as well as distinguished) by their respective styles, and most often the style of an athlete will set him apart. Putting it into a more germane level of discussion, Hohler (1974) states:

> In physical movement we recognize the personal qualities of the performer who not only masters but also realizes the corresponding technique of the movement. The performer's personality enriches the technique which he has acquired. In this connection we talk of an *individually mastered technique* or an *individual style* of the performer. (p. 51)

There is no doubt that superstars are recognized by their individual style. Walter Payton (see Plates 25a and 25b), O. J. Simpson, and Johnny Rodgers are all first-class running backs with identical roles to play in the performance of their skills, but each is clearly identifiable from the other in personal style. Each personal style reflects a personal beauty of action on the football field, both in isolation and in relation to other players. Style is the product of anthropometric qualities (which are hereditary) and the training required for the mastery of technique. The fundamental difference between style and technique hinges on the manner in which an athlete solves an immediate problem by recourse to creative faculty and adaptation.

THE "SPORT-AESTHETIC"

(The introduction of the concept of "sport-aesthetic" is done with some trepidation. The concept might better be introduced at the close of the book. The student should decide.)

Philosophers, accepting a generalized phenomenon, have held that relative to the sense-modality employed, one aesthetic may differ from another depending on the mode of art-form that is perceived. On the other hand, the investigations of psychologists suggest that individuals differ in their perceptual and cognitive styles and, therefore, in their receptivity to an aesthetic stimulus, irrespective of its art-form. The latter conceptualization provides the better form of reference for investigating a particular form of response which might be identified as a "sport-aesthetic."

Historically, the concept of a sport-aesthetic might be traced to the classic play theory of art expounded by Friedrich Schiller in his *On the Aesthetic Education of Man*. Earlier, both Plato and Aristotle believed in the generic connection between play and art, each regarding play as sensuous in character and as a natural expression of animal restlessness. Characteristically, play has an imitativeness and immediately pleasurable quality that can be put to the service of education through exploration and curiosity. Aristotle saw in play a recreational and cathartic function which, on the level of art, also had some value in the socialization of the child.

Schiller's "play impulse" is an expression of behavior intermediary between man's purely sensuous (animal) nature and his formal (rational)nature (Hein, 1968).

Aesthetic activity, according to Schiller, is the highest cultural form of play, since it is primarily the free exercise of the imaginative and intellectual faculties rather than exercise of the physical or affective qualities. Schiller's belief that play has both intrinsic and extrinsic value agrees with the contemporary view that the aesthetic has both implicit (behavioral) and explicit (observed) components. Extending on the Schillerian doctrine, Hein elaborates:

> Schiller does not clearly articulate the relationship between art and play, but it appears to be essentially a genetic one. Both art and play are manifestations of the play impulse, but aesthetic activity is the gratuitous exercise of higher level, i.e., intellectual faculties. Possibly it is a more mature or complex form of play. Consequently it also has a higher moral value than play, and play turns out to be a kind of apprenticeship to the aesthetic appreciation of the beautiful, which, in turn, is a stepping stone to morality. (p. 68)

Accepting the statement by Hein that aesthetic activity might possibly be "a more mature or complex form of play" invites the contention that sport, fitting that description, is also aesthetic activity. The logic of deduction is not precise, but the parallel is attractive.

Schiller's suggestion that play was initiated by an overflow of surplus energy was supported by the nineteenth-century psychologist Spencer, who contended that aesthetic activity is the play of the higher, more complex faculties and is found only among animals at a high stage of evolutionary advancement. Groos pursued Spencer's thinking, agreeing that play is functional in the maturation of ordinary instinctual processes, but he rejected Schiller's special "play impulse," and he adds nothing to the comprehension of the aesthetic.

Freud's psychoanalytic theory redirected attention from the exclusively biological nature of play, and suggested that play was not always pleasurable in an immediate sense. Play is regarded as an assimilative activity by means of which circumstantial impediments are overcome and the child or adult gains active mastery of a situation which he has passively undergone. Sutton-Smith (1969) applies these principles of Freudian thought in his interpretation of the disequilibrial function of play and sports as being concerned with redressing the balance of unconscious life. This line of argument could be applied to help explain the creative process of the artist and account in part for aesthetic experience. The contention that play is a form of conquest, and that this is the basis of pleasure derived from it, focuses on the aesthetic derived from problem solving which Emerson (1968) puts into the games and sports context. These psychological interpretations differ greatly from the phenomenological (Kaelin, 1968).

Huizinga (1950) avoids all reductive analyses of play and maintains that there is a primitive and nonreducible play instinct to which art and other forms of human culture may be attributed. For him, essential characteristics of play are "a feeling of tension, joy and the consciousness that it is 'different' from 'ordinary life.' " Emerson (1968) gives this opinion psychological veracity derived from learning theory, and Berlyne (1960) suggests that tension is a characteristic of arousal, which, in turn, is qualified by the aesthetic. This holds true for explicit and implicit factors. Further common ground is provided by Hein (1968), who draws attention to the shared quality of detachment from the real.

The fundamental problem behind the discussion of play as it relates to the aesthetic is the lack of elaboration or clarification of the concept *play*. Miller (1968) attempts to explain the function of play while avoiding the problem of definition. Definitions do not need to be a major concern here where sport is seen as a subset of play, at least to the point of inquiry where sport is performed for social or pecuniary reward. But sport as play, or sport as social reward, both apply to the explanation of the "sport-aesthetic."

The literature does not appear to carry any prior reference to the "sport-aesthetic." The "sport-aesthetic" is identifiable from the aesthetic experience derived from other art forms because of a closer empathetic relationship between the observer (spectator) and the sport as an art-form. As Susanne Langer (1957) states:

> The distinction between dancing and all of the other great arts—and of those from each other—lies in the stuff of which the virtual image, the expressive form is made. . . . As painting is made purely of spatial volumes—not actual space-filling things but virtual volumes, created solely for the eye—and music is made of passage, movements of time, created by tone—so dance creates a world of powers, made visible by the unbroken fabric of gesture. That is what makes dance a different art from all the others. (p. 67)

Indeed, one would expect a "sport-aesthetic" to correlate more with a "dance-aesthetic" than with any other aesthetic, owing to an implicit kinesthesis common to man. Applying the concept expressed by Langer, Maheu uses it to support his *a priori* assertion that sport is beautiful:

> I need hardly say that sport is a creator of beauty. In the action and rhythm which testify to mastery of space and time, sport becomes akin to the arts which create beauty. No athlete can accomplish a genuine feat without such perfect physical control, in time and space, that his movements and the rhythm of their timing are not to be differentiated

from the finest ballet, the most splendid passages of prose or verse, the most glorious lines in architecture. (p. 8)

The question of what constitutes the "sport-aesthetic" remains unanswered. It is suggested that empirical research into the nature of aesthetics is still in its primitive stages, and responsibility for deeper investigation of the "sport-aesthetic," if it is identified as being separated from aesthetics in the arts, rests with students of the sport sciences. If the concept of a "sport-aesthetic" is acceptable, it is necessary to know if it has both implicit (behavioral) and explicit (observed) components. These may be identified as subjective aesthetics and objective aesthetics of sport respectively. It is also important to find out if there is an interaction effect between them—which might help to account for "empathy."

s u m m a r y

This chapter has attempted to do two basic things: (1) to give an overview of questions to be discussed more fully in the book, and (2) to take one or two underlying principles which appear to link sport with both nature and art in the heritage of man. In the broadest sense, "beauty" as a concept is taken for granted (to be analyzed more closely in later chapters) with the exception of a brief comment on the historical derivation of the idea in primitive and Classical Greek times. Thus, the "natural beauty" of the body derives from narcissistic (or egotistic) speculation endemic to the thinking of those earlier cultures. The natural beauty of the body became identified with an "ideal" which had connotations with the supernatural through the deification of athletic heroes. From these sources of thinking there developed the "sense of proportion," a concept rooted (eventually) in all socio-cultural and political elements of Greek society.

A brief analysis of the present-day appreciation of the symmetry of the body can be instructive in educating us to perceive the beauty of asymmetrical performance. Some empirical evidence on the preferences expressed by groups for symmetrical or asymmetrical figures is presented.

The physical idea of the body differs largely from culture to culture. The present-day sense of the ideal human form derives to great extent from that held by Periclean society of Classical Greece. It appears that most cultures have used the physique of the athlete as the model for the artistic representation of the ideal human body.

Athletes are sensitive to the fact that they meet the physical ideal held by society, but more pertinently, they are aware of the beauty of action in their relative sports. They also know that the significant feature which distinguishes the superstar is a factor called "style." Style is a nondefinitive parameter describing sports-action and is as viable in its application to sport as it is in describing different forms of painting, sculpture, or music. Style is an additive, a distinguishing feature, superimposed on the mastery of technique.

The relationship of play and sport is drawn in an effort to determine root derivatives of the beauty of sport. Thus, if a case can be made for play being aesthetic (Schillerian), then we may be able to speak of a "sport-aesthetic." The concept of a "sport-aesthetic" is loose, but some further discussion of the beauty of sport as pursued by this book may help to bring better definition.

questions for discussion

1. Taking the assumption "sport is beautiful," why would anyone disagree?
2. Discuss the contention that there is no need for us to question the beauty of nature, and therefore the beauty of the human body.
3. To what extent did the Classical Greek sense of proportion pervade cultural and societal norms, behaviors, and institutions? How was it manifest in their sport?
4. Throughout history, and even today, man has accorded the athlete the best attribute of an ideal body. Discuss this in terms of the symmetry and asymmetry of the body.
5. Discuss the contribution of our concept of ideal athletic form made by R. Tait McKenzie.
6. Why do superstars look beautiful in action, and what is their own perspective of this beauty they produce?

The Relationship
of Sport and Art

The work of art is a self-sufficient, substantial
reality creatively produced and possessing
its own rationale.

PAUL WEISS

INTRODUCTION

"Principles of beauty in sports differ very little from principles of
beauty in art or architecture," states John Lawther in *The Psychology of
Sport*. What are those principles that Lawther refers to as being similar to
two areas of cultural interest which we often see as unrelated? One way of
attempting to answer this question is to look for common cultural derivations in antiquity, to see what social conditions must evolve in the formalization of society before art and sport can emerge as patterns of behavior.
This exercise would demand delving into the study of anthropology. Another way of attempting to answer the question would be to make an
etymological study of the derivations of the words, seeking to establish
agreements in the root meanings or cultural definitions of sport and art.
Both words are usually seen as "umbrella" concepts, and as such, they
satisfy the conditions of *construct* rather than pure concept—a *construct*
being more of an all-embracing or broader abstraction, cognitively speaking, than typically is ascribed to *concept*. Still a third way to approach the
question would be to take terms which can be construed to elaborate both
sport and art, and then to equate and differentiate the contexts in which
they are found. There are many other creative alternatives besides these
three.

27

Certainly, much of what we seek to explain as the beauty of sport depends on common elements in the relationship of sport and art, but we can find these without dependence on equivocational criteria. Let us accept sport and art in their broadest terms. By allowing ourselves this freedom, we leave open possibilities for creative exploration of constructs such as "sport as art," "sport in art," "athlete as artist," "art in sport" and many more options. There may be some criteria constituting the investigation of art which can be applied to the investigation of sport, such that, for example, if art implies "aesthetic" as a cultural norm for beauty, the "aesthetic" becomes a significant principle in our inquiry.

The study of the history of sport is vitally dependent upon artifacts from antiquity; pictorial illustrations of how man indulged in agonistic contest appear on coins, shields, ornaments, vases (kraters and amphorae), and in sculpted form and bas-relief. Without those graphic examples worked by the hands of pictorial artists, the history of sport would be dependent solely on the interpretation of written documents. To be sure, the ruins of buildings have something to say to the archaeologist about the behavior of man, but pictorial detail from artifacts (even shards and damaged relics) provides that conclusive evidence for posterity. Finely modeled metallic parts of harnesses, bits and bridles, tell of the sport of chariot racing, which is as old as the earliest myth ascribed to the Cyclic Poet writing before the fifth century, B.C. In that story, Heracles, driving the horse Arion, defeated Cycnus in a chariot race during games that King Copreus of Haliartus held in the temenos of the Pagasaean Apollo. Decorated chariot artifacts predate the earliest recorded words, and chariot racing was known at least one thousand years before the first recorded Olympic Games of 776 B.C. (see Plate 5).

Beside the sport and art relationship found on artifacts in antiquity, there exists to a lesser degree a similar relationship today. This relationship is explored more fully later in this chapter, and in Chapter 3. Some of the illustrative plates in this book, particularly those of the Greek amphorae, indicate the refined nature of the sport-art relationship in antiquity. Indeed, we can learn something aesthetically substantive both from the shape or form of such amphorae and from the athletic detail on their surfaces.

THE SPORT-ART PARADIGM

Today we do not give serious thought to the different historical developments of art or sport as they relate to each other. We have come to accept that such a relationship is a perfectly natural one. What concerns us most is the method by which we look at that relationship, because it will give us a strong basis for clearer understanding of the aesthetic of sport.

We do pay strict attention to the diversity of each of the categories "art" and "sport," and it is through teleological inquiry that we employ such attention to find a relationship between the arts (generically). Thus, we observe how painting and theatre are alike, how sculpture and dance are alike, as a process of uncovering elements which (hopefully) can be applied to sport—to see if sport can be brought within the purview of the arts, inferentially if not categorically. Expressive elements underpin "self-expressive" sport, and spectacle elements accompany sport for social or pecuniary reward. Both categories are satisfied. The extension of this feature of the sport-art paradigm is given greater scope in Chapter 4, Sport and the Performing Arts.

If there is agreement that the element of spectacle is present in sport, and therefore, spectators, there will be agreement as to the serious nature of sport. Acceptance of this stance precludes any discussion of sport being a recreational pursuit. Moreover, the recognition of art as serious enterprise which has as its object to win recognition for the artist, places both art and sport on definitionally agreeable planes. Elaboration of this theme can be found in *The Scientific View of Sport* by The Organizing Committee of the XXth Olympiad, Munich, 1972:

> Art and sport are both to be distinguished from play through the quality of earnestness; they demand hard work, and intense effort which can only be made by total commitment, and a great expenditure of will. The seriousness of sport is stressed by the presence of spectators. The spectator has a "connection" with the athlete, a "participation," which might be understood as a sort of initiating reproduction of the movements he makes. The "participation" is accompanied by a "distancing" (distanciation), for the spectator "never in fact intends to take part in the action." Both "participation" and "distancing" are equally characteristic of the reception of works of art: the latter can only be and has to be reproduced by the observer.
>
> The earnestness of the athlete and the presence of spectators is explained by the fact that sporting, just like artistic activity, is directed towards an *end;* both are directed towards a *result.* But what corresponds in sport to the work of art (oeuvre)? (p. 39)

The limiting nature of this question—what corresponds in sport to the work of art?—reflects our lack of understanding of both sport and art. This is not to say that obtaining a pure constitutive definition of the one will automatically give us the key to adequate definition of the other. But the serious question remains, both challenging and thought-provoking. It is wildly speculative to assume that the discussion of sport as aesthetic will bring us any closer to a real constitutive definition. However, we can claim that our level of inquiry is heightened and that, as a result, our critical perceptions are better focused.

That sport can be viewed as an art-form is being accepted more among the fraternity of physical education and sport sciences than among other disciplines. The pervasive and ubiquitous nature of sport in society, the greater exposure given to sport on television, and concomitant forces bringing greater attention to sport, all conspire to suggest that a broader vision be brought to bear on it. It is of little surprise, therefore, that sport be identified for its beauty, and for the cultural enrichment that it can bring through aesthetic appreciation.

The arts hold the traditional seat for the expression of aesthetic sentiment in the cultural heritage of man, and these have depended on the beauty of nature for inspiration. Beauty in nature has never been questioned—it has been revered. Man has developed the tools to express that reverence. He has painted and sculpted it, he has danced his admiration for it. Employing his creative skills, he has attempted to improve on the beauty of nature, but he could not do this before he had developed a conception of perfection. The concept of perfection is as much dependent on art as on nature.

For sport to be accepted as an art-form by a greater population, it must demonstrate its similarities with art in derivation of purpose as much as in its mode of expression. However, sport and art have become disparate as a result of traditional cultural forces lending weight to differing values. There is a strong doubt prevailing that predominant values associated with sport do not coincide with those of art. Sport is competitive, art not so. Exceptions occur, but the commonality is rare.

In his book *Soccer: The World Game*, Geoffrey Green (1953) suggests that commonalities and differences emerge in discussing sport and art. He believes there are more similarities than differences between the two forms of cultural expression:

> In order to appreciate the possibilities of aesthetic compensation in the sphere of sport and to grasp the meaning of the latter—especially the simple and beautiful pattern movements created in football—one can point to the very real nearness of sport to art.
>
> The two have three important things in common. Strong, emotional excitement; a system of conventions and rules by which an appropriate sphere of human experience is delimited and dominated, and which are just as serious and valid in their own particular way as the intellectual categories of philosopher and physicist; and last, exercise and creativeness within such a sphere.
>
> The essential difference between art and sport is that the latter is more external and everyday, more materialist and matter-of-fact. (pp. 214–215)

Accepting what Green says as a viewpoint, it could be forcefully argued (by an art educator or artist, for example) that the "essential difference" is not a difference at all but rather a strengthening of the argument for similarity. The exposure that is brought to contemporary art—the Chicago *Picasso* and the Calder *Flamingo,* both fine examples of monumental art in downtown Chicago—the field trips of schoolchildren to art galleries, and other methods of bringing art to the people, all make art "more external and everyday." Furthermore, the trends of Pop Art and New Realism, both recent and contemporary, are significantly "more materialist, and matter-of-fact." The similarities presented by Green can be given further support by identifying shared "negative" features common to both sport and art in culture. The editors of *The Scientific View of Sport* present the statement, for example, that:

> The "uselessness" of sport is a striking feature, identical with the "absence of purpose" in art. Sport, no more than art, responds to a need; neither has an immediate aim. If this or that jump had not been made, only the athlete and the spectators would have lost something—the pleasure in jumping or in looking on. The only justification for art and for sport is the "delirious joy." (p. 39)

Much the same can be said about the performing arts, which are a class of "art." The student of dance or drama will attest to this. Indeed, those students who have actively combined studies in theatre or in dance with their physical education and sport studies may well have come to a personal conclusion that the differences they see (if any) only serve to enrich their own perceptions. They see each form of cultural behavior all the more clearly because they have imposed severe questions pertinent to the one on the other. These questions may have contained underlying elements apropos of creativity. Certainly, creativity is recognized as the wellspring of artistic expression of any form. But so, too, creativity has been identified by psychologists as a feature of much problem-related life experience. Creativity is identified as one of the modes for learning about the world as it is experienced by the very young child. The behavioral component of creativity need not be aesthetic, but aesthetic expression in art always implies an origin in creativity. What of sport? Does the creative use of the body in solving a physical sports problem deserve the recognition of "art"? Component elements of creativity include "originality, openness, exploration, independence, and flexibility" among others. Sport endeavors that call upon the athlete to express his judgment, his emotions (nondestructive), his aesthetic perceptions, his spiritual impulses (metaphysical), and his symbolizing powers provide the range of expressive opportunities which can be readily identified with creativity as a process. Openness, or a freshness of perception, can keep alive the gift of originality in an unspoiled awareness of the most mundane of sport encounters, but more forcefully, it becomes significantly constructive in the intenseness of high-level competition. "Keeping cool under pressure" might be the vernacular expression, for in such conditions strokes of brilliance, superlative plays, can emerge for the thrill of both the athlete and the spectator. Through the creative process, independence frees the athlete from most of the typical social pressures of the stressful sport situation. Playfulness, the ontological precondition for sport, reflects the flexibility of the athlete of originality and of creative impulse and talent. Sport, ultimately, is a natural domain for the expression of creativity.

INTERPLAY BETWEEN SPORT AND ART

The two examples of writing that follow reflect a fine interplay between sport and art. The first is a quotation from the novel, *Pluche: or The Love of Art,* by French novelist Jean Dutourd. As the narrator of the story, Pluche is cast in the role of a painter.

> When I paint a picture there is nothing I cannot convey, and even with facility. Without wishing to boast, I am almost as good at it as the old masters. With my talent for painting I feel a complicity of the same nature as the champion sprinter has with his knees or the muscles of his thighs. The sprinter on his mark and getting set for the hundred yards knows nothing distinct about his body but he has an experience of this body: he knows how he must nurse a tricky muscle, how to control his breathing, and so on. These complicities give him confidence; he takes in his stride, so to speak, and with supreme ease, the distance to be run. Once past the post he perceives that he couldn't possibly not have won the race. This intimate union of heart and body, this secret understanding between self and self, I feel absolutely when I paint. (p. 3)

The piece is instructive, but it is also high-quality prose writing, the essence of the novelist's art. Indeed, the quality of the art is the reason for including the example; the simile drawn by the painter is incidental from an artistic or aesthetics point of view. In the second example the reverse becomes true. The quotation is taken from *Faster: A Racer's Dairy,* by Jackie Stewart and Peter Manso (1972), and it illustrates the way a sports event can be given aesthetic interpretation by a process of descriptive compatibility.

> Through the turns, though, is where the true character of the car shows itself. A Formula I car is really an animal; a machine, yes, of course, but beyond that an animal because it responds to different kinds of treatment. A highly bred race horse, a thoroughbred in its sensitivity and nervousness. To get the best out of it you must coax it, treat it gently and sympathetically. In a corner it's right on its tip-toes, finely balanced, on the very edge of adhesion, just fingertips on the road, and if you dominate it

or try to push it round, it will go straight on or slide off or do any number of things that leave you without control. So you coax it—gently, very gently—to get it to do what you want. You point it and coax it into the apex, and even after you've pointed it and it's all set up, committed to the corner which might still be fifty or a hundred feet away, you must be tender with it, holding it in nicely, because it's got an angle on it, an angle of roll, and it's building to its climax of hitting that apex. You've set a rhythm and now you must keep it. And as it hits the apex, you take it out nicely; you don't say, "You've got your apex, now I'll put my boot in it and drive however I want." No, your exit speed is very important, so you've got to maintain that balance or rhythm which you've been building all along. You've got to follow through, let the car fulfill itself. (p. 26)

The descriptive compatibility is between machine and animal, between machine and man, touching upon the finest expression of sensitive control. The langugae of this piece of writing, lacking the finesse of a novelist's style, nevertheless is couched in the terminology of aesthetic expression—the aesthetic expression of sport. The car loses its inanimate quality as it assumes the fingertip sensitivity of the athlete driving it; it takes on the poise of a man or animal balancing speed against control. In this example, the quality of the aesthetic in the sport is superlative to that of the writing. Indeed, by this example we are given some hint of what Bouet (1948) means by the "functional aesthetic" (see Chapter 8).

SPORT AND THE FINE ARTS

In his commentary on the "sport as a fine art" paradigm, Osterhoudt (1972) discusses the *medium* of a given art form. Osterhoudt must be viewed as a philosopher of a purist mold, who casts his observation in the Hegellian dialectic. Still, it is not difficult to sympathize with the unique way in which he draws our attention to the media distinctions operating between the fine arts. Paint and canvas are the media of paintings, written notations and musical instruments are the media of music, and with this knowledge the one art-form cannot be reproduced in any of the media of other art-forms. In the purer mode of expression that Osterhoudt employs:

> Each of the arts (from architecture to music) attends to a progressively higher level of consciousness, each characterized by its own distinctive uniqueness. As logically non-essential distinctions, however, both the differing media of expression and modes of embodiment offer revealing and instructive delineations. The arts differ in this regard by virtue of their being expressed in terms of media quite characteristically different from one another. These media are reflections (semblances) of the nature and quality of poetic contemplation associated with given art forms.

That is, they (the media) accurately manifest the notions which are of the arts, and existentially distinguish one form from another. Such that, that which is musically contemplative may not be painted; that which is architecturally creditable may not be expressed in terms of the theater. Similarly, with regard to modes of embodiment, one may not sculpt human movement, nor write sport. That some of the media are temporal in nature (performance dependent upon an extraction from art object—those of theater, opera, cinema, dance, sport, and music) and others spatial (presentation not dependent upon an extraction from art object, as presentation is art object—those of architecture, painting, literature, drama and poetry) is also of interest in this respect. In the case of the former, artificial (objective—spatial) modes of embodiment need accompany the media, while in the case of the latter the modes of embodiment are the media. The medium of sport is human movement; the mode of embodiment is the human body. (pp. 18–19)

The logical conclusion that "the medium of sport is human movement" is not pursued in respect to the suggestion that human movement is a fine art. Osterhoudt is careful not to say it even though it appears to be implicit in his thinking. What he does say, later, is that he excludes from "sport," activities which depend on automotive expression. Thus, he does not appear to allow that either (1) a racing car, hydroplane, or similar vehicle, or (2) the pilot of such vehicles in competition can be considered in his paradigm of sport as a fine art. It would be of value to approach Osterhoudt on his perceptions of nonautomotively powered vehicular sport such as gliding, sailing, and the like for a closer delineation of the frame of reference for his paradigm.

If Osterhoudt does not say that human movement is a fine art, he still contends that the athlete experiences a heightened awareness of himself and of the fleeting and static forms which surround him in his sport. Does the athlete see the architecture of the stadium as a part of his own aesthetic being? Osterhoudt would suggest that he does. Are both sailors and swimmers sensitive to the interpretation of aesthetic elements attaching to water? If they are, and Osterhoudt would assure us they are, would they give us independent or dependent conceptions of that beauty? To a large extent, these questions are rhetorical. If an answer is not already contained in them, then we quickly find our own answers for them. There are many alternative ways of approaching such questions, and we can choose to answer from a perspective of "beauty" or of "art." However, it is not sufficient to accept that "whatever their artistic merits, most sports cannot be compared to a painting or other deliberately created art object." (Gerber, 1972).

We might choose to make exceptions with reference to the so-called "form sports" of gymnastics: diving and figure skating. If we do, some challenge can be made that the comparison of sports with the fine arts is a valid one. Most certainly, the analysis of "painting or other deliberately created art objects," employing classical modes of dissection and interpretation, can be most rewarding in seeking deeper understanding of sport as art. Knowledge of the tenets of form, line, color, and chiaroscuro (tone), which instructs the student in estimating the aesthetic force of a work of art, can be effectively applied to sport. The analysis of a sports-painting, for example, can be done from two major perspectives: (1) the dissection of the painting as a viable work of art—the lines, colors, and general dynamics of the painting subscribing to the intrinsic quality—and (2) the analysis of the sports action as depicted. Clearly, the art student brings his skills to the former case, while the student athlete, physical education major, or student of sports sciences brings his skills to the latter case. Another typical way in which this is effected is through the analysis of sports photographs from newspapers and sports magazines. It should always be remembered that the photographer who took the original picture had some training in art and in "seeing," and further, the editor who selects the pictures is not totally naive of artistic presentation and layout techniques. The analysis of sports-sculpture follows similar principles.

Popular as it might be to draw associations (and dissociations) between certain sports and "painting and sculpture," we should be warned against this narrow perception of "art." More germane to the analysis of sport as art is the ready acceptance of "the arts" as the basis for comparison. Painting and sculpture are only two of "the nine basic arts" (Weiss, 1964). As Paul Weiss identifies them, they are: architecture, painting, sculpture, dance, music, poetry, musicry, theatre, and literature. To what extent we will find an interrelationship between sport and architecture leading us to a closer comprehension of the aesthetics of sport is open to speculation. The most obvious association to be made between sport and architecture, for example, is in the identification of sports stadia which add a touch of aesthetic flair to the skyline of modern cities (the Superdome of New Orleans, for example). By inspecting sports-painting and sports-sculpture, with the intention of better understanding the tenets of line, form, color, and the like, we sensitize ourselves to criteria transferrable to the analysis of sport as art. Logically, we move closer to this outcome the more we place line and form in the dynamics of active art (dance, acting) than in static art (the plastic arts of painting, sculpture, and ceramics).

In looking at the relationship of sport to art several factors can be considered. These are:

1. the problem of defining the "sports-painting" or "sports-sculpture"
2. the differential representation of sports by the athlete-artist and the nonathlete-artist

3. the differential representation of individual and team sports in painting and in sculpture
4. the changing modes of painting and sculpture, as they affect the representation of sports

Prior to a close inspection of these points it is worth bearing in mind that the study of the relationship between art and sport is bedeviled by a basic fact which is best summed up in the following quotation from *Art News,* December 31, 1938:

> Many of the paintings and the sculpture which immortalize the sportsman in pastimes dear to his heart go immediately into private collections. (p. 15)

However, in spite of this implicit limitation there are many other sources of information accessible to the researcher. Reproductions of paintings can be found in histories of American painting, biographies of artists, gallery catalogues, periodicals, and newspapers. Information about the sport involvement of artists can also be drawn from these sources. In some circumstances correspondence with curators of galleries, and, more directly, personal correspondence with living artists provides further information. Hence, evidence for study is available, but what do we mean by "sports-art"?

SPORT IN ART, OR SPORTS-ART

The study of sport in art would appear to provide subject matter for either the student of art or of sport. The fact that there are students whose lifestyles deeply concern them with both areas of study makes it a pertinent field of investigation. However, both areas are divided into a large number of subsets, each of which merit close attention. Thus there is the possibility of permutating a great variety of areas of investigation from the topic "sport in art."

The representation of sports by artistic expression is found in the heritage of many cultures. Sculpture, pottery, and mosaics have provided the sports historian with the earliest records of sports as they were performed by ancient civilizations. Oil painting, developed during the Renaissance, provided a further method for recording sports scenes. Ironically, the period of refinement of painting techniques was attended by a period of restriction in the development of sports. What Masterson (1974) says of the European schools of painting and sculpture is equally true of the American scene:

> . . . a superficial examination of the popular subjects of modern painting would confirm that sport is not amongst them—but if one looks be-

neath the surface, it is possible to find that many artists, amongst whom may be included some of the great masters of modern art, have at various times chosen to include sporting themes in their work. (p. 70)

Notably in America, George Bellows' boxing scenes reflect the truth of what Masterson says about Europe.

THE PLASTIC ARTS: PAINTING AND SCULPTURE

The success of the sport-sculptor or sport-painter lies in the fact that his intimacy with techniques in sport underpins the quality of art that he puts into his works. For any piece of art to succeed, there must be the selection of a critical moment when technique and aesthetic significance can be matched. R. Tait McKenzie, noted sport-sculptor, was able to catch the precise psychological moment of a sports action which summarized the totality of movement of the event. Actual sports movement is typically an extremely rapid event, when immediate balance is of necessity sacrificed to the balance of the totality of action. It goes without saying that the catching of this spirit of beauty in imbalance, the choice of the right psychological moment, is patently elusive to all but the practiced eye. The presentation of imbalance by the sport-sculptor and the sport-painter provides us with a clue to arrested motion in art. Furthermore, the capturing of the appearance of imbalance in an athlete—say, a running back as he cuts back sharply to turn inside a tackle or behind a block—where he appears to be falling, gives us a sense of dynamic force that the artist seeks to present in his work. The sports-photographer today often captures this same dynamic action of the athlete (see Plates 25 and 28), showing us an element of beauty deriving not only from the line of the body but also from the impression of centripetal force imputed to the straining, driving effort of the muscles in the juxtaposition of weight and balance. Good sports photography meets all the criteria of good painting and sculpture.

One of the most beneficial ways of looking at the sport-art relationship is to study the works of famous artists, painters, and sculptors who have successfully demonstrated that they can capture sports action. The pattern of inquiry requires the student to become familiar with sports-paintings and sports-sculpture, particularly those representing the major spectator sports of baseball, basketball, football, ice hockey, boxing, and horse racing. First, in this chapter a few thoughts are expressed on how sport appears in art, more specifically in painting and sculpture.

Sports-Painting

The looseness of the term "sports-painting" is compounded by two major factors. In the first place, sport can be loosely defined according to the source referred to: for example, whereas hunting and fishing are "sport" for one expert, they are excluded by definition for another. Second, and not so critical, is the question of what constitutes a painting, and this can be interpreted by reference to media used (oil, tempera, watercolor) on the one hand, or by reference to style on the other. This last point draws attention to the distinctions separating a "painting" from an "illustration." The narrow difference can be best understood when considering whether Norman Rockwell is an "artist" or an "illustrator." Many people would categorize him as an illustrator because his work was done mainly for magazines or "popular consumption" rather than for hanging in galleries, and his work is associated with a less-disciplined approach to the use of line and color. What features, then, make a painting different from an illustration? Artists tell us that the "quality" of the materials is one criterion, but there is a wide range of materials (as pointed out above) and a wide range of applying them to paintings. Oil paintings have a depth or solidity of appearance in the way the colors reflect the light, whereas watercolor paintings appear to be light absorbent and softer in tone. Two admirable examples of sports-paintings, executed in oil on canvas, are illustrated in this book: George Luks, *The Wrestlers,* and Frederic Remington's *Touchdown, Yale vs. Princeton, Thanksgiving Day, November 27, 1890, Yale 32, Princeton 0.* The painting by Luks is an excellent example of the use of tone (chiaroscuro), with the highlighting of the body of the athlete bridging to resist the pindown. In the Remington study there is a line, a directional force moving from the right-hand side of the picture toward the left lower corner. This "line" is reinforced in the action of the diving athlete and the watching eyes of the spectators. In neither of these pictures is there a tendency to force our attention out of the composition of the picture.

For the purposes of this book, a sport is pertinent in proportion to the amount of artistic representation it has had in painting. In other words, the painting must have earned critical acclaim and stand on its own right regardless of the fact that a sport is the subject of the art-work. Again, critical attention must be paid to the sport action in the painting. Is there emphasis on the style of sport performance? Is there any feeling of movement in the action of the figures? Does the picture capture the tension of the moment in the arrested movement? These questions demand that commentary be made both on the representation of movement in sport and on the quality of artistic expression and relative renown of the work of art.

If noncompetitive sports activity is considered, then greater weight is given to the pastime or recreation element in sport, and this allows for an expanded range of choice in interpreting what is a sports-painting. Take the case of swimming and skating. Research has not produced examples of paintings depicting swimming or skating competitions, but the subjects have been well-treated in comparison with other sports. Thomas Eakins painted *The Swimming Hole* in 1883, Yasuo Kuniyoshi painted *The Swimmer* in 1924 (see Plate 10), and Phillip Evergood painted *Lure of the Waters* in 1946. At least six paintings have been executed depicting skating: John O'Brien, *Moonlight Skating in Central Park* (1873); Everett Shinn, *Hoboken Skaters* (1905); William Glackens, *Central Park, Winter* (1905) and *Skating, Central Park* (1905); Louis Eilshemius, *The Skater, Central Park* (1906); and Kenneth Miller, *The Skaters* (1943).

From a different standpoint, portraiture is seen as sports-painting when the subjects are either athletes or others in sportswear. A variety of examples will serve to illustrate this point. In 1871 Thomas Eakins painted *Margaret in Skating Costume,* a three-quarter-length portrait of a seated figure; Yasuo Kuniyoshi painted *Self-Portrait as a Golf Player* in 1947, a full-length study of the artist; John Kane's *Self-portrait* (1929), is a half-length pose of himself as a prizefighter; Henry McFee painted *Japanese Wrestler* (circa 1935), study of a reposing nude; and *Howard Petterson of the Harlem Yankees,* a three-quarter-length portrait of a seated basketball player holding a basketball, was painted in 1940 by Edmund Archer.

Walt Kuhn painted many studies of athletes and strong men which are fine examples of athletic portraiture; among them are: *Athlete* (1919), *Top Man* (1931), *Wrestler* (1933), *Hand Balancer* (1944), and many studies of circus performers and stunt men. According to the notes in the Cincinnati Art Museum catalogue, Kuhn inherited a stocky build from his father, and "during the season he barnstormed country fairs as a professional bicycle racer (between 1897 and 1900), the great day of the bicycle."

Styles in painting, from dynamic action to reposeful portraiture, instruct the student in the breadth of presentation that this art-form offers. The quality of a painting is not always contingent upon the view of critics and galleries; we can find our own "quality" in a painting if we study it and enjoy it for its intrinsic elements of line, color, and form.

Sports-Sculpture

In sculpture, form and shape, as much as pure line, are seen in a dimensional way as we might see an athlete performing in a sport. To Hussey (1929), this concept of dimensionality in sculpture is given a dynamism by R. Tait McKenzie in his work:

> We need go no further than some of McKenzie's work to see how, by skillful choice of poise, the rhythm of a beautiful movement can be expressed in a motionless form. (p. 36)

Some people are of the opinion that the moving body has sculptural qualities, and these are emphasized by the perception of color and the subtle movement of clothing on the body. Such judgment could be applied to the action and appearance of the athlete, and this observation becomes particularly highlighted when we see two teams like Southern California (Red and Gold) and UCLA (Blue and Gold) run out onto the football field. The color heightens the movement in an artistic fashion and is as meaningful aesthetically as the ballet sculptures of Degas, who placed a tulle dress on his bronze art-work to add a sense of realism. In antiquity, paint was applied to sculpture, a fact no less significant than the painted decorations of the totem poles of primitive societies.

As with painting, recent trends in sculpture have brought representation from the literal to the figurative. Sport action, of course, depends on the literal if it is to be truly represented in this three-dimensional art-form. Hence, it is not surprising that rarely has sports-sculpture represented the human form in abstraction. The representation of the human form in sports action has largely followed the earliest tenets of Greek sculpture, although individual sculptors have often interpreted it in varying degrees of naturalism and realism.

According to Herbert Read, the stylistic integrity of sculpture was lost with the death of Michelangelo, but the revival of interest in sculpture began in the late nineteenth century with the work of Rodin. Rodin's visual realism gave sculpture an air of modernity, but it was the influence of Degas and Matisse that brought sculpture to maturity for twentieth-century expression. With sculptors of the twentieth century, an ideal of dynamism was injected into their work. For example, a particular group of sculptors, the Futurists, worshipped the concepts of power and speed which are both basic to athletes striving for excellence in their sports. European trends in sculpture have had significance for sculpture in North America, specifically with respect to the development of sports-sculpture. One important link is between modern sculptors and the sculptors of Classical Greece, who often showed athletes in action in wrestling, running, and the like. The sculpture of R. Tait McKenzie has a definite Greek influence.

In Chapter 1 we discussed how R. Tait McKenzie first became recognized as a sculptor. *The Sprinter* and *The Athlete,* his first two attempts at artistic form in the round after completing the masks of *Effort, Breathlessness, Fatigue,* and *Exhaustion,* had won for him recognition on an international level. He had successfully shown both studies at the Royal Academy of London in 1903 and at the Paris Salon in 1904.

In 1904 he left McGill University and took the position of Director of Physical Education at the invitation of the University of Pennsylvania, Philadelphia. The turning point is significant in his artistic career, for he elected to depend more on his own sense of form and proportion in sculpture and to reject his earlier scientific application of mensuration to his art. However, he continued to include athletic subjects among his works. Two of the best "breakaway" subjects are *The Competitor,* completed in 1907, and *The Relay,* 1909, both evocative of the work of Rodin.

Throughout the years 1904 to 1911 McKenzie worked on a study of a football scrum, *The Onslaught.* It illustrates a halfback carrying the ball supported by two other backs aiding his vaulting assault of the line, and to complete the wedge effect of breaking the line, two ends have come around in support of the backs. The attacking guards have taken out their opposite number to create the "hole," but other defensive guards are moving to block the gap, and the ball-carrier is sailing up over them. It is an event which occurs in almost every football game seen on television today.

It would appear that sculpture lends itself particularly well to the representation of sports, yet there might appear to be a limiting factor on the types of sport (or the focus of action) which are best represented. An interesting study of this question might well be made. Boxing and wrestling appear quite frequently in sculpture, for example. As the correspondent for *Art News* points out:

> For the last twenty years Mahonri Young has modeled the outstanding boxers of the generation with a sympathetic understanding of the machine that is the human body. "Groggy" contains all the elements of his series of interpretations in bronze. (p. 15)

Prominent sculptors from North America who did sports-sculpture include Mahonri Young, Joseph Brown, Sybil Kennedy, R. Tait McKenzie, Clemente Spampinato, and William Zorach among others. All these sculptors obtain a truly vital element in their works. An example of portraiture in sculpture is seen in the polychromed plaster figure of *Casey Stengel* by Rhoda Sherbell, completed in 1965; this is an example of the new realism school following the pop art period. Joe Brown was a boxer as well as a football player in his youth, and the relevance of this fact to his skill as a sculptor is discussed in the next chapter. An example of a boxing study by Mahonri Young is found in Plate 7.

The question may arise: Are sports trophies examples of sport-sculpture? In some cases they can be considered as such, but most often they are not. The distinction can be made in this way: The Heisman Trophy, showing a rushing ball-carrier, can be construed as sculpture, as can the Brancusi-like shaped football bronze known as the Grantland Rice Memorial Trophy. Less appropriate for the title of "sculpture" would be those trophies which show a miniature track athlete or a bowler set on top of a columnar structure. These trophies are intended as mementos rather than as works of art, and they should be equated with awards rather than with art.

At this point it seems appropriate to bring in the relationship of art to Olympism. Section Four of the Charter of the Olympic Games states:

> The Olympic Games must include the following events: Athletics, Gymnastics, Combative Sports, Swimming, Equestrian Sports, Pentathlon and Art Competitions.

Emphasis is added to this edict in Section Ten of Regulations and Protocol for the Celebration of the Olympic Games, which states:

> Art and literary exhibitions which may be organized during the Games and in connection with them are not fixed. It is desirable that they should be numerous and especially that public lectures should take place and also that the work submitted for art competitions and accepted by the jury should be exhibited in the stadium or in its neighborhood.

An account of the levels of support that such abjurations have received throughout the period of the Modern Games is given by Bland (1948). The record is not very good. However, de Coubertin held a firm belief in the cultural interdependence of art and sport and cited the rebirth of the Olympic Games as the potential impetus for the regeneration of a fine relationship to be exhibited. The views of de Coubertin, as analyzed by Dr. Erhard Höhne, are given in the following section.

COUBERTIN ON THE PLACE OF ART IN MODERN OLYMPISM*

"Modern Olympism,"† the complex manifestation of the modern Olympic Games, by definition comprises not only the greatest event in world sport and its four-year cycle of competition for victory and medals among the world's best athletes, in accordance with the endeavors and aspirations of its originator, the French humanist, historian, sociologist, and educationist Baron Pierre de Courbertin, but also—and very decidedly—boasts its own philosophically well-grounded idea. Briefly, the ideological roots of this idea are classical bourgeois humanism and respect for man's dignity.

---

* The author wishes to acknowledge the courtesy of Dr. Erhard Höhne for the use of his original article. Under the title above, the article originally appeared in the Bulletin of the National Olympic Committee of the German Democratic Republic, IV/1969, I/1970, and II/1970.

† *L'Olympisme moderne,* a term coined by Coubertin, includes everything connected with the resumption of the Olympic Games and with Olympic thought since 1894.

On this basis, Coubertin included in this modern Olympism, fundamental principles such as democracy, democratic internationalism, equal rights for all human beings and nations, civic education in the spirit of genuine patriotism and yet of mutual international regard—in spite of racial, religious, and political differences; he also included devoted service to peace and education for peace. Modern Olympism is thus essentially an educational program: education in the spirit of a humanitarianism which directly derives from sport and is characterized by fair play, sporting competition according to the motto *"citius—altius—fortius"* (ever faster, higher, stronger), recognition of the Olympic athlete as the model of every citizen's athletic way of life (*religio athlatae,* as Coubertin called it), and by thoughts and feelings based on scientific insights, political responsibility, and aesthetic values.

At the time when the bourgeoisie was beginning to give up and even disclaim the best traditions of progressive bourgeois movements, Coubertin hoped to preserve those fundamental ideals by integrating them into modern Olympism. But he also felt that the working class would one day take up, cherish, and perfect what his own class, the bourgeoisie, had ultimately failed to achieve. In his pamphlet "Entre deux batailles"—written in 1922, after the First World War—he expressed his concept as follows:

> . . . One could hardly expect that the working class will be reduced to its former lot. The only alternative in dealing with it is either to reach a compromise with, or to yield to, it.

> A variety of opinions is beginning to develop around this alternative. Some consider the debit side, the disintegrated state of our society, its failure to implement its own improvement—and thus take up the ideals of a new society, a juster and consequently a more Christian one. Others believe that the elements of restoration are there and will eventually manifest themselves. However, no matter whether the working class will, in the near future, exercise power completely or only share in it, its preparation for this task remains a question of prime importance. . . .

> Time has passed. The question has come to a head, in fact so much so that some people believe it is too late to deal with it successfully, and therefore put up with what they call the end of culture and an offensive return to primitive barbarism. I am not one of them. I expect much from the working class; it holds tremendous promise and seems to me capable of very great achievements. On the other hand, are we not deluding ourselves about that culture of which we are so proud? There is so much slag to be found in the pure metal, so much of the absurd and the artificial, so much insipid self-complacency and barely veiled pornography!

> Nevertheless, the problem, in my opinion, presents itself like this: Under no circumstances can the working class suddenly be faced with great

culture as defined during the preceding era: The working class itself must take stock so that the temple which holds the treasure acquired in the history of civilization is revered and preserved when it is placed in the hands of this class tomorrow! (1)*

I have quoted Coubertin at some length here in order to illustrate what I consider essential for the definition of his Olympism, namely this: The allegation advanced by some of the friends (but mainly by opponents) of the modern Olympic movement, that Olympism as understood by Coubertin is now an antiquated concept which must be replaced by new versions and new "isms," is either an idle contention with no thorough knowledge of facts to back it up, or a deliberate denial of Olympism's fundamentally humanitarian and humanist message. From the above I would argue as follows:

1. Coubertin's Olympism is a humanist concept based on classical bourgeois humanism and therefore subject to the idealism and historically conditioned limitations of this philosophy, but nevertheless a challenge and an obligation for us simply because Olympism will forever remain a humanist responsibility.

2. For us, to keep Coubertin's Olympism thus means to pass on and to surpass its humanist essence within real socialist humanism, since Coubertin wanted his idea to be understood in a context of time and place, demanding and practicing—as a historian—a historical approach not least toward and in his own work. His historical thinking was determined not only by his concept of an integrated world with an integrated social development, but also by a deep understanding of the continual and irrepressive development of man and mankind toward ever greater perfection.

3. Coubertin's Olympism also includes the particular mission of the working class now risen to power, to defend his heritage and his ideals—a fundamentally humanist message to the world—against any falsification, vilification, or even refutation from any quarter; to defend it in the same way as the exiled German writer Heinrich Mann did when, during the First International Writers' Congress in 1935, he revealed the character of the 1936 Olympic Games. Mann later wrote about that Congress:

> Humanists are useful only from the moment they start hitting out instead of merely thinking. Henri Barbusse, whose last act was the conception and implementation of the Paris Congress in 1935, was a militant man, and this is what we want to be. He had a grasp of realities to be used as the tools of spiritual concepts, and he sensed power that could be seized. . . . (2)

* Parenthetical numbers in this section refer to footnotes on page 55.

4.   Coubertin's Olympism is a universal idea, philosophically, historically and educationally well-grounded and paying particular attention to culture, i.e., to science and learning, art, and literature. As creator of the Olympic ideal, he hoped that culture would, in the course of time, be integrated into the more obvious manifestation and instrument of his modern Olympism—the Olympic Games—in the same way as it had been in Ancient Greece in the heyday of the Games at Olympia. This is what he writes in his "Mémoires olympiques":

> It was not by accident that the writers and artists of old assembled at Olympia around the ancient sports; it was from this incomparable coalescence that the prestige sprang which for so long characterized the institution. (3)

Nor is it by accident that we now undertake to deal with the question of what the position and role of literature and art have so far been within the Olympic movement of our day, and what their position and role ought to be according to Coubertin: This is, after all the twentieth year after the establishment of the first peaceful state on German soil, the German Democratic Republic; and it is the seventy-fifth year after modern Olympism was created. So I hope that the above introductory remarks will contribute to a full understanding of the complex situation.

Coubertin dreamed of inbuing the modern Olympic Games with the spirit and meaning of the ancient Greek games—in particular of those held at Olympia—"if not in technical detail, in principle." This meant grounding them on five "pillars," which he saw as interrelating elements forming a unity. Three of these were classical: the intellectual, the moral, and the quasi-religious one. The other two were modern: one signifying "technical perfections" and the other, "democratic internationalism." (4) This means that learning, art, and literature were to be accorded the same important position that they had so uniquely held in the classical games.

Coubertin himself said "it would have been childish" to demand such a degree of artistic and literary integration as early as 1896, or even to expect it from the 1900 Games, which were held in connection with the Paris World Exhibition. This meant that he was again reduced to planning progress in stages, which, incidentally, he considered the best approach "in any enterprise involving many-sided intellectual capacities and a spirit of durability." (5)

It was therefore not until 1906 that he called an "Advisory Conference on Art, Science and Sport," which brought together about sixty artists and writers in the Comédie Française

> to discuss to what extent and in what ways art and learning might take part in the celebration of modern Olympiads and, more generally, be

combined with the practice of sport, both to their own advantage and the latter's enrichment. (6)

At this conference, Coubertin gave the opening address, whose central idea was presented as follows:

The first point of our plan, which we are today submitting to you for criticism and advice, is the envisaged creation of five competitions, in architecture, sculpture, painting, music, and literature. In these competitions, previously unpublished works directly inspired by the concept of sport are to be honored once every four years. Entries for these competitions may at first perhaps be small in number, and they may even be poor in quality, simply because in the beginning such competitions will no doubt attract only artists and writers who personally practice some kind of sport. Indeed, should not the sculptor who wishes to create a fitting representation of the tremendous muscular excitement which such an effort produces in the athlete's body, himself have had some personal experience of it? And again: Are we going to be held back by that unfounded and thoroughly antiquated prejudice which alleges that certain professions are incompatible with sport? The strength and universality of sport—gained in so short a space of its renaissance—shield us from such apprehensions. As early as the next generation, there will be intellectuals and professional people who at the same time will be athletes. Is this not a common fact among fencers even today?

In this, time is on our side. It would, however, not be prudent to expect too much from the future alliance between athletes, artists, and spectators. So much still needs to be done, for eurhythmy* has been forgotten. (7)

Following Coubertin's proposal, the artists assembled at the Conference decided to call for the inclusion of those five art competitions in the modern Olympic Games. Their decision, however, was not effected at the London Games. It was first put into practice—although in the face of fierce opposition from the Swedish artists of that time—in Stockholm in 1912. But Coubertin and the International Olympic Committee (IOC) had meanwhile not been idle. They had, for example, organized a special international architectural competition in Paris in 1911, which was to produce detailed plans for a "new Olympia," which had previously been set out in principle in a series of articles published by the "Revue olympique" (October 1909 to March 1910). But this time it was the "indecision and cold indifference" (8) of young architects that Coubertin found to criticize, even if the celebration in honor of the prize-winners seems to have

---

* Eurhythmy, which was simply defined as "regularity, harmony, and just proportion" at the beginning of the twentieth century and is described as "beautiful, perfect harmony of the forms of life and expression" in a recent German dictionary, was in the latter meaning Coubertin's comprehensive term of the content and manifestations of cultured, perfect living. This style of living was to be a reflection of the aesthetic qualities of useful and materially beautiful things and it was to be achieved not least thanks to modern Olympism.

fully compensated him for this disappointment. In this connection, the following description of this celebration is well worth our attention:

> It was held during the night, in the quadrangle of the Sorbonne, which was filled with two thousand guests in spite of a threatening storm. An orchestra and choirs were hidden behind artificial shrubbery. The quad lay in complete darkness. Beautifully planned illuminations inside the cloister produced a variety of changing color effects. The musical program, the movements of one hundred gymnasts bearing torches and palm fronds, who formed the background to sixteen half-naked youths, whose exercises dominated the area in front of the Richelieu Chapel—all this served to maintain an uninterrupted harmony of sound, light, silence and silhouettes. . . . The architectural beauty of the surroundings made its own marvelous contribution to the effect. Then followed the interlude of a medieval and yet modern fencing match, the appearance of a small group of men with barrelorgans and bagpipes who accompanied the "Pas d'armes du roi Jean" by Saint-Saëns, a Hellenistic round dance performed by women, and finally the performance of the charming play specially written for this occasion by Maurice Pottecher, "The Philosopher and the Athletes," in which a genuine wrestling match had been included. The climax was reached when Bengal fires were lighted in the timberwork of the building and its cupola, while choirs sent forth the magnificent harmonies of Rameau and Palestrina over an enthusiastic and yet composed crowd. This tremendous effect had required no more than the cooperation of a gymnastic club, a fencing club, and of musical societies from one Paris quarter. For me, this meant not only the realization of a wonderful dream, but also a new, certain aim with regard to popular art. Civilization had gone astray, and only the "return to eurhythmy" would put it back on the right path again." Eurhythmy, a forgotten concept that one speaks about without having the least idea of what it really once was. (9)

Just how much Coubertin wanted art of this type—gayness, buoyancy, and an aesthetic harmony of life and expression—to be included in the Olympic Games, together with art competition proper, is shown in his account of the Stockholm Games:

> In the superb setting provided by the capital, the young people let themselves be carried away with the general elation. They hardly slept, but then nobody felt like sleeping. Fêtes and celebrations followed one another and yet did not interfere with physical achievements. The Gothic stadium with its pointed arches and turrets, its technical perfection, good organization, and general sense of purpose appeared to be a model of its kind. We saw it changed into a banqueting, a concert, and a dance hall, and yet it was always ready for the next competitions on the following morning. We saw it covered with thoughtfully prepared turf squares overnight, we saw obstacles erected and flowering shrubs embellish it for the equestrian events. All this happened without any fuss, without delays,

without a single oversight. In London, the life of the giant city had not shown the least sign of being affected by the vicinity of the Olympic Games; Stockholm, however, was steeped in them. The whole city took part in the general endeavor to honor the strangers, and one had a kind of vision of what the atmosphere at Olympia must have been like in ancient times—a vision which became the greater and the more beautiful through all the comfort and amenities—for once unspoiled—of our day, so that Hellenism and progress seemed to have united to receive the world. (10)

It was in this comprehensive sense then that Coubertin viewed the question of the role and position of art in the Games. He defined as one of the foundations of modern Olympism,

> . . . beauty, derived from the participation of art and intellect in the Games. Indeed, can one celebrate the festival of human vernality without inviting intellect?

And he answers his own question:

> But this brings up the important question of the interrelation between brawn and brain insofar as their union, their joint effort, must be given a definite shape. The brain is no doubt the dominant element; the brawn must remain its servant—though on condition that it is the most perfect forms of artistic and literary creation and not insignificant products of the kind that, thanks to the ever growing indulgence of our time, are obtruding themselves on us everywhere—much to the detriment of civilization, truth, human dignity, and international relations. (11)

To round this off, let me quote two more characteristic remarks by Coubertin on the position and role of art within modern Olympism, the former made in connection with the organization of artistic competitions during the Paris Games of 1924, and the second from Coubertin's Appeal to Youth of April 17, 1927, in Olympia.

> The Marquis de Polignac had made the organization of the art competitions his special concern, and it is thanks to him that at last they became worthy of Olympism. Feeling that this was still not enough, he managed to arrange an "Art Season of the VIIIth Olympiad" as well, held at the Theatre des Champs Elysées. This gave Parisians the pleasure of, in particular, listening to the Ninth Symphony—the one which I have personally always considered the Olympic symphony par excellence—performed by the orchestra and choirs of the famous Dutch Mengelberg Society from Amsterdam. . . . (12)

And his Appeal to Youth reads:

> We—this is my friends and I—have not put every effort into restoring the Olympic Games to you in order that they may be made into a museum-

piece or a movie spectacle, or that financial or electioneering interests may take control of them. By reviving an institution which originated 25 centuries ago we wished to enable you to become disciples of the religion of sport as our great ancestors understood it. In our modern world, which brims with immense opportunities but is also threatened by dangerous degeneration, Olympism can establish a school of noble-mindedness and moral purity as well as of perseverance and physical energy; but this will happen only if you continually keep aspiring to the same heights in your concepts of honor and sporting unselfishness as you attain in your muscular endeavors. The future depends on you. (13)

If we review again the position or role attributed by Coubertin to literature and art within modern Olympism—this is why these decisive passages have been quoted at length—we arrive at two basic, general conclusions:

1. Wishing to secure for the Olympism of our time both the humanitarian educational spirit of antiquity and that of the progressive bourgeoisie, and in particular to achieve the "rapprochement of the marital partners" art and sport, which he considered "of the greatest importance" for the fertility of that "remarriage" (14), Coubertin defined as the decisive instrument in this endeavor the art competitions (which were to be of equal importance with the athletic contests) and the planning of not only the Olympic Games program, but also of regional sports meetings, on generally eurhythmic and artistic lines. In his 1906 speech he said:

    This serves a double purpose: We organize the thought-provoking cooperation between art, science, and the revived Olympic Games on the one hand, and their everyday modest and limited cooperation with sporting activities at the level of local promotions on the other. There is no doubt, gentlemen, that we shall succeed. However, there is no doubt either that this will require much time and patience. (15)

    The position of art and literature within modern Olympism is therefore one of equal partnership with sport. Each should learn from the other, each should inspire his partner to excellence; they should acknowledge and elevate each other, since it is only in their combination that they can fully express genuine vitality and zest for living—the *mens fervida in corpore lacertoso** which Coubertin wanted to teach, in the course of time, to all mankind as their inalienable *raison d'être*.

2. This legacy, in fact, if we look only at the surface, has been kept alive in the modern Olympic movement, as was shown individually in the

---

* "A glowing spirit in a muscular body"—a motto specially coined by Coubertin to characterize modern Olympism, in contrast to the over-medical and hygienic *mens sana in corpore sano*. (16)

art competitions up to 1948 and again at the Melbourne, Rome, and Tokyo Games. But the Games held in Mexico City set new standards in the preservation of this heritage.

If we consider what the organizers of the Mexico Games added, on an equally high level, to the sports competitions in the way of artistic, scientific, educational and social events, we are struck not only by the scope of their effort, but in particular by their endeavor to stimulate man's social consciousness and contact between human beings at an international level, through the special means of art. Even if art and sport in Mexico City were by and large only loosely coordinated, with little joint effort or mutual encouragement, it was a definite beginning, and both the IOC and all the National Olympic Committees (NOC's) should take the hint that it is high time they thought again, and in a fresh way, about this complex of problems.

This will have to start with a reconsideration of the decision taken by the IOC session in Athens in 1954, which ruled that no further art competitions were to be held, and it will have to go as far as to consider how the best of art and literature at any time can be really integrated into the general program of the Games and into the lives of the competitors (athletes as well as artists) and spectators.

The role or function of art and literature within modern Olympism is therefore twofold:

• works of art created in the Olympic spirit are stimulated, compared, evaluated and exhibited as reflections of man's need and zest for physical culture and sport, through national and international art competitions;

• the "Festival of man's vernality"—the Olympic Games—as well as comparable regional games, are embellished and raised to the level of cultural festivals, thus providing, over and above the experience of sport, deep cultural impressions of the Olympic spirit which can be evoked only through the characteristically artistic forms and possibilities of expression.

Coubertin's concept of the Olympic position and role of art, however, permits us to come to still more concrete conclusions:

1.   The works of art or other artistic achievements presented at the Games are to reflect the highest ideals of modern Olympism; to put it in Coubertin's brief formula: they must "serve peace and respect life." He himself set an example of this in the first Olympic art competition through his "Ode to Sport," which was submitted under a significant pseudonym and, as we know, won a gold medal. He wished that

art would keep on dealing with this very tenet of modern Olympism and give to it educationally convincing expression in the future. What he had in mind was not any so-called work of art and certainly not art for art's sake, art as it were in a vacuum, individualistic or formalistic gadgetry. What he meant was art that was committed to the basic and progressive ideas of peace, international friendship, and human dignity which make up the essence of human progress.

2.   Art, which is so closely associated with ideas and objectives, is more than a platonic declaration of love for sport. It is a fundamental means of developing social consciousness, and as such is thoroughly partisan, choosing for its own standards the ideals of modern Olympism and taking up the cause of Olympism because it is a significant and even vital element in the social existence of our time. From this it follows that it is the mission of art to represent objective reality, as opposed to objectivistic generalizations; to take sides from the choice of topic onwards, through form, content, aesthetic values, to the entirety of philosophical conviction and expression. So-called "neutrality" does not, as we have discovered, belong to the concepts that Coubertin supported or even tolerated, either verbally or in active form.

3.   Through various experiences, Coubertin's conviction had grown that literature and art—including their Olympic varieties—can justify their position and fulfill their role only when they are linked with the people, when they do not avoid everyday life with its difficulties and inadequacies in order to escape from their social responsibilities, when they do not withdraw into abstract realms, into that "realm of uncensored emotions," as it was called by Johannes R. Becher at the 1935 Paris Congress mentioned above (17), but when art—Olympic art too!—understands and accepts its alternative position. This was defined by Bertolt Brecht in connection with modern popular drama as against the Victorian fustiness of narrow-minded, petty-bourgeois "folk plays" as follows:

In this era of decisions, art too must decide. It can make itself the instrument of the few who act as gods of destiny for the many and demand faith whose chief ingredient is blindness, or it can side with the many and put their fate into their own hands. (18)

It was this close connection between art and the people, this "people's art," that Coubertin was striving for in the Olympic field, too, even if he may not have visualized the details as we understand them today.

4.   The humanist mission of modern Olympism, largely shaped by Cou-

bertin, commits art to the mission of expressing and materializing this humanism. Like the Olympic Games themselves, this humanist content goes back to Greek antiquity, to Sophocles' declaration in his "Antigone": "Powerful things there are many. But there is nothing more powerful than man." It was thus basically in progressive bourgeois thinking and in classical bourgeois humanism, which he always acknowledged as the roots of his philosophy, that Coubertin expressed the essence of his Olympism—including its limitations and unattainability under capitalist relations of production. Of this, however, Coubertin was never quite conscious, although his realistic thinking, e.g., his historical insight, drove him—as we have seen—to work for a future which was to be governed by nothing but humanism. This was most clearly expressed in his speech on youth and the future, which he gave on June 11, 1932, at the Lausanne celebration of his seventieth birthday:

> May there be a threefold will within you to support and guide you: the will to enjoy physical pleasure, which produces intensive and even excessive muscular effort; next, the will to practice undiluted, undivided and constant altruism . . . , for, mind you, the society of the future will be altruistic or it will not be at all: you will have to choose between it and chaos; and finally, the will to understand the entities comprehensively. . . . (19)

This is why there is a particular obligation for us never to cease striving, on the basis of this heritage, for the real humanism that has become possible in a socialist society and in socialist realism, for the benefit both of modern Olympism and of the art integrated into it. We have, after all, the required revolutionized relations of production and a scientifically established philosophy of the world, which includes a scientific concept of man's nature and of the laws of his social development.

In addition, however, if a work of art created under different social conditions is characterized by a humanist content and artistic veracity, modern Olympism should be concerned—so far as such works of art fall within its scope—to acknowledge this progressive, hopeful force and to give it prominence and publicity; for the progress of mankind will be implemented the sooner, the stronger we can forge the alliance of all progressive forces against reaction and barbaric manipulation, so that it can make its strength and its decisive power felt in the worldwide ideological struggle of our time.

5. To think and act in the spirit of Coubertin also means not to limit ourselves in artistic competitions to the original group of five, but to

acknowledge historical developments and to recognize all forms and possibilities of artistic expression. And it means, in conclusion, that each Olympic Games must be guaranteed its own artistic content and program based on Olympism as well as on the principles of eurhythmy.

As regards the former instance, Coubertin himself lived to see the five originally suggested competitions subdivided into thirteen (introduced at Amsterdam in 1928). Having added to this list sports photography and sports philately, the IOC finally arrived at a total of seven basic events subdivided into fifteen medal-winning competitions, but subsequently robbed itself of an important sphere of influence (and modern Olympism, of a field of successful progress) through its unfortunate 1954 decision. It was not until the Mexico City Games that a new start—if in the form of side shows—was made. The essential point, however, about the efforts made by the Mexican Organizing Committee for the Games of the XIXth Olympiad was the possibilities that they opened up for further artistic competition, e.g., folk art, dancing, children's drawings, and film, that is to say, modern possibilities the wide range of which must be appreciated, but the full meaning of which is still waiting to be explored by modern Olympism.

As regards the actual integration of art and literature into the Olympic Games—a most important element in Coubertin's educational heritage—the great Frenchman wanted two things put into practice: first, the planning of the whole procedure of the Games from the opening ceremony to their conclusion on eurhythmic lines, following a well-thought-out protocol and solemn ceremonial, to the preservation of which he attached great importance,* (20) and second, the embellishment of this program through every artistic background and accompaniment of an Olympic nature which could be suitably employed to make the Games an edifying and lasting experience for both athletes and spectators.

In his "Olympic Memoirs," Coubertin frequently referred to this aspect of the Games and did not hesitate to praise or disapprove; but his criticisms were never destructive. (His own fellow-countrymen, however, who misunderstood these facts and Coubertin's motives, unfortunately repaid him with ingratitude at Grenoble in 1968!) It appears that Coubertin had a special preference—which he professed as early as 1906—for group displays, rhythmic dances, festivities after nightfall with torchlight and other lighting effects, and choral as well as orchestral performance, if possible in the open air.

* Cf. "Bulletin of the NOC of the GDR," 14, no. 2 (1969), p. 11.

Reviewing the above, we now understand that a universal and comprehensive program of artistic effort and creativity in the Olympic spirit could be achieved; that art, in all its forms and manifestations, could take a central place in Olympic and similar meetings; and that we shall have to take upon ourselves a variety of obligations if we want to adopt, critically assess, and develop this heritage. But it also becomes evident how great an obligation we in particular, but also all other progressive people and nations, have toward this heritage, in an era of worldwide conflict about what our Minister of Culture, Dr. Klaus Gysi, recently called the "fundamental question" of "the attitude of the working class and of the socialist society established under its guidance, toward the great humanist traditions in our own history and that of other nations. . . . The struggle for the great traditions is today proving to be a sphere of great intellectual and political explosiveness. Classical humanism is playing an ever greater role in the struggle of our socialist, humanist culture against dehumanized, manipulated culture." (21)

Coubertin's Olympism and the question of the position and role of art within it are part of this heritage and of the cultural struggles of our time.

It is a fact that close contacts between art and physical culture (and thus close contacts between art and literature and the Olympic movement) have always received great attention in the GDR, with appreciable results; but it is also a fact that not all the possibilities offered by our society have yet been fully exploited. It is hoped that this article will contribute a few basic ideas to the fruitful public discussion in order to ensure even steadier and more systematic progress, for art will be able to gain and maintain a proper position within modern Olympism only if and when it is given a chance of putting down strong roots on a national level. It is only the ripe fruits of such national efforts that can ensure for art international standing, forceful humanist expression, and general educational influence within modern Olympism. The national endeavor therefore is—and will remain—an essential but as yet not quite perfect element of our cultural policy, a mandate for all institutions and organizations connected with it—entirely in keeping with the mission delegated to us by Coubertin:

> The point is to reunite the bonds of a legitimate union which have been severed for so long: muscle and brain. I should risk distorting the truth if I were to claim that a burning mutual affection is driving them to return at once to a state of wedlock. Their union no doubt once lasted for a long time and was fruitful; but once separated by adverse conditions, they finally got as far as ignoring each other completely; separation had caused oblivion. But now Olympia, their principal former residence, has been restored, or rather, revived and renewed. The forms, it is true, are different and new, but they are still imbued with the same

life and content. They can thus return to their residence; meanwhile it is for us, and no one else, to prepare their return there. (22)

notes

1. Pierre de Coubertin. "Between Two Battles: From Olympic to University Worker." In Extract of the *Revue de la Semaine,* January 20, 1922, pp. 8–9.

2. Heinrich Mann. "A Memorable Summer." In *Internationale Literatur,* Zurich 6, 1 (1936), p. 22.

3. Pierre de Coubertin. "Olympic Memories." Bureau International de Pédagogie sportive, Lausanne 1931, p. 77.

4. *Ibid.,* pp. 77–78.

5. *Ibid.,* p. 78.

6. *Ibid.,* pp. 79–80.

7. Pierre de Coubertin. "Opening Address of the Conference of Arts, Letters, and Sports." In *Anthologie.* Aix-en-Provence 1933, p. 267.

8. "Olympic Memories," p. 113.

9. *Ibid.,* pp. 114–115.

10. *Ibid.,* pp. 122–123.

11. Pierre de Coubertin. "Philosophical Reflections on Modern Olympism," *Le Sport Suisse,* Geneva 1935. Tirage à part, p. 4.

12. "Olympic Memories," p. 195.

13. *Ibid.,* pp. 207–208.

14. *Ibid.,* p. 77.

15. *Anthologie,* p. 167.

16. "Olympic Memories," p. 115.

17. Cf. *Einheit,* Berlin, 24, no. 4 (1969), p. 431.

18. Bertolt Brecht. *Writings on Literature and Art.* Editions Aufbau-Verlag, Berlin/Weimar 1968, II, pp. 340–341.

19. Pierre de Coubertin. In "Address Given during the Ceremony Honoring Baron Pierre de Coubertin." Imprimerie du Léman S. A., Lausanne 1932, p. 14.

20. "Olympic Memories," pp. 195–196.

21. Klaus Gysi. "Art in the Struggle for the Socialist Community." In *Schriftenreihe des Staatsrates de DDR,* Berlin 1968, no. 7, p. 41.

22. *Anthologie,* p. 166.

summary

The relationship of sport with art has a respectable history, the foundations resting in prerecorded antiquity and deduced from artifacts of cultural life in Mycenaean times and earlier. This relationship gives rise to a determination of a sport-art paradigm which appears to have currency in the twentieth century and which appears to be entering a period of cultural ascendancy. Questions concerned with whether sport can be regarded as an art-form are entertained subsequent to further exploration of the interplay between sport and the arts; some derivation of common constructs is allowed to emerge, hopefully to the benefit of a new perspective for sport.

Primarily, Chapter 2 presents the major link between sport and the plastic arts (painting and sculpture), exploring the representation of sport conceptually in these media. To some extent, also, there is a minor discussion of definitional difficulties attaching to what is meant by sports-paintings and sports-sculptures.

Finally, the views held by Baron Pierre de Coubertin on the place of art in modern Olympism are presented (from the original article by Dr. E. Höhne of the German Democratic Republic). As is generally known, de Coubertin held a total cultural concept of the Olympics, one which he believed was a true reflection of the pervasive cultural role of the Classical Games in Ancient Greece. There seems little doubt that he perceived the festival nature of the Games, seeing the resurgence of Olympism as a part of a new life commitment. In one respect we can accord de Coubertin the title "a man before his time" since he presaged the development of "leisure for all," for a time when Olympism would be the ideal statement for life. Höhne states that we are entering that period now in the latter half of the twentieth century. If we are, we have a long way to go, but more pertinently, we owe de Coubertin a great debt of gratitude for his efforts and farsightedness in reinstituting the Olympic Games as a cultural symbol of hope.

questions for discussion

1. Under what circumstances in the development of society do both sport and the arts emerge as elements of culture?
2. The meaning of sport is as diffuse as the meaning of art, yet we may claim that sport can be regarded as one of the arts. Is this a paradox? Why should the meaning of one term include the meaning of the other?
3. What are the cultural antecedents of the reverence of beauty that man has held for nature?
4. What are the problems associated with the definition of sports-painting and sports-sculpture?

5. Categorize the difference between an artist and an illustrator.
6. It could be argued that R. Tait McKenzie made a greater impact as an artist than as a physical educator or athletic director. On what grounds could this assertion be made?
7. What major contribution was made by Baron Pierre de Coubertin in ensuring a closer link between sport and art?
8. How does Dr. Erhard Höhne classify the Olympism of Baron Pierre de Coubertin? To what extent is the classification value-based?

The Place and Role of Sports-Art in America

A careful survey of the field discloses a general lack of sympathy for sporting art.

K. W. ZOELLER

INTRODUCTION

Chapter 3 gives attention to the development and place of sports-painting and sports-sculpture in the United States over the past 100 years. The difficulty of painting and sculpting sports subjects is emphasized to account for the limited number of such works to be found in the cultural heritage of this country.

The representation of sport in the United States takes many forms and is expressed in a variety of media—painting, graphics, drawing, sculpture, and ceramics. The problem of representing action in art materials and the academic problems underlying instruction of this dimension of artistic expression have been known from the earliest times. In an article signed by Fairman Rogers, but attributed to the pen of Thomas Eakins, the following was written about "The Schools of the Pennsylvania Academy of the Fine Arts" (McHenry, 1945):

> From time to time, athletes, trapeze performers and the like have been secured. Originally the number of male models was greater than that of female models, as they are rather more instructive as to muscular development; but because the male figure is more familiar to the male students, at least, than that of the female, through opportunities afforded in swimming, for the past two years the sexes have been alternated so that the

class sees the same number of each during the season. . . . Poses representing action are difficult to keep and the moving of the model confuses the student. (p. 127)

With the arrival of an enlightened attitude toward sports, artists were able to represent man's participation in them with pictorial sophistication. The invention of photography superseded this function of the painter and sculptor who turned more and more toward exploring the use of their media in purer terms in representing their sports subjects. At that point, the artist ceased being solely a recorder of events for the sport historian, and the representation of sports by artistic expression took on new meaning. This view is strongly endorsed by Zoeller (1936), who states:

> But today's artist faces no easy assignment. His predecessors, the print makers, did not have the competition of portable cameras, and motion pictures did not exist; theirs was the only available record of sporting events and scenes and the public was forced to accept them as authentic. The modern artist confronts a sophisticated audience of men and women who are highly critical of form and technique. Almost every American indulges in some form of sport or is interested in one or more of the national pastimes. Hence the successful sporting artist must convey the emotions of play and the love of sports which the camera cannot reproduce. (pp. 12–13)

The sports-painting that is referred to by Zoeller is more typically the scene of hunting or fishing rather than the sports of industrial society. The role of the painter as recorder of the sports scene involves him in a very particular way, and this viewpoint is borne out by Metzi (1962), who tells us that "the artist no longer merely reproduces what he sees, he interprets and tries to involve [us] in his interpretation." Metzi adds that the artist is no longer merely a recorder of sports events, but that he is also a spectator whose commentary is often as interesting as the event itself. The differential approach of the painter and the sculptor to producing sports pictures and sculpture should be considered; examples of artists in each category will be cited in support of our discussion.

Historical Comment

Prior to the Civil War, society in the United States had not acquired sufficient cohesiveness to provide a basis for organized sport, and those games of a team or competitive nature which were introduced on a regional basis were loosely structured. Just as much of the game form of the first half of the eighteenth century was introduced from Europe, so were the predominant modes of painting and sculpture. As an art critic for the *Literary Digest*, November 1922, points out in an article discussing "Americanism in Art":

> In America, where native art was still in its infancy (in the nineteenth century), the artists began slavishly to imitate the models (hunting and horse-racing scenes) sent over from England and France. The elegance of foreign sport was stamped on the American product. (p. 23)

This speaks primarily to the "sports" of "gentlemen," who provided the main source of patronage to the artist at that particular time.

However, engraving and the sporting print had become well-accepted forms of recording sports scenes, but, says Zoeller (1936):

> When those capable artists exchanged engravers tools for the inspired brush or chisel, our academic bodies, emulating the British, frowned on all attempts to create a special niche for sports in the fine arts. (p. 12)

The transitional period in American history culminating in the Civil War saw the rejection of much that had rested in the roots of European traditionalism. It was as if America had found a new maturity and, in the process, had learned to make statements based on its own decisions. This outlook indicated a more cohesive structuring of society, and organized games reflected the direction society was taking. Furthermore, the post-war period saw American artists becoming more nationalistic, and the development of genre painting and sculpture was a natural outcome. Toward the turn of the century, American artists began to depict, according to Zoeller, "sportsmen in peculiarly American clothing, fishing in American streams or surf, jumping up to see who had been knocked down in the boxing ring, craning their necks to make a successful shot at billiards, hiding in a boat surrounded by decoy ducks, or whizzing downhill on skis."

There were two main figures in painting during this era, Thomas Eakins and Winslow Homer, and one major sculptor, R. Tait McKenzie, whose work appeared during the first quarter of this century. For the most part the period from the Civil War to the turn of the century was not as fruitful as the early part of the twentieth century in producing paintings or sculpture of a sports content. This latter situation is in part a function of the pace of the emergence of the United States as a nation.

PAINTING AND SCULPTING SPORTS SUBJECTS

Although paintings and sculptures depicting sports scenes have been more plentiful in the twentieth century, they have not appeared in the number that Zoeller would suggest (even allowing for his wider usage of the term "sports"). Writing in 1936, he states:

> There are several hundred living artists of outstanding genius who, having a flair and an understanding of exacting qualities of sportsmanship, are producing work that will always live, an art which is becoming a

permanent record of an important page in the history of America. With a trail blazed toward this new art, many established artists of the academic schools are finding enthusiasm in sports as subject for inspiration. And, when these masters of brush or chisel describe the joy they take in their favorite recreations, their work assumes national importance and the accolades of the public demonstrate the vital interest which America has developed in sports. (pp. 11–12)

This optimistic approach cannot be echoed for the interpretation of sports that this text holds. Indeed, something less than a hundred artists who have painted at least one sports picture have been found throughout the last 100 years. This may be because "capturing the essence of a sport makes great demands upon an artist" and "it is the artist's task to see beyond the literal moment and capture the summing up of the sportsman's total involvement." Zoeller endorses this viewpoint:

> Graphic art can no more than recall a result; it requires an artist of high calibre and a devotee of the sport to portray the emotions which live in the memory of a sportsman. (p. 14)

More generally, he states, "The whole subject of sporting art requires the bi-visual glasses of art and sport."

The Athlete-Artist

The first use of the concept athlete-artist can be traced to an article appearing in *Art Digest* in February 1942, when an anonymous correspondent discussed the work of sculptor Joseph Brown. Brown, who is presently a professor emeritus at Princeton University, was a football player and boxer in his youth; his work is discussed fully later in this section.

The term athlete-artist has significance in the study of sports-art from many perspectives. It is reported that Leonardo da Vinci could twist horseshoes between his fingers, bend bars of iron across his knees, disarm every adversary, and in wrestling, running, vaulting, and swimming had no equal. This illustrates adequately the construct "athlete-artist," which allows for the exploration of the question of whether an athlete-artist depicts sports better than the "nonathlete artist." In this context the term is similar to what Zoeller speaks of as "sportsman-artist." To quote Zoeller (1936):

> Every phase of the active recreations and national pastimes has its group of sportsmen-artists, high priests of a cult who mix the "feel" of the chase or the spirit of games with their paints; not as graphic artists, nor illustrators, but academicians of the fine arts without portfolio. (p. 11)

More central to the idea of "athlete-artist" (and stated in support of the construct "sportsman-artist") is Zoeller's claim that

> . . . if an artist approaches the subject of sporting art in the same mood in which he takes to sport, there is bound to be a freedom from the illustrative and an improvement in the inspirational quality. . . . Hence contemporary artists who are also sportsmen are painting sporting subjects in a spirit of relaxation from their usual commissions and are able to "see" the sporting subjects through the eyes of sportsmen as well as artists. (pp. 14–17)

Fundamental to this thinking is the question of the relationship to the man's life of his art or his sport. How much is he involved in, or concerned about, his art or his sport? Will his preference show through his product, or will a blending of the separate skills conceal this? These questions, and similar ones, will be answered to some extent by a consideration of both artists who were athletes and those who were not. Three artists who were athletes are Thomas Eakins, George Bellows, and Joseph Brown.

Thomas Eakins. The viewpoint expressed by Goodrich (1933), Eakins' major biographer, is that: "When we think in terms of art in athletics, and athletes in art in America, there is certainly no one single personality that more surely symbolizes both phases than that of Thomas Eakins."

Thomas Eakins (1844–1916) was recognized to be a strong youth, standing some 5 feet 10 inches tall and built powerfully but not heavily. "One of the simple factors of Thomas Eakins himself," says McHenry (1945), "was his ancestral heritage of strength and an admiration for strength." In adult years his boyhood love of outdoor life remained with him, his recreations being simple, natural, and close to the earth: hunting, fishing, walking, riding, skating, sailing, rowing, and swimming. He had grown up in that period of American history which saw the renaissance of sports and science. This new concern for the body, its function and description, found no greater advocate than Eakins; this becomes particularly evident when his painting of sport subjects is considered.

Of Eakins' ability in the sports domain, Goodrich (1933) says:

> Both he and his father were beautiful skaters, the older man remarkable for fancy figures, tracing calligraphic flourishes on the ice like those he made on paper; the younger for speed, power and endurance, being able to skate backwards as fast as others could forward. . . . He owned a small sailboat, and loved to go sailing on the Delaware, often being out on the river at four o'clock in the morning. Above all he enjoyed swimming; the water was a sort of passion with him, and he would strip and go in at every opportunity, without worrying about the sense of propriety of those who might see him, for he was as natural and unashamed about nakedness as a child or savage, liking to swim, sail, and bask in the sun nude. (pp. 6–7)

The influence on Eakins' becoming such a good athlete was his father. Porter (1969) states:

> His father (Benjamin Eakins) lived with him all his life. They spent a lot of time together engaged in all kinds of individualistic outdoor sports —swimming, sailing, hunting and skating. Benjamin Eakins was an excellent skater, tracing calligraphic flourishes on the ice. Thomas could skate backwards as fast as most people could forwards. (p. 15)

Eakins' way of life was definitely reflected in his art; indeed, his sporting subjects are positive statements of his own involvement, his sympathy for the sports milieu. And, of course, his subject matter extended beyond his own interests in sports participation. McKinney (1942) writes that "Eakins believed almost fanatically in the old adage 'a sound mind in a sound body,' and went frequently to the Schuylkill to row or to the Delaware for a day of sailing." Eakins was also fond of that newfangled sport, bicycling, and it is reported that when the Academy of Fine Arts decided to show *Between the Rounds* after having rejected it for ten years, he turned up at the event wearing red bicycle pants and riding a high bicycle.

The scientific origins of the photographic study of human movement can be traced to the efforts of Eakins, in 1884. Eakins sustained the belief that the naked human body was the most beautiful creation in nature, and he blended this artistic outlook with a fine scientific mind for the solution of physiological and anatomical problems attaching to movement. Movement, for him, was beautiful, but he had to understand better why this was so. Eakins improved on the Muybridge technique of using many cameras for successive action shots by inventing his own device which could get ten exposures of movement on one plate. With the new device, he took pictures of running and jumping nude athletes in his quest for analyzing the motion of the human body. His experiments and results were purely for artistic purposes, for he did not pursue the technological development of the motion picture.

In his role as teacher, Eakins proposed to use the last half-hour of his life classes in noticing and sketching the action of movements made by a model—that model already being familiar to the class with regard to general form. Eakins had the sense of the need to capture or reproduce action accurately for the depiction of sports subjects.

McHenry (1945) relates accounts of Eakins' students and how they responded both to the teacher and the man. "Tommy Eagan remembered Eakins as a great ice skater: 'He skated as he painted, "broad," ' Tommy Eagan would say. 'None of the boys could keep up with him.' Eakins would come to the school and want the boys to go skating with him."

Eakins would have been about 42 years of age at that time, and therefore still an active athlete or sportsman.

George Bellows.   Writing while Bellows was still alive, Cortissoz (1922) seems at first unflattering in his specific criticism of his subject, yet the insight he affords of the living artist is very real:

> Life as Bellows sees it is singularly barren of charm. Whether he is study-ing the nude or drawing the heroes of the prize-ring, he appears to find form an affair of brute strength, never of beauty, and this view of the matter enters the very grain of his art. (pp. 178–179)

Writing more recently, Richardson (1956) is critical of Bellows the artist in much the same vein, and is able to make a statement based on hindsight. Albeit slightly disparaging, this criticism offers the same kind of informa-tion that is vital to an understanding of the artist's style of life in terms of the criteria that this study is investigating. Richardson writes:

> George Bellows (1882–1925) was an artist who preferred the strong, hearty, pungent flavors of life—prizefights, religious revivals, or the drama of the great rivers that surround Manhattan. Time has not sustained Bellows' contemporary form, which was based in part on big, violent pictures of boxing matches that seemed at the time very bold and excit-ing. (p. 366)

George Bellows grew up in Columbus, Ohio, where he attended the public schools and graduated from Central High School in 1901. At school he had shown outstanding athletic prowess, and in his final year threw half the touchdowns thrown by Central, besides playing a good all-round game. However, the idea was already established in Bellows' mind that, despite his being an athlete, he was destined to follow a career in the arts.

Bellows entered Ohio State University in the fall of 1901 and con-tinued his athletic career. He was especially noted as shortstop on the university baseball team, but he continued his activities as an artist through various types of illustration for the college paper. Throughout this period he kept a scrapbook of newspaper clippings of athletic events, accounts of art exhibitions, and reproductions of works he admired.

A description of Bellows appeared in a catalogue of his work shown at the Art Institute of Chicago in 1946:

> George Bellows was six feet tall and weighed around one hundred and eighty pounds; he looked and moved like an athlete, which he was. (p. 6)

Upon leaving the university, Bellows went to New York, which was quickly becoming established as the main art center in the United States. In order to continue with his artistic career he turned to professional sport as one means of livelihood. Edward Keefe (1946), in F. A. Sweet's *George Bellows,* recalls his acquaintanceship with him:

Bellows was a fine athlete, baseball and basketball. We played together with various pro basketball outfits in and around the New York area, which helped to keep a skylight over our heads. Bellows interests did not include prize fighting rings at that stage [circa 1906—the prize-fight paintings are circa 1911] of his career. It happened that a lad from New London, one Mose King by name and lightweight boxer by profession, was appearing at various New York fight clubs. Being a home town boy, I watched his progress with great interest and eventually prevailed upon Bellows to enjoy the pastime. (p. 13)

During these early days in New York, Bellows was living at the hub of two of the city's most lively centers of interest—the art world and the sports world. The linking of these two worlds was realized one day when he met Eugene Speicher, who wrote in *Contemporary American Painting* (1948):

George Bellows and I first met one late afternoon in October 1907 in a gymnasium on West 57th Street, New York City. I was watching a basketball game and asked an attendant who the tall, vigorous fellow was—unquestionably the best player. After the game he introduced us, and I found myself talking to "Ho" Bellows from Columbus, Ohio—a star player on the Ohio State University team.

We talked for a while about basketball, and finally went out to a restaurant for dinner, where we continued discussing athletics in general. . . . He then divulged that he was a painter, studying with Robert Henri, and I explained that I also was a student at the Art Students League, and we talked far into the morning about art. (p. 5)

The reference to Robert Henri is pertinent here, because it was under the influence of Henri's philosophy and criticism that Bellows began to paint the American scene wherever he found it interesting; the prize ring, the swimming hole, the field (see Plate 16), the waterfront, the parks and beaches. And, as W. F. Paris points out, "His sports are city sports." The prizefight pictures illustrate this extremely well, and although he played basketball, Bellows never painted any aspect of this sport, nor of baseball or football.

Bellows' first prizefight picture was shown in 1908 at the Carnegie Institute and marked his debut as an artist at Pittsburgh's great International Fair. However, his first important picture of the human body in action was inspired by the children he saw swimming in the East River and the Hudson. Masterson (1974) is precise in his interpretation of George Bellows when he states that the artist's interest in boxing reflects the most intense elements of his athletic background:

Dempsey, being knocked through the ropes by Firpo (1924), was a famous incident which appealed to him [Bellows], but his approach in earlier pictures, such as "Both Members of the Club" (1909), and "Stag at Sharkeys" (1909), displayed a "Goyaesque" quality absent from the later work. The slashing attack of the brush strokes in these pictures, the colour and harshness combine to show a disregard for subtlety and elegance, and are in themselves reminiscent of the contests. (pp. 83–84)

Joseph Brown.   Joseph Brown must be rated as the most prominent sculptor among the class athlete-artists. While still a student of R. Tait McKenzie, Brown had been a practicing athlete, a boxer and a football player. Brown claims he became a sculptor by accident, but the events leading to his professional position can be traced to the fact that he was a boxer. Recognizing that he had a good body and that athletic muscular definition and posture were good for an artist's model (and being temporarily out of work), he found casual employment in the Pennsylvania Academy of the Fine Arts. Looking at the work done by the students, he felt that he was not being truly represented, and in his dissatisfaction with what he saw, he attempted to model a small figurine of a boxer. He then tried to cast his model but failed. He visited a metallurgist, where he saw how casting should be done, went back and sculpted another small study of a boxer, and successfully cast it. R. Tait McKenzie gave him the encouragement he needed to continue to develop as an artist, but he also gave him the type of severe critical judgment that has assured Brown's emergence as a major American sculptor of the twentieth century.

As a professional boxer he fought nine winning bouts, then retired. His brother had been a boxer for eighteen years and showed the effects of it, a fact which was significant in Brown's early retirement from the ring. In some of his work, Brown evinced great sympathy in portraying the effects of many years' boxing, and his finest work must include his boxing studies. Commenting upon his work with the subject "boxers and boxing," Brown has said (in a private interview with John Donnelly):

> I thought I could make a better boxer than anybody who ever lived. I've seen some lousy attempts and thought about people who did not know what it was to get hit. I got my lumps honestly, and quit the year before they were unnecessary lumps. I was poor during the Depression, but I knew I could do something else since I had an education. A lot of kids never had the least opportunity to go to school. For me things were tough during the Depression, but not that tough. I've known too many kids that had their brains knocked out and that was not for me.

> I spent seven months working on the boxer. I was doing it in my bedroom. The room was surrounded with mirrors and I would go through the motions of the boxer. Because of my own unique experience, I was going to make boxers that nobody in the world could ever do.

In recent years, since 1970, Brown has been working on a commission to complete six 15½-foot sculptures of baseball and football players to decorate the newly completed Veterans Stadium in Philadelphia. The statues depict moments in sport "when the outcome is in doubt," which finds agreement with what Kaelin (1968) believes to be the epitome of aesthetic performance.

It must be emphasized here that the term "athlete-artist" implies an ongoing involvement both in sports and in artistic expression. Thus, Walt Kuhn was renowned as a professional cyclist, although most of his physical activity paintings were of circus performers. Also, John Kane, a sometime professional fighter, must be included in this category although he did not paint sports action pictures specifically. Other artists, who indulged in school sports activities but ceased upon graduation, must be excluded. Hence, the following discussion of the "nonathlete artist" embraces a construct of wider definition.

The Nonathlete-Artist

Within the framework of this construct, consideration must be given to all other artists who have painted one or more pictures of sports subjects but whose participation in sports is of a vicarious nature. This aspect is more difficult to trace in the artist's life, since in biographies, emphasis is given to activity involvement only if it existed. Thus, the "negative" aspect (for the purpose of this study) is usually not stated, and noninvolvement must to a great extent be imputed from other evidence. Again, lesser-known artists of whom little is known (unless it is discovered that they were sports-involved) must be included in this more loosely structured category.

Winslow Homer. According to W. H. Downes (1911), one of the major biographers of Winslow Homer:

> Winslow Homer at the age of nineteen was rather under the average height, delicately built, very erect, and performed most of his work standing for the purpose of avoiding the tendency to get round-shouldered . . . he would rise at three o'clock and go out to Fresh Pond (two miles distant) to fish before breakfast. (p. 28)

The indication from this account is that Homer was not built "like an athlete," yet he would be considered a "sportsman-artist" by Zoeller on account of his fishing interest. However, in 1857 Homer made a series of drawings entitled *Life in Harvard College,* one of these depicting a football game. He is also one of the most prominent American artists of the nineteenth century, and his painting of sports subjects are extremely well-documented both in a sports context and in terms of artistic execution. This is endorsed by Samuel Isham (1927):

> . . . pictures of Winslow Homer's representing motion suggest another
> and a very personal characteristic—his exact feeling for weight and
> force . . . and we can feel the momentum that in "Snap-the-Whip"
> hurls the youngsters at the end over on the grass. (pp. 353–354)

The painting referred to here is a picture of a group of children
playing a vigorous game, the action represented most accurately, therefore
demonstrating the artist's perception and painterly skill to a degree that
shows a strong sympathy for participation in the action.

Two other painters of diverse backgrounds may also be considered in
illustrating the construct "nonathlete artist." Eilshemius was born into a
wealthy family, grew up on a large estate, and was accustomed to gentility.
His *Croquet* (1906) reflects this very well. At a different level of society,
Fletcher Martin struggled for an early existence and developed much in the
tradition of a garret artist. Again, this is reflected in his work, and some
indication of his background interest is given by William Saroyan in
Contemporary Art in the United States:

> . . . on Friday nights for a couple of weeks Fletcher Martin and I went
> to the Hollywood Legion Arena to see the fights . . . we sat far back,
> so that we saw both the fights and the people at the fights . . . But at the
> same time, Fletcher Martin went as a painter, and I as a writer. (p. 14)

It must be repeated that the limitations of information about artists
who have done paintings of sports subjects must set the boundaries for
categorical statement, and, at the same time leave wide open the possibility
for speculation based on the way they depict human movement in the
competitive sports settings.

R. Tait McKenzie. In his youth, McKenzie had attended McGill
University in Montreal to complete his studies in medicine. He held a deep
and abiding interest in physical activity, and participated in interscholastic
and intercollegiate sports, winning gymnastics and high jump championships in his second year at McGill. However, he did not pursue athletics or
sports beyond those early years at college. Upon completing his degree he
served for a short time as the Director of Physical Education at McGill,
also being responsible for teaching anatomy at the Medical School. His first
attempts at sculpture were the four masks representing facial expressions
of effort, breathlessness, fatigue, and exhaustion. These he executed for the
purpose of illustrating an article he had written for the *Journal of Anatomy
and Physiology* in 1900; thus he was in his early thirties when he began his
artistic development as an avocation to his career in physical education.
The major thrust of McKenzie's sculpture was motivated by scientific
inquiry and to assist him in instructing his students in physical education
and anatomy.

MAJOR SPECTATOR SPORTS IN PAINTING AND SCULPTURE

The fact that a sport may appeal to the public does not necessarily mean that it will be proportionately represented in any given art-form. Football and baseball, probably the most popular American sports, hardly appear at all. An examination of the painting and sculpture representing the major spectator sports leaves much to be desired in an appraisal of this aspect of cultural heritage.

Painting

The examples cited in this section represent the research findings of a six-month survey of texts on art, and correspondence with major galleries of the United States. Thus, no claim is made for the complete representation of these sports—nor that there is proportional representation; the assertion is held that sports-art is very limited in amount.

Basketball. Although basketball is recognized as one of America's most popular sports, only two examples of paintings depicting basketball were found, one of which might better be categorized as an "illustration." A picture of *Luisetti Scores Again,* painted in 1936 by James Bingham, appeared in *Art News,* October 1, 1944. This is a portrait-in-action of the 1936 Stanford captain; it was written of the artist:

> Bingham captured with all the vitality of a motion-picture camera that intense moment when Luisetti easily outleaped his opposing guard and with one of his confident, one-handed shots tossed the ball into the basket to turn the tide in favor of Stanford. (p. 240)

In 1961 Jerome Martin was commissioned by *Sports Illustrated* to paint a double-page illustration on basketball in Indiana. This watercolor merited a place in the exhibition of sports illustrations held in 1962, and earned the following remarks from Metzi (1962):

> With an entirely different technique, Jerome Martin creates the essence of a basketball game. The players' bodies are flat quadrilaterals, serving as sockets for the exaggerated arms and legs which do the running, throwing, blocking and passing. Telling lines repeat the players' motions in ceiling and floor to converge and focus on the ball and basket in the background. (p. 32)

The style of art in this painting most proximates what is known as "cubist," which originated in France in the nineteenth century.

Baseball. Ethel Barrymore once said: "The inspiration to be found on a baseball diamond for paintings seems to me to be completely ignored." She judged correctly. The first painting of a baseball scene is ascribed to Thomas Eakins, whose *Baseball Players Practicing* was completed about 1875. *Sports Illustrated* reproduced this painting in color in May 1955, and subheaded the picture with a quotation from "God's Country and Mine" by Jacques Barzun:

> Whoever wants to know the heart and mind of America had better learn baseball, the rules and realities of the game. . . . That baseball fitly expresses the powers of the nation's mind and body is a merit separate from the glory of being the most active, agile, varied, articulate, and brainy of all group games. (p. 9)

The Eakins painting is a rather formal pose of a batter standing majestically with the bat held across his shoulder at the ready, but without any anticipatory lean in the body, while the catcher crouches behind ready to receive. This painting is a watercolor and is presently owned by the Rhode Island School of Design.

It appears that no other baseball paintings were executed until the Thirties, when a number of action and still pictures captured a broad cross-section of aspects of the sport. Such examples are: *Babe Ruth, King of Swat, Two Umpires,* and *In the Dugout* by Paul Clemens (the first being a swirling, twisting impression of a batter in midstroke; the second, two figures in conference; the last, a frontal reportage of several players awaiting their turn for play). *Baseball Catcher* by James Chapin is a composite portrait providing a record of protective wear and equipment but not representing sports action. *Batter Up* by James Chapin is adequately described in *Sports Illustrated,* September 13, 1958:

> "Batter Up" portrays the umpire-batter-catcher group in a small town baseball game. The three figures silhouetted against the little sun-lit grandstand await with intentness the delivery of the ball from the unseen pitcher. This community of intentness is expressed both in the characteristic individual poses and in the continuity of line developed through the umpire and batter, who are inwardly inclined toward the balanced figure of the catcher. (p. 20)

Ben Shahn's *National Pastime* is an action picture of a dive for the plate demonstrating the scuffle which takes place as the point is contested. *Dizzy Dean,* painted by Fred Conway, is a "festival" picture, a large canvas of a stadium and the crowd's response to a fine piece of play (which is not immediately evident in the picture). In the same vein as Conway's picture is that by Edward Laning, entitled *The Greatest Moment in Big League Baseball, 1941.*

Jacob Lawrence painted *Strike* in 1949, a picture that catches the moment in midswing when the batter hits the ball. Lawrence appears to be the only black painter depicting sports scenes in America.

Between 1950 and 1955 Thomas Meehan, an abstract expressionist, painted at least three pictures of the baseball theme. *Through the Screen* shows a catcher stretching to catch a high ball. Speaking of this same painting, the correspondent for *Sports Illustrated,* on June 13, 1955, wrote:

> His enthusiasm and knowledge of the game of baseball, combined with his eye for color and design, bring a fresh excitement to these paintings of America's national game. (p. 64)

Catcher at the Plate and *Waiting for a Decision at Home* are not sports action paintings but do carry the feeling of tension which is part of the sports setting. This "tension" can be said to represent the transmutation of beauty between sport and art.

From 1950 until today, the depiction of baseball appears to be the sole prerogative of those illustrator-artists commissioned by *Sports Illustrated.* One exception stands out, Ralph Fasanella, a primitive artist whose work, however, appears in that same magazine. Both pictures, untitled, have the unmistakable primitive style, are all-embracing in content (the sandlot game seen from an artificially elevated viewpoint), and are heedless of perspective.

Edmond Kohn was commissioned on two occasions, in 1957 and 1958. The former painting, *The Long-Ball Hitter,* is accompanied by the following, written by a staff reporter in *Sports Illustrated,* September 12, 1956:

> Edmond Kohn's big southpaw stands in the batter's box with the brooding intensity of one man alone against nine. The bright and shadowed stadium, the crowd on the fretful edge of suspense are fused into a kaleidoscopic back-drop. (p. 88)

The latter painting, *The Late Throw,* catches more potential action and is given a more expressionistic interpretation. Kohn has a strong sympathy for the physical movements involved in the sports subjects he depicts—thus, for example, there is a more accurate treatment of the anticipatory stance of the *Long-Ball Hitter* than is seen in the Eakins posed treatment. Kohn is quoted as saying: "I've always loved baseball, and now with the Dodgers here, I practically camp on their doorstep."

Robert Gwathmey was commissioned by *Sports Illustrated* in 1958 to paint scenes relating to the World Series. Only one of the pictures actually depicted the game. *County Stadium, Oct. 7, 1957* caught the moment in the fifth game which brought victory to the Milwaukee team. This scene is a panoramic view of the field, the stadium, and the game in progress at the point where the winning run is made. The picture was also used for the cover illustration of September 20, 1958, *Sports Illustrated.*

A painting by Byron Thomas, *Night Ball Game* was reproduced in a

January 1960 edition of *Design,* but no indication of when the picture was executed is given. This painting, another panoramic scene similar to the Gwathmey, appears to be the only scene of the floodlit game.

The picture is subheaded with the statement:

> Another summation of America's national sport with the eerie bath of floodlights to pick out every memorable detail. Here is rich detail painted broad and simple, with all the nostalgic clues of the ballpark. . . . Are these teams down in the cellar, as the sparse crowd seems to indicate? (p. 126)

The figures in both the Thomas and the Gwathmey paintings are diminutive enough to evade discernment of sympathy for the action of the players.

Football. Football, claim some observers, is rapidly superseding baseball as the major spectator sport in the United States. In spite of this popularity, only eight paintings of football were found for the period of time extending back to 1865.

Faithfully representing the actions of a tackle and a block, Frederic Remington's *Yale-Princeton Football Game, Thanksgiving Day, 1890,* painted circa 1891, shows a strong understanding for the dynamic postures experienced in play (see Plate 24).

In 1912 Gustave Rehberger painted *Big Jim's Biggest Day,* a football action picture showing Jim Thorpe running with the ball, swerving around a group of defense players.

Rico Lebrun's painting of a running back, *Red Grange: Houdini of the Gridiron,* executed in 1924, demonstrates a new approach to sports action painting in which the representation of the swerving figure and the blocking tackles is given sharp relief. Describing the inspiration for the painting, Paul Gallico (1938) writes:

> The first run itself was one of the greatest demonstrations of deception and elusiveness ever seen on a gridiron, for Grange crossed the field twice from sideline to sideline, ducking before he broke into the clear.
>
> It is this run that Rico Lebrun captured in a dynamic painting, depicting one of the great moments of American sport. (p. 13)

John Stuart Curry's *Hitting the Line* (circa 1930) shows the absolute embroilment of bodies blocking and tackling with abandoned vigor. The subject matter is highly reminiscent of *The Onslaught,* by R. Tait McKenzie (see the section on "Sports-Sculpture" in Chapter 2 for a description of this sculpture). Of the Curry painting, a correspondent in *Time,* May 22, 1960, wrote: "As John Stuart Curry's powder-puff oil, *Hitting the Line,* showed, football is a mighty hard sport to picture convincingly." The painting is more forceful in both its representation and impact than this correspondent would seem to imply with his reference to "powder-puff."

The Four Horsemen by James Bingham, completed about the same time as the Curry study, carries similar overtones to *Hitting the Line.* The painting records a play action of the "four horsemen" of the 1923 Notre Dame team, in which a feeling for team play is caught by the subtle positioning of the players executing a driving move through an opposing defense. The skill with which the play is recorded demonstrates a sympathy for action involvement on the part of the artist.

W. M. Boyd's *Rutgers versus Princeton, 1869,* painted in 1932, is a stylized picture illustrating an aspect of the sport as the painter imagines it to have been. While action is shown, it is not really convincing in its presentation.

Football Game was painted by Hedda Sterne in 1952. This painting, executed in the abstract expressionist manner, gives an impression of the force felt by contact or combat sports. No really definitive body outlines exist, so no comment can be made regarding the depiction of the body's shift of weight or balance. The correspondent for *Sports Illustrated* wrote in the September 13, 1958 issue: "Her response to football's motion and strife is seen in this painting . . . (she) has dared to catch one of the humourous sides of the game: football is a traffic jam."

Both of the last two mentioned paintings have more of a pure painterly quality than a representational element.

Ice Hockey.   In 1931 June Knabel painted *Hockey,* a high grand-stand view of diminutive figures playing ice hockey. The location of the sport and the spectator support for the game is more apparent in this painting than are the forms or movements of the players.

In 1956 *Sports Illustrated* commissioned Russell Hoban to paint a series of ice hockey scenes. In its November 12, 1956 issue appeared:

> Russell Hoban visited Toronto Maple Leaf camp (ice hockey) where he made sketches for paintings—paintings that give the true feeling of hockey, not necessarily as exemplified by any one team or player, but rather of the sport, itself, which he here describes in his own words: "During the morning and afternoons of training the shouts of the players echo in the frosty air of the empty arena. This is the time of the veterans fighting for their jobs and rookies trying to move up. . . . The coach with sharp eyes and sharp voice skates after the players with a whistle in his mouth. . . . In this first picture he is snapping at forward's heels like a terrier." (p. 36)

Boxing.   The prizefight, or boxing, has been a popular topic for many artists since the period beginning 1865. The earliest example is *Bare*

Knuckles painted by George Hayes in about 1865, a somewhat stylistic or posed subject, lending little or no feeling of the action of the prizefight.

In a similar vein, Thomas Eakins painted three or four fight pictures such as *Taking the Count* (1898), *Salutat* (1898), and *Between Rounds* (1899), when he was about 55 years of age, but none of these pictures is an actual scene of combat (the nearest being *Taking the Count*). Eakins carefully observed many boxing matches so that the details of his paintings would be correct. McHenry (1945) writes: "Eakins painted prize-fights in that spirit of love for anatomy in which his former teacher Gerome had painted gladiators."

The best-known and most representative paintings of boxing are those by George Bellows. Edward Keefe of the Art Institute of Chicago reported in F. A. Sweet's *George Bellows* (1946):

> Being a ball player himself and a great admirer of sports, he got a big thrill from observing trained athletes at work. This constituted a really worthwhile life class. His three early fight pictures were all inspired by scenes at Sharkey's Club Night. . . . The combatants in "Both Members of the Club" are believed to be Kid Russell and the Negro fighter Joe Gans. . . . Such violent action and dynamic force had never been expressed in American painting before. (pp. 15–16)

Tom Sharkey's Boxing Club in New York was half a block down West 66th Street and just across Lincoln Square from Bellows' studio. As noted previously, Bellows was introduced to the Club by Edward Keefe, and subsequently spent many hours watching the fighters in action. Speaking of his works, Breuning (1945) writes:

> "Both Members of the Club" and "Stag at Sharkey's" are the high points of Bellows' paintings of ringside scenes. The later canvases of similar themes suffered both from a dimness of visual memory and from an apparent loss of interest in the subject matter, which to such a continually questioning mind as that of the artist, had become "old hat." "Both Members of the Club" represents a prizefight. . . . It is evident that Bellows executed this painting at a white heat of interest, vivid memory and imagination both contributing to its impressive effect. It may be recalled that he wrote to a young artist that "I am still satisfied with 'Both Members of the Club.'" That is really an understatement for such a magnificent performance, which conveys such an immediacy of dynamic power, not only through the rhythmic play of the muscular bodies integrated into coherence of design, but further through the dramatic play of brilliant lights and darks that intensify the emotional excitement of the scene. (p. 22)

This is essentially true of the earlier fight pictures, but a different impression arises from the later works as Sweet (1946) states:

Bellows was commissioned by the *New York Journal* to cover the Dempsey-Firpo fight in Jersey City on September 14, 1923, at Boyle's Thirty Acres, and made sketches on the spot. He also did a lithograph of the subject and ultimately the painting (1924), but in each successive version he lost both freshness and vitality. None of the force of the early fight pictures is left. "Ringside Seats" (1924), though not an action picture, is far more convincing in giving the excitement of the prizefight. (p. 25)

The strange phenomenon which emerges here is that some ten or eleven years separate the fight studies; in the latter series Bellows would be about 42. In addition to the years separating the two groups of fight paintings, there were different motivational forces at work in Bellows.

Mahonri Young, who is better known for his sculptures of boxers (and other athletes) in action, painted one small study, *Two Men Boxing*, in 1936. (This picture is catalogue listed number 95 in the Boston exhibition. No reproduction of it appears.)

More recently Umberto Romano has taken boxing as a theme in his *Image of Man* series. In a personal communication, he writes: "I have done several paintings of *The Knockout* theme (circa 1942–1945) and many paintings and lithos of *Horses*." Accompanying the reproduction of *The Knockout* in the *Encyclopedia Brittanica Collection*, he writes:

> I have always wanted to paint the "knockout." The crowds at a prizefight—the hot, harsh, glaring lights, the heavy blue smoke—the yells, the jeers, and the tense restlessness of people. . . . I have been stirred, moved, aroused, by the hot sensuous light on human bodies in the ring, by the powerful savagery of two, taut, brutal forms in combat, by two violent bodies—at times human, at times animalistic, prancing, pacing, calculating, waiting, waiting for that one great climactic moment, the opening for the punch, that terrific murderous punch—the Knockout. (p. 92)

Romano's *The Knockout* shows the closing of two boxers at the point of delivery, the action filling the canvas (as a referee might witness the action). There are no extraneous details to detract from this forceful subject.

It is known that Fletcher Martin did some fight scenes in materials other than paint, but no reproductions of boxing subjects have been found illustrating his work in that media.

Horse Racing. Paintings of horse racing are not as common as portrait paintings of thoroughbreds. This is evident from the catalogue of the National Museum of Racing. Resort is made to this catalogue for the most extensive list of nineteenth- and twentieth-century racing paintings. Correspondence with the Museum provided illustration of only one racing (action) painting: *The First Futurity Stakes* painted by L. Maurer in 1888, catalogue listing number 70. Other racing paintings of horses in action, catalogue listed, are:

44. *Steeplechase at Cedarhurst*, 1885, Frederic Remington.
59. *Jumping Race at Saratoga*, 1882, Junius Fuller.
63. *Match Race at Monmouth Park*, 1885, C. L. Zellinsky.
69. *The Brooklyn Handicap*, 1887, Henry Stull.
84. *Domino Winning the Futurity*, 1893, Henry Stull.
108. *The Brighton Cup*, 1900, Henry Stull.
111. *Mon's Park*, 1902, Henry Stull.
113. *Finish of the White Plains Handicap*, 1903, Henry Stull.
114. *Brighton Handicap*, 1904, Henry Stull.
115. *Champion Stakes*, 1904, Henry Stull.
116. *Futurity Finish*, 1904, Hemment.
118. *The Suburban*, 1904, Henry Stull.
134. *Man O'War Defeating Sir Barton*, 1910, T. Martin.
144. *Over the Liverpool, Challenge Cup*, 1927, Gordon Ross.
145. *Over the Post and Rail at Virginia Gold Cup Steeplechase*, 1927, Gordon Ross.

(No reproductions are available for the above; thus, recourse for their assessment must be made to the National Museum of Racing.)

About the turn of the century, Albert Pinkham Ryder painted *The Race Track*, a painting of a solitary rider on a race course. However, the picture appears to have more allegorical meaning than sports content.

In 1920 Frank Boss painted *Man O'War Beating John P. Greir*, a representative picture of a finishing post with several riders approaching the line.

Dark Secret's Last Race, painted by Harold Von Schmidt in 1934, is similar in presentation to the Boss picture. In both of these paintings the skillful observation of the artist has caught the action, but as if in a photographic still, demonstrating the high quality of technique developed in representational art.

John Grabach painted *Taking the Hurdle* in 1939, an almost photographic representation of steeplechase riders coming out of a jump. The skillful representation of this action is almost as a sports photographer would catch the scene. Writing in reply to correspondence relating to his painting, John Grabach states: "In reply to your recent query on my painting *Taking the Hurdle* which has been exhibited throughout the country, my interest was not for the sport but for the beautiful motion and graceful action and the formation of a composition of movement of the horses."

The first break away from photographic representation of horse racing comes in 1956, in a painting by Jon Corbino, which *Sports Illustrated* reproduced in March 1956. The painting, *Race Track Lineup,* is subheaded with the following note:

> Straining to be away, jockeying for position under the guidance of strong hands that control them, highbred horses on the track compose themselves into a magnificent spectacle in this Corbino painting. (p. 64)

The painting is important because it marks a beginning in the change of policy in *Sports Illustrated* from purely commentator to innovator. The painting is accompanied by an article entitled "Fantasy of Horses," in which the critic writes:

> The exhilaration and excitement that vibrate like a shimmering layer of atmosphere over a race track when the horses are keyed up for a race have been transposed into a quality of painting by Jon Corbino. . . . His artistic roots lie in the styles of Delacroix and Rubens, his subject matter often in the world of carnivals and race tracks, where color and movement are inseparable. [In *Race Track Lineup*] Corbino has produced immensely sensitive and decorative patterns of elegant mobile creatures, muscles straining, in a richly colored world, half fantasy, half fact. (p. 63)

Subsequent treatments of horse racing also appear in *Sports Illustrated. Down to the Finish Line* was painted in 1960 by Morton Roberts, and Tomi Ungerer painted a series of watercolors for a *Sports Illustrated* feature article on the Kentucky Derby in 1962. Both are painted in the abstract expressionist vein and symbolize the atmosphere of horse racing rather than giving a photographic presentation. As Metzi (1962) writes of the Ungerer series:

> Tomi Ungerer's impressions of the Kentucky Derby are expressed in simplified color; horses and jockeys become squared bodies with single legs, all taut and fleeting to create the impact of speed and motion, nothing else. (p. 32)

Depictions of sport have not always reflected a close understanding of the movements involved in athletic participation, although there are a number of truly accurate representations of action. Often compensating for a lack of sports form, an artist has attempted to catch a mood or feeling involved in the sport, particularly the abstract expressionist painter. Thus color has been used when form has been forfeited.

Sculpture

As pointed out in Chapter 1, the representation of the human form in sports sculpture has followed the traditional approach first set by Classical Greek sculptors. Each artist interprets the human form in sport in varying degrees of naturalism or realism according to his individual style.

Basketball. Seven works of art depict basketball in sculpture. Two of these were executed by Clemente Spampinato, both called *Basketball Group.* One of these is a bas-relief in bronze, the other a group composition which is uniquely balanced so that one figure is jumping for the ball with both feet completely off the floor. Three of the basketball sculptures are by Joseph Brown. These are: *Pivot,* a bronze illustrating a player preparing to pass the ball; *Break,* showing a tall, slender player in the act of bouncing a ball with his right hand and poising the left hand as if to hold off an attacker; and *Bill Bradley,* showing the athlete in a state of total awareness of an opponent who may be attempting to take the ball. In a sculpture entitled *Bob Cousy in Action,* executed by Stanley Martineau, it can be said that the artist has accomplished a most difficult sculptural feat in representing the movement of the body in space. One other basketball sculpture, *Vertical Line* by Rube Goldberg, is a Giacometti-type work of art in which the figure of the athlete is elongated to emphasize the height of the player who is holding the ball aloft.

Baseball. Nine studies of baseball in some part of the action have been depicted in sculpture. Clemente Spampinato executed two works, entitled *Baseball Batter* and *Baseball Pitcher (Blazin' One In),* both finished in 1950. Joseph Brown executed six studies, making him the most prolific sculptor of baseball. These are: *Hook-Slide,* showing the athlete at the completion of the slide with his toe on the bag; *Pop-Foul,* in which a naked figure of an outfielder is poised ready to receive a falling ball in his open glove; *Hurler,* another naked figure in the act of winding up for the pitch; *Sandlotter,* showing a young man wound up and ready to hit the ball; *Double-Play,* another naked athlete moving forcefully into a throw, poised on one foot—an extremely dynamic sculpture; and *Big Stretch,* showing a first baseman with his foot on the bag and reaching for a ball. The last sculpture, *Casey Stengel* by Rhoda Sherbell, is a portrait of the coach and manager standing in his typically aggressive stance.

Football. Nineteen studies of football executed by sculptors show a broad range of the sports action. Nine of these were done by Joseph Brown, North America's most noted sports sculptor. Two of his studies depict the concentration necessary for the place-kick; these are *Extra Point* and *Holding the Ball,* finished in 1947 and 1949, respectively. His *Punter* portrays the punter in the follow-through position watching the direction and flight of his kick. Also extant is a finished sketch of *Punter,* executed in 1952, which appears to be a better and alternative study to *Punter,* 1947. *Jump Pass,* also done in 1949, shows the quarterback up on his toes, with his arm cocked, ready to release "the bomb." Two of Brown's sculptures are examples of tackling: *Cutting Down a Back* is a frontal block on the man running with the ball, and *Attempted Spin* is a side tackle on the running ball-carrier. Lastly, *Center, Vintage 1930* shows the athlete grasping the ball between both hands, poised for the snap, and *Lineback #1* shows the linebacker in an inclined forward charging position, the ball locked tightly in his arms and pressed against his chest as he thrusts forward with his head lowered into the defensive line.

Clemente Spampinato is also celebrated for his football subjects, four of which are described here. *Forward Passer* shows the quarterback raised on his toes, with his arm cocked at the point of throwing the ball; *Football Runner* illustrates the runner carrying the ball, but half-turning with his left hand outstretched to push away an attempted tackle; and two studies are called *Flying Tackle,* one a bas-relief, the other a bronze, both expressing the strength and power of the tackle and the deceptive reactions of the man with the ball resisting the tackle.

In 1930 William Zorach completed a small granite sculpture entitled *Football Player,* which shows an athlete in a half-kneeling position.

Football is a game for large groups of men, yet there are very few sculptures which show groups of athletes in contest for the ball. The most noteworthy studies showing groups of football players are those executed by R. Tait McKenzie in 1911 and 1927. Two particular works are of note: *The Onslaught* shows a pile-up of both lines as the ball-carrier attempts to leap-charge over the defensive line; and an untitled frieze commissioned for a memorial to Percy D. Haughton shows two bas-relief views: one of the ball-carrier trying to break the line, and the other, the attempted blocking of a punt.

Ice Hockey.   Hockey has not been a particularly popular subject with sculptors. Joseph Brown executed a small sculpture entitled *Hockey Player* illustrating a forward leaning toward the goal and glancing back as if in anticipation of receiving the puck. Less dynamic than Brown's study is the work by Sybil Kennedy entitled *Hockey Player,* which represents the activity but shows little concern for anatomical reality.

Boxing.   Boxing is represented by at least thirty-one sculptures in twentieth-century sports art. Again, Joseph Brown is the most notable among the sculptors, having executed twenty-one of the thirty-one. As a young man, Brown was a boxer at college, and later a boxing coach at Princeton. One of his earliest sculptures, *Boxer Bandaging His Hands,* shows the power and strength of the boxer's body in a preparatory stage of dressing for the bout. Brown's *The Supplicant,* executed in 1951, shows a boxer acknowledging his opponent with a gloved hand raised to his forehead. Four of Brown's sculptures focus on the fallen, fatigued, or defeated boxer: *Pieta, 1944 A.D., Not a Word, Fighter,* and *Dropped,* Antaeus 1951. All these depict the listless look of dull eyes, open mouth, and apparent loss of control which contribute to a picture of the frustrated athlete striving to continue against overpowering opposition. The majority of Brown's sculptures, however, are of action as it would appear in the ring, with single boxers shown in stances, or with two boxers exchanging blows, counter-punching or defending themselves. Such works include *Thein Myint, Kioshi Tanabe, Oone Kingpatch, Leroy Haynes, Thai Boxer (Kio Wan), Mickey Walker, Sugar Ray, Counter-Punch #1, Counter-Punch #2, Counter-Punch #3, Boxers, Upper-Cut, Left Hook Counter from Outside, Left Hook Counter to Body,* and *Jab-Counter.* Many of these read like a text of sculpted lessons for the young boxer since they depict specific technical aspects of the sport. Primarily, Brown was concerned with the representation of the action of boxing in these works, rather than with pure anatomical detail.

The single-figure studies of boxers by R. Tait McKenzie include *The Boxer, Why Not—II,* and *Invictus. Why Not—II* shows two poses in one (the figure has four arms), an attacking and a defensive position. *Invictus* shows a boxer crouching or half-kneeling and supporting himself on his right arm presumably as he takes the count. The alertness of the figure in *Invictus* shows him ready to return to the bout before being counted out. *Boxer,* executed by Richard Bartre in 1942 illustrates a pose in which the weight of the body is held defensively back while a right-fisted forward center-punch is being delivered. This study shows a Giacometti-like figure in the pose of a boxer moving around the ring in the early rounds, getting the measure of the opponent, and there is a freshness in his poise, with plenty of spring in the heels and the impression of tonic reaction in the body.

Lastly, the works of Mahonri Young and Clemente Spampinato should be mentioned. Spampinato's *Boxer Group* illustrates the point of contact made with a lunging right cross to the jaw of the opponent. Mahonri Young completed four works: *Right to the Jaw, The Knockdown, Groggy,* and *Joe Gans.* Young obtains a fluidity and rhythmic freedom of action, as well as a determined concentration in his art.

The significance of this section has been to direct the student to sources of art (painting and sculpture) in which the major spectator sports have been represented. The study of these art-works makes a substantial contribution to understanding what is meant by the beauty of sport. Color, line, and form as the artist presents them can teach the layman much about aesthetics in general, but when the artist applies these elements to the dynamics of sport, he not only takes on a difficult task of representing motion with still effect, he provides the student with the understanding of that difficulty, and at the same time invites the student to see things his way. The process of the acquisition of aesthetic education is complex but the artist does all he can to assist the student in achieving this knowledge of the underlying elements of beauty. Then, the student of sport studies is able to meet the artist part way by virtue of his intrinsic knowledge of sport. In this fashion, one of the major steps to the recognition of the sport-aesthetic is acquired.

SPORTS-ART IN EXHIBITIONS

The first indication of a Sport in Art exhibition that has been found is mentioned by Maurice Raynal (1953):

> Artists cast an observant eye on the beginnings of the craze for sporting events,—athletic contents of all kinds, tennis, foot-races, and especially bicycle-racing, about 1885. In January, 1885, the Georges Petit Gallery ran an exhibition on the theme "Sport in Art." (p. iv)

The interest that Raynal speaks of is not surprising when it is remembered that the late nineteenth century saw the rebirth of the Olympic Games. That the modern Olympic Games was conceived as a wider cultural pursuit to include artistic festivities is not generally known, yet this fact is well demonstrated by the 1932 Games held at Los Angeles. Raynal wrote:

> The Olympic International Exhibition of Art opened on July 30th in the Los Angeles Museum of History, Science and Art, in a city gay with the flags of all nations and agog with enthusiasm over the great sport competitions which began the next day. . . . There were, in all, over eleven hundred exhibits: painting, sculpture, architectural projects, and decorative arts . . . and every work included therein represented sport and was assembled for the most part by sportsmen.

> It should also not be forgotten that this was primarily not an exhibition but a competition. . . . No work could compete for the honors that was not by a living artist . . . related to sport and approved by the Olympic Committee of the nation of which the artist claimed citizenship.

> The exhibition continued for a month, ending the last day of August. The attendance approximated fifteen thousand daily—twenty-five thousand on Sunday afternoon. (p. 136–137)

Despite the insistence of this journalist on the "competitive" aspect, there can be no doubt that as an exhibition (the end result), it brought a finer appreciation for the topic "sports in art" to a wider circulation than mere "competition" would suggest. This did not prevent commentators and critics from holding to the sports-competitive orientation of the exhibition. Thus, the correspondent for the *Art Digest,* September 1932, wrote in an article appropriately titled, "America Scores Victory in Olympics Exhibition of Sports in Art": "As in the track and field games, the United States carried off the lion's share of the honors with three firsts, four seconds, a third, and seven honorable mentions."

Also taking place in 1932 was a "Novel Exhibition of Paintings, Prints and Sculpture Evoking Glamorous Moments in the Manly Arts of Boxing," held at Knoedler's gallery in New York, in which "the rigors of the prize ring, as set forth by artists of various epochs, are assembled for your edification." Works by Luks, Eakins, and Bellows were included in the exhibition. The correspondent of *Art News,* April 1932, wrote of the Bellows paintings:

> George Bellows, more determined to get the smash and quiver of the ring into his work, takes you right up into the very thick of things, and his large "Club Night" (incidentally one of the best things of the sort he ever painted) and his numerous lithographic studies are vivid souvenirs of a pastime that Bellows delighted in to the full. The strong, straight arm reaching home was something he could grasp in all its dramatic significance. I remember him saluting a friend on Fifth Avenue one afternoon with the advancing maneuvers of a boxing expert, just as lacking in self-consciousness as possible. It is doubtful if anyone has ever quite caught the full flavor of prize-fighting as Bellows has. Beside his striking commentaries, other representations of fighters in action seem pale and somewhat loitering. (p. 5)

Finally in 1932, although not really classified as an exhibition, was the acquisition by Yale University of the "Whitney Collections of Sporting Art," specialized collections which had evidently been in existence for a number of years. The following is from *The Yale Review,* Spring, 1932:

> An announcement was made at Commencement last spring of the gift of the "Whitney Collections of Sporting Art," presented by the Gallery's constant benefactor, Francis P. Garvan, '97, in memory of his friends, Harry Payne Whitney, '94, and Payne Whitney, '98. A small but representative selection of these large and varied collections of prints, paintings, drawings, sculpture, and ceramics—perhaps the finest of its kind ever assembled in this country—was placed in the three north rooms of the Gallery last June and remained on view until last month. Almost every sport is represented—football, baseball, track, bicycling, swimming, rowing, cricket, tennis, boxing, wrestling, boat racing and yachting, hunting and fishing of various kinds, including dogs and game, horses and horse-racing and even billiards and card playing!
>
> The collections are comprised of twenty pieces of sculpture by Tait McKenzie, Paul Manship, and others; forty-nine paintings, eight hundred and eighty-five prints, including a great many by Currier and Ives, as well as several of the original paintings from which the prints were made; besides such modern work as George Bellows' prize-fighting series; three drawings, three amusing mugs illustrating cockfighting; and one prize-fight announcement. These will ultimately be hung in the Payne

Whitney Gymnasium, and in the adjoining Ray Tompkins House. (pp. 140–141)

Clearly, the holding of a major athletic festival such as the Olympiad at Los Angeles in 1932 had been well in tune with the prevalent image of the "Golden Age of Sport." The period spanning the late Twenties and early Thirties, economically disastrous for the United States, can be reflected upon by the student of sport with some sense of wonder and accomplishment. Moreover, the impression is given by the spate of exhibitions of sport in art that there was a greater cultural acceptance of the notion that sport had artistic appeal than actually was the case.

In 1938 an organization called The Society of American Sporting Art sponsored an exhibition entitled "The Art of Sports." A reporter for *Art News,* December 1938, made the following comment on the exhibition:

> To promote the idea of sporting art as a branch of the fine arts there is being held an exhibition of paintings and sculpture in a gallery at A. G. Spalding and Bros. It is under the auspices of the Society of American Sporting Art, a newly formed organization whose title is self-explanatory and which has held a show both here [New York] and Chicago. In this particular one the artists exhibiting are both successful in the world of art and are active participants of the sports portrayed. That accounts for the enthusiasm which is apparent in the work on view, as well as for the fact that as descriptions of the sports themselves they carry conviction. (p. 15)

According to the correspondent of *Art News,* the Society of American Sporting Art intends that "work which has artistic merit shall be available to be enjoyed by fellow sportsmen." The Educational Division of the Philadelphia Museum of Art assembled an exhibition in 1940 entitled "The Art of Games" in which "some four thousand years of art are spanned in fifty pieces inspired by the design of games."

In 1944 the Boston Museum of Fine Arts held an exhibition entitled "Sport in American Art." The extent to which the organizers went in acquiring exhibits shows the seriousness with which they compiled this exhibition. Thirty-one agencies (art museums, private galleries, private owners) were approached, and a most comprehensive forty-page catalogue was put out which contained a scholarly introductory essay discussing the origins and meanings of the word "sport." C. H. Edgell (1944), the writer of the introductory notes, draws the distinction between informal and organized sport:

> Sports can be divided into two categories, interlapping to be sure but recognizable, which we might call the informal and the organized. Fishing, hunting (in the American sense), boating, swimming, skating, riding, and many others are informal sports, though when the sport of

> riding goes over into racing it becomes organized. Football, baseball, polo, boxing, and many others clearly belong to the category of organized sports. The choice of adjectives may not be wholly happy but the general distinction is clear. (p. 6)

(Edgell here illustrates the fundamental difference between popular understandings of the term sport, and endorses that essential meaning which has been selected for this book.)

Emphasizing the precision and care with which the exhibition was set up, Edgell writes:

> I cannot too strongly emphasize, therefore, that this exhibition is literally of sport in American art and not an illustration of the history of American sport. In selecting the material if, for example, the Curators were confronted with choosing an indifferent picture of a great trotting horse and a fine picture of a less important trotter, the less important trotter won. Unless this is clearly understood the exhibition would appear to have grave limitations. (p. 7)

The paintings ranged across a period 1758 to 1915, although from the painting by Benjamin West (a portrait) executed in 1758, "we have to go forward to Thomas Birch, about 1830, before sport really reappears in American art." As a justification for the period covered, Edgell says:

> Mr. Constable deliberately decided not to include the work of younger contemporaries and to stop with artists who were established not later than the last World War. He felt, and I think correctly, that if the younger contemporaries were admitted and justice done them it would be impossible to do justice to the wealth of material offered from an earlier period. (p. 8)

Allowing for this breadth of interpretation, some 196 exhibits were hung, the media ranging across the entire scale of two-dimensional illustration, not merely painting. Writing in the *Art Digest,* October 1944, a correspondent states "This is the first extensive show of its kind ever attempted in this country, as far as we know."

In 1950 Gump Galleries of San Francisco put on "the world's largest exhibition" of sport in art entitled "Pageant of Sport." Richard Gump, the director of the Galleries, is quoted in *Time,* May 22, 1950, as saying:

> Why not baseball or football pictures? Those frozen hunting prints have become purely functional, like doorknobs. Pictures mean nothing unless they make sense to the man who looks at them. (p. 63)

According to the newspaper columnist Bob Goethals, there were "more than 300 exhibits," all but one of which were for sale. Goethals writes:

> . . . on exhibit are paintings and prints of unforgettable sports figures, some still living; some dead, brought to life on canvas by famous artists.

There are scenes of the "greats" at their best and, in some cases, of the "greats" at their worst.

It took Gump's three months to assemble the world's largest all-sports exhibition. (p. 114)

Gump Galleries also put on an exhibition of sports in art entitled "The Art of Golf in Art," in June 1955. As their advertisement of the event indicated, the exhibition comprised "original oils and watercolors . . . etchings, drawings, cartoons . . . and a *Sports Illustrated* collection of photographs depicting exciting moments in the history of championship play." The background to this particular specialized exhibition within an already specialized area of expression is given by Harry Phillips of *Sports Illustrated,* June 13, 1955:

> The idea for the exhibit was born some months ago when *SI*'s Sport in Art editor, Elaine St. Maur, met with Richard Gump, a member of the U.S. Open Committee and president of Gump's unique emporium in San Francisco, where the exhibit will be shown. The result is a selection of 57 items ranging from a contemporary abstraction down to a 17th Century Rembrandt etching of the game of *kolf,* and includes photographs from *SI*'s own black-and-white and color files.
>
> During the summer the exhibit will appear as a sidelight to some of the nation's big golf tournaments. In July it will move to the J. L. Hudson Co. in Detroit in conjunction with the PGA Championship; and in September to Thalhimer Brothers in Richmond, Va., during the playing of the U.S. Amateur. (p. 8)

This "functionality" of a sports in art exhibition is a unique venture from the popular conception of an art exhibition. As an example of relating sport to art it comes much closer to an ideal statement for a broader cultural experience than the same type of exhibition given in isolation. This concept has since been repeated by Katharine Kuh in the *Saturday Review,* December 1962, in which she discussed the first sports in art exhibition sponsored by the National Art Museum of Sport: "It may not be long now before we find boxing arenas and football stadia depending on adjacent exhibitions of provocative modern art to increase attendance." Although seemingly harmless out of context, this type of statement may act as a destructive agent in the realization of refined cultural mores.

When the IBM Gallery arranged its exhibition "Fine Art in Sports," sponsored by the newly organized but not yet permanently located National Art Museum of Sport, the main source of critical comment was, again, Katharine Kuh.

> Unfortunately, the National Art Museum of Sport's debut show did not measure up to the most discriminating standards. Granted that the ground rules were pretty difficult, what with each work being limited to some

specific sport, still the choice could have been less indulgent. Too often the exhibition seemed more conscientiously related to subject than to esthetic discovery. Otherwise how explain the inclusion of such obvious potboilers as Germain Glidden's "Redwings vs. Rangers," Norman Rockwell's "The Rookie," and other banal works that scarcely qualified as good illustrations.

There were, at the same time, a number of fine pieces, often borrowed from prominent American museums, but emasculated by the frequent proximity of indifferent works that made the exhibit meaningless as art —and, curiously, meaningless as sport. Though activities ranged from baseball, boxing, golf, and skating to lesser known sports like jousting, jai alai, kayak racing (and, inexplicably, chess), as a rule the theme song came through only dimly. (pp. 30–31)

The point that Katharine Kuh makes about some paintings being merely illustrations reflects a direction which some established (and emerging) contemporary artists pursued in the late Fifties and early Sixties. "Pop art" was, in fact, just that type of painting which emphasized the illustrative aspect of the advertising or commercial world. Indeed, prominent artists of this style were then engaged by *Sports Illustrated* to provide pictorial documentation of sports in their contemporary context. Out of this source was derived the last exhibition of sports in art undertaken during the period 1865 to today. A critical account is given in the *American Artist,* November 1962, by E. Metzi:

The current show at the Society of Illustrators is an exhibition of sporting illustrations by more than thirty artists done for *Sports Illustrated* from 1956 to the present. It is significant that these works are being honored by the Society of Illustrators, for *Sports Illustrated* has worked consistently to bring the artist into prominence as a reporter. Recognizing the camera's limitations, the editors have, from the first issues, added interest, variety, and scope to their publication by utilizing the artist's ability to add his own interpretation to what he sees. The truly creative artist stores visual impressions in his memory, enriches it with his intelligence and imagination, and then projects an emotional impact, a personal interpretation that often immortalizes an event. (p. 32)

The Sports Reporter and Sport in Art

The earliest indication that can be found of a sportswriter's interest in the artistic expression of sports focuses on the paintings of George Bellows. William Paris, writing in *The Hall of American Artists* comments:

The prize-ring pictures established Bellows, interestingly enough, with a group seldom concerned with art galleries—the sports reporters who therefore watched his work and commented upon it with an interest as great as that of their exhibitions. Art and sport had, for one of the first times in America, established a rapprochement. For sport it may have been a matter of minor significance; for art it was development of unusual interest. (p. 94)

Recalling Bellows' role as an athlete-artist, it is not difficult to see that he must have had the respect of the purely sports-oriented newspapermen. Indeed, his sports activities must have been commented upon in their columns if the games in which he played were reported.

Again, recalling the Boston Museum's "Sport in American Art" exhibition, a correspondent for the *American Magazine of Art* wrote in December 1944:

> The most interesting comment on the Boston Museum's extensive exhibition of "Sport in American Art" was that furnished by the sports writers. The exhibition of 196 paintings, prints and drawings by American artists ranging from Benjamin West to Edward Hopper was calculated to appeal both to museum and stadium habitués. So a special luncheon was given for the sports writers in the frank hope that they would review it in their columns and deflect some of the stadium trade towards the museum. It worked. The sports writers wrote, and new faces by the thousands appeared at the museum. (p. 297)

Notwithstanding, the sportswriter retains his own style in writing about sports in art. The emphasis is on the action as depicted, or on the event as it occurred, and very little or no attention is given to the mode of artistic expression. Thus, a classic example of the sportswriter on sport in art is drawn from a full column account of Gump's "Pageant of Sports" exhibition; the article appeared in the *San Francisco Examiner,* May 10, 1950:

> Possibly the best known American work in the group is one of the Dempsey-Firpo fight by the late, great George W. Bellows. This is a striking illustration of brute strength, but can be criticized, we think, in that he gives a misleading picture of who was beating h--l out of whom.

> Bellows' effort shows Firpo knocking Dempsey through the ropes. That happened, all right, but if you merely viewed the painting without reading the account of the battle, you'd have a completely erroneous idea of what took place.

> The truth, of course, is that Dempsey all but murdered Firpo ere knocking him colder than a wedge in the second round. The way Bellows has it, Dempsey is the loser.

> For our dough, the best things in the collection are a number of watercolors by a contemporary artist named Joselph W. Golinkin. This guy Golinkin is at home in any sport and we were for acquiring an armful of his colorful and decorative creations until a man told us they were priced at between 300 and 400 clackers apiece.

A touch of local interest is given the exhibit by Lou Macoulliard, who is showing an oil of the "Fifteenth Hole at Lake Merced." If you look sharp, you can see a hacker in one of the sand traps. The figure could be Lefty O'Doul. He plays at Lake Merced all the time. (p. 38)

Given this kind of appeal, it comes as no surprise to learn that exhibition attendances show a marked increase when a sports in art exhibition is being shown at a city gallery. The cultural role of the sportswriter is expanded beyond the "commonplace" of his specialization in circumstances like this.

Sports in Art in Periodicals

In the nineteenth century such periodicals as *Frank Leslie's Illustrated Newspaper, Harper's Weekly,* and *The Illustrated Sporting and Dramatic News* used graphic illustrations of sports action to give pictorial significance to games reports.

Sports Illustrated published a series of features called "Sport in Art" from 1954 until 1959 in which they showed paintings representing or interpreting sports. Included in the series were recorded events associated with the history of sport as represented in painting. Their concept of sport was all-embracing, as illustrated by such diverse subjects as *Tut Ankhaman Hunting Lions* (a decoration from the lid of a box found in the young Pharoah's tomb), to *Les Bagneuses* by Honoré Daumier, to *Winter Evening* by Fred Uhlman (a contemporary English artist), to *The Game of Skittles* by Pieter de Hooch and Ben Marshall's *Peace* (a portrait of a fighting cock).

The feature was regular in the first few years of publication and became intermittent and infrequent between 1956 and 1959. During this latter period, however, another sports in art direction was being pursued in the feature entitled "Spectacle," for which the magazine began engaging artists to document outstanding sports events. In 1960 *Sports Illustrated* began to use paintings occasionally to illustrate their feature "Spectacle," as in the five paintings of Golf of Masters Tournament by Daniel Schwartz, and Morton Roberts' paintings of the Kentucky Derby. John Lahr speaks about Richard Gangel, the art director of *Sports Illustrated,* in his *Print,* September 1966, article:

The wide range of artists sought out by Gangel has been instrumental in capturing subtle textures of experience in the variety of sports worlds. . . . Gangel hopes to take the art of his magazine in still newer directions. "Illustration," he says, "in a certain way is part of the grand tradition, but still part of the past in magazine pages. The future as I see it is to reproduce the work of the most exciting painters who are showing currently throughout the world. These painters are the ones I plan to use in my own future and the future of this magazine. This is not to say that the present illustrators will be left out—only that the more dynamic, exciting gallery painting will be included as part of our illustration."

The painters whom Gangel has most recently engaged are R. B. Kitaj, Wayne Thiebaud and Bob Stanley. Thiebaud is in the painterly tradition —a sensualist who directs his oils on pop-art objects. . . . The interesting aspect of Gangel's choices is that these painters who might be said to represent the second-string of the pop-art world are influenced by the artful illustration of magazines. Their work for *SI* is a curious return to the source of their inspiration. (pp. 17–21)

Thus the role of *Sports Illustrated* (in the short history of its place in the period discussed) changed from documentor to innovator in its involvement with sports in art.

summary

The representation of sports in art did not begin to show much evidence prior to 1865 apart from a few isolated examples. With the new spirit of nationalism there developed a singularly American way of painting and sculpture, epitomized in the work of painters Thomas Eakins, Winslow Homer, and sculptor Joseph Brown. The acceleration of the development of organized sports toward the turn of the century provided wider opportunity for choice of subject matter, an opportunity that was not wholly taken. Sports subjects were painted and sculpted by both athlete-artists, such as George Bellows, and nonathlete artists, such as Fletcher Martin and R. Tait McKenzie.

Fewer than half a dozen exhibitions of sports in art were held throughout the past 100 years. Such exhibitions were reported by sportswriters, as well as by art critics, and this exposure served as a cultural expansion of interest for many people. Pursuing this thought, *Sports Illustrated* ran a series of features on "Sports in Art" and explored the talents of contemporary artists as illustrators to document notable sports events.

The optimism of W. K. Zoeller (1936), expressed in the opening paragraphs of this chapter, is reinforced in his comment on the hope for the future:

Living or contemporary artists have caught the spirit of Americans at play; posterity will see and feel our enthusiasm for fishing and hunting; yachting; polo and racing. Dog fanciers will appreciate the breeds popular in this day. The sport of flying has its contributors; golf and tennis will go down in history with their colorful traditions as will college sports and athletes. Baseball, football, boxing, and even prizefighting will be an open book to the grandchildren of this age. (p. 11)

The 1970's represent that future, and we may claim to detect that some of what he says has validity today. Clearly, this book is a part of that message and hope. When John Tunis wrote in 1958, "Sociologists of the future may wonder why we paid so much attention to sports," he was speaking of the "Golden Age of Sport," the Roaring Twenties and Depression Thirties. The lesson that we, as students of sport, have learned from that era is that they were well aware of the beauty of sport, and that we, as their future, have much to benefit from their vision.

questions for discussion

1. How does the study of sports-art reflect the cultural heritage of the United States?
2. What is the difference between an athlete-artist and an artist-athlete?
3. Assess the contributions to sports-art made by painters and sculptors. Was the contribution of Eakins or Bellows any greater than that of McKenzie or Brown?
4. Can a case be made for stating that one particular art medium (painting, say) is any better than another for the best representation of a particular sport in art? Put another way, is sculpture better than painting for showing sports action?
5. Discuss the cultural contribution made by sports-art exhibitions and the reports of such exhibitions made by sports reporters.

Sport
and the Performing Arts

 Athletics implies exercise of the body; art, function of the brain. These two forms of endeavor constitute a sort of Siamese twins existence, which makes for health and sanity and such reasonable fulfillment of our cravings for perfection as we may hope to realize.

C. H. BRADNER

SPORT AS ART

Upon entering the discussion of whether sport can be seen as an art, some questions arise as to process and product. Conceptually, sport implies both process and product; art, too, implies both process and product.

The process of sport is in the playing of the game, in the contesting of the match, and in the play action in the most general and specific terms. Sport as product is more abstract and harder to define. It is sometimes signified in the victory, the tournament championship, and the symbol of trophy. The interactive effect of spectators attending a sports event, for which they have paid an entrance fee to watch athletes earning their salaries for performance, comprises a case of confusion in which sport simultaneously is both process and product. Business or entrepreneurial interests in sport recommend the interpretation of sport as product.

The process of art is in the action of painting, sculpting, designing, dancing, acting, writing, composing. The product in some cases is easy to identify, such as the finished painting of a landscape or portrait, the sculpture, the poem, and the symphony. In other cases, it is as difficult to identify as for sport, as in the dance and dancing, the play and acting, and architecture (designing and building). The confusion merits only our attention and cognizance of it, not our efforts to explain it. Our need to

91

acknowledge art as a process is intrinsically bound up with our objective study of sports-art for the instruction it brings to the beauty of sport. Beauty in the various forms of art is a given, and from that given, we hope to adapt the lessons of the major arts to our study of sport.

Kovich (1971) expresses the opinion that "the definition of art needs to be expanded to include the skilled athletic performance." She reinforces her judgment by referring to the superlative athletic performances of Arthur Ashe, Bob Seagren, and Vera Caslavska as artistic, suggesting further that skill in movement, whether by top athletes or by schoolchildren, expresses beauty. Kovich elaborates on this concept thus:

> The spectator cannot divorce man from his movements. Sport is a truly human form of art, for it is not just the product of man's abilities which is on display; it is man. Research in electromyography has shown that observers mimic in a minute way the movement patterns of the performer, thus inducing a form of restrained participation. As the performer feels the art he is creating, so can a perceptive spectator feel this same quality, although not to the same extent. Whether intended or not, there is silent communication between the performer and the spectator. Empathy with the elements of force, space, and time in the world of the performer and his movements can account, in part at least, for the spectator interpreting the movement as meaningful and beautiful. (p. 42)

The sense of empathy is introduced in the concept of identification between athlete and spectator. Parenthetically, Kovich uses "product" as we are using "process" in our context, but by focusing on the principle of empathy, she reinforces our observation that there exists an interactive effect of process and product (as we mean it) when people pay for a ticket to watch sports performance. The principle thus brings us to similarities that exist (if superficially) between the stadium and the theatre. On the basis of these similarities, we can explore possible sources of support for justifying our consideration of sport as an applied art or as one of the performing arts.

SPORT AS AN APPLIED ART

In the Foreword to *Man, Sport and Existence* by H. S. Slusher, Edgar Friedenberg expresses the thought that "Sport is a kind of applied art." He suggests that sport is most like ballet of the performing arts since the body is the medium for artistic expression. However, he believes sport as an art is more formal than other performing arts by virtue of being convention-bound. Within the rules, the function of the human body is to accomplish the task, not necessarily just to create or regulate a contest. Hence, the limitations binding the athlete in the production of his art-work (an action, a strategy, or the game) are more like those which bind the sculptor designing a work as part of the grander design of a building. "The expressive function of the athlete," states Friedenberg, "is subordinate to spectacle and profitability, while his performance must fit completely within a framework of rigid conventions if it is to have any meaning at all." He adds, finally, that the athlete who insists on virtuoso performance, disregarding the place of that action in the total structure of the game, runs the risk of spoiling the total effect of the game as a work of art. Friedenberg thus distinguishes between the beauty of the individual performance (virtuoso performance) and the beauty of the total game, suggesting that the emphasis on the former can interfere with the effect of the latter. Can we agree with this? The more explicit interpretation is that the virtuoso and the total game are two different things, which, except by value judgment, need not interfere with each other at all. More relevantly, the one can heighten the effect of the other as in the case of Bobby Orr, the National Hockey League top-scoring defenseman, who has "saved" games by his virtuoso performances. Punt-return touchdowns are always virtuoso performances, and, simultaneously electrifying if they "turn the game around." It is "sour grapes" not to extol the beauty of individualized virtuoso performance by suggesting that it spoils the total effect of the game. The case is stronger when argued to the contrary.

If the argument is now taken up that the constraints in ballet, as one dance form, are physically more restrictive than in sports, then the sports must be differentiated for comparison purposes. This is not "begging the question," since just as ballet is one dance form, so is jazz dance or modern expressive dance, and in their demands and options they are as separable as fencing, football, and gymnastics. Dynamics of movement and action differ between dance forms, as they do between sports. Mental and physical applications of the body to both dance and sport, in their own unique instances, can be practically indistinguishable in any chosen set of comparisons. To draw distinctions, we must assess the affective or emotive (emotional) input of dance and sport, and we may concur then that for dance the affective element is important in the process and in the product, whereas for sport it is more difficult to make this case. This is not to say that emotional discharge does not take place either in the process or product of sport. Further discussion of this acknowledged fact is found in Chapter 8. Here, suffice it to say, if sport is to be considered as an applied art, the component elements of artistic quality (process and product) must be better understood first.

SPORT AS A PERFORMING ART

Wesley Pavalon, the founder and chairman of the board of the Milwaukee Bucks basketball team, was quoted in *Look* magazine, April 6,

1971, as saying: "I have given this city a performing art, I have given them the ultimate in basketball, yes, a performing art."

What are the performing arts? For our purpose they comprise the dance, the theatre, and music. They are those media of human expression in which physical movement predominates—the dance being expressively more movement dependent than the theatre, which in turn employs greater movement options than music. Where is the similarity between these forms of cultural expression and what Pavalon calls a "performing art"—basketball? Basketball has been called balletic by some observers, but we might presume they carry the same bias as Pavalon himself.

John Dewey, the author of *Art as Expression,* has said: "Dance and sport are activities in which acts once performed spontaneously in separation are assembled and converted from raw, crude material into works of expressive art." While this provides us with a baseline for comparison purposes, we should not be unquestioningly acquiescent to this thought, even if it looks agreeable to us in our search for the beauty of sport. We need only turn to René Maheu (1962) for some challenging counterargument which, curiously, does not set counter-argument at odds. The tacit statement of Maheu is that: "Sport consists wholly of action; art, on the contrary, by its employment of the sign which frees it from the object and from life, moves into eternity—thus, sport and art face in opposite directions." He adds that in his opinion there is "a contrast between the beauty of sport and the beauty of art." The riddle is spoken. The clue to solving it lies in separating the beauty of nature from the beauty of art (see the section on the Beauty of Nature in Chapter 1).

Ernst Jokl has expressed agreement with Maheu on philosophic grounds, but he appears to be perplexed by the riddle set by him. In his own right, Jokl (1974), in Whiting and Masterson's *Readings in the Aesthetics of Sports,* holds that: "One of the great cultural attributes of sport is that it creates beauty." In saying this, he reflects his alliance with Maheu, who, he frankly admits, taxes his own deeper comprehension of sport as beauty. The problem that Maheu presents for Jokl is stated in the separation conceived as "a contrast between the beauty of sport and the beauty of art."

However, Jokl does see one way out of his difficulty. He takes the viewpoint that sport can be interpreted similarly to music or the stage for its implicit artistic content:

> Is the beauty that is derived from ice skating and dancing, from gymnastics and water diving, from soccer, hockey and horseback riding categorically different from that of, say, music and of the stage? Is it true that only in sport the beauty which the performer's action begets is immanent in the very act which creates it? I believe that the answer to these questions is in the negative. The esthetic implications of the acts

that engender beauty in sport are fundamentally the same as the acts that engender beauty in music and on the stage. They all belong to the present, as Maheu has rightly pointed out in respect of sport. Like the performing athlete, the performing musician and the performing actor merge completely with their action. Esthetics in sport and esthetics in music and on the stage also have the same double character in that on the one hand they appeal but for a "fleeting movement" while on the other their performances can be rendered permanent: in music through staff notation, in literature through the written word; in sport through graphic symbolization, e.g., in choreography. All these forms of esthetic revelation can therefore be reflected upon and repeated; all three thus attain a quality of the "eternal." (p. 32)

The Jokl statement will be recognized as both incomplete and evasive. Evasive, because he does not challenge the Maheu riddle. In this book the riddle is solved by drawing the distinction between beauty in nature and beauty in art, the clues for which were first presented by Baumgarten and the eighteenth-century German poet-philosophers. Jokl does not complete his pursuit of "sport as a performing art" by virtue of his not continuing the analysis of the performing arts to show how many of the fundamental criteria both sport and the performing arts meet. To do this, we must digress for a moment to a brief discussion of "form." Basic to any discussion of the arts, "form" can be either static or dynamic. In the performing arts, we are speaking of dynamic form rather than of static form.

Form in Art

The concept "form" has been of interest to man since pre-literate times before Aristotle. For Aristotle, "form" was as important to understand as "nature." Today, we tend to take the terms for granted much as we take "beauty" and "sport" for granted. It is when we find people, ourselves included, using such terms as "form" or "harmony" or "grace" in their efforts to describe what is meant by beauty that we realize that little in the way of real explanation is taking place. If form is elusive for us to explain, then we need to seek clarification for a basis of agreement, at least, before we discuss its relevance to the beauty of sport.

Parallel words that we might identify with form are shape, configuration, pattern, structure, organization, wholeness, and unity. Immediately we can see the weakness of our case. None of these parallel words imply the *dynamic* function of form; to do this, we must add descriptive location focusing on a particular referent, such as "musical form" or "mathematical form." If we mean harmony when we say musical form, we may be one step nearer our objective of clear definition of form, but only one step, and even then we may be slipping into the trap of circuitous description rather than coming closer to explanation. Similarly, if we mean geometry or algebra when we think of mathematical form, we may find ourselves pursuing a path which leads only to explanation by mathematical symbol.

The classical parallel terms of shape, configuration, pattern, and structure mean much the same as form when put into terms like the definitional clause, "certain elements in certain relations" (Bell 1958). To test the underlying notion of form, the student is invited to consider the difference between "form" and "pure form."

Implicitly, the category "pure form" qualifies as smaller than the category "form." This deduction equates with the artistic criterion. Bell states that people who are of refined aesthetic judgment and who can be said to experience deep aesthetic emotion "are concerned only with lines and colours, their relations and quantities and qualities; but from these they win an emotion more profound and far more sublime than any that can be given by the description of facts and ideas." Bell claims to be "transported" (emotionally elated) equally by "pure musical form" as by "pure visual form." Students of an artistic turn of mind will feel comfortable with the evocative nature of what Bell is saying, whereas the student who seeks empirical satisfaction to his inquiry will question him further. Barry (1970) accords Bell his "youthful position," but is uncomfortable about the place of form in nature and form in a painting, sculpture, or theatrical presentation as these might fit Bell's schema. He sidesteps the circular discussion of "pure form" in his efforts to bring a better understanding to what he calls "structure," a preferable and less ambiguous term than "form." The four-part alternative that Barry brings to structure is based on Bell's definitional clause of elements and relations, and is a nice demonstration of deductive reasoning which the student of empiricism will relish. With the understanding that "pure" means "as found in nature," and that "representational" means "as found in art," Barry recommends "four cases of pure or impure art which are rarely discriminated." Since he is writing about the theatre, one of the performing arts, it is highly likely that his four cases are applicable to the analysis of sport as dramatic production. By satisfying the artistic conditions of dramatic production, perhaps we can deduce essential bases of common form contributory to the beauty of sport. The four cases given by Barry are:

1. Pure elements in representational relational patterns.
2. Elements seen as representational in representational relational patterns.
3. Pure elements in pure relational patterns.
4. Elements seen as representational in pure relational patterns. (p. 94)

Incidentally, motion and movement are not omitted from the Barry schematization of form or structure. While this has not been elaborated in the foregoing statement on form, an underlying presupposition of readers of this text is that they find implicit statements pertaining to the beauty of the movement of sport, as well as to other elements of form and structure dependent on motion and movement (strategy, for example). Temporal parameters are as functionally formal or structural as are the spatial parameters.

Sport as Pure or Impure Art

Does sport satisfy any of the four cases of pure or impure art? To answer this question we may have to make some assumptions which are clearly within our framework of what is meant by athlete as well as what is meant by sport. It is possible, therefore, that sport will satisfy one, more than one, or none of the four cases, but for us to interpret meaningfully, we must sustain some integrity in what we define as components in the sports domain (elements and relations). Thus, is the athlete a man/woman in the purest sense of person, or is the athlete representational of some other role? For our needs, the athlete is man/woman, and hence is pure element, not "element seen as representational." Is the sport domain (playing field, court, mountain face) an element or a relational pattern? (This question is neither specious nor spurious.) Viewed as objects, a football field, baseball diamond, mountain face, tennis court, or boxing ring may have aesthetic quality and may be viewed as elements (just as colors, lines, shapes, etc., are elements). They are as much the elements of sport as are men and women (athletes) until the point of interaction between both groups of elements is staged. At this point a transformation takes place when such elements take on representational meaning—their shapes become patterns by virtue of the symbolism ascribed to them. For example, the basketball court is no longer a rectangle with lines painted on it; the "key" takes on meaning, as does the halfway line, and the shape takes on a rule-bounded pattern. This pattern becomes a relational pattern due to prescriptions called "sport," a movement from the purely spatial (shape of the sport domain) to the temporal contiguity of action and interaction. Thus, the sport domain is a relational pattern.

   Now we must establish if sport can be either a pure or representational relational pattern. What else in life, nature, or society does sport represent? Typically, nothing. It is not representational of any other form of behavior. We do not represent love, hate, power, honesty, ambition, greed, lust, or any other manifestation of emotion in behavioral terms. To be sure, some will say that sport is like religion in today's post-industrial society, others will say that it is the civilized alternative for internecine violence and subjugation, yet apart from providing a few outstanding individuals with a means for making a living it does not even represent work. Sport is a form of entertainment, but not by representing some other real-life alternative. Sport, then, is pure form, pure action. The only constraints or contrivances are the pseudo-social rules that set boundaries within which that pure action should be prescribed. But wait! If so, is not sport representational of the ethical and moral code of our society, is it not the "unreal" model by which we socialize our young? If it is, and some sport sociologists aver that it is, then, sport is indeed a representational relational pattern. Let us agree then that *physically* sport is pure, but that *socially* it is representational. Conclusively, we can state that sport satisfies two of the four cases for form in art:

1. Pure elements (athletes) in pure relational patterns (sport—physical activity).
2. Pure elements (athletes) in representational relational patterns (sport—quasi-social activity).

It is interesting that Barry (1970) describes the first case above as "the purest pure form" of art. The deduction that we have attained can be taken as applicable for the interpretation of sport as a performing art of the purest kind also.

Form in Sport

Lawther (1951) uses the term "form" in agreement with Lascari (1973) when speaking of form in sport. Whether Lawther or Lascari view sport as a performing art is not patently evident. Lawther states:

> Form . . . is a design or pattern of performance. Efficient form is the way that is best adapted to accomplishing the purpose of the performance. The purpose may be beauty, grace, and apparent ease as in gymnastics, diving or figure skating. (p. 286)

This functionalist interpretation that he gives to the meaning of "form" is no less valid than meanings given by an artist in explaining his art-work, or by a philosopher employing the term "aesthetically" to explain certain features of all art. Lawther puts the element of form into a vocabulary of movement much as a theoretician of the performing arts would do. Furthermore, he speaks of "good form" as economy of motion or "a minimum of wasted energy." As an instance of his functionalist perspective, he cites the example of a skilled runner as one who may have less than an inch of rise or fall in his center of gravity in the execution of his sprint. Similarly, the beauty of the hurdler is often attributed to the fact that he shows little evidence of vertical momentum as he takes the hurdles. However, variations in force and speed, which can be referred to as component movement patterns essential for the interpretation of skill, are also categorical in explaining form as beauty in athletics.

A further approach to investigating form in sport is to take the dance as a performing art, and to draw meaning from it either uniquely or in comparison. Before doing this, it is worth calling upon the authority of Kaelin (1968) to add substance to our reasoning. Kaelin states:

> If I were to use a model of a completed developed aesthetic activity which is understood on its own terms, my choice would not be of a totally dissimilar medium, such as dramatic literature, which works its wonders by the articulation of words and by their meanings, but by the similar medium of dance: human effort expended in kinesthetic response to the growing needs of a physical situation. In dance, of course, the situation and the responses are mutually determinant and self-contained. My argument will be that competitive sport is capable of the same kind of development, that it achieves the same sort of mutual determinancy and self-containedness as the most abstract of dance. The "drama" of the sport may indeed produce a more effectively expressive vehicle than what is usually achieved in dance. (p. 309)

What, then, is the difference between sport and dance? The difference lies in the purpose of the movements. The athlete is concerned with efficient results and must be governed by real properties of space, time, and mass. The beauty of the movement is a by-product of the efficient coordination. The dancer (and perhaps the artist, as well) expands on time and space limited only by a personal limitation of body mass, and uses energy extravagantly to maximize emotional involvement. Between dancers (artists) and athletes, communication can take place based on mutual appreciation of each other's purposes. Sport motifs can be used for dance. Through the sport motif the artist (dancer) can expand the meanings and emotional values of the movement. Through dance experience an athlete can increase his satisfaction in movement and expand his understanding of the need which drives a person to conquer space, time, and mass.

It is well known that many athletes have taken dance lessons, notably ballet, to enhance their athletic ability. Athletes have gone on record claiming that the dance exercises have been beneficial for improved sports performance. Conversely, some dancers of national and international recognition, namely Villella and Nureyev, have been acclaimed for the "athletic" appearance of their skills in the ballet, although this is not to say that their dancing looks athletic (see Plate 11).

Sport as Aesthetic Performance

The perceptive observation by Hein (1970), that theories of aesthetics are largely bereft of commentary on performance as artistic expression, is valuable to the student of sport since, when commentary is made it usually accords little fundamental importance to the performer. Thus, where reference is made to the performer at all, it is usually as an interpreter. The status and role of performers as expressive artists appear only rarely in the historical literature on aesthetics. As if to be expected, commentary typically focuses on the dance, acting, performing music, or "happenings." Again, since most of these art-forms of expression are dependent upon written or prepared work by composers, choreographers, and the like, analytic interest has been paid mainly to these rather than to the actual performer. Thus, we would speak of a beauty of interpretation for the performer as opposed to the beauty of the art-work. It is this challenging concept of the beauty of interpretation which has most value for the study of sport as a performing art.

The scenarios for throwing the javelin, or for running the mile, or for pitching a ball, or for lifting the weight remain similar for each sport or athletic event from one occasion to the next (notwithstanding minor exceptions for variation in climate, altitude, crowd size, or environment). The more complex the sport, the more possibilities for variance and hence the need for "choreographers" (coaches in professional league sports). Hence, what can be predicted of the performance of a given sport is much the same as what can be predicted from the reading of a score of music or the directions of a play. Sport and athletics slip very well into this category.

Hein (1970) tells us that authors and composers are regarded as "primary" artists, and that those who perform the plays or conduct and play the music are designated "secondary" or "derivative" artists. Accepting for the moment that sport can be called a performing art, who are the "primary" artists of sport and athletics? Although most are lost in antiquity, we can point to Naismith, the founder-orginator of basketball, as one example in our literature. But because he was innovative and creative in designing the new game of basketball does not mean to say that Naismith was an artist—or does it? Perhaps it is time for a reconsideration. For many, at least, he created a beautiful game, a "performing art," as Pavalon put it.

Performance as an aesthetic category is a curious phenomenon since it is relevant only to certain art-forms, such as dance or drama or music. With very little excuse, we could find good reason to include sport. However, that is the seat of our inquiry, and we must avoid begging the question by acting on such an assumption. Performance is a temporal as well as a spatial art form. Temporally, many sport forms can be compared with performance arts, and insofar as those arts are performed in a particular theatre or auditorium, so the spatial dimensions of the arena, stadium, or court might be seen as not grossly dissimilar.

Hein cites notation or instruction as intermediary elements between the original "primary" artist and the "secondary" performing artist. In sport and athletics we have rules and boundaries, the infraction of which results in poor sport. Poorly performed violin sonatas and badly acted plays destroy the artistic effect intended by the composer or author. Infractions of sports rules are poor social behavior, the "author" of which is the tradition of society to sustain social control. Beautiful behavior in society is not a commonplace concept but we all know what it means. Sport and athletics are the symbolic (artistic?) seats of what is beautiful social behavior. This social-function interpretation of the role of sport sets it aside from the other performing arts in that one respect. We still have the other respect to contend with in what we recognize and define as "graceful, harmonious" athletic performance. The athlete-as-artist interprets his "art" on two major levels: (1) *technical performance,* employing speed, strength, strategy, and physical skill, and (2) *symbolic performance,* employing generalized ethical values, attitudes, and social behavior. Both have equal weighting in our judgment of good sport. In interpretive performances of music and dance, technical performance is counter-weighted with aesthetic (as opposed to ethical) value; in drama, technical performance and aesthetic performance outweigh the symbolic performance of social behavior. In sports and athletics, the social symbolic performance is the stuff of real emotion, the involvement of the spectator often being on very real terms. In the other performing arts, the sense of distance between self and action is far greater in socially symbolic terms, and the emotional involvement is situational and nonthreatening. Sports performance, on the other hand, can be seriously threatening to every fiber of our social identity.

Sport as Dramatic Performance

When the musician, dancer, or actor performs, of course, the intention is to heighten aesthetic awareness by bringing beautiful interpretation to what is culturally accepted as a work of art. Hein notes, "The concept of work of art as creative process, or performance, might also evoke the doctrine of art as experience which also identifies the work of art with a subjective process." This suggestion that a certain experience can be interpreted as art raises the question posed as to the "subjective aesthetic" of the athlete. This suggests, too, that sport can be viewed as dramatic performance.

On the issue of whether drama can be considered one of the aesthetic qualities of sport, Elliott (1974) is tentative. He states that dissension about dramatic qualities of sport should not mislead us into assimilating sport to the drama. This counsel is directly contrary to that held by ourselves in our search for explanation. Drama (theatre) is one of the nine basic arts (Weiss, 1969). Drama presupposes a whole range of human response to theatrical action which can manifest itself in aesthetic reaction to comedy, tragedy, or any other form of theatre. If we assume that "aesthetic" in some way means pleasurable (as some writers do), then we have difficulty assimilating tragedy with the aesthetic, but if aesthetic response is given parallel with empathy, then concordant emotional response can fairly be termed aesthetic. Largely, our search for explanation of sport as aesthetic leans little on interpretations of empathy and centers more on pleasurable response, but the option of empathy is not discounted. Also, traditionally people have claimed to have "had a good time" at the theatre even when the show has been dramatically "tragic." Elliott is not totally unaware of this, but he refutes the purely dramatic context of sport by drawing the paradigm of "sport as real life." In his own words: "In the sporting contest, something of importance is at stake, and we deceive ourselves if we say that defeat in sport does not matter." The difficulty is easily recognized. For his option in this instance, Elliott has taken "sport as real life," as opposed to Huizinga (1950), who holds the thesis that sport is only symbolic of real life. This argument about sport in society is classic, and it is important to be aware of, but it is unwise to base opinion on one side of it at the expense of the other side.

To repeat, Elliott is not totally unaware of the predicament: "There is no *mimesis* in sport, but if in a sense the tragedy in sport is real, it is not of the kind which involves death or serious suffering." The Spanish bullfight may be an exception, but if so, it is one which provides a focal point for the discussion of the *definition* of sport (see Plate 24). To accept the broadest cultural perspective of sport, some assumption must be made that the bullfight is sport, for there are elements of aesthetic content which we must examine in deference to the analysis of Roland Barthes. The death of the bull, symbolically, is no more important than a goal scored, except in the sense that the act of killing the bull reaffirms for man his potential ability to triumph over the forces of nature (survival) greater than himself. Killing the referee in a South American soccer match is not quite the same thing, of course, even though some may see a symbolic parallel.

So, although sport may or may not be seen as a drama, depending on one's particular perspective, many people experience it as though it were. This presupposes that those who witness a sports event take with them a special attitude which it is appropriate to adopt when spectating. Elliott calls this "disinterested contemplation." The difference between "disinterested contemplation" and "sport as real life" is hard to reconcile in his argument, but disregarding this, disinterested contemplation is the attitude that allows for dramatic aesthetic interaction between the sports event and the spectator. This attitude must be prevalent for the tragic and the triumphant events in sport to assume an aesthetic aspect. The spectacle of sport is only spectacular within an attitude of disinterested contemplation. The frame of reference within which this precept is presented is very valuable to our overall understanding because it offers a challenge to the way in which the role of the spectator is perceived.

The dramatic impact of sport as spectacle must be viewed differently from the way in which a ticker-tape parade or the Mardi Gras is seen as spectacle. Attendance in the crowd at any of these events is exciting, as is attendance in a large capacity-filled stadium or arena. It is as if there is an "electricity" in the air, and the sense of presence is stimulating. This phenomenon has been identified by psychologists seeking to explain collective behavior (Turner and Killian, 1957; Blumer, 1957; and Lang and Lang, 1961).

Two authors who have drawn similarities between sport and drama are Keenan (1975) and Maheu (1962). Both point to the social role of drama in its purpose to be presented before an audience. From an instructive perspective, the functional comment by Maheu builds on the structural account made by Keenan. Keenan states:

> The drama is an art form developed with spectators in mind. It is perhaps in the drama that sport reaches its closest affinity with art as process. The audience at athletic contests behave similarly to those at dramatic stage productions; there is applause for performers who are skillful, as well as overt manifestations of disapproval for poor performances. We speak of "players" in both athletics and drama. The attitudes and experiences surrounding stage and arena are also similar in that we take pleasure and delight in exciting performances which deliver an organized sequence of action executed with skill. (pp. 41–42)

The reverse also can be true, especially when the spectating crowd actively identifies with a team or an athlete. Riots of jubilation have been noted as well as riots resulting from the frustration of defeat. There is very real emotional relationship, as Maheu points out:

> In the theater the audience involves itself in the drama being enacted befor it, thus becoming, after a fashion, actor as well as spectator, and similarly in the stadium, an intense empathy develops between spectators and performers. (p. 41)

There is, of course, one vital difference. Spectators have a "home" identity with "their" team and "their" stadium which theater-goers never proclaim. On the other hand, both groups go to their respective performances with the psychological set to have and receive entertainment. Whether they go with differing or similar emotional expectations is open to question. The theatre-goer might attend plays to obtain cognitive stimulation in preference to emotional-affective response, and this may or may not differ from the intentions of the sports-spectator—the question remains speculative. The fact that both groups can be emotionally aroused, regardless of intentions of the visit (attendance), is testament to the dramatic impact of each event, the play or the sport.

s u m m a r y

Sport has been explored for its relationship to art from the perspective of similarities existing between it and the performing arts. This exercise links the discussion of the broader sport-art relationship with due consideration of the athlete as artist. If the athlete is to be regarded as an artist, it must be as a performing artist. Hence the parameters defining similarity between sport and art which focus on performance provide a foundation for the realization of that objective.

It is possible to equivocate on whether sport can be considered an applied art, and the case for argument may rest on firmer ground than the case made for its being a performing art. Even so, the framework of the question, germane to the total sport-art paradigm, focuses more exclusively on the body and its potential for action as the manifest medium for creative expression. As paints and canvas are to the painter, so the body is to the athlete in the demonstration of his art. His art can be both process-centered (self-expressive) or product-oriented (social or pecuniary reward-induced), which is to say that it is no different from the artistic enterprise of any artist. Certainly, end results (the work of art) differ—a painting and sculpture serving for posterity, a dance living only for the duration of its execution—and into this spectrum of "differences" sport may take a place. Most suitably, this is closer to the dance (or nonfinite product) end of the spectrum.

The dynamics of sport are more akin to the dynamics of dance or the theatre, the subtle difference appearing in the exploitation of the absolutes of strength, endurance, speed, and similar extremes of man's physical potential (typically applied to a value structure founded in competition). The agonistic factors typically take sport some conceptual distance from consideration as fitting into an arts spectrum. This factor demands further exploration if a classification of human activity attributing the implementation of beauty is to be postulated. The concept "the arts" appears to do this already, yet the exclusion of sport from the arts tests the strength of this supposition.

Sport as one of the performing arts depends on an understanding of underlying commonalities such as "form." What is form for the performing arts should have some agreement with what is form in sport. Form is explored more fully, distinctions being drawn between pure and impure form for the detection of elements or structure which give art the basis for a substantive claim to being contextually separated from nature. Putting this into a context drawn from Chapter 1, the beauty of the athletic body (form) is natural and therefore "pure" in artistic value, whereas the representation of the athlete that R. Tait McKenzie made in his study of *The Sprinter* reflects "impure" form by virtue of being art and not of nature. The question of whether sport satisfies more or fewer conditions of pure or impure art is answered affirmatively as "the purest pure form" of art. This leads us logically into what is meant by form in sport. On the basis of this discussion, sport is viewed first as aesthetic performance and then as dramatic performance. In each of these instances, a sense of empathy is conveyed such that aesthetic and dramatic force felt at sport events translates to the experience of the beauty of sport.

questions for discussion

1. Both sport and art are process-related and product-related. Discuss the similarities for each in respect to process and in respect to product, and consider the value of each product for the cultural heritage of society.
2. Is sport an applied art? Answer this question by referring to sections of the book which discuss sport as the beauty of art and sport as the beauty of nature.
3. The virtuoso athlete and the virtuoso violinist have many things in common (some bad, some good). What are they?
4. Do you support the contention of Wesley Pavalon that baskeeball is one of the performing arts?
5. There is agreement that form can be either static or dynamic, and we can speak of musical form and mathematical form. But what do we mean when we speak about "athletic form"?
6. Discuss the conditions and circumstances of life, nature, and society in which sport plays a representational role. In what way does it represent art?
7. There appear to be differing foundations of emotional effect associated with sport and with dance. How can these differences provide the basis for the argument that sport cannot be classified as dance?
8. How does "aesthetic performance" differ from "dramatic performance"?

The Athlete and Artistic Performance

5

Esthetics govern all of Ali's actions and conclusions; the way a man looks, the way he moves is what interests Ali. By Ali's standards, Frazier was not pretty as a man and without semblance of style as a fighter. Frazier was an affront to beauty, to Ali's own beauty as well as to his precious concept of how a good fighter should move.

MARK KRAM

INTRODUCTION

The subject of whether sport can be viewed as one of the performing arts leads logically into the discussion of whether the athlete can be regarded as a performing artist. Is the running back, the sprinter, the centerfielder, or the welterweight as much an artist as the violinist, the ballet dancer, the orchestra conductor? From what we have deduced in the foregoing chapter, we might save ourselves the trouble of further discussion with a self-congratulatory affirmation. Yes, indeed, the athlete is a performing artist!

Before we are accused of arrogance, let us spend a few moments investigating what we mean by our expression of affirmation. Let us ask if athletes view themselves as performing artists, or if sport theorists have any opinion on the subject. Let us also look closer at a form-sport (gymnastics), for the lessons it affords.

ATHLETE AS PERFORMING ARTIST

The late Steve Prefontaine, the gifted distance runner, claimed that he wanted people to appreciate his running as art. He is quoted as saying: "I'm an artist, a performer."

106

The discussion of sport being interpreted as an art-form is given more impetus by Paul Frayssinet (1968), who insists that the experience (as opposed to the observation) of sport is an art like music, poetry, or the dance. His definition of sport describes it as "an activity in the form of a contest requiring an intense muscular effort which demands great expenditure of energy [with] this contest [being] usually turned into a spectacle." Frayssinet refers to all phenomena as art which fall under the discipline of the fine arts, i.e., whose purpose lies in the creation or active achievement of beauty; thus he states from the outset his value orientation. In support of Frayssinet, the editors of *The Scientific View of Sport* (Organizing Committee for the Games of the XXth Olympiad, Munich, 1972) assert:

> This assumption only seems strange to those whose thinking is still under the influence of the mind-body dualism. Connoisseurs of sport, particularly the athletes themselves, are opposed to the reduction of sporting activity to the "physical"; sport is just as much a "cosa mentale" as painting, to quote the phrase with which Leonardo sought to liberate the latter from the stigma of "manual labour." (p. 39)

But Paul Weiss states that the athlete is not actively interested in creating beauty. Weiss contends that the struggle, the "agon" of contest, does not allow the athlete to be concerned with being artistic. On the more obvious plane, we can turn to gymnastics as one of the sports in which "aesthetic surpremacy" can often decide the outcome, and this is discussed more fully later in this chapter.

With the introduction of the concept of virtuosity—another word for skill—we come to a point indicating that the athlete can be regarded as an artist. The virtuoso musician is one who plays well the music as written but who adds his own flair, his own style to the delivery of the written score. The following quotation from the *New York Times,* January 21, 1925, describing the virtuoso playing of the violinist Fritz Kreisler clearly states the sense of solo virtuosity:

> . . . For I know of no virtuoso whose playing gives one to such a degree the feeling of being in close communication with a great and rare spirit. Paradoxically, the overwhelming power of his personality springs in part at least from the very selflessness of his attitude toward what he plays. Hearing him, you think: "Here is a man who thinks more of music than he does of playing the violin, and who thinks more of playing the violin than he does of himself." He stands behind the music rather than in front of it, and you are thus able to see that, unless it be very great music indeed, he is the greater of the two.

By implication, the virtuoso performing artist adds something extra to the art-work presented for his performance. Athletes are sometimes described as "virtuoso" by analogy.

But is sport "art" or "oeuvre"? A painting or a piece of sculpture can be referred to as "a work of art," and so can the dance sequence in a particular ballet. To come to an acceptance that a sport event can be regarded as a work of art, it is safer to approach the problem from the standpoint of accepting that a dance or similar choreographic sequence be so regarded. The moving characteristics of both the dance and sport provide the basis of commonality upon which to ground intuitive association. Yet, some caution should be counseled first.

Caution is presented by Paul Frayssinet, who suggests that some distinction be recognized between the English term "work of art" and the French term "oeuvre." The sense attributed to "oeuvre" is more appropriate to our discussion here, since it is broader in its scope than "work of art." It is better to think of "oeuvre" as a product of artistic activity: a dance sequence can be an oeuvre but we might not typically think of it as a work of art. Thus, the distinction is fine but it allows us to inquire into the nature of an athletic oeuvre.

Allowing that the ballet as oeuvre cannot be identified with the body of a particular dancer, it is safe to say that the athletic oeuvre cannot be so identified with the athlete. Perhaps the quickest way to comprehend this is to select any given athletic event (a mile race, a stolen base, a jump) and to recall your two or three favorite memories of it. From the viewpoint of the spectator (objective aesthetic), the athletes who performed on those occasions tend to blend into one "abstract" or generalized athlete in consideration of the *event* as a beautiful experience. Or, in unique instances, the *athlete* is described as being beautiful in the execution of the event. From the perspective of the participant (subjective aesthetic), successive experiences of personal successful performance—which may or may not be identified subjectively as "peak experiences"—tend to blend into an "abstract" or generalized occasion. Again, the unique circumstance can be singled out, but here there are other associative elements at work also.

To illustrate, let us consider the mile race. Focusing on world record runs since 1954, we can say that Bannister, Elliott, Ryun, Bayi, and Walker are all distinctive in their running styles. Students might freely argue which one has the most "beautiful," most artistic style. As individual athletes, they are beautiful to see in action, and this claim may be made based on different criteria (see Plate 6). Considered collectively, they bring to the mile a quality, perhaps a folkloric mystique, which adds something to the event whenever it is performed by any group of highly skilled athletes. By their action, the mile race becomes infused with dramatic potential. It is the *dramatic potential* which separates the mile race as oeuvre from the mile race as commonplace track event. Insofar as many paintings, sculptures, plays, musical compositions, poems, and the like cannot claim aesthetic distinction, so sport performances are equally restricted. From the subjective perspective, and taking batting as the example, the athlete knows that he does not always connect on the "sweet spot," but he remembers and recognizes afresh those occasions when he does. Hitting the ball just right has a personal dramatic impact, the experience of which is often claimed as "beautiful." The style of the miler, the way the batter hits the sweet spot, these are the criteria distinguishing our purpose or intention in calling the athlete an artist.

Returning to the exposition of Frayssinet on the athletic oeuvre, it is worth examining the bases upon which he rests aesthetic distinction for sport. In his dependency on Souriau, he accepts the duality of an oeuvre's being both illusory and real. The oeuvre presents a representation of reality and therefore serves the purpose of creating an illusion while, coincidentally, the oeuvre is a thing of substance in the real world. This duality focuses on the space-time separation sometimes referred to as a "purpose" of art. The illustrators of amphorae in Classical Greece, more than two thousand years ago, bring home to us today the lesson of the duality of art in the service of sport. More importantly, they tell us that sport was seen as an art, and that the athlete was regarded as an artist. Space and time, as contributors to the dimensions of the oeuvre, are distinguished by different manners of observation. They contribute to aesthetic observation as the replacement of normal perception. In relation to the oeuvre, time and space are seen differently from events of everyday life. Perception now becomes selectively "aesthetic." The "reality" is not attended to, but rather attention focuses on the "illusory" component.

Frayssinet (1968) identifies four levels of existence in his exposition of the oeuvre: the material, the sensitive, the ontic (ontological), and the transcendental. The *material* existence is the athlete, the person who has subjected his body (given) to the rigors of training (product). The athlete "masters" skill through repetition and refinement. The *sensitive* existence is the knowledge that the athlete has of his material existence as refined product. Frayssinet suggests that the spectator has the power of recognition of the sensitive existence of the athlete. He submits that the spectator employs vision as the vehicle of communication between himself and the athlete, and can tune into the "tactile-muscular" sensations of the athlete. The *ontic* existence describes the presence of sport as a cultural discipline of specific behaviors (changeable and adaptable with technology) which reflect a given time and space of reality for man and society. The *transcendental* existence is manifest in the unification of the material, the sensitive, and the ontic. There is no precise formulation for better understanding of the ontic, according to Frayssinet, and none is attempted here. The question of the ontic existence proposed by Frayssinet is discussed only sparingly in other sections of this book, for example, in the discussion on "subjective aesthetics" and "peak-experiences" in sport.

It is assumed that the artistic experiences of the athlete include that which we mean by subjective aesthetic and peak experience, and these questions are explored more fully on theoretical and empirical levels as appropriate. Here, in agreement with Weiss (1969), the athlete is *equated* with the artist, as with the thinker and the man of religion. What separates the athlete from being an artist, according to Weiss, is that the athlete shows ideal form with his body whereas the artist uses other extraneous equipment—and here we must disagree with Weiss. Following Weiss's logic, a dancer (who uses his body alone) is separated from the artist. Further, a batter or javelin thrower reserves the right to consider his bat or javelin as the instrument of his art. The point that we can agree with, if this is what Weiss implies, is that the athlete represents that which can be outstanding in the nature of man, the call to excellence and the demonstration of excellence through the body. Lastly, there is no reason why the athlete, like the dancer, should not regard the body as his instrument, even though this duality might be heinous to present-day philosophers. Norman Mailer refers to the boxer as "a *body* artist," but this is not to say that boxers regard their bodies as the instruments of their art. In an article for *Life,* March 10, 1971, Mailer wrote:

> The notion of prizefighters as hard-working craftsmen is most likely to be true in the light and middle divisions [where] they know their limitations [and] are likely to strive for excellence in their category. The average fighter is a buried artist, which is to say a *body* artist with an extreme amount of violence in him. Obviously the better and more successful they get, the more they have been able to transmute violence into craft, discipline, even body art. (p. 19)

The athlete most commonly seen in the role of artist is the one who earns his living by his performance, traditionally referred to as the "professional" or league athlete. He is there to sell his art, no differently from an architect, a musician, or any other artist earning a living by his performance. Kupfer (1975) makes the statement: "A man who has no motive other than to play the game well and enjoy himself in such play would sooner lose a well-played game than win, when playing poorly, through luck or the utter weakness of his opponent. [while] the latter eventualities would not phase the 'professional' since his concern *is* with matters extrinsic to the game itself." He acknowledges the weakness of his argument by making the following footnote:

> The case of the professional athlete includes the following objection: One can play ungracefully and score, or gracefully and score, or gracefully

and fail to score. My response is simply that as a function of human anatomy the very *best* plays and players (those who score most and in the most crucial situation) are graceful. Economy and efficiency in effort is always an asset to one's play. To be sure there have been fine athletes who lacked in grace of form but their achievements were not made *because* of awkwardness. (p. 90)

It is regrettable that Kupfer allowed himself to drop into the trap of assumed agreement on terms, but as discussed elsewhere, "grace" is that kind of word which lures the unwary.

Athletic Creativity

Establishing that the athlete can either (1) be equated with the artist or (2) legitimately be a so-called "artist," thereby making athlete and artist synonymous terms (like dancer and artist or painter and artist), demands an analysis of components common to both. Creativity is one such component. From the realm of skiing, an example of creativity can be drawn in which Jean-Claude Killy invented the vaulting start driving the body up and out from the starting gate, a trick which gains perhaps two-hundredths of a second before the ankle trips the little arm which starts the clock.

One of the methods for analyzing creativity in this regard is to take conditions characterized by time and space and, applying them to the sport domain, ask how creative the athlete is. Time and space are recognized as somewhat "false" essentials when we discuss sport in operational terms, but the fact that sport allows for "time-outs," and that the dimensions of any given sport arena are space-bound (court, field, ring, track, fairway, mountain, course, circuit), tells us that the constraints on *reality* impose demands for creative solutions. We see athletes doing this every time they perform; we do this ourselves every time we set ourselves the conditions of sport. In other words, every time we induce ourselves with the physical, psychological, and sociological conditions of stress (which is an alternative operational way of defining sport), we set ourselves problems to solve. This holds true of any enterprise upon which we embark.

The confining nature of the field, court, and ring set by prescribed boundaries of play defines limits for the athlete as precise as the stage is for the dramatic actor. In fact, in team sports the athlete must function within more restricted yet looser boundaries. The difference between athlete and actor is the demand placed on him to exhibit strength, speed, and the broader physical components of man's potential. The broader boundaries of the stadium, plus the rules of the game (regulations of technical performance plus social-moral contingencies), specify and delimit the athlete much as the painter is delimited in his specific use of a surface (canvas, board, wall) and colors (paints, tempera, collage materials). The confining nature of sport and the way in which the athlete can be expressive and creative like an artist are commented upon by Kupfer (1975):

> Within the confines imposed by the rules, which define the play of the game, and the spatio-temporal boundaries, often precise and geometrically exact, the resolution of these tensions requires invention in the exercise of the athlete's talents. Sport instantiates man's capacity to improvise in the midst of structured stress. (p. 89)

The discussion of whether the athlete or actor is the "freer" in the expression of his art is an open question.

To call a certain athlete an "artist" is often to refer to the craft or skill of his game, to the perfect functional efficiency of the strategy and movements, and to aesthetic moments in the performance (Reid, 1974). Reid asserts that the production of beauty in movement need not be art (thus separating art and aesthetic intent), and that strategy should not be confused with art. Similarly, skill is not necessarily art, but all art requires skill. Hence, he infers that the football player is not an artist in the same sense that a cellist or dancer is an artist. It is clear that this level of discussion is rooted in a temporal cultural dialectic which ignores the possibility that the Classical Greeks regarded athletes as artists or that at some future time athletes could be classified again as artists. The contention held by Reid that the purpose of games is "winning" is further evidence of his narrow perspective. His assertion that games cannot be art rests on the premises of value currently held for games; the student has the right to challenge such premises. However, Reid does concede:

> There are some sports—diving, aquabatics, skating, some gymnastics—in which some performances seem to have at any rate a *prima facie* claim to be called artistic. Putting it in a slightly less radical way perhaps, they are complex, or compound, activities, part sport with a defined achievement-aim, part art, with an embodied-expressive aim which allows, or requires, some individually devised free creativeness. (p. 18)

And what of the creative strategist of a game? Some team captains are noted for their creative potential, for their ability to quickly sum up the ability of the opposition and to establish counter-strategies for success. Can we not say that such a leader has artistic quality, that he demonstrates aesthetic refinement in the way he sets up situations of play? In fairness to Reid, it must be allowed that he considers this question from the standpoint of the individual athlete, not team captain. He points out that although the athlete must work within the rules "he is freed to give his movement an expressive form which is his own creation, and which *embodies aesthetic meaning*" (italics added). The major point that Reid makes is that the individual athletes like gymnasts, skaters, and divers are freer to be artists than team-sport athletes. Students of the aesthetics of sport may agree or disagree, but they should be cognizant of conflicting viewpoints.

Self-expressive Athlete

In *The Game,* Jack London wrote:

> He lacked speech-expression. He expressed himself with his hands, at his work, and with his body and the play of his muscles in the squared ring; but to tell with his own lips the charm of the squared ring was beyond him. Yet he assayed, and haltingly at first, to express what he felt and never analyzed when playing the Game at the supreme summit of existence. (p. 38)

Tom Sullivan, running-back for the Philadelphia *Eagles,* is a painter. He is quoted as saying: "Running with the ball, you can express yourself in motion; the gestures, the moves are creative and spontaneous; it's poetic [and satisfies] a need for self-expression" (see Plate 25).

Jack Scott, author of *The Athletic Revolution,* has been called an iconoclast, a revolutionary, and an innovator among many other flattering and unflattering names. One of the first publications that brought prominence to his name was a limited edition book called *Athletics for Athletes.* In that book, Scott attempted to bring a perspective of self-expressive sport to the attention of athletes. His best statement is one of hope:

> The athlete would be viewed as an artist and he would be taught how to express himself through the use of the body. . . . For some this self-expression would come from primarily esthetic activities such as dance and gymnastics, while for others it might come from long-distance running, weight-lifting, or some other physically exhausting activity. . . . Athletes would be more concerned with expressing themselves as well as possible rather than with proving themselves superior to their opponents. (pp. 90–92)

Such thinking is the forerunner of such ideas as doing away with the flag ceremonies, the national anthems, and the opening day parades of the modern Olympics. The day will surely come when the last record to be broken will stand like all the others, and it may be that future generations will entertain themselves in attempting to "equal" them. Sooner than later records will cease to be personal things, and will be shared by all those who perform to its absolute standard. Ernst Jokl has documented from time to time in his writings the asymptotic effect being created by the constant efforts of man to express his superlative abilities.

The humanist artist, claims Hussey (1929), "can raise both the practice of and enthusiasm for athletics on to the aesthetic plane." How true this might be is debatable. Most of the breakthroughs in athletic skill and ability have come from athletes who exhibited creative qualities. Take, for example, the two great technical advances that have improved shot-putting over the last fifteen years. Both Parry O'Brien and Brian Oldfield have shown a creative approach to this effort. Along one line of argument, both might be referred to as artists, even humanist artists, but not in the sense of creating a piece of sculpture or a painting.

Both the builder of shells for crewing and the boat designer of *Intrepid,* defender of the Americas Cup, might be considered artists. In the film *Rowing,* S. Pocock, who builds boats for eights, says: "The whole idea is to make a very delicate thing go fast." The pure artist will chide the form and function philosophy which underpins these examples, but he will find it hard to disparage the aesthetic qualities built into a fine yacht or crew shell. There is no doubt that these designers have been athletes in their own right and that they know the peculiarities of demand placed on a well-designed boat by champion yachtsmen and oarsmen. The application of their athletic knowledge to the design of better craft places them in a category of athlete turned artist. It is the considered opinion of S. Pocock that it is "a great art, rowing, searching for perfection; when you reach perfection, you are approaching the divine which is the you of you, the soul."

If a yacht or a shell can be regarded as a work of art, so too can a baseball bat, a golf club, a javelin, a tennis racquet, and so on. The superior athlete uses superior equipment, and the closer a player gets to excellence of performance, the more likely he is to treat his equipment as a work of art. In principle, this applies equally to the way in which a gymnast will view a high-bar or the rings, to the hurdler viewing the hurdles, and to the pilot of a soaring glider. The oarsman talks about "understanding the water" through having a "relationship with your boat." The rhythm of a crew rowing together creates what the oarsmen call "swing." The "sense of swing" is achieved when the oarsman feels two things: (1) he has the impression that the shell is being lifted out of the water on each stroke by the combined power of the crew (as if the shell were to "hydroplane"), and (2) he feels as though he is doing it all alone, as though the power effecting the lift is the work of his own oar, thus giving him an illusion of supreme power and speed which he finds exhilarating. These experiences and similar ones are the motivating feelings which drive men and women on to seek new limits of physical capacities, sometimes found in the form of records.

What happens when records are no longer perceived in their present-day value? What difference do flags make to the brotherhood of athletes? The rhetorical nature of these and similar questions is already evident. The question of records is neither rhetorical nor consequential in the discussion of gymnastics, one of the pursuits to excellence in self-expression known as "form-sport."

FORM-SPORT: GYMNASTICS

One of the conclusions deriving from the interpretation of sport as beauty is that sport more proximally assimilates the beauty of nature than the beauty of art. Testing this conclusion, we should examine those sports which bring artifice into their construction. Notably, diving and gymnastics are sports that impose demands for action in accordance with prescribed constraints. Dives and gymnastic moves have names and qualifications (A through C difficulty, for example) and those who participate must perform to standard conditions. The only freedom for the athlete is selecting and piecing together his moves (which he will do to maximize scoring potential based on the prescribed component parts), beyond which he searches for presentation—the "aesthetic" component (the artifice). Hence, the diver or the gymnast imposes on nature certain open-ended demands fabricated by man. Typically, the gravitational effect of nature on a falling man is interrupted by the diver who defies this phenomenon by spinning, twisting, or tumbling with deliberate, calculated movements.

Brown and Cassidy's (1963) deduction to the same conclusion stems from a closer look at gymnastics. Brown and Cassidy use the term "expressive form," taken from Susan Langer, to describe aspects of movement in the service of the creation of sensory illusion—"as the dance is described." For Brown and Cassidy, "designed" or "structured" movement, even of "a beautiful gymnast performing," is not expressive form and is perceived as being *part* of the movement with an "actual named physical self in space." Thus, they support the contention that the artistic product of the gymnast is one of art, not one of nature (see Plate 20).

One of the exercises recommended to us for the substantiation of qualifying sport as beautiful is to take a sport that claims aesthetic content as a part of its execution. Gymnastics satisfies this requirement, and there is a 200-year legacy upon which we can rest our confidence. Per Henrik Ling, 1776–1839, known as "the father of modern gymnastics," originally classified gymnastics into four groups: educational, military, medical, and aesthetic. According to Ling, the objective of aesthetic gymnastics was to express thoughts and feelings through physical movements which also should be attractive for others to observe. In this respect, Ling (who was also a poet of national renown) was putting into physical movement expression much of his sympathy with what Baumgarten and the German poet-philosophers were exploring in the spoken and written forms of aesthetic expression. More than that, Ling wanted his notion of "aesthetic gymnastics" to pervade all forms of gymnastic activity, and for that reason he could set no fixed demarcations on its performance. In this, he was faced with precisely the same problem that still exists today. In his strength of purpose, Ling made it clear that to ignore aesthetics would mean the end of gymnastics itself.

The implicit interpretation that gymnastics has aesthetic content is subscribed to not only by gymnasts and enthusiasts of the sport, but also officially and internationally. Millman (1969) has attempted to provide some understanding of the nature of aesthetics in gymnastics. However, the criteria of aesthetic excellence have either eluded experts in gymnastics, or else the attempts of those experts to apply aesthetic criteria to gymnastics have proven barren on account of a fundamental lack of comprehension of what constitutes aesthetic performance in human movement. Upon closer inspection, many aesthetic criteria traditionally associated with understanding the arts (plastic and performing) are extremely useful in understanding aesthetic excellence in skilled human movement, yet there also appear to be other dimensions which may be unique in their contribution to an interpretation of "aesthetic" in sports action. Focusing on gymnastics at this point, and attempting to isolate relevant aesthetic criteria, should help to establish differentiations of an aesthetic nature between the performing arts (ballet) and sport (gymnastics).

Since the term "aesthetics" originally meant anything that had to do with perception by the senses, this would include by inference the contemporary concept of "kinesthetics," a term which describes personal interpretations of proprioceptive stimuli, as well as visual or emotional responses to stimuli from the other sense modalities such as sight, hearing, taste, smell, and touch. Current uses of "aesthetics" as it applies to gymnastics have avoided drawing the distinction between the proprioceptive experiences and the emotional experience. From the time of the Greeks, the aesthetic quality of physical movement has been described by terms such as "joy," "beautiful," "grace," "harmony," "elegant," and "natural."

Only recently has the necessity for clearer comprehension of such terms with respect to physical movement been given serious attention. More importantly, only during the last twenty years have the aesthetic components or "elements of artistic creativeness" of human movement been considered for study, and only during the last ten years have educators begun to emphasize beauty and enrich students and scholars in the awareness of it.

Initial study of the aesthetic content of gymnastics demands that three assumptions be made. First, man gains physical and psychological enjoyment from rhythm and movement. Second, such enjoyment becomes more acute as the rhythm and movement become more refined; that is, *if* the individual is sensitive to the refinements and is aware of the abilities required for such expression, then the type of finesse considered here probably finds its highest expression in dance, particularly ballet. Third, one *cannot* agree with the view often expressed that since the ideas of what constitutes beauty vary from one individual to another, it is futile to attempt an objective assessment of something which appeals to us subjectively. On the contrary, experts in the arts and those who appreciate artistic endeavors can and do agree on the aesthetic value of various works of art, be they painting, sculpture, music, poetry, or prose. There are essential recognizable qualities of production which are readily identifiable depending on the particular field of aesthetic endeavor. This represents a total experiential sensation to the realm of artistic interest which reflects itself psychologically in the perceptual style of the individual.

One of these "qualities of production" which rests purely on aesthetic interpretation (and therefore is a nondefinitive term) is *amplitude*. It is suggested by Dowsing (1975) that the concept "amplitude" has real meaning and validity of purpose in describing gymnastic performance. The given definition for amplitude is "performing any element to its fullest and best." Asking others what it means will bring responses like "stretch," "reach," "extension," "tightness," and "height," all of which add some sense to the concept, but none of which aid in refining the definition.

To illustrate, amplitude in the free hand balance is shown when the gymnast holds a straight rather than an arched pose. Thus, the effect of overbalancing (archedness) is reduced and replaced by a more purely balanced pose. Balance, as opposed to overbalance, lends amplitude. Further, stretch without strain (or overstraining), tonic tension (extension with tone) without the appearance of tension, adds to the definition of amplitude. Strength and flexibility are the means by which tension and stretch are modified for amplitude. Amplitude in gymnastics comes only after the basic skills (backbends, splits, rolls, walkovers, and aerials) have been perfected. Thus, amplitude can be defined as the essential aesthetic quality that the gymnast searches for in the fullest realization of his sport.

GYMNASTIC PERFORMANCE AND AESTHETIC MOVEMENT

With the introduction of the concept of "amplitude," the fine bridge between gymnastic performance and aesthetic movement is suggested. Performance has been a feature of gymnastics since the inception of the activity originating with Guths Muths and Ling. Throughout the ages, gymnastic performance has meant different things to different groups, and the classic four-part categorization that Per Henrik Ling formulated essentially highlights this. Further, what Per Henrik Ling recommended as "aesthetic" gymnastics, or more precisely aesthetic movement in gymnastic performance, was probably very different from what later generations would term aesthetic or beautiful. Ling did not mention the "beauty" of gymnastics when he spoke of aesthetic performance, but he did stress the power of "nicely executed" movements to evoke emotional response in both the performer and the spectator. As interpreted today, the aesthetic function of Ling's gymnastics probably was closer to dance or what has become known as "educational gymnastics" or "movement education." We can only speculate.

Since the 1820's gymnastics has been evolving from the acrobatic to the artistic—from harsh, dull, limited, and virtually static movements, where brute strength, mechanical precision, and sterility of action were the hallmark of performance, to provocative, personal, free-flowing movements in which the illusion of ease and flight are valued. In the vernacular of the performer, the gymnasts have developed "style." Within the last twenty years this style of execution has brought to life gymnastic performance as artistic. Kunzle (1956) suggested that the elusive quality of beauty in gymnastics can be accounted for by the acquisition of style. For Kunzle, "style" is synonymous with "line or effect, and rhythm of execution," and with "form," "aesthetic," "class," or "a quality of difference." The philosophic interpretation of the relationship is presented by Slusher (1967):

> The gymnastic routine might be "style." The kip, turntable, giant swing, thief vault, etc., all have their "rightness" in the heavens of the ideal. Yet each man must give "style" to the movements. To a degree, it brings both unique "self" and awareness of "other" to realization. To look at the movement objectively is to divorce the performance from the man. This type of dualism leads to isolation of man from his self. What is needed is relationship between man and his movements. The gymnast and the movement meet each other. (p. 70)

On the more pragmatic level, the "dualism" that Slusher fears becomes a question of separating the aesthetic effect from the mechanical principle. Efficiency of movement in the language of mechanics raises some questions which seriously test value opinions of what is and what is not more beautiful in gymnastic performance. The very real problem, from the perspective of a nationally ranked coach of gymnastics, is presented by Lascari (1973):

> Certain principles have, however, been generally accepted which can form the rationale for one's gymnastics preferences. An accepted principle of artistic gymnastics is that a gymnast must make a movement "look" effortless. Whether or not the performance actually is effortless is not the pertinent factor. A reasonable corollary to this principle is that if one looks as though his movement is effortless he will be mechanically

efficient *relative to the task involved;* i.e., a double back somersault in floor exercise may look effortless compared to what one might expect, even though most observers would agree that more effort was visible compared to a single back somersault. The reciprocal is that if one performs in a mechanically efficient manner he will concomitantly look beautiful. This may be the rationale why a top echelon track and field performer looks beautiful even though there is seldom a conscious effort to look beautiful. (p. 1)

The principle cited breaks down for the example of the back somersault because of differences of opinion separating height as aesthetic from layout as aesthetic. The height obtained is dependent on the tuck of the body, yet the general opinion is that the "line" of the body is lost in the tuck, thereby forfeiting aesthetic effect. The elements of controversy thus become endemic, the problem as much for the judge as for the coach.

INTERNATIONAL FEDERATION GUIDELINES

According to the International Gymnastics Federation, the aesthetic content of gymnastics can be explored through three major and three collateral elements of an artistic gymnastic performance, each of which plays a vital role in this form of expression. The major elements are (1) *difficulty* or the natural value of the exercise, (2) *composition,* the structure or formation of the exercise, and (3) *execution,* the correct form and technical performance. The collateral aspects are (1) *risk,* danger, or hazard—the possibility of loss of points in case of failure, (2) *originality*—new movements, new exercise parts or combination of parts that go beyond the areas of what is traditional classic, customary, or outdated, and (3) *virtuosity*—blending elegance of execution, richness, freedom of movement, amplitude, and flight. Where "difficulty" is seen as the natural value of the exercise in the F.I.G. guidelines, Lawther (1951) suggests that there is in reality an underlying "unnaturalness," a quality which is veiled by the *training* of the gymnast:

> The training for concealing a slight error in a gymnastic routine . . . is to have the unintentional variation flow into an appropriate continuity as if it were all part of the total plan. The gymnast merely draws on his repertoire for a variation that permits continuity and *seeming* unity to conceal the slight lapse in perfection. Never does he permit himself to reveal by his face or tensed musculatore "forced" movements or signs of difficulty. (p. 292)

Difficulty

Difficulty, according to the International Gymnastics Federation, is worth 3.4 points out of a possible 10.0 points. Thus, in judging the artistic content of a gymnastics exercise, one-third of the criterion of "good art" must be based upon the relative technical skill of the artist. Charteris (1969) makes the point that

> Difficulty has been correctly rated 3.4 out of 10 by the F.I.G. and it is *this* that gives our sport the respectability it deserves as a link between sport and art. Difficulty rightly is, and must always remain, quite subservient to the aggregate of good form and combination. Only by this means will gymnastics retain the respect of persons well versed in the appreciation of poetry of motion. (p. 214)

The separation of difficulty from the aesthetic which Charteris implies detracts from the element of risk which is identified as an intrinsic component. Charteris receives general support throughout the gymnastic world, although Kunzle (1956) states that the beauty of gymnastics "depends *not* on difficulty, but on line or effect and rhythm of execution." Further, the F.I.G. cautions against the indiscriminate use of difficulty, so that "the difficulty of an exercise must never be escalated at the expense of correct form or technically correct execution. The exercise must be adapted to the ability of the gymnast . . ." (Gander, 1968).

Flawless aesthetic execution of a skill of *major* difficulty should provoke a greater measure of intensity of the aesthetic experience (visually and experientially). In support of this interpretation, Kunzle (1956) elaborates:

> Every alteration in the body's position must be prepared for by the preceding one, and prepare in turn the following one. This principle obviates any clumsiness or lack of grace. (p. 8)

Kunzle goes further by drawing a parallel between the skillful gymnast and the painter or composer, each of whom, without the essential abilities in the use of their eyes or ears would fail in their search for the aesthetic as much as would the gymnast lacking the perception of his own physical qualities. Much the same can be said of the performing musician, with whom a closer analogy to the gymnast can be made. Yet, difficulty *is* a major factor to be considered in defining the aesthetic content of gymnastics. It is also apparent that the greater the performer's repertoire of difficult and complex parts, the greater is his creative potential.

Composition

Composition may be considered in terms of two conceptual parts. First are the requirements for the *contents* of an exercise. F.I.G. states that "the parts of an exercise must be connected in an elegant and fluent manner without superfluous movements or intermediate swings" (Gander, 1968).

In the discussion of the potential for aesthetic content in particular gymnastic routines, it appears that Charteris and Kunzle hold differing views. Charteris (1969) specifies "free standing: more than any other event the gymnast has the opportunity to display his sense of the artistic flow of movement." Kunzle (1956) says, "the pommel horse is the hardest piece of apparatus to master thoroughly, yet despite this, or because of it, the exercises are of the most beautiful (see Plate 20b). One cannot join this controversy at its current level of discussion, since it is believed that beauty is an absolute and cannot be qualified on a value continuum dependent on event content.

More relevant to artistic expression, composition might be thought of in terms of a second component, *complexity*. Berlyne, Ogilvie, and Parham (1968) empirically tested the aesthetic in terms of complexity, interesting-ness, and pleasingness. Interestingness and pleasingness (the aesthetic) were determined in large part by the level of complexity of the stimulus. These studies, and others conducted by Rump (1968), indicate that there is an optimal level of complexity for experience of aesthetics beyond which the stimulus becomes merely confusing.

The complexity studies take on more importance when viewed in the light of Wober's (1968) theoretical analysis introducing the notion of "aesthetic unit." The "aesthetic unit" is considered to be a nonreducible bit of information in the computational sense which, when perceived in se-quence or series, forms an impression which is dependent uniquely on the criteria of "difference" or "belonging." In the long run, the rules determin-ing the phrases of aesthetic units depend on the extent to which cognitive skills have been developed by an individual in particular sense modalities. This may be illustrated in the case of a gymnastics routine in which the performer combines highly integrated and difficult combinations in such a manner to produce an overall gross or ugly performance even though each individual part may in itself be artistically interesting and pleasing. Geb-lewitz (1965) comes closest to the broad interpretation of beauty in all events when, speaking of the superiority of Japanese gymnasts, he com-ments on their rhythm, tempo, and elasticity—all elements of aesthetic production. He says, "Each of their exercises showed, besides an amazing complexity and versatility of technique, a wonderful artistic integrity of performance, the thing we call *imagery* in art." (p. 23)

The role composition plays in the aesthetic of gymnastics is at once a limiting factor, setting the bounds in which the performer as artist may express himself, and at the same time a component for establishing com-plexity as an artistic quality of performance. The creative gymnast who modifies the usual or expected into the novel or unexpected approaches his performance with the psychological set of an artist.

The significance of unique perceptual-cognitive styles relative to specific art-forms is given further elaboration in the sport context by Lowe (1971), who states that "an individual socialized in sport may acquire in the development of his perceptual cognitions a recognition of sport as an art form." By extension, the perceptual mode of proprioception, an important facet of the aesthetic experience of cultures in which dance is a major means of expression, suggests itself for further empirical inquiry. A clue is provided by Wober (1968), who comments on the time-awareness involved in the perception of rhythm. He says, "in other senses, time can be, but is not necessarily being perceived. But for rhythm, which importantly involved proprioception, tune is an essential prerequisite." (p. 237)

Closely akin to the idea of time-awareness is the concept of "tuning." While it is believed that tuning is important in the realization of efficient movement and combinations of movement, as a concept it speaks only to efficiency which can in turn only be regarded as the ultimate stage in performance *prior* to the injection of the aesthetic quality. Lascari (1973) contends that if a gymnastic movement is mechanically efficient then "it also possesses beauty." The controversy that this provokes is not taken up here.

Execution

This is the third component, and the single most important criterion for the official evaluation of an exercise. Section D of the *Code of Points* (Gander, 1968) under "execution" states that deductions of points should be made for "poor form" and "incorrect technical execution." Poor form and incorrect technical execution can be, conceptually, two distinctly separate or highly similar criteria of movement, depending on the definitions attached to them. The fact that form can mean a relationship of component parts or structural appearance (objectively validated), as well as an artificial contrivance for the creation of a particular impression (subjectively validated), indicates the ambiguity which can foul definitive interpretation in an evaluative context. "Technical execution" interpreted only as mechanical precision makes a robot out of a gymnast; interpreted as a reproducible pattern it is the key to artistic gymnastics. The former destroys the potential of the aesthetic, whereas the latter enhances that potential.

The essence of "style" in artistic gymnastics adds to execution another dimension, that is, the unreal, the deceptive, or the illusory. Illusion as a dimension of the aesthetic can be traced to Platonic thought. To create the illusion of linearity in architecture, the Greeks tapered the columns and supporting pillars as a standard aesthetic feature of their temples. Robinson (1948) tells us:

It is probably impossible for any but the trained eye of the architect to appreciate such a temple as the Parthenon to the full. To such lengths of subtlety has the design been carried that almost every line, which is apparently straight, has in reality a scarcely perceptible upward convex curve, thus avoiding the appearance of sagging. Some of these modulations can be detected only by the touch, not seen by the eye. No people, a modern architect has said, ever built like this; and it is in the last degree unlikely that any will build so again. (p. 185)

In like manner, Gothic arches and flying buttresses add a dimension of illusory ease in their support of the visual and real weight of European cathedrals. The painter or sculptor can create the illusion of noise, movement, excitement, confusion, etc. So, too, the stylist gymnastics performance, beyond correct technique, provides the illusion of difficult movements executed without effort, yet with excitement. Balance is said to correlate with the tension and, in balance, tensions appear to be minimized. Thus control creates an illusion of ease both for the performer (proprioceptively) and for the observer (visually). Further, while it is recognized that tensions are established throughout a gymnastic exercise, the appearance of such tensions must be eliminated. The "grace of execution" that Kunzle (1956) speaks of is an illusion, the absence of perceived tension. In execution, the proper control of tensions, as the forces acting upon balance adjust, can be described in terms connoting "harmony" (Gander, 1968). When such control creates an illusion of ease, the perceptual presence of tensions is eradicated. In this respect, the apparent *ease* of performance of a gymnastic routine provides an illusion of a difficult movement executed without effort.

GYMNAST AS ARTIST

In gymnastics the subtleties of the presentation distinguish the virtuoso, the performer who exhibits an unusual talent for artistic execution, from the technically sound performer. By extracting himself from his physical self, the gymnast must, as artist, refine the tools of his trade—his physical structure—to the creative process of an artistic end-product, the art-work. In this respect the total experience of the routine should be sublimated by the performer for the aesthetic content to emerge and be recognized. The fleeting nature of his art-work makes it nonetheless valuable as an aesthetic experience for the perceiver, as Picasso may make a drawing in the sand only to have the tide wash it away.

Any artistic endeavor is a personal expression of one's own aesthetic nature. Yet within limited bounds, one can describe qualities in gymnastics that, when applied with skill and sensitivity, produce the masterpiece of human movement. Gander (1968) alluded to this in his remarks on the evaluaton of virtuosity in the finals of a gymnastic competition:

> When the gymnast succeeds in blending elegance of execution, richness, freedom of movement, amplitude in flight, the mastering of difficulty and risk in an impressionable dynamic, he creates a presentation which radiates an inner experience and harmony which characterizes the virtuoso. (p. 163)

Risk, Virtuosity, and Originality

Considering risk, virtuosity, and originality as the artistic subtleties of perfection in an elite gymnastic exercise, some discussion centers on their interpretation. If risk is seen as contributing to the aesthetic, and if risk is seen as synonymous with difficulty (or at least as a closely related concept), then there is an addition to the confusion in terminology. The F.I.G. offers freedom of interpretation which mitigates heavily in favor of the creatively artistic gymnast, and this must be the seat of much controversy when competition is close. The quality of control does not appear to have reference in either the philosophical or psychological literature pertaining to aesthetics. Much the same applies to risk, and where virtuosity may be synonymous with "flair" and suggest a dilettantish taste for skill (control), at least "originality" has connotations of creativity which in turn bespeaks the production of the aesthetic. This does not mean that control has no relevance to the interpretation of aesthetics, since closer inspection of aesthetic demands for perfection in gymnastics may well provide a few points of departure from inquiry into an ancient phenomenological problem (Feibleman, 1949; Langfeld, 1920; Mead, 1952).

JUDGING AESTHETIC GYMNASTIC PERFORMANCE

Allowing that "artistic" and "aesthetic" have synonymous meaning when applied to gymnastics, a closer inspection of the demands placed on a judge of gymnastics can be made. The gymnastics judge is advised and guided by the F.I.G., which adjures him to look for "general beauty," "elegance," "rhythm and precision," "harmony," and "perfect artistic execution." It is clear that, besides begging the question of what is aesthetic, this advice omits much that the judge should be aware of and, at the same time, presumes that the judge is an aesthetically sensitized individual in this particular category of appreciation, and that he differs very little in quality from the other judges (Child, 1964). This presumption is not so categorical, of course, but the point is made to emphasize the difficulty faced by the judge of top-class or international competition. Are all judges the culturally enriched beings that Geblewitz (1965) and Nasmark (1963) would have them be? Or are there other facets to the judgment of aesthetic gymnastics which the judge can call upon?

With respect to the former question, the interpretation of "cultured" in this context applies to a wider comprehension and appreciation of the arts, and it is recognized that to make such a universal demand for judges of gymnastics would be too presumptuous to defend, either on logical or sociological grounds. However, in consideration of cross-cultural differences where judges of international competitions come from different parts of the world, there is some evidence that there is a degree of universality of good taste in aesthetic judgments (Child, 1964).

Concerning the second question regarding other facets of judgment, and focusing on the qualities a gymnastics judge does have for evaluating the artistic content of a movement, several factors suggest themselves. There can be a basic assumption that the judge has been a performer of some note in his younger years. Hence, he is familiar with the elements of bodily control, is perceptive of the demonstration of skill from an empathetic standpoint, and recognizes qualities of difficulty and risk. These attributes, while being fundamental to the judgment of ability, also provide a foundation for the refined perceptions demanded for the recognition of the aesthetic attributes of human movement.

The routine of gymnastic movements is set and is therefore identical for all. The distinguishing features, then, which must separate the aesthetic from the nonaesthetic performer depend on the gymnast's creative use of the variables remaining to him (e.g., timing or pacing). This applies both to the ongoing execution of one particular skill, and to the transitional integration of two or more skills. Thus, it is not sufficient to speak merely of harmony, since harmony means different things for a unit of movement and for a collection of units of movement. The obvious demands for a "time-style of information articulation" (Wober, 1968) are apparent for both performer and judge, and the phrasing of units of movement (equivalent to Wober's "aesthetic units"), recognized as belonging to (or different from) the preceding and succeeding units, decides the aesthetic. To some extent this is what Kunzle (1956) has said:

> The good gymnast must be graceful in movement, that is to say, have a sense of rhythm allied to control; he must have feeling for the plastic, decorative effect of a posture and for beauty of combination.

When the "aesthetic actuality" of the gymnast's movements are no longer outside of the judge, when he becomes one entity with the gymnast, the aesthetic has been created. And in the purest sense, the judge perceives a movement as aesthetic at that same moment at which the gymnast experiences his aesthetic, his own recognition and inner appreciation of the success of his performance. The judge should exult in the performance to the point where the emotional content supersedes the purely technical.

Indeed, an emotional response to aesthetically executed gymnastic performance should be an experience akin to inspiration, due to its being a recognition and acceptance of the unexpected. Under these circumstances, the judge experiences the feeling that his attention in the psychological sense is reduced to zero, even though the act of judging implies paying particular attention. Thus, attention to the beautiful becomes spontaneous, relating to elation and a feeling of oneness with the performer.

s u m m a r y

Whether the claim of Prefontaine or the aspirations of Olympic gymnasts satisfy the conditions for what we understand by performing artist remains for the student of sport to judge. The presentation here has been analytical and only tentatively theoretical.

Consciousness of performance (as aesthetic) is incidental in the one case (Weiss, 1969), and intentional in the other (Kunzle, 1956; Charteris, 1969; Lascari, 1973). The athletic "oeuvre" is both repeatable and unique, difference of style often being the sole separating factor. Dramatic potential heightens the likelihood of aesthetic performance in all sports; this potential in turn sets distinguishing characteristics attributable to the athlete as a performing artist. Supreme or superlative performances by athletes reflect athletic creativity, no less inspired than that of dancers, painters, or sculptors working within the constraints of their art-forms. Athletic creativity can fairly be judged aesthetic creativity, particularly when the self-expressive athlete sets standards of human action and movement outside the physical realm of a majority of the population. Indeed, this is the major objective in competitive gymnastics, where the separating criteria are those sublimating technique and skill in the aesthetic domain.

The performing artist in dance and the theatre represents facets both of beauty as nature and beauty as art. This same fact holds true for the athlete. We can separate the art of Prefontaine from the art of the Olympic gymnast comfortably into statements representing each form. The beauty of Prefontaine is the beauty that Weiss states is nonintentional, and therefore is of nature; the beauty of the gymnast is created by intention, and therefore is of art. This deduction solves the riddle that Maheu posed Jokl, who could not understand Maheu's statement that "sport creates beauty" and, yet, contradictorily, that sport could not be art, for art and sport face in different directions.

questions for discussion

1. What is the difference between "a work of art" and "an oeuvre"? Why is it pertinent to comprehend the subtleties of difference in respect to sport?
2. Discuss the "folkloric mystique" surrounding a particular sports event, and state why that sports event earned a place in the folklore of a society.
3. What are the "four levels of existence," and how can they be accounted for in behavioristic terms for the analysis of the aesthetics of sport?
4. Make the case for categorizing a tennis racquet, a baseball bat, a javelin, and a racing shell as works of art.
5. Why should the beauty of gymnastics be classified the beauty of art rather than the beauty of nature?
6. What are the difficulties faced by the judge of gymnastics in respect to qualifying aesthetic performance?

NOTES TO THE PLATES

The selection of the Plates to illustrate this book is prompted by several considerations. In each case, an illustration should serve at least two purposes, and this is evident from the notes relative to each Plate. The Plates show most forms of art—painting, sculpture, pottery (ceramics), mosaic, drawing (pencil, chalk or ink), lithography, as well as the art of photography—and in all cases sport is the subject. The sports photography contains evidence of thematic points made throughout the text. Every effort has been made to cross-reference the Plates with the text, and vice-versa. In some instances, Plates are cross-referenced with each other to emphasize a given point.

Many sports are not represented and some sports might appear over-represented. For example there are no pictures of soccer (the world's most popular game) or handball (one of the fastest growing games), among other noteworthy sports not represented. But, those sports shown are comprehensive, and more importantly, they get across the major ideas presented in the text.

PLATE 1   (Leonardo da Vinci drawings of Man)

The natural beauty of the human form is illustrated in these two pencil drawings (1a and 1b) executed by Leonardo da Vinci. The model for the drawing may or may not have been an athlete, but it is evident that he has a classical mesomorphic build. Note the fine use of the pencil line, the quality of the draftsmanship, and the toning (shading) to highlight the muscular form of the body. See Chapter 1, "The Body as Natural Beauty." Has the model adopted an "athletic" stance? Do we obtain a sense of strength, or of poise (balance) from the pose? See the discussion on "Symmetry" of the human form, Chapter 1; "Poise," Chapter 6; and "Strength," Chapter 7.

PLATE 2   (Two sculptures: Classical Greece and R. Tait McKenzie)

These two sculptures are examples representing the Greek and the twentieth-century physical ideals of the athlete. It is widely believed that contemporary man obtains his sense of the "ideal" body from the heritage of Greek sculpture represented here in the *Athlete from Ephesos* (2a). This process is called "transcultural communication." The *Standing Athlete,* by R. Tait McKenzie (2b), was constructed from a scientific analysis eliciting the mean of measures made on many athletes. Typically, *Athlete from Ephesos* represents a mesomorphic somatotype, whereas, *Standing*

Athlete more closely approximates the meso-ectomorph. See Chapter 1, "The Physical Ideal of the Body" and "The Ideal Body of the Athlete"; Chapter 2, "The Plastic Arts–Sports–Sculpture."

PLATE 3   (Mosaic of athlete)

The technique of making mosaic pictures with small pieces of glass or ceramic known as "tessare" was as popular with decorators of houses of the Roman nobility as was the interest in athletics. This mosaic of an athlete illustrates the strength typically found in a Roman athlete, the strength needed for combat "sports," the spectacle of the Roman circus. See Chapter 7, "Strength."

PLATE 4   (Two Hercules statuettes)

The strength of Hercules was recorded in the poetry of Homer, and is here ascribed to in this pair of sculptures (4a and 4b) executed by Giovanni de Bologna (circa 1550 A.D.). The details of the muscles—serratus anterior and gastrocnemius, for example,—the athletic and tonic definition of the muscles flexing in the struggle, attest to the appreciation that the artist had for the beauty of human athletic form. Equally significantly, the sculptures are a pair, perhaps to be placed symmetrically (one at each end of a mantel or on a bureau dresser), thus they help us understand the closeness of symmetrical and asymmetrical form. See Chapter 1 for the discussion on "Symmetry and Asymmetry"; see also Chapter 7, "Cultural Antecedents" and "Strength."

PLATE 5   (Two Greek vases—chariot and runners)

Classical Greek pottery is renowned the world over for the beauty of its form, as the two amphorae here show. Functional, as well as decorative, such vases usually have two handles, each one set symmetrically opposite the other. Besides the craftsmanship seen in the shape of the vase, there is the immaculately detailed draftsmanship of the illustrated panels on the sides. Note especially the fine line-work of the musculature of the athletes and the harnesses of the horses in the chariot (5a). The artist who drew the athletes running (5b) has carefully observed the action of the sprinter in this case, thus demonstrating that the Greeks were obsessed with running speed. See Chapter 7.

PLATE 6   (Classical Greek vase and modern sculpture—runners)

The action of the distance runner is distinctive. Both of these examples, the three runners on the panel of a Greek amphora (6a) and the modern sculpture of Paavo Nurmi by R. Sintenis (6b), illustrate the beauty and control of the stride that is noted as being distinctive. Once again, as with Plate 2, a sense of transcultural communication is manifest. It seems perfectly relevant that there is less emphasis on muscle definition in these examples, such is the nature of distance running and the gracefulness of the easy stride. The process of etching the lines on the figures on the vase to emphasize muscle definition is called "graffiti," (literally, in translation, "scratching"). This method for illustrating the surface of vases is called "slipping" (a slip is a refined viscous clay which can be applied like a paint and will bond chemically with the clay of the vase when fired), and the slip can be scratched for linear definition and detail. See Chapter 5, "Athlete as Performing Artist," and also Chapter 6.

PLATE 7   (Boxing—vase and sculpture)

Boxing, both ancient and modern, is depicted here in a vase painting (7a) and modern sculpture (7b), again illustrating the transcultural communication across more than 2000 years. In Greece, they used the "cestuses" in that style of boxing called "pankration," the formal nature of which is depicted here. Contrast the poise of the boxer (who has just knocked his opponent down in the Mahonri Young sculpture) with that formal depiction by the Greek artist. See Chapter 2, "Sports-Sculpture," and Chapter 3, "Sculpture—Boxing."

PLATE 8   (Javelin-thrower and Hurdlers)

Here is one more example of transcultural communication, but this time the focus of attention is on the fact that the artist in both cases is dealing with a circular form. Both artists, constrained by the limitations of the circular shape, have made best creative use of the space available to them. The javelin-thrower (8a) has been drawn in the interior center of a krater, a flat open dish or bowl, typically with handles on the sides. The hurdlers in the bronze plaque designed by R. Tait McKenzie (8b) represent the athletic concept of *The Joy of Effort*. Note the attention to detail in the tonic definition of the musculature of the athletes, as well as the overall fluidity and rhythm of the hurdling stride. See Chapter 6, from "The Joy of Effort."

PLATE 9   (Olympic Shield of Athletic Sports)

The best description of the Shield is that given by Christopher Hussey, and is quoted in full in Chapter 7 under "Citius, Altius, Fortius."

PLATE 10   (Swimming—painting and photograph)

This painting of the swimmer by Yasuo Kuniyoshi (10a) probably has some symbolic or allegorical significance. Purists of swimming as a sport will challenge the athletic form and the position of the body in the water, but they will not dispute that the artist conveys a thorough sense of buoyancy and a sense of aesthetic pleasure that swimming provides, both competitively and recreationally. The sense of beauty in symmetry is the most apparent feature in the illustration of swimmer Sharon Stouder (10b). An implicit poise is made evident by the angle of the arms in relation to the water, and the position of the hands might suggest such grace in the ballet. The relaxed posture of the hands and wrists at the point of recovery from the water lends a compositional completeness to the directional force of the outstretched arms. See Chapter 1, "Symmetry and Asymmetry," and Chapter 6.

PLATE 11   (Dancer)

Edward Villella, a dancer with the New York Ballet, has sometimes been referred to as the "greatest living athlete." The illustration here shows his athletic form, his muscle definition (sartorius and quadriceps) implying great strength, the suggestion of which is that there is a close proximity between sport and the performing arts. The dance action that he is demonstrating is evocative of many situations in which the athlete finds himself (see Plate 20). See Chapters 4, 5, and 6.

PLATE 12   (Sculling—photograph and painting)

The idea of a transference from symmetry to asymmetry (postulated in Chapter 1) is given added force in these two pictures of sculling. The photographer is exploring the beauty of symmetry (12a), whereas Thomas Eakins, in *The Pair-oared Shell* (12b), has taken the subject matter as an exercise in perspective. In both instances the sleekness and lightness of the shell is brought out, the fragile beauty of something designed to go very fast. See Chapter 1, "Symmetry and Asymmetry," and Chapter 8, "The Most Beautiful Sport."

PLATE 13   (Baseball etching and golf swing photograph)

Two examples of imputed dynamic form are given here. In the Ben Shahn etching, *Baseball* (13a), the sense of drive and swing is given by the expressive array of lines and tones indicative of the moving hitter. Shadowy effects in the ink-work add to the swirling, punching drive of the batter. In the stroboscopic photograph (13b), the flashing strobe has caught the sense of rhythm and dynamics of the golfer's drive in the shaft and head of the club. See Chapter 6, "Dynamics" and "Rhythm," and Chapter 7, "Power."

PLATE 14   (Water-ski and Ski slalom)

Although both of these pictures show slalom techniques, and give a sense of man defying gravity by the effect of centrifugal force, they have been chosen for their graphic quality as similar to drawings (art-work). There is a similarity in the lines of the "rooster-tail" spray of the water-skier (14a) with the lines of the shaft of the golf-club in the stroboscopic photograph (Plate 13b). It is not a one-to-one relationship, but it is possible to detect a dynamic pattern similar to both. The muscle tension in the upper torso of the water-skier has a finely molded quality comparable with the sculpted figures in Plate 4. Both photographs of the slalom action show the classic style of the expert and therefore are aesthetically pleasing to see. Note the dynamic angle of the body in the skier between the flags (14b), similar to that of Walter Payton in Plates 25a and 25b and the attacking hockey-player in Plate 28. See Chapter 6 and Chapter 8, "The Objective Aesthetic."

PLATE 15   (Wrestling)

The major purpose for presenting these two illustrations of wrestling is to point out the technique a painter employs in preparing a finished oil painting. The "unfinished" painting by Thomas Eakins is an oil-sketch (15a), of which the finished work of art can be found in the Columbus Gallery of Art in Ohio. The George Luks finished painting (15b) is shown to demonstrate the differences in style between the painters and also to emphasize the difficulty of the subject matter, namely the action sport of wrestling. Both artists show the muscular build of the wrestlers, and although these are relatively static poses, there is a sense of struggle and dynamism (more especially in the finished painting). George Luks has employed the technique of *chiaroscuro* to heighten the symbolic nature of the struggle. See Chapters 2, 3, and 7.

PLATE 16   (Horse-racing and Polo)

The close similarity of these two paintings underscores what is meant by "composition." In both instances, the center of action is held within the framework of the painting (the eye does not want to wander off the canvas because there are no optical forces working on the perception of the viewer to carry his attention away). George Bellows, the painter of *Polo at Lakewood* (16b), is better known for *Firpo Knocking Dempsey Out of the Ring* and other equally well-known boxing pictures (see Chapter 3, "Painting-Boxing"), but the quality of his art is never illustrated to better effect than in this dynamic study of the sport of polo. The style of an artist is as distinctive as the style of an athlete. Refer to Plate 24 for the art-style of Frederic Remington, and Plates 2, 8, 9, 19 for the art-style of R. Tait McKenzie. See Chapters 2 and 3, and Chapter 1, "The Beauty of the Body in Sports Action—Why Superstars Look Beautiful in Action."

PLATE 17   (Horse-racing)

The excitement of the close finish is captured in the picture of these two horses racing neck-to-neck down the home-stretch at Sportsman's Park in Chicago. The interrelationship of the rider with the horse defies the separation of roles in the race; perhaps this is effected by the poise of the jockey, mounted strategically for best control in relation to the horse's center of gravity. The sense of drive and speed is evocative in spite of the fact that only the rider and the neck and shoulders of the horse are shown in the picture. The composition of this picture is excellent, the eye of the photographer is very artistic. See Chapter 7.

PLATE 18   (Lacrosse)

This picture illustrates two girls, evidently in a practice session, competing for possession of the ball. The action is instructive from several viewpoints. Most obviously, the action has a particular balletic quality, especially in evidence in the posture of the unsuccessful challenger for the ball. But note how the challenger compensates for a lack of height, effecting a personal body strategy which she employs with marked control and poise. See Chapters 6 and 8.

PLATE 19   (Speed-skating photograph and plaque)

The concept of "art improving on nature" is very apparent from the comparison of the group of skaters in *Brothers of the Wind* by R. Tait McKenzie (19a), and the photograph of speed skaters in a tournament race (19b). The sense of speed is given both in the art-work and in the photograph. In the former case, it is the forward lean, the appearance of a total body commitment, whereas in the photograph, the effect is drawn from the centrifugal forces working on the athletes as they round the bend. See Chapter 7, "Speed," and Chapter 8, "The Subjective Aesthetic."

PLATE 20   (Gymnastics)

The "strength-hold on the rings" (20a) and the "scissors on the pommel-horse" (20b) represent classic "still" and "action" poses in gymnastics. Further, these contrasting "poses" illustrate the symmetrical and the asymmetrical beauty of gymnastics (see Chapter 1, "Symmetry and Asymmetry"). The muscle definition in the upper arm sections of the athlete doing the strength-hold compares favorably in its beauty with that of the water-skier in Plate 14. Again, a sense of similarity (this time, of form or action) can be noted between the gymnast performing the scissors and the dance action of Edward Villella in Plate 11. See Chapter 5, "Form-sport: Gymnastics," *et seq.*

PLATE 21   (Sprinters)

In this picture of Wilma Rudolph winning the Women's 100-meter race at Rome in 1960, a fine sense of speed is conveyed. Certainly, the driving force of the left leg exhibits a strong notion of power, but this is superseded by the obvious lightness and fleetness that her body action illustrates. She has power in reserve, it seems, unlike the impression of weariness given in the postures of the other two competing athletes. Furthermore, the tilt of Wilma's head and her apparent "smile" adequately express what we understand by "the joy of effort." See Chapters 6 and 7.

PLATE 22   (Baseball player with angel)

Lithography, as an art-form, would appear to lend itself well to the depiction of sports events. In this lithograph, the artist has attempted to bring out the mythological quality of the superlative athlete, the situation in which a catch is "heaven-sent." Mythological powers were ascribed to athletes in Classical Greece, and the same applies today in a so-called sophisticated industrial society. The artist has also caught the sense of "the perfect moment" in sport. See Chapter 7, "Cultural Antecedents," and Chapter 8, "Great Moments in Sport."

PLATE 23   (Baseball pitcher and base slide)

These two classic sports-action pictures from baseball show the pitching skill of Vida Blue (23a) and the slide into second base (23b). In this slide, the runner was forced out (not evident from the picture), an indication of the fine timing and the strategy of the play. See Chapter 7, "Precision" and "Strategy."

Plate 24   (Bullfight and football)

Frederic Remington is recognized as one of America's greatest *genre* artists. He caught the spirit of the times and recorded many aspects of American life. In these two examples of his work, evidence of his artistic skill is presented both from the standpoint of the composition of his works and from the perspective of his skill with a paint-brush. Bullfighting (24a) is not discussed in the text, although it is acknowledged that in some societies this is regarded as sport. Certainly many writers have attested to the beauty of the bullfight, and here Remington has painted a superb picture. The football painting (24b) is interesting in its composition for the immense dynamic flow of the action on a diagonal line from right to lower left in the picture. See Chapter 3, "Football."

Plate 25   (Football)

The superlative skill of the sports photographer can give the sport-aesthetician great scope to explore his ideas of what is beautiful in a given sport. Here, two examples from football are taken, and the study of the skill of the running-back can be made. In these pictures, Number 34, Walter Payton, of the Chicago Bears, is the subject. In the Cardinals' game (25a), he is driving hard with his right leg, thereby committing the opposition end to remain poised on his right foot, but Payton reserves the option to (i) continue through, or (ii) to drive hard down on his left foot to come round the left side of the end. The Cardinals' end should close option (ii) so that the pursuit by Number 50 is effective. In the Cardinals' game, the *power* of the running-back is emphasized, whereas in the Colts' game (25b), his *gracefulness* is most evident. See Chapter 1, "Why Superstars Look Beautiful in Action," and Chapters 6 and 7.

Plate 26   (Football—quarterback 19)

"Socking the quarterback" is a beautiful play in football because (i) the defensive tackle has "taken out" his opposite number to get to the quarterback, or (ii) the defensive end has been so fast, the quarterback did not estimate his arrival so soon, or (iii) any number of other reasons showing beautiful defensive strategy. See Chapter 7, "Strategy—Defense."

PLATE 27   (Tennis)

Joseph Brown, the noted American sculptor of athletes, has caught the point of delivery in the serve in this study of champion tennis player, Arthur Ashe. The weight of the athlete has been effectually reduced to the point where he appears about to float effortlessly from the ground. Such qualities of illusion, the mark of great art, speak directly to the beauty of sport. Note also the relaxation in the left arm and hand, compensating the striking angle of the right arm with the impending force of the poised racquet. See Chapter 3, "Joseph Brown," and Chapters 6 and 7.

PLATE 28   (Ice-hockey)

A perfect "draw-play" on the goaltender is shown in this action photograph of Chicago Blackhawk right wing, J. P. Bordeleau, 23, slipping the puck past the California Golden Seals goaltender. The offense-man has indicated going across the front of the goal, then seeing the goaltender come out to meet him, allowed the progress of the puck to slow (all the time dropping his body back) and gently steering the puck into the goal behind the goaltender. Centrifugal force carries him on, and he employs the blades of his skates to check the forward action of the feet. Note the relation of the upper body to the position of the feet (the blades of his skates actually "biting" the ice to allow him upright recovery from this shot). The result looks controlled and graceful. See Chapter 6 and Chapter 7, "Strategy—Offense."

PLATE 29   (Motor-racing)

The speed of racing car Number 32 is approximately 150 m.p.h. at the time this picture was taken (29a). The dynamic lines of the machine are pleasing, but the illusion of speed is not accurately given, even by reference to the blurred landscape. The picture showing cars Number 65 and Number 2 (29b) illustrates the concept of "slip-streaming" or "drafting." See Chapter 7.

PLATE 30   (Basketball)

The composition of this basketball photograph is the most significant aspect since it demonstrates so effectively the concept of the "balletic" quality of that sport. The relative positions of the nonjumping players, leaning in towards the center of play-action, their eyes looking up at the ball, support the emphasis on attention focused on the jumping players. From the viewpoint of an artist, this formation represents a classic "triangular" shape in the figures, a format used frequently throughout the history of painting and sculpture. See Chapter 8, "The Objective Aesthetic— The Unforgettable Game."

Plate 31   (Hang-gliding)

Although this picture provides a side-shot of hang-gliding, the most implicit message is one of symmetry. The symmetry of the giant kite is essential for the athlete to have maximum control over the maneuverability of the kite in changing air conditions. Both Leonardo da Vinci and Goya, artists who lived before the time of winged flight in any form, sketched their ideas of man flying, but powering his own wings. The story of Daedalus and Icarus, from Greek mythology, tells that the idea is older than recorded history. The beauty of hang-gliding is attested to by those who engage in this relatively new, ecological sport. See Chapter 1, "Symmetry and Asymmetry," and Chapter 8, "The Subjective Aesthetic."

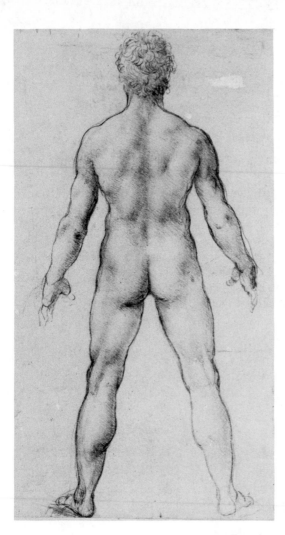

PLATE 1a

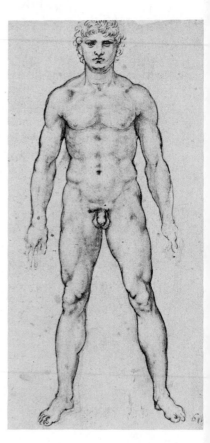

PLATE 1b

PLATES 1a and b. *Reproduced by Gracious permission of Her Majesty the Queen. Copyright reserved*

PLATE 2a. *Kunsthistorisches Museum, Vienna*

PLATE 2b. *Courtesy Lloyd P. Jones Gallery, University of Pennsylvania*

138

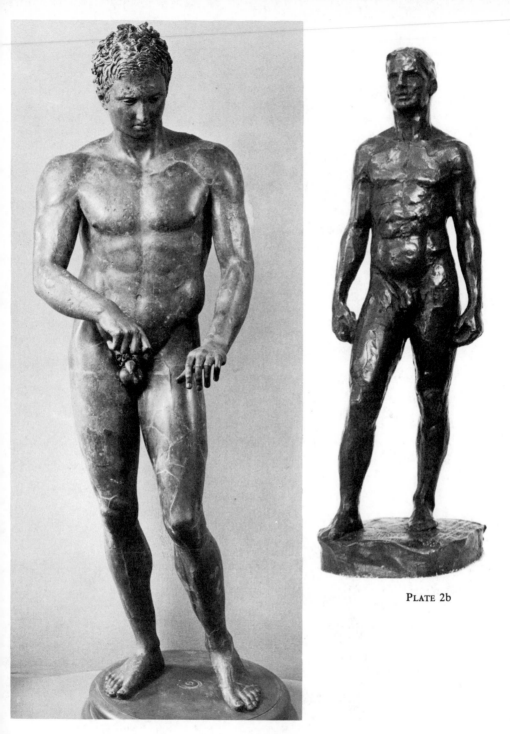

Plate 2a

Plate 2b

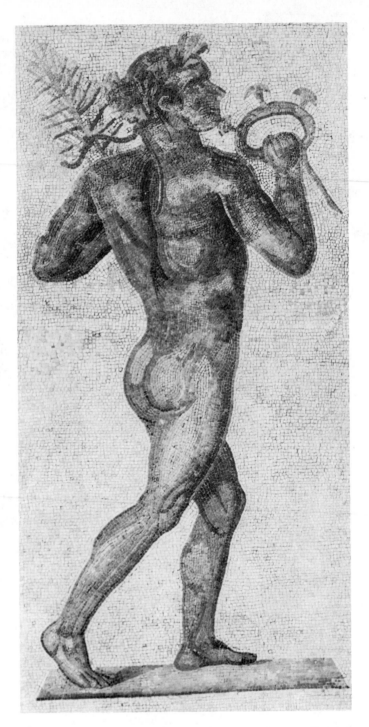

PLATE 3

140

PLATE 4b

PLATE 4a

PLATE 3. *Monumenti Musei E Gallerie Pontificie*

PLATE 4a and b. *Courtesy Art Institute of Chicago*

141

PLATE 5a

PLATE 5b

PLATE 6a

PLATE 5a. *By courtesy of The Trustees of the British Museum*

PLATE 5b. *The Metropolitan Museum of Art, Rogers Fund, 1914*

PLATE 6a. *The Trustees of the British Museum*

PLATE 6b. *Museum der Bildenden Künste zu Leipzig*

PLATE 8a

PLATE 8b

145

PLATE 9. *Courtesy Lloyd P. Jones Gallery, University of Pennsylvania*

PLATE 10a. *The Columbus Gallery of Fine Arts, Columbus, Ohio, Gift of Ferdinand Howald*

PLATE 10b. *Time-Life Picture Agency © Time Inc.*

146

PLATE 10a

PLATE 10b

147

PLATE 11

PLATE 11. The New York Times

PLATE 12a. *Photo by Georgi Busching, Terra Magica, Reich Verlag, Luzern, Switzer-land*

PLATE 12b. *Philadelphia Museum of Art: given by Mrs. Thomas Eakins and Miss Mary A. Williams*

PLATE 14a

PLATE 13a. *Courtesy First National Bank of Chicago*

PLATE 13b. *Courtesy of Dr. Harold Edgerton, MIT, Cambridge, Massachusetts*

PLATE 14a. *Courtesy of American Water Ski Association, Winter Haven, Florida*

151

PLATE 14b. *Photo by Malcolm Reiss*

PLATE 15a. *Philadelphia Museum of Art: Bequest of Fiske and Marie Kimball*

PLATE 15b. *Courtesy Museum of Fine Arts, Boston*

PLATE 16a

PLATE 16b

PLATE 17

PLATE 16a. *Courtesy Art Institute of Chicago*

PLATE 16b. *The Columbus Gallery of Fine Arts, Columbus, Ohio*

PLATE 17. *Photo by James Dupree*

155

PLATE 18

156

PLATE 18. *Courtesy of Chelsea College of P. E.*

PLATE 19a. *Courtesy Lloyd P. Jones Gallery, University of Pennsylvania*

PLATE 19b. *Courtesy of Amateur Skating Union of the U.S.A.*

PLATE 20a

PLATES 20a and b. *Courtesy of University of Minnesota Department of Athletics*

PLATE 21. *Time-Life Picture Agency © Time Inc.*

158

PLATE 20b

PLATE 21

PLATE 22

PLATE 22. *Courtesy First National Bank of Chicago*

PLATE 23a. *Photo by James Dupree*

PLATE 23b. *Minnesota Historical Society*

Plate 23a

Plate 23b

PLATE 24a. *Preston Morton Collection, Santa Barbara Museum of Art*

PLATE 24b. *Courtesy Yale University Art Gallery, Whitney Collection of Sporting Art*

PLATES 25a and b. *Photos by Donald Lansu*

162

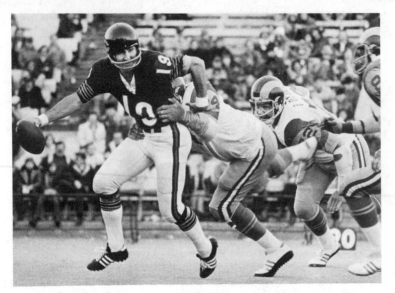

PLATE 26

PLATE 27

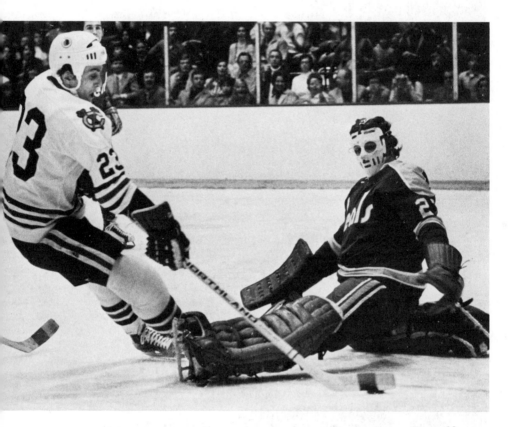

PLATE 28

PLATE 26. *Photo by James Dupree*

PLATE 27. *Courtesy of Joseph Brown; Photo by Jonathan Tang*

PLATE 28. *Photo by James Dupree*

165

PLATE 29a

PLATE 29b

PLATES 29a and b. *Courtesy of Lloyd De Grave*

PLATE 30. *Photo by Donald Camp*

PLATE 31. *Photo by Leroy Granis*

166

PLATE 30

PLATE 31

Symbolic Communication: Nondefinitive Parameters

The judgment of taste is not a cognitive judgment, that is, it is not logical, but aesthetic.

IMMANUEL KANT

INTRODUCTION

The beauty of movement is often *felt* as much as perceived, felt not in a personal action sense—although this is true also—but in a sense of witnessing in a total comprehensive capacity. This phenomenon can manifest itself in a number of ways and can be sponsored (or triggered off) in us by several alternative means. The evocative power that the beauty of movement has obliges the description of it to the use of *nondefinitive* terms. Among the more common of these terms are such words as "rhythm," "harmony," "form," "flow," and "gracefulness." They are, of course, applicable in describing dance and sport.

"Nondefinitive" does not mean that the words do not have definitions. Typically, a nondefinitive word may have several meanings, may be constrained by referential criteria, may be limited by explication resting on elaborative tautology, or may be otherwise loosely defined in interactive effect. Nondefinitive words appear to be culturally sound; they are words for which we learn the meaning very early in life, and we have very little difficulty in using them to convey ideas to each other. Such words as rhythm, harmony, gracefulness, and the like are admirable for the descriptive power they bring to shared communication on the beauty of sport, but for our purposes we need to seek substantive basis for why they are so admirable.

The beauty of movement is clearly perceived in the moving film, is better registered in the slow-motion replay (but not necessarily gaining or losing the quality of beauty), and can be grasped in our imagination by the phrasing of a good writer. Carlos Castenada, author of the *Don Juan* series of books dealing with anthropological studies of the Yaqui Indians, has the writing capacity to capture the effect of the beauty of movement in the choice of his words. The quotation here is from an article he wrote for *Esquire,* in March 1971, in which he describes a leap made by don Genaro:

> Suddenly don Genaro jumped onto the water. It was such a thoroughly unexpected action that I felt a vacuum in the pit of my stomach. It was a magnificent, outlandish leap. For a second I had the clear sensation I had seen a series of superimposed images of his body making an elliptical flight to the middle of the stream.
>
> There was something truly exquisite about his posture, his body seemed so nimble, so frail. I thought that don Genaro with his headband and feathers and his dark poncho and his bare feet was the most beautiful being I had ever seen.
>
> He threw his arms up suddenly, lifted his head, and flipped his body swiftly in a sort of lateral somersault to his left. The boulder where he had been standing was round and when he jumped he disappeared behind it. . . . Don Genaro's masterful feat had thrown me into a state of profound emotional excitation. I felt he was a consummate artist. (p. 82)

The applicability of rhythm, harmony, and similar nondefinitive words is recognized in his description of the leap by don Genaro, even though none of them is used by Castenada in this passage. Observing slow-motion replays of filmed sports action, even watching the action itself at the event or on television, we may be drawn to express ourselves about what we see by recourse to such nondefinitive terms. This is the power of communication between people, and such words do have sound cultural value.

To illustrate how nondefinitive words can be used to bring meaning to those interested in sport, we can turn to the description of pitching greatness given by Leonard Koppett (1967) in his book, *All about Baseball*. Allowing that Koppett is being sardonic, that he is using the special vernacular of baseball, the point he makes about the four major attributes of pitching greatness, "stuff, control, craft, and poise," not only provides food for serious thought, but touches upon the beauty of sport into the bargain. He summarizes his definition of these four attributes as follows:

> Stuff is the physical element: how hard can he throw, how big is the break on his curve? Stuff is the product of strength and exceptional hair-trigger coordination, and seems to be an innate quality, perhaps improvable by practice and technique, but not acquirable.

Control is the ability to throw the ball—with stuff on it—exactly where the pitcher wants to, with extraordinary accuracy.

Craft comprises the knowledge that comes with experience, analytic power, meticulous observation, and resourcefulness. Craft is what tells a pitcher where and how to apply the stuff he can control.

And poise includes the ability to apply one's craft under the most severe competitive pressure, to rise to an occasion, and to produce best when the need is greatest. (p. 308)

In Koppett's estimation, Sandy Koufax was the greatest pitcher that he ever saw because he demonstrated the "greatest combination of stuff and craft ever seen." Koufax had perfected his control and mastered his tactics, all the while sustaining a phenomenal speed which showed in the mastery he had over both his "blazer" and his "monster curve." These are the elements of pitching that Koppett says caught the admiration of the fan, what the man in the stands found beautiful in baseball.

The point is made. There is a freedom of expression associated with the use of the nondefinitive vernacular. The terminology is based on a commonly accepted associative basis; such words are culturally locatable, agreeable, and nonthreatening. Moreover, they allow for shared symbolic communication, most significantly with a population of limited vocabulary, and are facilitative of interaction rather than restrictive. In all frankness, it seems a little effete and even unnecessary to explore the meanings of such words, and the only saving argument seems to rest on the issue that the beauty of sport will not be adequately grasped without the test given to them for their substantive contribution to our overall inquiry. Classical Greek philosophers like Plato and Aristotle concerned themselves with such terms and their referents in nature, and we should not assume ourselves too sophisticated to probe the concepts anew for the possibility of shedding further light on the subject.

Nondefinitive words are both revealing and obscuring or veiling. Taken at face value, they appear glib, superficial, and untrustworthy. Tested for their innate or inherited (cultural) meaning, they reveal a depth meritorious of a broad and strongly interwoven fabric of ideas and associations. The revelation provided by nondefinitive terms is offered in this chapter, where etymological constituency serves as the major foundation for what we can derive from them today.

UNITY

Rhythm, harmony, form, flow, gracefulness, and such terms are usually subsumed under the concept of "unity." The unity of any artistic expression, be it in the plastic arts, the literary arts, or the movement arts,

SYMBOLIC COMMUNICATION: NONDEFINITIVE PARAMETERS   171

is an alternative statement of its wholeness or totality, and therefore of its aesthetic presence as an entity. Several levels of interpretation operate in any reasoned explanation of unity. For instance, unity belies the mind-body duality; further, unity is *homeostasis* or psychological balance. Unity can be symmetrical or asymmetrical, so long as the balance of forces acting in the aesthetic expression are not overwhelmingly discordant or dissonant.

"Unity in one shape or another is the ultimate goal of all human thought or endeavor." With this conclusion in mind, Robinson (1948) builds a historical rationale based on Greek origins:

> With (the Greeks) Unity of Design was the first condition of Beauty. . . . Exact symmetry, in short, was essential. Contrast, of course, there will be. . . . In the use of the spoken word, no less than in the visual arts, Unity of Form was the invariable aim. Speeches were planned from prelude to peroration with an eye to their total effect. The Greek orator was a master of balance and symmetry. . . . In Drama the Law of Unity was carried still further. The Unities of Time and Place served to enhance the unity of the plot. (pp. 183–186)

The mind-body principle, absence of a separation of what we accept as two entities, pervaded Greek life sufficiently for us to believe that athletics was not independently regarded for its emphasis on physical performance. We can accept that sport for the Greeks was a total mind-body experience just as today we can accept the message of karate and *mushin*. *Mushin,* we are reminded, is "the moon on water," an entity that is neither the one nor the other. There is harmony between the two component parts, found only in the image created by the reflection—a reflection caught only by one in a position to see and, upon seeing, perceive. Ripples on the water make the "moon" dance gracefully; the rhythm is one with a cadence that we do not find disturbing, either visually or psychologically. If the rhythm were to break, be splintered by a splash, the unity would be destroyed, all graceful-ness vanish, and the harmony lost. We have no difficulty in reading and understanding this language, nor do we have any difficulty knowing that this imagery could be applied by analogy to the dance or to sport—if our sensitivity will allow us the pleasure. Nondefinitive terms such as rhythm, harmony, gracefulness, and flow do not threaten us, nor should they in our search for better understanding of them.

We might assume that these nondefinitive terms refer to the concept of unity in a directional sense. That is, if man pursues values and behaviors most typically associated with the concepts they describe, and put them into a frame of reference which has a steering quality, he not only will be better for that pursuit but, with effort and conviction he can eventually *achieve.* Achieve what? Unity of body and spirit? Perfect happiness and contentment? The aim is set by the nondefinitive descriptors; perfection or

172 SYMBOLIC COMMUNICATION: NONDEFINITIVE PARAMETERS

unity is the goal. Unity and perfection depend much on the same parameters, spiritually and behaviorally, for their realization.

Is perfection ever realized? The answer to this question is pursued further in Chapter 8, in the section, "Beauty and Excellence." Here we are concerned with a brief observation of the concept, and it is appropriate that we turn to the judgment of a golf professional for his sense of perfection. The appropriateness of leaning on the expertise of Jack Nicklaus is self-evident in the recognition of golf as a precision sport, one which, hypothetically, should be commensurable to the finest degree of perfection.

Jack Nicklaus (1974) claims that a part of his personality is a desire for perfection in all things. However, he fully understands the nature and meaning of perfection when he states: "Of course, I never have played golf perfectly, and there is a mighty good chance that neither I nor anyone else ever will." Virtually the same comment has been made about archery. In her opening remarks for the instructional text, *Archery*, Lorraine Pszczola (1971) states: "There has never been a perfect archer—the challenge is to see how close to perfection we can get." Herrigel (1953) restates this view in *Zen in the Art of Archery*.

The definition of perfection that Nicklaus elaborates is stimulating for our study of the beauty of sport, and his basic premises may be transferable. For Nicklaus, perfection translates as "100 percent golf," and 100 percent golf, given in the example of a par-72 course, means "shoot birdies on the fourteen par-3 and par-4 holes, and eagles on the par-5 holes." In tournament terms, this amounts to an eighteen-hole score of 50 for one round, repeated four times for an overall score of 200. (Nicklaus holds the record of 271 for 72 holes, the all-time best championship winning score.) For Nicklaus, there are three elements necessary for perfect golf:

> First I would have to have achieved 100 percent analytical objectivity—recognized the ideal shot for each situation. Second, having recognized the perfect shot, I would have to have resolved to play it—no compromises. Third, having recognized and resolved to play the perfect shot, I would have to have executed it perfectly—no technical hitches. (pp. 253–254)

Nicklaus reckons that he has never gotten closer than 75 percent to the goals he set himself, and he thinks that execution is the primary hindrance. As he states at the outset of his fine book, *Golf My Way*, "I certainly don't claim perfection—I'm too frequently reminded of my imperfections on the course." Even with his "lack of perfection," few would dispute his excellence. That excellence and perfection are closely related concepts is explored further in Chapter 8. Excellence, from one or two exemplary perspectives, is introduced here to whet discussion.

Most typically, *excellence* in sport has been equated with victory and triumph. Such quantitative grounds for excellence place constraints attendant on the wider value base for qualitative assessment. Interpreting excellence as the beauty of performance places it in the qualitative rather than the quantitative realm. Aesthetics resists efforts by man to quantify, and such concepts as beauty and excellence, whether interpreted as comparable or otherwise, remain as values only. The scientific study of values, pursued most notably by psychologists, appears to be a fruitless operation, all the more frustrating by virtue of the apparent simplicity of the project. What is most beautiful, like what is best, is always an open question.

George Santayana gave recognition to the fact that athletics is one of those realms of human activity in which man strives to achieve excellence. In 1888 he wrote an article for the *Harvard Review* entitled "Philosophy on the Bleachers." In part, he stated:

> We are dealing with an art in which only the few, the exceptionally gifted, can worthily succeed. Nature must be propitious, circumstances must be favourable, patience and inspiration must not fail. There is an athletic aristocracy for the same reason that there is one of intelligence and one of fashion, because men have different endowments, and only a few can do each thing as well as it is capable of being done. Equality in these respects would mean total absence of excellence. (p. 184)

The paradox he addresses is that for excellence to emerge, there must be competition—this was systematic thinking in nineteenth-century American "ivy league" universities (Curti, 1951). Because it was systematic thinking in those days does not mean that it must remain so today. Surely, this line of thinking is acceptable as one mode of address in sport, but it is only one. There are others, as those who explore the mind-body unity concept through contemplation, and apply this to sport, will attest. It is a reflection of the narrowest mode of thinking to believe that competition, and only competition, sponsors excellence.

The suggestion has been made in several contexts that the beauty of sport is a derivative of contemplation, whether contemplation in action or at rest. One of the sports that adheres to this concept as part of the philosophy of its exponents is karate. Karate, a "defense" sport, is never truly attained without the state of mind called *mushin,* or "no-mind." Hidetaka Nishigama, quoted in the *Minneapolis Tribune,* November 27, 1970, explains it this way:

> It is often likened to the lunar reflection in water. Neither the moon nor the water has any preconceived idea of producing the incident designated by us as "the moon in water."
>
> The water reflects accurately all images within its range—so a mind calm as undisturbed water can apprehend all movements physical and psychological of an opponent, and react appropriately.

The implications given here for the mind-body unity concept of the beauty of sport are stated in poetic terms. For the ancient Greeks, the mind-body unity principle was value-based, resting on the concept of *areté,* or "nothing to excess." *Areté* was, for the Greeks, excellence in living, the balance of physical and metaphysical forces which measured the fine distinction between excellence and perfection. The balance of forces in nature and in man bespoke the harmony of life and of existence. As an objective, harmony was well-known to the Greeks, as their folklore testifies.

HARMONY

Harmony, in Greek and Roman mythology, was the daughter of Venus and Mars, representing the social balance between Love and War. Robert Thuma (1897), in his *The Grace of Man,* identified harmony with flexibility of the body, the physical component in his "concept of trinity." He spoke of the "harmony of poise," which he based on the Delsartian Theory that there can be traced a system of infinite harmony in all things (man, animals, and nature), and which he claimed takes one toward a theological harmony. "Oneness with God," interpreted here as Unity in Nature. This is but an extension of the thinking of the eighteenth-century German philosopher, Leibnitz.

The theory of the nature of harmony that Leibnitz developed in the seventeenth century found its inspiration in the belief held by the Greeks that musical harmony was reflective of a more inclusive universal or cosmological harmony. To substantiate his new theory, Leibnitz had to develop a new dimension of mathematics accounting for the selective teleological choice of the most pleasingly perfect tones and combinations. He believed that the highest possible degree of perfection of harmony could be achieved by dependence on a selection of principles more limited in scope than those associated with ordinal sequence. In other words, harmony as perfection reflected the beauty of simplicity. In the twentieth century the Leibnitz-Thuma development of reasoning on harmony found statement in the thinking of Huizinga (1950), who applied the underlying theoretical construct to his analysis of the role of play in culture. Huizinga stated:

> In play, the beauty of the human body in motion reaches its zenith. In its more developed forms [viz., sport] it is saturated with rhythm and harmony, the noblest gifts of aesthetic perception known to man. (p. 7)

In the language of the physical sciences, wherein physical laws are established, harmony is defined as a "continuous function." A harmonic (the irreducible bit) is defined as "a continuous function which satisfies Laplace's equation, and whose first derivative is also a continuous function." Thus, science adds little of value to our cultural use of the term harmony, and we might deduce that musicians are closer in touch with harmony than are scientists. Musicians, we may recall, are more concerned with aesthetic criteria and experience than we might expect of the typical scientist, exceptions allowing.

Ultimately, of course, harmony can be explained in mathematical symbol, suggesting that form as an elemental process is also an abstraction. That form ultimately may be an abstraction should not deter our analysis because we know that many abstract thoughts can be expressed figuratively or graphically. For example, we know that a parabolic curve is imputed with dynamic force or thrust if it is drawn in such a way, the line graphically illustrating an abstract mathematical function. The same dynamism of potential force that we impute to the graphic mathematical curve is imputed to the body of an athlete when we observe his musculature, although the cognitive and affective sources from which we pull our referents would appear to be intuitively different.

Culturally speaking, we tend to attribute more potential power or dynamism to the mesomorph than to the ectomorph or endomorph. We appear to have inherited this from the Greeks, for they are equally aware of the difference. Vase drawings depict the ridicule of overweight and indolent youth by others of a more active or athletic build. For some unaccountable reason (other than potential dynamic energy?), the triangulated upper torso and slim hips inspire a consciousness of admiration not usually accorded the ectomorphic and endomorphic body types. The concept of "ideal" body, not necessarily identifiable with mesomorph (but strongly assimilative), is treated in Chapter 1.

The very real sense in which harmony is explored in the athletic domain can be traced to the statement made by Arthur Gander for the *Handbook of the Federation International de Gymnastique*. Based on the dictionary definition of "accord, agreement, the correct relation of the parts to the whole," harmony has distinct and clear meaning for the gymnast. For him there is the implication of a sequencing of parts comprising an exercise in a harmonious manner to bring about a harmonious whole. Harmony in gymnastics tests a context of "belonging" and "difference" which characterizes the linkage of "aesthetic units" formulated by Wober (1968). As the *Handbook* states it:

> Transition from one part of the exercise to another forms an agreement which equals a curved-like line corresponding to the character of both parts. This line is short as far as movement is concerned. It becomes more pronounced when two parts of slower rhythm, or larger movements which are pronounced, follow one another. This curved-like line can expand itself also from a small curve into a relative larger one, especially when one such pronounced movement with slower rhythm fol-

lows a relatively short and rhythmically limited first part, or vice versa. This can be seen in combinations consisting of several parts with very different rhythms, and finally, this is also the case in the presentation of a complete exercise. While in all exercises on the apparatus we are always involved with harmony, this concept and evaluation factor will have to be given even greater attention in the floor exercises, where handsprings, Saltos and kips are combined with pauses and gymnastic elements; where strength and movement have to follow in a harmonious manner, harmony will play an ever greater role. (p. 186)

The discussion of "harmony" cannot be complete without considering "contrast" and "comparison" and the ways in which a sequence of elements in a routine are blended according to the satisfaction of these criteria. The contrast and comparison of such elements is as important for the production of an artistic routine as would be the correct selection of colors and lines for the success of a painting.

FORM

A similar argument seems to hold true with practically all the nondefinitive aesthetic terms that we can identify for the elaboration of aesthetic and artistic unity in expressive form. Indeed, the definition given to "form" by the scientific community is no better than it being an entity having "intrinsic anisotropic properties as substance or object." The wisdom of David Hume (1964) surpasses that of the scientific community, for he notes that beauty is nothing more than a form (shape) which produces pleasure. Pleasure is the essence of beauty and the power of producing pleasure is beauty, according to Hume. "That shape which produces strength," he states, "is beautiful in one animal, and that which is a sign of agility in another." The quaint and archaic way in which Hume expresses himself does not detract from the sense of his meaning:

> The strength of a horse, and the swift-sailing of a vessel (boat), form the principal beauty of these several objects. (p. 576)

For Hume, strength is both form and beauty. (Strength, for us, is a definitive term, and is explored more fully in a later chapter.) Strength in the beauty and form of a horse or a yacht is equivalent to force, solidity, firmness, and steadiness. Strength as form and beauty denotes resiliency, the quality of tempered or toned plasticity, animate or inanimate. (Strength is defined in physics in relation to the resistance to a factor of stress— hence, strength is also a physical manifestation of resilience).

Form, viewed as a psychological process of perception, is a relationship between two or more units simultaneously perceived to provide a consciousness of the coexistence and distinction of those units. The suggestion by Wober (1968) that, for the purposes of analysis, such units be conceived as irreducible "bits" is useful but not structurally instructive. Such an analysis demands a recognition of constituent elements, in which abstractions as well as material components be given appropriate weighting. This implies a dynamic relationship, but how do we assess what is dynamic? The question is rhetorical here, since we all believe that we recognize the dynamic in relation to the static. But, for reemphasis, form has both static and dynamic components, the most essential nature of which was discussed in Chapters 1 and 4.

DYNAMICS

Dynamics is the study of the behavior of objects in motion, particularly objects acted on by forces and having variable velocity. Thus, the observation of acceleration or deceleration in an object (or in an athlete) can be interpreted as being dynamic by description. We impute the dynamism in the motion or action relative to perceived force, which in turn may be ballistic, explosive, or of a more controlled nature. A still photograph of a running-back in the act of changing direction to avoid a tackle, a picture of a yacht tilting in response to the wind, the sculpted stride of the runner, all fixed in their respective eternal images, evoke a sense of dynamic force, movement, and action. We know, as certainly as we walk upright, that forces of specific power are at work.

In the nondefinitive use of the word dynamic, we imply force and direction (vector qualities). The angulation of the body of a skier tells us that centrifugal forces are working to set him upright even when we perceive that he is making a 30-degree angle with the horizontal plane (see Plate 14b). There is a thrust, an implied tilt, a power of expression in the still photograph of moving action which relays information tapping into our experience of muscular force and control. We know that muscles exert power and force, and we know, even as children, that a tensed muscle, a muscle defined in fibrous outline under the fine skin of the body, transmits the communication of strength and dynamism. The analogy of the muscle being a coiled spring is incorrect, of course, since anatomically muscle fibrillation does not work like a spring; but to say that the relaxed, or tonic, muscle is springlike in its readiness to flex gives us a better feel for underlying dynamic forces at work in skeletal muscle. We grow up with this knowledge, tested in childhood, acknowledged in adulthood.

The coiled body evokes a similar sense of tensed dynamic potential. But what of other dynamic forces in relation to the body? The sky diver picks up weight the higher he goes in the plane carrying him aloft for his fall. But shortly after leaving the plane, his body takes on new facets of dynamism—aerodynamics. With the body curled he falls one way, with it outstretched he falls another, and he learns the control of his aerodynamic torso. In similar vein, the ski jumper who leaves the ramp at 60 m.p.h. headed for a 300-foot jump inclines his body and skis in such a way that he both looks dynamic and acts aerodynamically, both in the use of his skis and of his body. Likewise, the water skier, most evidently in slalom racing, sets a dynamic between himself and the water, opposing at the same time a dynamic that the towing boat places on him (see Plate 14a). In all these conditions we use the sense of dynamism to explain our awe, our acknowledgment that what we see is beautiful. Yet, if we question ourselves, we find it difficult to account for beauty in terms of angulation, vector, and other attributes we accord as dynamic.

Students of dance will speak of the dynamics of line and form in choreographic sequence. Students of painting and drawing are taught the elements of basic design, usually interpreted as the dynamics of visual form (de Sausmarez, 1964). Art lecturers speak of visual kinetics, by which they mean that lines and even dots or spots have energy when placed in relation to each other. The Miller-Lyer Illusion illustrates the effect of visual energy, in which we are obliged to see parallel lines as concave, simply because they are interfered with by intruding or co-relative lines. Visual kinetics suggests that forces operating in pictorial display can be likened to those of the pull of gravity, the swing of a pendulum, the opposing forces of pulleys, principles of levers and counterbalancing—the principles of which are learned by the child as part of his comprehension of number, weight, volume and mass, and the principles of relativity. Equally fundamental to those observations taken from developmental psychology are questions arising from the psychology of perception. Figure-ground studies and relationships bespeak a source of dynamics, the nature of which is still being investigated. The student interested in analyzing the dynamics of sport for aesthetic value and interpretation should not avoid these avenues of inquiry.

FLOW

Flow, another nondefinitive descriptor of expressive movement, is sometimes used to categorize a form of action reflecting reduced dynamism. Flow suggests gracefulness, "graceful" having origins stemming from analogies with divinity. However, flow recommends two basic lines of interpretation for consideration: (1) the reduction of meaning in physical law, and (2) the comparative perception of highly dynamic action.

In the reduction of meaning, flow (used in the sense of streamline or laminar flow in physics) is a state between the surfaces of two objects in which there exists little or no microscopic mixing. In the strictest physical sense, flow occurs in sport at the interface between the surface of the ski and the snow, the shell of the skiff and water in sculling, and the surface of the body and the water in swimming. When flow is used to denote line of movement in dance or sport, it equates more similarly with harmony by virtue of its sense of meaning as "continuous function."

As comparative perception, flow replaces dynamism of action as typically found in the slow-motion replay of intense physical action. Thus, flow derives from dynamic form, and presents an impression of exaggerated control, balance, timing, and the like. Flow in this exaggerated time-sense is closely akin to flow in real time. Time becomes the primary and necessary condition for the subjective evaluation of flow, and, once again, the poetic or aesthetic significance is greater than the scientific.

GRACEFULNESS

Whether the concept of gracefulness has remained the same etymologically over the past two millennia is disputable. The origins of conceptualizations attaching to "grace" are rooted in closeness with the divine, the spiritual recognition of one godhead (as in Christian belief) or a host of gods (as on Mount Olympus). One who had grace, and who therefore was graceful, was a person endowed with behavioral attributes which others saw as being exceptional—more from a social and dispositional aspect than from a physical sense. Monks and others who lived lives of grace usually conducted themselves in public in such a way that their behavior was ascribed "graceful." It was a small psychological "leap" to describe their physical behavior as graceful, thereby implying that a person who moved with measured step, with controlled deportment, was physically graceful. Physical gracefulness equates with physical poise, the impression given of tonic deportment suggesting sound muscular tonus and control, belying all effects of strain of movement. Gracefulness implies perfection of controlled physical behavior. An athlete can look graceful even when his muscular exertion is at its greatest, although this is rarer than would be found in a dancer fully exerting himself (see Plate 11). Whether race-horses look graceful at full tilt down the home stretch is also open to discussion. What we do know of the "form-sports" is that they seek gracefulness at the point of extreme exertion, and thereby create illusion.

Extending on the concept of gracefulness equating with divinity and perfection, we can draw upon the opinion of S. Pocock, a master boatbuilder, who states in the film *Rowing: A Symphony of Motion*: ". . . a great art, rowing, searching for perfection; when you reach perfection you are approaching the divine which is the you of you, the soul." Jack Grant, commenting on the playing ability of the golfer Jack Nicklaus, has said: "that many people get the impression his skills are heaven-sent rather than self-developed." Perhaps the etymological derivative for gracefulness does still have connotations in present-day language. The observations made by Dick Cullum regarding the boxing ability of George Foreman bear testimony to this. In the report of Foreman's fight with Aaron Eastling, which appeared in the *Minneapolis Tribune,* February 5, 1971, Cullum stated:

> At that moment Foreman made an odd move, an unusual kind of feint, and his left hand darted out. It was a lightning jab which must have carried a sting because Eastling's knees softened and Foreman seized him lest he fall.
>
> At the end of this round, and in appreciation of that one *beautiful* punch, the crowd roared its approval.
>
> When the exhibition ended Foreman was held in the ring for a long time by the enthusiastic applause.
>
> He had done little, really, except to display his *quickness and grace* and, somehow, project his personality.
>
> Still he had that crowd in a *worshipful* state. (p. 4C)   [Italics added.]

Consciously or unconsciously, the sense of divinity in relation to grace comes through in Cullum's statement. The fact that the witnessing of speed and gracefulness in the boxer brings what Cullum calls a "worshipful state" to the crowd tells us a little more of the mesmeric effect that quality performance has on those who see it. There should be little doubt in the mind of the student that this is a fruitful area of research directly applicable to collective behavior and crowd studies in sport as well as to the beauty of sport.

RHYTHM

According to the literature of dance, that form of expressive movement antedates words, music, and all other art-forms. Rhythm is virtually synonymous with dance; the literature emphasizes that the wellsprings of the dance are emotion, rhythm, and communication. That dance predates sport, even the athletics of Minoan and Mycenaean times, goes without question, yet we see (and often, seek) in sport evidence of the rhythm of human performance, if not of communication. But fundamental differences occur separating sport from dance, at least as far as rhythm and emotion are concerned. In dance, rhythm is injected, it is part of the intention of communication and is an undisputable attribute for the very reason that it is intended to transmute feeling or emotion. Sport differs, for even when athletes or teams obtain a "rhythm" in their efforts, that rhythm has developed as much by the coincidence of circumstance as by intention. But more importantly, the athlete does not typically take into his sport the release or communication of emotion—this is evident from our witnessing the breakdown of emotional control when other values have impinged on those which sport was originally designed to manifest. The discussion of emotions in sport should not undermine the discussion of rhythm in sport, but the separation between the two is more obviously patent than occurs in the dance. The objectives of dance and sport are clearly separable when the discussion of rhythm is entered, yet this does not detract from the speculation that sport can appear extremely dancelike, probably because of how we perceive rhythm in sport.

The sense denoted by rhythm is that it is a continuous, therefore time-related, phenomenon. Surely, if we call rhythm a "continuous function," either formally or physically, we note that the terms rhythm and harmony are synonymous and are logically interchangeable. Thus, we see tautology entering into our language if we define rhythm in terms of harmony or harmonious function. Most typically, rhythm, when applied to a game situation, usually implies an unbroken cadence in the play. A team can pick up a rhythm of counterplay as a result of turning the game around—or they can lose that rhythm by jarring or disjointing elements entering to break up the rhythmic flow of coordinating sequence. The rhythm of play in sport is attested to by many athletes, both within a game and even in a series or season. The component elements of rhythm in such cases are the recognizable satisfactory and successfully pleasing parts of the sport. More often, the rhythm in a game is a happenstance, something which is not sought or engineered, but rather which occurs due to a sequence of two or three nondiscordant events. The sequence of these few events strikes the players as presenting both some unity in themselves and yet, paradoxically, a small complete part of a greater unity. The sensing of this effect sets the scene for great motivational impulse to continue it and to be part of it.

The rhythm of a game is like the rhythm in any art-work. There is linearity, form, color, cadence, nuance conforming to make a wholeness, and the rhythm of the expressive art is a part of that wholeness.

Sport has a wholeness as works of art have a wholeness. According to Kupfer (1975) this is bound up in the sense of unity and completeness that man typically seeks. "The wholeness and finality possibly in competitive sporting events, paradigmatic in the artistic, answers the human desire for completeness and unity, if only in symbol," says Kupfer, echoing a Gestalt theory for explanation of the psychic needs of man. Closure, as a necessary component of an art-work, has long since been challenged in painting and sculpture, just as Gestalt psychology has been exposed for the limitations it imposes on explanation.

The sense of rhythm, cadence, and tempo that is ascribed to athletes in some sports is a statement of their control. For Jack Nicklaus (1974), rhythm describes "the *texture* of the swing, the variations of speed within the over-all pace" of the clubhead prior to the production of maximum speed at impact with the ball (see Plate 13b). As an elaboration of what he means in the actual process of addressing and hitting the ball, Nicklaus gives this instructional sensate and emotive pointer:

> Feeling the weight of the clubhead against the tension of the shaft helps me to swing rhythmically.
>
> As the backswing progresses I like to feel the clubhead's weight "pulling" my hands and arms back and up. Starting down, I like to feel the weight of the clubhead lagging back—resisting—as my thrusting legs and hips pull my arms and hands down.
>
> When I can "wait" for these feels, I am almost certainly swinging in proper tempo. I am giving myself enough elapsed time to make all the various moves in rhythmical sequence. (p. 170)

Much of what Nicklaus refers to as rhythm has parallels in comments made by people associated with rowing. Oarsmen speak of a sensitivity to the oars, to the boat, and to the interactive effect of oars, boat, and water. (Curiously, oarsmen do not normally feel they are pulling with others, but that they are alone, and that they alone are responsible for the reaction they obtain from their sport.) In the movie *Rowing: A Symphony of Motion,* Cleve Livingston speaks of a phenomenon which oarsmen call "swing," the action of the boat thrusting forward, giving the impression of being lifted out of the water with each stroke and this occurring with a rhythmical cadence of surging harmonious repetition. For statesman Averell Harriman, the beauty of rowing was "the rhythm of the crew rowing together."

POISE

The discussion on symmetry and asymmetry in physical terms provides the basis for an approach to psychological balance or poise. When a football quarterback like Bart Starr says of his opposite number, "he showed me a lot of poise Sunday," he is speaking as much for the psychological balance of the athlete as for his physical ability. Psychological balance in these circumstances equates with demonstrable social poise. Put in social terms, "personal poise," state Gross and Stone (1964), "refers to the performer's control over self and situation, and whatever disturbs that control is incapacitating and consequently embarrassing." In football, the fumbled ball is a perfect example of loss of both physical and social poise. On the social side, athletes lose poise when they find themselves in positions not normally prescribed for them. Take the classic case of Garo Yepremian, who, finding his kick blocked and knocked back toward him, picked up the ball in a midfield position with advancing tackles from the opposing team descending on him; Yepremian is a beautiful kicker but in that instance he lost the social poise he needed in the game situation since he did not know that he should have run for the sideline and gotten himself out-of-bounds. Sustaining poise in the game situation can be an exciting and beautiful experience, particularly when playing out of position, as Willis Reed, the basketball star, illustrates (*Look,* April 6, 1971):

> To go out hunting in the woods and outwit a deer, an elk, a bear, it takes savvy, it takes patience. You come out of your environment and into his. This excites me, just like it does *when I play out of position and outwit another ballplayer.* (p. 70) [Italics added.]

In their analysis of embarrassment, Gross and Stone (1964) cite five criteria for distinguishing social poise: space, props, equipment, clothing, and the body. A salutary borrowing of their five criteria is appropriate here, and they are applied to poise as a contributory descriptor of beauty in sport.

To some extent, the Yepremian example dealt with *space,* the first of the five criteria. But when we consider the nature of space in sport (the boxing ring, the football field, the lane in track) we note the boundaries within which the sport takes place. Often the boundaries are explicit, but occasionally they can be implicit. Explicitly, the rules and regulations of track and field state: you shall not step into another lane in the dashes or hurdles; the explicit (marked) boundary is always defined in the book of rules governing a sport. Implicitly, the football and soccer fields, the baseball diamond, and all larger sports arenas have within their explicit boundaries those other positional areas with unmarked but readily recognizable "social(?)" boundaries. The attacking defenseman (hockey, soccer) is an example of the athlete overstepping implicit boundaries attaching to his role on the field: if his play is successful, he is beautiful; if his play is poorly executed, he is the embarrassment of all. Sustained poise, even in losing situations, is beautiful in sport. In the purest sense, psychological space, as Gross and Stone suggest, parallels to a great extent physical space. The delimitations of the ice hockey arena oblige occasional body-checkings on the boards—these do not typically result in the checked athlete feeling his psychological space has been infringed, and so, only occasionally does an outburst of violence ensue. When fighting does ensue from such a play, the frustrated player has interpreted the body-check as an infraction of his psychological space also. He loses poise accordingly in his attempt to sustain it or win retribution.

Race position at the start is crucial for many athletes, be it track, lane, pole, or gate starting number in time trials. Thus, for example, in downhill skiing it is better to be number 15 than 150, to be on the snow before the *piste* becomes scraped and rutted from the traffic. Taking the pole in Formula I and Grand Prix racing may not be so critical in the sense of damaging the track, but the risk of accident is not diminished just because the best times were clocked in the trials. Race position for some athletes thus becomes measurable in terms of their chances which they regard as "beautiful" or disadvantageous.

In skiing, again, especially the giant slalom when gates are approached at 25 to 30 m.p.h., coarse snow and temperature conditions can place unexpected demands on racers, obliging them to adjust their speed accordingly. "Winning," Billy Kidd is reported as saying, "is mostly who's best at handling all the variables."

Race-car tracks are meticulously inspected and cleaned prior to races because at flat-out speeds, the smallest piece of debris or trash on the track can produce disaster. For the race-driver, the environment (his space) begins with the machine that surrounds him, yet paradoxically, it is also part of him. The reaction of the race-driver to the eventuality of loss of control on the track is summarized by Bruce McLaren in *Life,* August 7, 1970:

> When you do get into trouble, or see trouble ahead, you do two things. You immediately realize you are frightened but you dismiss it. Then, if your car is going to go off the track, you try to pick the softest place to aim for—between the trees rather than at them. And you start concentrating on controlling the car, not necessarily by just putting on the brakes, because the first thing that happens if you put the brakes on hard is that you lock your wheels and can't steer the car. You also have to turn, and this is more important. It is part of the racing driver's stock-in-trade. (p. 34)

The poise that the athlete has to display in these conditions both separates himself from the machine and unites himself with it. The power of the machine, out of control, can destroy the athlete; the athlete does not want to be destroyed, he loves his sport too much, and so where lack of control mechanically looks hazardous, he compensates with quick and ready knowledge and actions from his repertoire of emergency contingencies. He relies less on luck, and by his success, shows what a beautiful driver he is. Spin-outs, like other recoverable accidents, mature the athlete. Maturity is confidence.

Props, the second criterion for poise, refer to the fixed surroundings, to what Gross and Stone call the "decor." We might consider several examples in sports. In boxing, the athlete who uses the ropes (fixtures) to rebound, as Muhammad Ali did in taking the world heavyweight championship away from George Foreman in Zaire in 1974, employs the ropes as props to his advantage and therefore adds to his poise. His use of the ropes is beautiful. Norman Mailer, reporting on the first Ali-Frazier matchup for *Life,* March 19, 1971, wrote:

> So Ali lay on the ropes and wrestled him off, and moved his arms and waist, blocking punches, slipping punches, countering with punches—it began to look as if the fight would be written on the ropes. (p. 32)

Most typically, however, the boxer against the ropes has lost his poise, and, unless he regains it, he has lost his beauty as a fighter, at least temporarily. A more general case to illustrate the beauty of sport employing space and props can be seen in the airborn catch made by a wide-receiver who just manages to touch his feet in-bounds or in-goal before his momentum carries him out-of-bounds. Changes in climate, the heavy downpour, high winds, and similar weather factors become unpredictable props in sport. Thus, when Green Bay played a division-clinching game on their own field in minus 15 degree weather, the opinion was generally held that such conditions favored them better than it did their opponents from a milder clime.

The third criterion of poise is *equipment*. Equipment is distinguishable from props, and in sport it means just what it usually means in sport—equipment (excluding clothing). Thus in football, the lines on the field are props, yet the ball is equipment; in sailing, the yacht is equipment, the wind and the condition of the surface of the water are props. Thus, the equipment can hold up to sustain the poise of the athlete which might be lost if he finds he cannot cope with the conditions imposed by the props. We can state the example of Seagren, at the XXth Olympiad in 1972, who showed that he was embarrassed from two aspects by the necessity to use the "official" pole. As sport equipment it interfered with his technique, and as social equipment he employed it to thrust his embarrassment at the officials. He lost poise in both settings, but perhaps in his own view he had lost both in his sports performance and had nothing more to lose.

An expertly thrown discus is a beautiful action, and many beautiful throws took place at the 1975 Pan-American Games in Mexico City; yet the overall discus event was spoiled by the action of officials who "turned a blind eye" to the Cuban competitor who used his own discus to obtain a silver medal, forcing Jay Sylvester into third place. (Sylvester later appealed this action.)

Socially, state Gross and Stone, "equipment can range from words to physical objects (moved about, handled, or touched), and a loss of control over such equipment is a frequent source of embarrassment." The tauntings of Ali at pre-fight weigh-ins and the like are equipment he uses to distress his opponent, to reduce the poise of the opponent and therefore to build an edge on him during the fight. The opponent with "class" ignores such equipment. Norman Mailer once described Muhammad Ali as "the fighter who invented the psychology of the body." He meant by this that Ali employed techniques to upset the poise of his opponent. Mailer cites a classic example in his *Life,* March 19, 1971, article:

> Ali taunted black majestic king-size Liston before the fight and after the fight. "You're so ugly that I don't know how you can get any uglier." "Why don't you sit on my knee and I'll feed you your orange juice," Liston would rumble back.
>
> "Don't insult me, or you'll be sorry. 'Cause you're just an ugly slow bear."
>
> They would pretend to rush at one another. They were building the gate for the next fight. (p. 28)

Mailer states that Ali "knew that a fighter who had been put in psychological knots before he got near the ring had already lost half, three-quarters, no, all of the fight could be lost before the first punch."

In the novel, *The Natural,* Bernard Malamud writes about the baseball skills of Roy Hobbs. Hobbs' great skill is as a hitter, but we are told that the bat he uses was carved from a willow tree which had been struck by lightning. The inference that there are "other-world" powers operating in its use is of interest to us when we note that the Classical Greek mythology is replete with examples of such equipment. There is no doubt that social value derives from sport value in any particular piece of equipment. Who has touched Hank Aaron's bat or Johnny Bench's glove? The beauty of sport can occasionally be examined through anthropological consideration, particularly in light of the mythical significance of the modern athletic hero.

The effect felt by *clothing,* the fourth criterion of poise, is for the athlete a crucial part of his composure. The appearance of clothing must be maintained and controlled for coherent communication purposes. This is the reason for distinctive uniforms for teams, as well as the color adding to the beauty of the game. But when two English rugby teams play in the worst of muddy conditions so that their separate identities get lost under the mud, all sense of communication gets lost visually and the game degenerates through lack of recognition as much as by poor play. Golfers are particularly meticulous in their dress, and the dress code for horsemen is explicitly stated. The officials at football and boxing check the shoes for cleats and the gloves for loose laces. Yastrzemski constantly adjusts his hat and the fit of his shirt over his shoulders whenever he is at bat. You could say it was nervousness, but when he connects for a homer, he is a beautiful hitter; and he hits homers only when he feels his clothing is comfortable.

The fifth criterion of poise is the *body*. The social role of the body, as expounded by Gross and Stone hardly bears consideration in our exposition. Total body control and the readiness to act are part of the natural makeup of the athlete. Body poise is by definition athletic, a good muscle tone supporting a sound posture. The social communication that this imparts is always evident, according to Gross and Stone. In the athletic role, however, body poise is a constant feature of good performance. When two good athletes confront each other in an one-on-one situation, the man with the better body poise, whether offense or defense, will upset his opponent. Superlative body poise in the athletic arena is what we call beautiful.

EFFORT

Like the other nondefinitive parameters, effort claims the distinction of our recognition to the extent that we can speak of physical or social effort and agree on what we mean. If we try to set definitive limitations on the term, we are forced into analogies with the expression of power. Effort is energy expenditure, both directed and misdirected, individual and collective. We speak of "war effort" and "industrial effort," and usually associate it with a broad thrust of purpose for grand ends. In the best sense of the term, "team spirit" in sport means "collective effort."

Effort, for Laban and Lawrence (1947), meant attitude toward particular components of movement. Effort provides for the analysis of movement, taking into consideration *weight* (strength and lightness), *space* (directness or flexibility), *time* (suddenness or sustainment), and *flow* (bound or free quality). Laban originated the use of these variables for the analysis of physical movement as expression, particularly for dance and theatrical movement. Recognizing that sport usually demands the extremes of man's dynamic capacities, we might be tempted to reject the breadth of possibility for analysis that is provided by weight, space, time, and flow. However, we are reminded that *strength* (weight), *speed* (space), *precision* (time) and *flow* are all dealt with in this book. The student is referred again to these sections of the text as well as to the original writings of Laban and his associates. In some respects, the student will detect that effort is a fine link concept between the nondefinitive and definitive terms that we have identified. Furthermore, the sense of effort in R. Tait McKenzie's *The Joy of Effort,* substantiates the power of the poetic over the scientific, expressing a demand that the nondefinitive term be given equal if not greater weight in the analysis of the beauty of sport.

THE JOY OF EFFORT

The primary purpose of analyzing *The Joy of Effort* by R. Tait McKenzie is to take an artistic term and to apply scientific inquiry to it at least to the point where measurement techniques might appear to become necessary. In other words, by closely looking at it both as an art-work and as a poetic idea, we shall be forced to that position of impasse where science and art meet, or fail to meet. Words have meaning for the cultural transference of communication between people; art-work has the same function. In *The Joy of Effort* we find the message being transmitted through both media, the word and the art-work. One question we might ask in our search for aesthetic meaning in sport is: How true is the message of McKenzie's *The Joy of Effort?* By our examining this question closely, it should reveal the symbolic meaning it conveys and the relationship it has to athletic achievement (Plate 8b).

The Joy of Effort is one of six athletic plaques in a list of 283 works of sculpture executed by R. Tait McKenzie. The original plaque, measuring 46 inches in diameter, was set in the stadium wall at Stockholm in 1913 to commemorate the 1912 Olympic Games. Pendleton (1970) describes it as "a graceful depiction of three hurdlers skillfully portrayed in, but not restricted to, a circular form."

Being poetically conceived, the title *The Joy of Effort* is artistically apropos to the work. One other of the six plaques was given a poetic title: *Brothers of the Wind*. This provides a clue to the truly basic *artistic* nature of McKenzie, who could just as easily have titled his works with more patently descriptive names. McKenzie is reputed to have described the rippling muscles of struggling wrestlers as "the artistry of effort."

Etymological history is replete with examples of shifts in concept and meaning of words over time. "Sport" is one such word; it has shifted its meaning from something equivalent to frolic and light entertainment in pre-industrialized society to agonistic contest in mass society. "Joy" and "effort," however, have retained their early cognitive associations, irrespective of the contextual limitations placed upon them. Since the global interpretation of the term "joy" conveys many facets of human experience, we should guard against specifying that patterns of physiological reaction are clearly identifiable as visceral responses of excitement. Baxter's (1660) elaboration of the concept of joy obtains strength from its association with such words as "meekness, humility, forbearance, self-denial, and mercifulness." There is no "glory" or "self-gratification" associated with the true experience of joy, just as connotations of "victory" and "triumph" are totally unwarranted. This comes remarkably close to underlying assumptions about "sportsmanship" and *areté*. A similar conceptualization pervades the interpretation given to "joy" by Schutz (1969) in the concept of "personal functioning," a *credo* which must appeal quite favorably to physical educators of a phenomenological turn of mind:

> . . . Joy also arises from the full development of personal functioning. The parts of the body may be taught and trained, exercised and sharpened. The senses may be made more acute to discriminate smells and sights. Strength and stamina can be increased in the muscles. Sensory awareness and appreciation can be awakened so that more sensitivity to bodily feelings and natural events can be developed. Motor control can be cultivated so that development of mechanical and artistic skills result, and coordination and dexterity improve. (pp. 16–17)

Interpreting phenomenological analyses, Herbert (1969) deduces that "joy contains a hint of infinity, a hint of eternity. Even when its source is strictly temporary . . . it carries with it the perfection of a moment which is eternal." The mystical interpretation of joy describes the experience as being so powerful that it makes life worthwhile, as rarely as that may occur, and the identification of the mystic with his experience takes the individual outside of time and space, gives him a oneness with a world perceived as a single rich, live entity (Bouet, 1948). By contrast, an experience of aesthetic pleasure characterized as joy might make a whole world out of one small unit or object. More pragmatically, Maslow (1965) characterizes such experience as constituting a process he calls "self-actualization," a process deriving from "peak-experiences." Blanchard (1970) interprets Maslow's peak-experiences as "a radical, instantaneous, global reorganization within the individual." Maslow contends that peak-experiences are relatively infrequent, and that they are difficult to produce or deliberately pursue at will. The peak-experience, then, is clearly distinguishable from joy, which ostensibly can be produced as a result of physical effort in sport.

Herbert's view that several terms are required to do justice to the qualitative and quantitative differences in mood which the broad emotional concept of joy covers, can be countered by reference to Reuning (1941). Herbert cites such words as "pleasure, gratification, happiness, elation, and ecstasy" in support of his viewpoint, which Reuning is able to categorize, respectively, as "neutral," "static," "neutral," "kinetic," and, in the case of ecstasy, both "strongly kinetic" and "trance." As Ryle (1963) points out, there exist certain *feelings* which are associated with *moods,* such as might be expressed in "a surge of joy." Since joy is relativistic and is understood only in terms of another idea or experience, then the term "effort" must imply certain sensations or feelings contributive to the mood *joy.*

Eberlein (1918) believes that McKenzie's empathies with the Hellenic spirit were brought out as a result of his own self-motivated "Spartan" or ascetic lifestyle:

> The Greeks did not divorce mind and muscle. They gladly dedicated their bodily strength and grace to the honor and service of the gods. They honored Zeus and Apollo with races and wrestling, the action and beauty of trained bodies. The gods gave their blessing by enhancing that beauty and grace and filling them with divine euphoria. This exaltation of spirit resulting from gymnastic exercises and the deep respiration that went with the activity imparted a feeling akin to divine happiness. (p. 167)

Eberlein further recounts the difficulties the sculptor placed on himself in his attempts to reconcile his understanding of the Greek concept of the athlete with his own concept of the modern American athlete, the ideal of which he attempted to represent in sculptured form. This perfectionist attitude toward his work is given further embellishment by Holbrook (1967), who states:

> McKenzie's figures in art truly portray something that people can understand and sympathize with for their representation, their quality, and their realism combined with idealism. Not only do the modeled figures please the public taste but they stand the test of the practiced critic's eye. (p. 33)

Almost certainly, McKenzie would have subscribed to the Delphic idea that self-discovery derives from the experience of joy *through effort*. He would have found it more difficult, perhaps, to accept the Schutz theory, and may have regarded it as pseudo-active in its nature. McKenzie may have had difficulty resolving Classical Greek and modern American concepts of the athlete, but he was not unaware that the Greeks held agonistic contest in high esteem or that they were physically prepared for the effort demanded in combat and war. Superlative effort would be more likely to result in joy, he might argue, than would be effected merely by searching for improved sensory awareness through exercise.

But the discussion of joy focuses precisely on the stated impasse where art and science meet or fail to meet. Joy, as a concept, is more acceptable to the artist than to the scientist; the artist is prepared to equate joy with the knowledge of aesthetic awareness, his own area of study and interest, whereas the scientist (who may recognize the feeling of joy resulting from his work), intrinsically and by training, seeks to understand causal and other relationships for the satisfaction of his inquisitive nature. This applies equally for the behavioral and social scientist or for the natural scientist. McKenzie was that admirable human conclusion, a cultured scientist and man of letters. He *understood* the joy of effort both poetically and scientifically.

In an analogy with the experience of scientific insights (intense intellectual awareness), which is described as being essentially passive, Blanchard (1970) provides an interpretation for man seeking the joy of effort through sport in which "joy" takes on definitive aesthetic attributes. He says:

> It appears to be an experience in which his ego, personality or character, as we commonly use these terms, are not operative. Later, however, when he interprets such an experience, a man's own personal style may become manifest. He may proceed to express or utilize his experience mathematically, in stone, in words, or *in wonderful action.* (p. 10) [Italics added.]

Relating joy with the notion of effort in a definitive context helps to focus attention on particular aspects of the concept, but since not everyone's bodily activity can be said to be identical, the emotional nature of such activity may be very different between individuals. Assuming the concept of success to be a constituent part of joy, a winner of a race may experience a surge of joy concomitant with the climactic (moment) of recognition of that success, yet sometime later, mounting the podium to receive a medal, may have a similar experience of joy. Clearly, the physiological conditions attendant relative to time and place are different. Allport (1955) related feelings of pleasure with excitation of the parasympathetic nervous system, and feelings of displeasure with excitation of the sympathetic nervous system. He speculates, as do Genasci and Klissouras (1966), that the pleasure derived from physical activity and exertion in sport are due to the unimpeded conduction of nerve impulses from the body periphery. This speculation leads to the posing of typical questions, such as: Are there measurable differences between the heart rates of the winner and a loser in a race which might be associated with success? Do differences occur in the alpha rhythms of those who claim an elation through sports effort, compared with those whose sports efforts are otherwise motivated and experienced? Would galvanic skin response measures provide clues to differences? These are the questions for which science seeks the answers. Advances in technology will allow those measures to be made which will solve the mystery of the joy of effort.

The speculation by Genasci and Klissouras, that athletes "have a feeling for the beauty of their movement creations but are often unable to explain their love of creating this kind of beauty," reflects the kind of thought that might have been attributed to McKenzie. If "catharsis" is what Genasci and Klissouras call "purification," then this concept is accounted for in the transcience of the fleeting moments in which joy and self-discovery are both attained, simultaneously and spontaneously, through effort. Attempting to specify the spatio-temporal locus of the effect, by its very nature, restricts or impedes definitive recall in detail. This is so, both behaviorally and dispositionally.

Pursuant to this, questions raised by interpreting *The Joy of Effort* as representing *aesthetic* value in the personal experiential sense demand that the literature reporting empirical findings relative to this interpretation be given closer scrutiny. Alderman (1970), employing Kenyon's (October 1968) attitude inventory with 136 Canadian champion athletes, 81 male and 55 female, demonstrated that "male athletes showed a surprising strength of attitude toward physical activity as an aesthetic experience."

A close examination of R. Tait McKenzie's *The Joy of Effort* reveals a depth of meaning which eludes exact explication. Perhaps a title of a sport-related sculpture has poetic immunity, but the significance of the term serves as a challenge to those who seek meaning in sport. However, the relevance of *The Joy of Effort* for sport extends beyond the sculptural and poetic, and directs attention to empirical research in the social psychology of sport.

Effort, of course, is a nondefinitive factor in the symbolic communication of the beauty of sport, and thus it is not surprising that it has greater poetic value (like gracefulness and harmony) than analytic value. However, as was stated earlier, it is the ideal concept to serve as a link between discussions of the nondefinitive and the definitive parameters in the study of the beauty of sport.

s u m m a r y

In this chapter, the principal focus of discussion centers on the validity of nondefinitive terms usually employed in the description of beautiful sports action. The list of words examined here is not exclusive, but rather representative of the most typical descriptors used when human movement is analyzed for its aesthetic components. Implicitly, this chapter recommends that an empirical approach be taken to fully test the construct validity of such terms. As symbols in the communication process they appear to be "tried, tested, and true."

Starting with the concept of unity, an attempt is made to discuss words which appear to have a logical sequence. In this exercise, Chapter 6 is presented as one-half of a total unit on symbolic communication, Chapter 7 being the other half—the definitive parameters. While it is believed that a spectrum of ideas is embraced by the total unit, from "unity" (the opening section of Chapter 6) to "strategy" (the closing section of Chapter 7), there is no claim that the spectrum is pure, either in content or in weighting. Several flaws present themselves in the discussion, perhaps the most noteworthy being the deduction that "rhythm" is synonymous with "harmony" in the final analysis. This deduction suggests at least two lines of thought: (1) that the discussion of nondefinitive terms is a spurious exercise, and (2) that further inquiry, empirically sponsored, is the next logical step. The one acknowledges a hollowness, the other a challenge.

Some of the nondefinitive terms lend themselves to interpretation by physical law, others by reference to anthropological analysis of myth. Perhaps this is as much a function of the fact that some of the terms have validity in the physical sciences as they have in poetic application to beauty (humanism). Overall, however, we find the physical use or explanation to be nonconstructive in seeking foundation for the validity of the poetic use. Our conclusions, in some instances, suggest that the poetic use of a term in symbolic communication is more powerful than its scientific use. While this assertion may be challenged as being too value-loaded in a favored direction, the observation does at least retain some salutory significance for our purpose in the cross-disciplinary analysis of the beauty of sport.

Lastly, the so-called "cutoff" point separating Chapter 6 and Chapter 7 needs to be considered. Is it arbitrary, or is there a feature of the spectrum which now begins to show evidence of the shift of emphasis toward "the other end"? The spectrum of ideas is a conceptual whole, not necessarily clearly formulated but retaining much flexible alternation for abstraction. Yet, one-half is designated "nondefinitive" and the other "definitive." Here again we touch upon the potential for flaws to appear in our analysis, for the discussion of "poise" in this chapter might be classified as perfectly definitive under the sponsorship of Gross and Stone (1964). Thus, in each instance, the introductory remarks of both Chapters 6 and 7 are important to the student wishing to know more about symbolic communication of the beauty of sport.

questions for discussion

1. What does the term "symbolic communication" mean, and why is it a valuable concept for the study of sport?
2. Discuss the way in which symmetry was such a fundamental factor for the Classical Greeks in their concept of the Unity of Design. Express the best points of this discussion in relation to what we detect as the beauty of sport.
3. Are the concepts "rhythm" and "harmony" synonymous, or does the study of sports action focus attention on some subtle differences?
4. What is "dynamic form"?

5. State the five component concepts defining poise in human behavior and give examples of how poise is beautiful in the sport setting.
6. How does Laban categorize effort, and what does his categorization tell us about component elements of the beauty of sport?
7. Should *The Joy of Effort* be subjected to scientific analysis? How would a construct analysis of this phrase add to our knowledge?

Symbolic Communication: Definitive Parameters

"You would defend the game, of course, since you excel in it. That is what you love, Bellarion; to excel; to wield mastery."

"Do we not all? Do not you, yourself, madonna, glory in the power your beauty gives you?"

RAFAEL SABATINI, *Bellarion*

INTRODUCTION

The acquisition and recognition of symbols is the statement of our knowledge. When we see or hear things that we do not fully comprehend, even when we think we recognize them, we respond either with a sense of curiosity, or with a sense of humility or fear, or with the experience of emotional and cognitive uncertainty usually described as "awe." We are awed equally by the mysterious, which we cannot comprehend, and by the superlative, which we think we can comprehend. These responses have been common to all men since prerecorded time and have been the basis of much ancient myth. This phenomenon was known by the eighteenth-century philosopher David Hume (1964), who wrote:

> There is commonly an astonishment attending every thing extraordinary; and this astonishment changes immediately into the highest degree of esteem or contempt, according as we approve or disapprove of the subject. (p. 166)

Hume was speaking in a new "age of enlightenment" and his observations presaged much that later developed into psychology, the study of the behavior of man. The behavioral sciences of today still cannot fully explain "awe," yet it continues to manifest itself in man, no less so than when he witnesses superlative athletic achievement.

195

Sport is one of the domains for the search for and expression of the superlative. The Greeks of Ancient Hellas were cognizant of this, as shown by their art, literature, and philosophy. Their gods represented specialized forms of human behavior, usually value-based, and served the purpose of demonstrating superlative qualities. Also, the gods were modeled in the image of the *idealized athletic form,* hence the gods were that much better than man, even as athlete, could attain. He could aspire to that degree of perfection because it was recognizable but, being perfection, it was awesome, just out of reach. We owe our cultural heritage to the Greeks, and especially to their artists, for the recognition of the symbol of ideal man. Today we claim to have a more sophisticated comprehension of the forces of life and the universe, yet there are still experiences which we regard with wonder and awe. Paul Weiss, in his book, *Sport: A Philosophic Inquiry,* states very succinctly the obsession that man has with that which borders on the incomprehensible, and he puts that obsession into comparable terms in the world of sport:

> We read with awe of explorers, climbers, sailors, and trappers who kept on acting, or just living, despite extreme thirst, hunger, injury, disease, cold, and enemies, both natural and human. While engaged in some other activity, they incidentally revealed man maintaining himself for a while against the background of a remorseless time. Because we want to know at what point failure inexorably arrives, we take note of such unusual cases of endurance, even when some other result is the main issue. They tell us what man's ultimate boundaries are. The results achieved in a contest will normally fall far short of what these heroic figures accomplished, but the contest will teach us something that these men could not —what men can do in well-defined situations, governed by impersonal rules and a presumably humane set of conditions. (pp. 120–121)

Perhaps the most explicit of traditional values recognized as contributing to the beauty of sport are grace, harmony, form, flow and similar terms of acceptable significance, as discussed in the preceding chapter. The language of these terms is culturally sound and therefore "unquestionable"—often, a student will discourse on the inherent assumption that such terms are unchallengeable.

To enter into argument on the meanings of such terms as grace, harmony, speed, power, and the like is seen by many as an affront to the true sense of discourse. Some students will argue forcefully using "beauty" as a term of sound premise; taking the stance that, "If you don't know what beauty means, you should not be in the discussion!" Beauty, as a given, is for texts other than this one. Beauty as grace, speed, form, power, harmony, and strength moves us one step closer to what we are searching for. To be told: "The most arresting aesthetic feature of sport *is* the grace of the human form" (Kupfer, 1975) is an interesting, if speculative opinion—one with which we might agree or disagree. However, when Kupfer (1975) elaborates on it by stating, "Economy and efficiency of effort is accomplished in movement which is continuous and fluid; [and] sport provides us distinct balletic values," he excites our curiosity by putting "grace" into behavioral focus to some limited extent. The picture is still fuzzy, but the image of explanation appears to be taking better definition. To play "Devil's advocate" for a moment, one might argue that graceful weightlifting hardly bespeaks "economy" of effort, but in most cases agreement can be made with the sense implied. Thus, we are brought to a discussion of the definitive terms identified for their value in seeking to explain or otherwise account for the beauty of sport.

It is perhaps presumptuous to claim that strength, speed, and power are descriptive of the beauty of sport, yet such presumption does two things, at least. In the first place it offers a challenge to the thinking student who will be prepared to enter the argument (in the Greek sense), and may sponsor from him sounder discourse less dependent on presumption and more grounded on premise. From such lines of discussion we can all learn. Secondly, and as an outcome of the first effect, it will provide new criteria for consideration due to the strength of argument and discourse stressing either the resiliency or the weakness of those terms offered here.

The essence of the Greek attitude toward perfection is recorded in poetry, sculpture, and ceramics. For athletic events to have so inspired artistic production such as the *Iliad* of Homer, the sculpture of Praxiteles, and the nameless potters of vases, amphorae, and kraters decorated with athletes, we can deduce that there must have been an aesthetic association made with athletic performance (see Plates 5–8). How that aesthetic association was interpreted is beyond our speculation here except insofar as folkloric importance might have been granted to particular concepts. Was "strength" beautiful for the Greeks? Did they perceive "speed" and "fleetness" as qualities of the beauty of athletics? What features of athletics inspired the Greeks with a sense of beauty? Greek mythology would have us accept that such concepts were inspirational from an aesthetic standpoint, but that is a matter of interpretation, not scientific veracity. The major lesson we can learn from the Greeks is that strength, power, speed, precision, and the like were significant to them; they were ideals to which the Greeks aspired. The Greeks made attempts to explain these phenomena by reference to mystical entities and to the mathematics of proportion (see Chapter 1). The values represented by these ideals sponsored the earliest scientific inquiries made by man. But first they found substance and meaning in mythology.

How do we relate to this precept today? Surely we are closer to understanding the physical and psychological limits of human ability, and we expect to advance in our knowledge through both improved reason and improved technology. Nowhere is this more patent in sport than in the thinking of the innovative coach. Man's abilities are not necessarily sport-specific, and the broader a coach casts his net for ideas on speed, strength, power, precision, strategy, and other manifestations of human capacity, the more likely he is to stay ahead of his field. Such a coach is found in the person of Warren Witherell. In his text on ski-racing, Witherell (1972) recommends a new approach to learning how the body can best obtain the elements of balance and speed *from other sports*. Stating that all previous skiing techniques have been either "stylish" or commercial, he reinforces his belief in a new mode of learning: "Coaches must learn from the experience of other sports—like gymnastics, figure-skating, water-skiing, track and field, fancy diving, modern dance, etc." It is significant that he cites some of the "form-sports" as his major source for new notions of ski-racing, particularly when ski-racing, by definition, rests on speed as the major operative concept.

CULTURAL ANTECEDENTS

More and more today we are made conscious of human potential for achievement. Sport, or athletic competition, as Keenan (1975) reminds us, "qualifies as art as it raises the limits of insight and expectancy and [creates] ever new levels of human achievement." The role of the superior athlete is given greater cultural significance through media exposure and the attention paid to him by psychologists of sport (Vanek and Cratty, 1970).

The common cultural elements of sport and art, claims Whorf (1971), lie in the concept of kinesthesia:

> It would seem as if kinesthesia, or the sensing of muscular movement, though arising before language, should be made more highly conscious by linguistic use of imaginary space and metaphorical images of motion. Kinesthesia is marked in two facets of European culture: art and sport. European sculpture, and art in which Europe excels, is strongly kines-thetic, conveying great sense of the body's motions; European painting likewise. The dance in our culture expresses delight in motion rather than symbolism or ceremonial, and our music is greatly influenced by our dance forms. Our sports are strongly imbued with this element of the "poetry of motion." (p. 155)

With these comments, Whorf touches upon the reason why we delight in speed, power, and strength in sports. The symbolic function of these factors is as real to us as they were to the Greeks of Ancient Hellas, but their interpretation is different for us today. Whereas for the Greeks they represented a religious significance of proximity with a pseudo-abstract entity (the gods), the closest representation given today, by interpretation, is with technology. Both interpretations are equally speculative since they reflect figurative reasoning stemming from symbolic meaning based on fundamentally cultural values. Aspin (1974) writes of sports performances and activities in Whiting and Masterson:

> [They] are seen and appraised by us as a sub-set within the general class of "values" (the activity falling within the category of valuation), and in which certain terms, such as beautiful, classical, graceful, elegant, powerful, skillful, clever, economical, sparse, effortless, and so on, typically function as standards of excellence that are characteristic of, and operate within, the various diverse *genres* of artistic activity and production. (p. 132)

We can test the truth of this for the Greeks by reference to the art-work of Ancient Hellas (Gardiner, 1930). There will remain some margin of error, since we must interpret our deductions cross-culturally as well as historically. The discussion on *strength,* on the following pages, illustrates this difficulty. But we know that the Greeks pursued "excellence"; that they equated "excellence" with "beauty"—or with strength, grace, harmony, power, speed, and form—is interpretable by us only insofar as they held these as values. We can enter the Classical Greek mind only through their art and their literature, their ideas and their social system. Beyond that, we must ask ourselves: How much of the Greek heritage have we absorbed into our own systems of cultural perception? How far do we know that what they held as beautiful is so held by us today? The answers to these questions are of less importance than the warning they give for us to be on our guard against gross overassumptions. In the same vein, we may suppose that we know what values are held in society today. This supposition is only as sound as our knowledge of ourselves and of our values allows us to be. The value premise that we hold for this text, namely that sport is beautiful, would not find acceptance among a measurable proportion of the population. Furthermore, the proposition that speed, strength, precision, and power can be interpretable as component elements of that beauty is intended to be challenging.

CITIUS, ALTIUS, FORTIUS

Whatever the values held for beauty and excellence, speed and power, or strength and harmony, in Classical Greek culture, there do exist references to be drawn from modern man. We may turn to de Coubertin and to R. Tait McKenzie, as two notable figures cognizant of the aesthetic attributes of sport, for our endorsement of such valuation by modern man. De Coubertin gave the motto "Citius, Altius, Fortius" (Swifter, Higher,

Stronger) in support of his reinstitution of the Olympic Games, and while the historical justification for this motto may be rooted in his belief that a resurgent France would find its strength in major athletic competition, he was of the firm conviction that such ideals contained aesthetic overtones (Höhne, 1969). R. Tait McKenzie contributed "Celeritas, Agilitas, Fortitudo, Aequitas" (Speed, Agility, Courage, Fair Play) to the language of athletic achievement. These words appear on *The Olympic Shield of Athletic Sports,* executed by R. Tait McKenzie in 1928. Christopher Hussey, the biographer of R. Tait McKenzie, describes this work as "the apotheosis of the athletic ideal, an epitome of the track and field sports of the modern Olympic Games." Besides the many finely modeled figures decorating the shield, there are seven basic concepts and an epigram inscribed. The seven basic concepts are Citius, Altius, Fortius, Celeritas, Agilitas, Fortitudo, and Aequitas. The inscribed epigram reads, "Mens Fervida in Corpore Lacertoso" (An eager mind in a lithe body). The seven basic concepts provide for the student basic ideas for exploration of the beauty of sport hitherto not found in the literature (see Plate 9).

The description of *The Olympic Shield of Athletic Sports* by Hussey (1929) is as follows:

> In the centre is shown the Spirit of Olympia, helmeted and garbed in archaic drapery. Her outstretched hands are bringing together two athletes representative of the modern Olympic revival, who shake hands in token of the friendly spirit in which athletic competition should be conducted.
>
> These figures are in high relief and are surrounded by a laurel wreath and border. Immediately encircling this are panels depicting field events: throwing the hammer, casting the javelin, the pole vault, the high jump, putting the shot and scaling the discus, while below are a group of hurdlers in full flight.
>
> Four small octagonal panels containing figures of a broad jumper, an athlete crouching for the standing high jump, and two athletes preparing for competition break the continuity of the border surrounding this panel, a border which contains lettering above and below, with a running ornamental design at the sides.
>
> Above the central medallion is a winged figure. Surrounding the lettered and enriched border is a frieze of runners. In this frieze are nearly one hundred figures, showing every phase of the stride, as well as the starting positions and the finish of the race. Peculiarities of stride or style shown by famous athletes are here displayed, from the long experienced and accurate observation of many years. (pp. 48–49)

The "four small octagonal panels" contain the words "Celeritas," "Agilitas," "Fortitudo," and "Aequitas." These words, translated into English, give us a better sense of what de Coubertin meant by "Faster, Higher, Stronger," and add a socially acceptable dimension. R. Tait McKenzie has served us admirably in our initial steps to make beauty accounted for when we speak of the beauty of sport. Upon his recommendation we will look closer at "speed." From our own deductions, we will inquire further into strength, power and precision.

STRENGTH

The embodiment of strength in man is as old as the story of Hercules, the roots of which are lost in Mycenaean myth. Hercules, the patron of boxers and wrestlers, was also figured in constant combat with Phobos (Fear), illustrated in the decorated center of the shield, as described by Hesiod in the poem "The Shield of Hercules."

The value of strength in man is determined by the agelessness of the mythos in which it is couched. By the time the feats of Hercules were on the lips of people, he was already "the living example of the indomitable human spirit engaged in the never-ending struggle to rise above its own limitations." As the positive example of all human aspirations involving the expression of strength, the power to survive, Hercules was a figure to be emulated. He represented the anthropomorphism of an abstract quality, the full nature of which was incomprehensible to man at that time. Strength in quantity was easily recognizable—in great quantity it was awesome. The poet-storytellers added the rest, finely holding the amount of strength within the cognitive grasp of man, simultaneously singing its virtues and thereby imbuing it with beauty. Homer's *Iliad*, sometimes described as "a poem of force," extols the use of strength that Hercules uses to win recognition from his peers. But this strength is circumscribed by a well-defined discretionary code; namely, he cannot win glory through his strength without deference to a code of honor. There is procedure in his displays of strength; they are not merely unbridled expressions of force—which even in Homer's time was differentiated as violence and denigrated as an asocial or immoral act. The beauty of strength, then, was (and is) viewed within the social milieu. Society grants strength the prescription of beauty according to the code of values that pertain for social order.

Even in the recognition of strength as beauty there dwells a paradox, as evident to the Greeks as to us today. The embodiment of strength in Hercules was his birthright as the son of Zeus, who in turn was the son of Kronos (Creator of Chaos). Both Achilles and Odysseus, heroes of the *Iliad* and *Odyssey* respectively, visited with Hercules in the underworld and obtained his respect for the strength that each had. But in each case, the hero was meeting with a demi-god, man transformed to god through the recognition of his superlative powers and deeds, a recognition given by both men and gods (in myth). Achilles and Odysseus, in turn, know that they will follow this pattern of canonization. As a group, then, Hercules,

Achilles, and Odysseus comprise a small sample allowing us to make empirical deductions apropos the value attaching to strength in Greek society. They provide us with a model of the place and role of the strong man, and the paradox of their grandeur is noted in their strength, for each lives a life of loneliness at the pinnacle of society. The mythopoeic quality of strength is manifest in them. Today, we find the same paradox of strength allied with loneliness in the role of the world champion athlete. None can beat him, but the transitory nature of his success is understood, for sports are seasonal, challengers numerous, and the memory short. Repeat performances of championship success based on strength recommend athletes for enshrinement in Halls of Fame but athletic feats of magnitude are restricted to the very few, and their names persist in the folk culture. However, the heroes of sport in industrial society lack Homeric substance.

The discussion on ideal form and the beauty of the physical structure of the athlete adds to our perception of the potential for strength as beauty. The muscled torso, arms, and legs depicted in sculpted form contribute the vision of the artist to what we perceive as the potential ability for strength embodied in the athlete (see Plate 2). The Greek sculptors illustrated this in their work and it is found also in the work of Rodin and Joseph Brown.

Strength transformed into power by the application of speed, as demonstrated by Muhammad Ali or by a finely constructed Formula I racing-car driven by Jackie Stewart, broadens the scope of the interpretation of power as beauty. We know that power is the product of strength and speed, so before we look at power as beauty, we will turn to "speed."

SPEED

In some measure, speed can be interpreted as hereditary. The speed of contraction of the muscle, and the speed of delivery of the nervous impulse from the motor cortex to the muscle, vary between individuals. "Speed," says Floyd Patterson, ex-heavyweight boxing champion of the world, "separates the superstars from the stars."

Speed in humans, like speed in animals or in machines, is a fascination. The "fastest human" has true symbolic significance, although Lewis Mumford would describe the action of such a person as an "ostentatious display of speed." Conceptually, speed is both relative and absolute—relative due to the fascination man has with time, and absolute in the abstract sense that excellence or perfection is an absolute. The discussion of speed is fraught with trouble, but for some, speed is beautiful. Norman Mailer is one who believes that the speed of the boxer is beautiful; he wrote in *Life* (March 10, 1971):

> Ali worked rounds of dazzling speed, rounds which displayed the high aesthetic of boxing at its best . . . he would flash a tattoo of light and slashing punches, mocking as the lights on water, he would dazzle his sparring partner. (p. 28)

The symbolic nature of speed is attested to by Weiss (1969):

> We are interested in knowing how fast man can run. Later, we may also interest ourselves in knowing the speeds of other living beings, in order to satisfy a scientific curiosity. Long before that time, a knowledge of the speeds of different kinds of beings is wanted in order to enable us to see how man compares and contrasts with other quickly moving beings. Directly or indirectly, we then learn what man is, in a way and to a degree that is not possible by other means. (p. 110).

But the appeal of speed is not just centered in the comparison of man against man. The symbolic power of the concept speed permeates many other features of cultural interest.

"Speed is our god, a new canon of beauty." This phrase is attributed to an Italian artist, Filippo Marinetti, who, writing in 1909, also stated, "A roaring motorcar, which runs like a machine gun, is more beautiful than the *Winged Victory of Samothrace.*" Marinetti was implying that the car is a work of art and can be regarded as mass-produced sculpture. It is not clear whether he was obsessed with racing cars, the style of which was often classic in concept; but speed in the first decade of motor-racing was very much a relative force by today's standards. The artist's interest in speed must be one of his self-selected frustrations. It is difficult enough for him to represent motion in his art, without his imposing on himself the problem of accelerated motion. But the artist who does successfully represent speed in his art is well aware of countervailing elements, and he applies these to his expression of speed within the constraints of his media. The photographer is no less conscious of these elements than is the painter or the sculptor. Interviewed for the Baltimore Museum of Art text, *Man in Sport: An International Exhibition of Photography,* Horst Baumann explained his vision of sports photography:

> I was especially interested in the aspects of design, form and shapes coupled with speed and motion. The fascination with patterns in motion became the basic initiative for my entering this field because a turning wheel at a certain speed in color is something like a kinetic sculpture. In racing, this element is combined with highly dramatic action. (p. 17)

For an aesthetic effect of speed to be impressed upon us, we must be given perceptual evidence denoting lack of balance. To bring home the significance of this precept, it is worth recalling that a still photograph of a Formula I at great speed (see Plate 29) provides little in the way of aesthetic appeal (background blur does not provide it), whereas a picture showing the forward lean of a racehorse down the home stretch, much slower by contrast with the racing car, does have that aesthetic appeal. A newspaper picture of a slide into a stolen base gives an even "faster" impression. Yet, in real terms, a racehorse is at least twice as fast as an athlete at full speed and the Formula I is five times faster than the horse. A better understanding of perceived speed should contribute to our knowledge of the relationship of sport and art.

One of the fastest sports in which man propels himself by his own efforts is skating. The great appeal that League Hockey has for so many people can be found in the speed of the game, and this speed is often caught by the sports photographer. Fortunately, we have access to two works of art by R. Tait McKenzie which allow us some analysis of the concept "speed." These are *Brothers of the Wind* and *Speed,* a bronze medal. Following is Christopher Hussey's (1929) description of the major work, called *Brothers of the Wind:*

> In this frieze McKenzie may again be said to have touched the highest limit of athletic art. Its unquestionable beauty gives it a place of its own among the masterpieces of relief. Skating is an exercise beautiful in itself, and, as has already been remarked, peculiarly well suited to sculpture. But McKenzie's design, whilst taking its rhythm from the movement, possesses high qualities in the abstract. The design is essentially a swift flowing one, and is so handled that the continuity of its rising and falling lines is uninterrupted. They interweave like those bands in ancient northern ornament, the endless untiring linear rhythm of which gradually developed into Gothic art.
>
> Though the design is fully satisfying in itself, it is also cogently composed. A flight of eight skaters is represented in a long-distance race. The two leaders, unsuspecting any immediate rivalry, are skating easily, their heads well up. But a third skater is sprinting, preparatory to taking the lead, his arms swinging like two pendulums, first to the right then to the left, as each leg comes into action. He is closely followed by number four, who has not brought his arms down into the sprinting position, but is "trailing" number three easily—that is, taking the shelter of his wind. The last man is in difficulties, and will doubtless drop behind rapidly. Three others are seen in veiled relief.
>
> The chief line in the composition, in which many others can be traced, begins at the leader's head, and runs via No. 3's lower arm and No. 4's arm to No. 5's heel. A possible break in the line is amended by putting No. 4's hands over No. 5's head. Another line runs more or less along the backs of the figures to the same point. . . . The relief is low, with well defined but softly rounded planes, so that though the dominating lines are clean and distinct, the forms are full and very subtly moulded. As seen in plaster, the veiling of the lowest plane suggests vividly a misty atmosphere while the whiteness of the material implies ice and snow.

These are Brothers of the North Wind, supple, clean-limbed youths, fleeter and more deadly than the blizzard out of which they sweep in unearthly beauty. (pp. 46–47)

Plate 19a illustrates the above description.

But what does it feel like to be a skater, and what are the elements of skating at speed which bring a sense of beauty to the skating athlete? Barbara Lockhart was a world class and Olympian speed skater before becoming a professor of sport studies at Temple University. Asked to describe what it felt like to be a speed skater, she replied:

> Achieving speed in speed skating is a phenomenon that is hard to compare with any other feeling. . . . For instance, there is a real exuberance, a real feeling of joy, of lightness, at one with yourself . . . it's a really ecstatic feeling; you are extremely happy mentally, your body feels it is working for this one effort . . . you get the amount of force, the amount of momentum that you need, and you hit a speed that is phenomenal, and you would never believe you could go that fast . . . the exhilaration that you feel as you just slip across the ice. . . . The amazing thing is that with all the effort you have put into it, at this one point, as you are completely exhilarated by this speed you have generated, it seems effortless. . . . Of course, there are just a few times in a lifetime that you are going to feel speed to this point.

This personalized account adds to the sense of fascination that man has with speed, but it also significantly adds to our understanding of the subjective aesthetic in sport. (See Chapter 8.) This fascination is manifest both in experienced speed (vertigo in physical performance) and in observed speed, which some would suggest has mesmeric appeal.

The speed of the athlete in action has both symbolic beauty and artistic beauty. This appears to hold true more so for one-on-one agonistic confrontations than for group sports or sports dependent on instruments. Boxing is the sport, *par excellence,* in which adulation is expressed for the speed of a man. In 1921 Georges Carpentier fought Jack Dempsey for the heavyweight championship of the world. In the words of Irvin Cobb, the *New York Times* reporter:

> . . . Carpentier shows a flash of the wonderful speed for which he is known. With the speed he couples an unsuspected power, and shakes Dempsey with a volley of terrific right-handed clouts which fall with such speed you do not see them.

The speed of a right jab delivered by Muhammad Ali has been timed at three one-hundredths of a second.

In a *Time* article devoted to Vida Blue, pitcher for the Oakland Athletics, the generalized comment deriving from the opinions of many "sluggers" was that "five feet or so from the plate his fastball picks up speed and 'pops' or 'explodes' past them." Yet Blue is described as having a loose, flowing grace which allows him to "snap off" his pitch with seemingly effortless ease (see Plate 23a). Speed, in this sense, is an elusive force; it can deceive us. The sense of speed of the batter in baseball is given in a description of Claudell Washington of the Oakland Athletics. In another *Time* report it was stated that he "whips his 34-oz. bat across the plate with a fluid, level swing, rifling his line drives in all directions." The notion that the ball speeds away like a bullet is given by the image of "rifling." Similarly, the speed is given added effect by introducing a sense of precision. Accuracy seems to embellish, to add a further dimension to speed. This is not surprising since our common knowledge tells us that going for speed usually takes away from accuracy. Thus, when we see speed highly correlated with accuracy, a sense of mystique permeates our perception of the event. Claudell Washington is also credited with "startling speed" in his base running, particularly when he is stealing base. When Charlie Greene, a sprinter of national rank, spoke of "running on razor blades," he was attempting to give the sensation that a sprinter feels when running the 100-yard dash.

Speed and Risk

The interplay between speed and control is crucial to the understanding of the beauty of sport. Speed with full control is essential for beautiful performance, particularly in skiing. Physical control of self is one aspect, usually the one that championship athletes have least concern with, but another aspect is control of the environment, the external conditions of performance. Most typically, a downhill racer, like a Formula I or Grand Prix racer, will learn the elements of the environment (the terrain, the track, the *piste*) for the likelihood of error. What happens thereafter is subject to immediate changes in condition (lack of fresh snow to cover a worn *piste,* a rainstorm to slick the race-car track), and the athlete is then put on his mettle to employ his physical control for successful maneuvering of the new environmental problems. An excellent example depicting this phenomenon appeared in a *Life,* March 6, 1970, article about Billy Kidd, gold medal winner in the 1970 World Skiing Championships held at Val Gardena:

> Until he saw his time, he thought he had a good run. But coming over two bumps with a steep pitch on the other side, Kidd had hit a stretch of choppy snow where spectators had crossed the track. Traveling at about 65 m.p.h., he was thrown off balance and as he left the ground at one hump, he crossed his skis in the air, landed in more rough snow, almost fell, recovered. He decided this had happened because he was going too fast—that either the course or his skis were faster than

in practice. On that basis, at two critical spots later on, he slowed down. (p. 64)

In auto racing (Formula I, Grand Prix, drag, or stock car), it has been said that "speed is the essence of racing" and that "drivers rate other drivers on how fast they *want* to go." Race driver Sam Posey was quoted as once having said: "There's almost no limit to speed; you can go as fast as your mind lets you." The distinction is clear. Jackie Stewart, the 1974 Formula I World Champion, freely admitted that he would not want to be racing in a stock car championship in which Richard Petty and Glen Yarborough, or A. J. Foyt and Bobby Unser might be seen slip-streaming with less than a car length between them at 180 m.p.h. (see Plate 29b).

Just before he died on June 2, 1970, test-driving one of his own cars, Bruce McLaren was asked to comment on the way he saw automobile racing. McLaren focused on the fine relationship between speed and risk in his commentary "Don't Take That Extra Risk" (*Life,* August 7, 1970):

> The challenge for a driver is always to see if you can go that little bit faster and still come out of the corner with everything pointing in the right direction, and perhaps to outthink or outwit the driver alongside you, or just plain outdrive him as you go into the corner. Another challenge is to be sober enough not to take—or to have the courage not to take—that extra risk at the wrong time, just for the glory. The fear is what will happen if you do. (p. 34)

The equation that risk implies is one where speed and accuracy must be seen as separate components, but this separation becomes more blurred with the probability ratio specifying the success of outcome of any given action. Stated another way, success is indirectly proportional to risk, and risk is directly proportional to the inverse relationship of speed and accuracy. We can explore this fine relationship between speed and risk. Speed for the sake of a record being entered in the *Guinness Book of World Records,* or the speed associated with the efforts of man to test the physical limits of some machine, is fraught with risk. The potential for a wheeled vehicle to be driven at the speed of sound on the Bonneville Salt Flats sets specific demands on vehicle design calculated to reduce the risk of lift. The potential for lift in such circumstances is reduced by designing the machine so that the laminar flow of air over the exterior surface does not set up severe pressure differentials. We cannot see the effect of compacted air and the force that it exerts, but our experience tells us of its implicit danger. For this reason high-velocity vehicles are designed in a fashion we describe as "streamlined," or, more technically, aerodynamic. Aerodynamic design is often associated with a sense of aesthetic proportion, the beauty of "pure form." However, the fine balance that takes place between opposing forces and stresses introduces an element of risk which is heightened with each new attempt at an increment in speed. In 1961 Donald Campbell, several times holder of the world water-speed record, lost his life when the boat he was piloting, a speedboat fitted with a jet engine, lifted from the surface of Lake Coniston, flipped, and plunged to the bottom. Campbell ran a first lap at 297 m.p.h. and, on entering the gate for the return run, was clocking 305 m.p.h. and gaining speed when the boat lifted. He would have been the first man to have traveled at a speed of 300 m.p.h. on water, and his record would have stood for at least ten years.

The relationship of speed and risk takes a different perspective when, in the competitive sport context, we see a distance of less than a car length separating Richard Petty and A. J. Foyt traveling at 180 m.p.h. on the NASCAR Stock Car race circuit. We identify the follower as "slip-stream-ing," waiting for his chance to "whip" into a lead. The strategy is clear, but the margin for error is so slim as to be breathtaking (see Plate 29b).

In both the foregoing instances, speed-risk for the record, and speed-risk for competition, the parameters defining what we identify as conditions of severe danger hold us spellbound. The less our initiation into the workings of speed exploration or adaptation, the greater our amazement upon perceiving success. It is very often a sense of awe preceding a sense of relief which evokes the exclamation: "Beautiful!"

PRECISION

While precision typically means accuracy, in the sport domain, it can mean speed with control. Precision has a wider embrace of meaning including "timing" and "tuning." Both timing and tuning contribute to the sense of control that is indicative of top-level athletic performance. Control, however, has farther-reaching significance; it is bound with a knowl-edge of equipment as well as a knowledge of self.

Champion athletes know their equipment thoroughly and in many instances prepare their equipment themselves for competition. The top-level athlete usually has custom-made gear designed to his own unique specifications—taste and comfort, as well as fit and performance potential. But the distinguishing feature of the champion is that he brings to his equipment a knowledge of its use. On the basis of experience, he modifies, tunes, adapts, and in other senses assures himself that the equipment will work perfectly for him. Perfect response in the equipment, to his total satisfaction, will bring him his sense of aesthetic accomplishment, whether it be in a "win" or in "self-expression." The case is taken of the world-class skier who takes personal care in waxing his skis early in the morning of the day on which he can fairly analyze snow conditions; who waxes the sides of each ski for more speed once they are edged; who files the steel edges of each ski, carefully leaving parallel ridges running lengthwise along the steel to make the ski track better in a straight line on the runs; who bevels the edge of the ski at the tip so that the ski, when flat, moves more easily across the snow; and who tests the sharpness of the edges with the sensitive parts of the back of the fingers, and uses emery paper to take off too sharp an edge which would grab the snow. All these things Billy Kidd does for himself, not allowing the ski-equipment representative to do it for him, as so many others do. According to the *Life,* March 6, 1970, article:

> I psych myself up by getting my skis in fantastic condition. So, I have that little bit of extra confidence, knowing I have the best prepared skis on the mountain. (p. 56)

The precision is obviously very necessary, particularly when differences in timing of fractions of a second are so important.

The terms "timing," "tuning," and "synchrony" can be read as synonymous for the purpose of seeking explanation of what is beautiful in sport. Tuning the engine of a racing car or Test Trial motorcycle means more than getting an aesthetic sound from the engine. What is music to the ears of a Formula I mechanic may be a cacophonous, intolerable roar to someone else, but the point is made, the layman does not understand the finer elements of engine tuning. In the same respect that a violinist will tune his instrument to obtain the most accurate pitch for the production of his musical experience, so the Formula I mechanic will tune his engine knowing that the best performance, the most beautiful result, will come from it. Like the parts of an engine, the parts of the body can be examined for the way in which they work together to produce highly skilled performance. The greater the skill, the better the timing, and vice versa. This is but one more way of saying that the timing of a movement, the precision of motion of the component parts, leads us closer to the definition of movement as beauty. This is true for the performing arts as much as for sport, for in both, perfection and excellence are the ultimate objectives.

The skilled athlete is conscious of his timing in many facets of his sport. The discus thrower, the tennis player, the wide receiver in football, all know the limits of their own intrinsic timing. *Intrinsic timing* refers to the feeling of kinesthetic coordination in which the parts of the body work together to produce the best result that the athlete can ever expect of himself. Separating the discus thrower from the tennis player and wide receiver is the element of extrinsic timing. *Extrinsic timing* is another way of saying "strategy," the playing of the sense of timing of one athlete against that of another athlete. Extrinsic timing comes into play wherever athletes face each other in conditions of offense and defense. Intrinsic timing is often a great contributor to the successful effect of extrinsic timing. Thus, it could be safely speculated that the quarterback with deficient intrinsic timing will always get "sacked" by the tackle with superlative intrinsic timing (see Plate 26). Such an example in a real game is all the more beautiful to see because the tackle has already disposed of his opposite number, the guard. From the point of view of the tackle, the experience is beautiful perhaps because the experience of sacking a quarterback (who typically is not deficient in intrinsic timing) is a rare and rewarding one.

The rarity of an event in sport can provide us with a definition of the beauty of sport. Double plays in baseball, pick-offs in basketball, interceptions and punt returns leading to touchdowns in football have the particular quality of rarity that comes from extremely precise timing. All sports have some special facets of their performance in which precision decides the outcome.

In Formula I and stock car racing, timing is not restricted to the working of the engine. Often the outcome of a race will depend on the pit crew. Pit crews can make all the difference in a win, especially when it is recalled that 500-mile races can be decided merely by a car length, which is equal to one-tenth of a second. Typically, pit crews can change all the wheels and refill the gas tank in 15 seconds. To do the necessary adjustments in less than 15 seconds is to place your man nearer the winning place than the man whose crew takes longer. This time differential can turn a race around, and the excitement runs high when the pit crew "wins the race" for the driver. The fact that the driver is averaging better than 180 m.p.h. and negotiating all the "real" parts of the race loses significance in light of the crew effort—except that the driver now carries the added burden, to hold the lead given to him.

The focus of precision found in baseball centers on the fact that it is the only game in which two rounded surfaces (ball and bat) must meet at a point where the axes of each must conjoin in a straight line. When the ball is known to be traveling at approximately 100 m.p.h. and the head of the bat only marginally slower, the significance of the precision of a line drive to a designated part of the field is prodigious. The batter has less than one-quarter second to decide the path that his bat must follow to hit the ball, and he has a lateral range not exceeding one-half inch to ensure a good connection. The "sweet-spot" is quantitatively limited in area, and is all the more beautiful due to the infrequency of the occurrence of "finding" it in game play. Recalling what was said about the hitting ability of Claudell Washington (see the previous section, "Speed"), it becomes manifestly clear that his control and precision in having ball meet bat and go where he wants it to go embellish the most flamboyant interpretations of precision as beauty.

There are, of course, a number of sports that can be called "precision sports," such as riflery, golf, and archery. The preceding discussion has been more a dissection of elements than an analysis of the obvious. Shooting at a small target may be an obvious expression of "precision," but we should not deceive ourselves into believing that the exercise is facile. Precision, in these cases, becomes a matter of ballistics enjoining accuracy in the service of speed. The beauty of ballistics is offered to the student for further inquiry. Here, we may consider ballistics as a category of power, "explosive power," and attempt to place it in the correct relation to other categories of power.

POWER

Power, as the concept "potency," has roots in Aristotelian philosophy where it has been recognized for its physical as well as its social laws. In man, and particularly in the citizen-athlete-soldier of Hellas, power finds physical, psychological, and social representation. Physical power was manifest in the order of nature, psychological power was found in the man of honor (citizen-athlete), and social power derived from the political order (sovereignty and law).

Plato put power in the sport context when he said: "In order that we might come as near to reality as possible, instead of cestuses, we should put on boxing gloves that the blows and the wards might be practiced by us to the utmost of our power." Once again, "power" is one of those words which is culturally sound, and therefore may be perfectly applicable to the beauty of sport. However, power is also more complex than strength and speed—one definition of power is: "the product of strength and speed." We must subsume many other concepts, which should aid us in understanding power as beauty.

Power is defined by the Pergamon Press *Concise Dictionary of Physics* as "the rate at which work is performed." Work is "the transfer of energy from one system to another," and the unit of work is the same as the unit of energy. When we see the muscular or sinewy build of an athlete we speak of his "potential energy," implying a similarity to what is defined as potential energy in physics. There is a fine distinction between the perception of power and the exercise of it. "Power has always a reference to its exercise, either actual or probable," states Hume (1964), adding that we fall back on experience in our judgment of the exercise of power. We impute in a person with an athletic-looking body the power that he can perform athletically. It is the probability of a given action occurring that tells us what "power" lies behind it. This sense of potential energy in the athlete is exemplified by McPhee (1970):

> Graebner happens to be as powerful as anyone who plays tennis. . . .
> He is righthanded and his right forearm is more than a foot in circum-

ference. His game is built on power. His backswing is short, his strokes are compact; nonetheless, the result is explosive. (p. 2)

Power, as an idea in man's mind, is a restatement of vitality, of the life process, and therefore is a dynamic entity. With the sense of recognition attaching to the concept of power, there is an assurance of a possibility for order in the world—there is given to man the sense that perfection exists. We know that man has used athletics as a means of seeking this perfection since prehistoric times, thereby acknowledging both the power of his being in nature, and the power that exists in the abstract or metaphysical and religious sense of perfection.

In our discussion that power might be considered a criterion value for the interpretation of beauty in sport, we can turn to Roger Bannister for authority. In Bannister's mind there is a distinct relationship; he said, as a result of his athletic running experiences, "I found a new source of power and beauty." In another context, rowing has been described as "a surge of smooth, eye-pleasing power" (see Plate 12). Jim Dietz, a single-scull oarsman of national reputation, adds his notion of power in rowing by describing the start of a 2,000 meters as a time when "you explode." Explosive force, or ballistic power, is what coaches of many sports stress to their athletes.

Sports like archery, golf, baseball, hockey, and cricket illustrate the effects of ballistic explosive force which the athlete generates during a very brief span of time. Arrows, balls, and pucks become ballistic projectiles at the point of release or impact. The study of these effects, through the disciplines of physics or kinesiology, can be made exciting by virtue of the information that is revealed. Thus, the suggestion that the impact of the baseball on the bat is the result of summing the speed of the ball (which can be 100 m.p.h.) with the speed of the head of the bat (say, 50 m.p.h.) prompts a sense of astounding force. Measurements made on the impact of the golf club with the golf ball (Cochran and Stobbs, 1968) resulted in several revealing facts. The sensation that golfers feel of "holding" the ball on the clubhead over what appears like a measurable period of time is an illusion—the ball and clubhead are actually in contact for one-half millisecond (0.0005 second), during a span of three-quarters of an inch when the clubhead is traveling at 100 m.p.h. Ballistics is the study of the behavior of projectiles, but of most significance to the athlete is the amount of time and control that he puts into the action preceding impact. Once impact has been made, no amount of effort, persuasion, or incantation can change the path of the projectile. The wind can, of course, and the athlete's ability to predict and compensate for wind direction and velocity can provide him with both levels of satisfaction, the "win" and the "joy." When the head of a golf club strikes the ball, the human body has generated a four-horsepower swing for the point of impact, with the clubhead traveling in excess of 100 m.p.h. (a speed gained from rest to full acceleration in one-fifth second). The professional golfer has a smooth and graceful action, a seeming effortlessness which belies this great force (see Plate 13b).

The power of an athlete is relative to many other things, perhaps the most important being balance. The physical balance of an athlete is a flexible part of his deportment, dynamically as well as at rest. His balance is a statement of his composure, particularly when he is at that point of exertion which demands all-out effort, the extreme witnessing of his power. The power-balance relationship is neatly summed up by Sugar Ray Robinson (1969), one of the greatest boxers of all time:

> Slowly, my balance improved, and it saved me many times. In addition to enabling me to put all my power behind a punch, good balance enabled me to keep my feet when another man might have been knocked down. Balance is so important to an athlete. Joe Louis would have been an even greater champion if he had developed better balance. . . . Balance is hard to describe, but if you've seen Willie Mays catch a fly ball, or Joe Namath throw a pass, you know what balance is. (p. 49)

The nondefinitive nature of balance in the human is what Sugar Ray refers to; it is that tonicity of the body musculature which refutes any discussion of static balance in humans or other living animals. Balance in the athlete is a dynamic force, one which the gymnast seeks to veil in his "static" poses (see Plate 20a, the "iron cross"). In his efforts to illustrate symmetry, the gymnast employs great physical power to aid him in his creation of illusion. The image he creates is illusory, but we know intuitively, if not experientially, that the gymnast is exerting great power. The power of the running-back, the ball-carrier in football, is largely dependent on his balance. The interactive nature of balance and power ensures success in any sport, and well-controlled, well-balanced powerful form in athletics provides the basis for a real yet mysterious beauty.

The use of power as a damaging force in football is emphasized in a comment reported to have been made by John Brockington, running-back for the Green Bay Packers football team: "It's exploding, exploding every 30 seconds—that's why guys get so nervous, why they throw up before games, and why a lot of them quit." On the other hand, the use of power by a running-back like Larry Csonka appears like a superhuman quality. It has been said of Csonka, as a Miami Dolphin playing against the New York Jets: "Three of our guys hit Csonka head-on, and he put all three out of the game—he is unbelievable." At the time this was said, Csonka weighed 240 pounds, and while it is unlikely that the three he "took out" were much less in weight, we should closely inspect how he applied his weight to his power, perhaps in relation to the momentum he achieved. If any of the other players who hit him head-on were equal to his weight or heavier, then pound-for-pound, he is the more beautiful football player—in the "power" sense. A similar case of the power of an athlete can be taken from the Foreman-Frazier world championship fight held in Jamaica in 1973. A newspaper photograph of the fight showed Frazier literally lifted off the canvas by an uppercut from Foreman. At the time of the fight Frazier weighed 214 pounds, a fact suggesting that the power behind the blow that hit him must have been at least 220 pounds. If a registered punch of 220 pounds is not seen as "beautiful," whether in boxing or elsewhere, it is at least awe-inspiring.

Other than the intrinsic realm of power, the power of the athlete himself, consideration should be given to the extrinsic sources of power, that is, the power of the environment, the wind, gravity, and water in its manifest form (flowing or relatively still). The wind is one of the manifest forms of air, of course, and air currents provide the power needed in soaring, gliding, hang-gliding (see Plate 31), and similar sports. Wind power drives sailing boats and land and ice yachts, and the aesthetic experience derived from these sports becomes dependent on that form of power. In lake sailing, the power of the water resists the power of the wind, and the skilled sailor learns the balance between these two forces. Again, the power of air becomes manifest to the sky diver who, by reaching an altitude of 12,000 feet, adds power to his body for the fall. During the fall he is able to judge, manipulate, and enjoy the differentials of air pressure. This kind of pressure, at maximum velocity, becomes akin to the water pressure that a swimmer or a canoeist feels either against the body or against the canoe. At great pressure there is little difference between air and water (relativistically, of course) for the dynamics of flow are similar for both. In very real terms, the water skier in the classic pose of the slalom turn, when the "rooster-tail" spray is at its maximum, employs the pressure created by his speed, his centrifugal force, and the fine edge of his ski on the lake surface to maximize the potential power resistance that he needs to execute the turn accurately and safely (see Plate 14a). The sense of intrinsic power felt by the athlete in reaction to such pressure serves to endorse his sense of reality and personal limitations. These effects are sometimes interpreted as the subjective aesthetic experience of sport. It restates "the joy of effort."

The power of beauty to move a person to emotions of ecstasy and joy to the point of tearful release has often been explored in the arts. This type of response has been initiated both by the beauty of nature and the beauty of art, but the power of impact on the perceiver has never been fully understood. Fellini has explored it in film, George Orwell touched upon it in *1984,* but more obliquely. The mesmeric power that we speak of here sets a challenge for understanding the symbolic communication operating between athlete and spectator. That sport has this effect is further evidence that it can be interpreted for its component of power as beauty.

A parallel term with power is "effort," a word which derives from the Latinization "et fortius," or "with power." We identified *fortius* at the outset of this chapter when discussing the symbolism of "Citius, Altius, Fortius." The way that R. Tait McKenzie introduces us to effort is as a poetic statement of athletic achievement.

Explosion is defined as a rapid increase of pressure accompanied by heat, light, sound, and mechanical shock, arising as a sudden release of energy. This could explain by inference the body metabolism response of the "joy of effort" in the shot put or the discus throw.

Power, Risk, and Joy

Where an activity has the potential for great danger, and some sports *suggest* this to the layman, the dangerous qualities assume symbolic power —the power to take life away. With the introduction of a concept of *threat,* we can move closer to behavioral analysis of the symbolic power of danger. Psychologists speak of goal-oriented behavior and threat-oriented behavior to distinguish between that which we seek typically to approach or to avoid, respectively. Furthermore, probabilities of risk can be stated in such terms. Sky divers tell us that there is little or no risk in their sport; one death in ten years would automatically give us a different perspective about that sport (even though deaths recorded in conjunction with sky-diving are more frequent than one in ten years). When we are faced with risk in any venture, we are weighing very carefully what we want to approach against how much we should avoid. Confidence comes with the learning that attaches to success in approach behaviors. That is, through our learning we achieve the power to estimate the level of threat contained in a particular goal. That power is as real, psychologically, as is the physical power acquired through weight-training.

The sense of accomplishment that comes with success in a sport situation, the elements of which seemed overwhelming, is accompanied by a feeling of joy. This joy is the aesthetic, the beauty of power, derived from the successful challenge of symbolic danger. In this respect, we can restate "the joy of effort" in behavioral terms as a change in behavior (learning). Not only do we learn more about ourselves through the joy of effort, we learn more about others and about the environment (sport domain). As an expression of power, the joy of effort brings us closer to a self-actualization geared toward perfection of the self. The recognition of our own limits of power becomes the yardstick by which we measure power, real or imputed, in others. The symbolism of power becomes couched in the language of our own learning and may be termed "strength" or "confidence" depending on whether we are referring to physical or psychological power. Exhaustion of physical and psychological resources reduces emotional resistance associated with poise or composure, and exposes the individual to interference with perceptual process. Typically, this interference might be interpreted as halucinatory, visionary, or "spiritual" experience. The study of fatigue would clarify this question and throw more light on the phenomenon known as "the joy of effort."

STRATEGY

Strategy is recognized by many as the art of deception, and, as an "art," it reveals levels of skill usually associated with cognitive process rather than physical ability. Strategy is a pattern of tactics; Weiss (1969) is careful to make this distinction:

> Strategy needs support from tactics, the art of ordering and using one's forces. . . . There is no strategy for parts of a game, any more than there is a tactics for the whole of it. Tactics is strategy divided into steps and specified in the form of particular acts which give the strategy body and vitality. Strategy envisages an entire enterprise. It refers one to the anticipated pace of the venture, and points up the vital joints in it. Tactics, instead, concerns itself with the producing of effective means for realizing the strategic plan. (p. 87)

It is significant that Weiss accords strategy the status of an art, and we may read the significance in the same way we recognize the meaning of such terms as "the art of war" or "the art of self-defense." But, pursuing Weiss further, we see that tactics involves specific plays (football), drives and covers (basketball), punches and counters (boxing), holds (wrestling), thrusts and parries (fencing), tacks and jibes (sailing), and all similar specific parts of a sport in which basic skills apply. Put together, the parts comprise a strategic whole, and when the sum of the parts exceeds the whole, the true *art* of strategy has been achieved.

So good games, like good art, can be defined in terms of parts to wholes, and when the whole is greater than the sum of the parts, art has been created. In sport a "great" game is remembered for being more than the individual inspirations of the athletes summed into strategies of offense and defense to a closely contested and unpredictable outcome. Kupfer (1975) states this particularly well:

> In (competitive) sports the part can be brought to dramatic and athletic completion within the whole in two senses. The athlete realizes his excellence in relation to the team (as the team does collectively in relation to its opposition); the momentary funds [i.e., that which is momentary

in athletic action can be summed] and is in turn located within the temporally protracted whole. In the context of the opposition necessary for engaging in such sports, individuals come together to form a whole. . . . The individual's performance, a delight in itself, is organized and directed in the interdependence called forth by the demands of competition. The team as a whole is pushed and pressed to its limit by the performance of the opposition, [and] this mutual enhancement through opposition surely adds an aesthetic quality. (pp. 87–88)

The sense of "opposition" appears to be endemic to agonistic competition in sport, but there is no guarantee that it will provide an aesthetic product. The history of sport is replete with "flat" games, even championship encounters, in which little of aesthetic value emerged from the playing or the witnessing. Kupfer is indicating an ideal which is often the case but is by no means a complete generality.

The strategy of any given game or match may recommend the deployment either of plays or of players. Typically, an assessment of strengths and weaknesses must be made, and these can rest in styles of performance, again, either of skills or of the players. Hypothetically, a season-closing game between the team with the greatest record on offense and the team scoring highest on defense should produce a tie, or at least a very close match-up. Similarly, as Baumbach (1970) illustrates, the match-up may be between two given players:

The Baltimore-New York play-off figured to be a meeting between the two hottest teams in the league. . . . Baltimore was stronger on offense, New York better on defense. . . . In this sense, Frazier and Monroe probably best exemplified their teams' styles. Frazier directed the Knick attack, handled the ball perhaps eighty per cent of the time, although he seemed to prefer playmaking to shooting, defense to offense. . . . His most imaginative and heroic play was on defense. Where Monroe, hot, would hit a number of dazzling shots in a row, Frazier's thing was to steal the ball. . . . In any event, the strategy was repeated in the play-offs so Monroe and Frazier rarely got to go head to head. In control of the rhythm of the game, New York won convincingly, 113 to 101. (pp. 145–146)

Baumbach suggests that the superlative team was the one which developed a rhythm to the execution of its strategy. Implicitly, the rhythm must have been in the piecing together of the tactics of the game to give the overall strategy of play an artistic smoothness or flow—the elements of artistic expression. However, it is not forgotten that the strategy was dependent on the foundation of competition, and competition should be examined for the contribution that it makes to the beauty of sport through strategy.

Much of athletics presupposes competition. The opportunity for one person or group to test skills against another person or group is often the greatest attraction to an individual. Sport provides the arena for that opportunity.

"The winning or the losing of the game is irrelevant to its aesthetic evaluation," writes Kaelin (1968), "but the desire to win is never aesthetically irrelevant." The desire to win invokes the use of whatever skills and techniques are at the disposal of the athlete, the team, or the coach. One technique at hand is the principle of deception or strategy. When the definitive components of ability (strength, speed, precision, power) are balanced, the strategic skills and techniques of deception assume an overriding importance. There are levels of performance in sport and athletics from the relatively unskilled to the top-level performance of Olympic and professional league athletes. At each level the competition is tougher, the demands on ability are more exacting, and the rewards more appealing. Competition sharpens the best athletes as they progress up through the ranks. This process of the refinement of skill toward levels of supreme excellence is noteworthy for the social recognition that it merits. For that greater segment of the population which is more concerned with winning than with witnessing, the outcome of a game is most important. Current values in sport are most disposed toward winning because for many people "that is the American way." Not only the American way, however, for the people of Classical Greece were equally cognizant of winners. But for them, winning was a value of equal merit with other values, and not revered purely as a superlative. The Greek ideal of moderation in all things did not interfere with the spirit of competition to the extent that winning was not important; but though victory was important, the way in which it was recognized and enjoyed was tempered. A beautiful winner was modest in his triumph. Competition is equally important today, but how does it relate to the beauty of performance? According to Elliott (1974):

> The goddess of sport is not Beauty but Victory, a jealous goddess who demands an absolute homage. Every act performed by the player or athlete must be for the sake of victory, without as much as a side-glance in the direction of beauty. A game is a good one if it is played hard and skillfully, irrespective of its aesthetic merit or lack of merit. It is under this condition, the subordination of beauty to victory, that sport achieves the beauty that is proper to it. (p. 111)

It is significant that beauty in sport is dependent on victory in sport, for, were the emphasis on winning to be diminished by some erosion of values held by society, then mankind would lose much that is beautiful in sport. Victory does not mean only vanquishing opposing athletes. The conquest of a mountain, the scaling of El Capitan or the north face of the Eiger in winter, provide the same conditions for the recognition of victory—the use of superlative skill to overcome a formidable challenge. Even in team games, Roland Barthes tells us that man is not competing with man but that the symbol of opposing force lies in the nature of the ball.

The agonistic basis of competitive sport, whether between individual opponents, pairs of opponents or teams, subsumes the creation of tension. In pair, partner, and team sports the tensions are multifarious by virtue of coordinating counter-efforts between members. Thus, a so-called "good" game includes elements of both team cohesiveness and of equilibration of definitive component parts (structures, strengths) of each team. The better the balance between the opposing teams, the more unpredictable the outcome. This is qualitatively arguable only from the standpoint of relative components of *offense* and *defense*. The case is presented by Kaelin (1968):

> A change from defensive to offensive strategy in football is allowed by the interception of passes, in which the defensive player himself assumes the offensive; in the recovery of fumbles; and in effective punting, which may put a whole offensive squad on the defensive if the ball may be downed within the five-yard line. The tempo and rhythm of the game are defined in terms of the building up and the release of dynamic tensions, created ultimately by the opposition of equally capable teams.
>
> Controlled violence in which the opponent is not destroyed, but only defeated, and yet somehow morally edified—such is the essence of competitive sport. It reaches its aesthetic heights when the victor narrowly surpasses a worthy opponent. The game itself considered as an aesthetic object is perceived as a tense experience in which pressure is built up from moment to moment, sustained through continuous opposition, until the climax of victory or defeat. The closer this climax occurs to the end of the game, the stronger is our feeling of its qualitative uniqueness. Sudden death playoffs—and perhaps extra-inning games—are as close as a sport may come to achieving this aesthetic ideal. (p. 312)

The interception in football or basketball is a good case to make because it reflects several facets of strategy. Primarily, the interception reflects better defense than offense, either from the perspective of timing (precision, speed, etc.) or of position. In both cases, the offense has been outwitted on the basis of predictability of outcome. The interception is a rare occurrence, yet is always "expected" as a possibility; thus it is beautiful by definition (the aesthetic being defined as "the expectation of the unexpected"). In football, the opinion is generally held that offense plays are only as good as the blocking that is afforded the ball-carrier and that defensive alignments are predicated on the strength of the tackling. With this premise in mind, the creative coach sets about building into his plays patterns of deception to throw the opposition off balance. This is equally true for offense or for defense. But when the deception works, and the pattern is run, say, on an end-around reverse to gain a first down on the first play, the effect for the successful ball-carrier, for the offensive line, for the coach, and for the crowd of fans is beautiful. The study of deception as an art-form in sport merits close attention for what it can teach us of strategy.

The typical play-book of today may list as many as sixty or eighty formations, both offense and defense. Yet several plays will be gotten from each formation giving the coach and his players a permutation for a repertoire of some three hundred or more plays. By presenting a variety of formations in any single game, an offensive line creates problems of display and recognition for the opposing defense. Put into psychological terms, when the display is constantly changing, probabilities of predicting the outcome are reduced, thus interfering with intentional response behaviors. It might be suggested then that the variety of offensive formations will oblige an opponent to reduce his defense functions to a basic two or three. This reaction loosens the defense to allow the creative linebacker to get to the quarterback through the hole created by a tackle taking out the center; stacking the linebackers behind the tackles and playing only one loose-end and sending four backs to cover pass reception gives a defense the creative flexibility to deal with a variety of offensive plays.

This brief discussion on strategy has led naturally enough into the consideration of offense and defense. It is argued by some observers of sport that both offense and defense in all sports have their unique qualities of beauty. Others place a bias on one form of play over the other and forswear the supremacy of their choice. In baseball, most coaches agree that pitching is 70 percent of the game, lending the onus of play to offense. An interpretation of defense is arguable, of course, since, if the batter is seen as defense (and therefore in the 30 percent success probability bracket), his precision in connecting should be all the more beautiful by virtue of the overwhelming odds. What are those odds in the hands of the pitcher and what is meant by the beauty of the pitcher? The beauty of the pitcher in baseball can be summed up in the strategy he employs to keep the batter off balance by alternating (in random sequence) curve balls with pitches of straighter trajectory and varying velocities. How success-fully the batter responds to this "display" measures the beauty of his performance. The fine interplay of offense and defense provides an interac-tive effect, the strategy, which is in itself beautiful. Now let us turn to offense and defense as unique subjects of inquiry.

Offense

One of the major objectives in offense is to provide conditions that create a split second of hesitation for the defense to handle. The mobile tight-end who on certain play formations stays where he is reduces the predictability of the defense. His shifting, or his decision not to shift, provides the hesitation needed for the defensive back to know what to do to cover him.

A second major objective is to effect the opposite of hesitation, an overreaction. Typically, this might be done by the quarterback's drawing opposing tackles into an offside foul. The quarterback sets up a particular cadence of "hut-hut-hut," and when he has repeated it several plays using the same pattern of action accompanying his voice, he puts in a variation to slow the play down. The rookie tackle might bite and draw a foul—so might the veteran, but it is less likely. When George Allen openly admits to preferring to play veteran ballplayers as opposed to rookies, he is telling us that he does not want the mistakes the rookies will make—he wants the maturity that develops with years of service in the game. "Not wanting to make mistakes" is a statement of conservatism, and we do not normally think of conservative people as being creative. They are usually more concerned with defense. However, creativity is not the sole prerogative of the offense; if anything, the creative offense demands greater counter-creativity in defensive play. This seems to be true for most sports. But creative offense is a joy to see, and the best of creative offensive plays are adopted by most coaches and remain as solid play options season after season—until the rules change or a better defense is created. Creativity in sport is, of course, another facet of aesthetic behavior, just as creativity in any cultural pursuit.

One of the curious paradoxes of refined offensive play in basketball is to culminate a drive on the basket with a finely drawn foul from a defensive guard. The outcome is worth two shots rather than the one to be obtained from the lay-up. Draw plays in any sport are creative techniques of the offense to play a deceptive tactic against the defense. The defense, in turn, learns to read the signals and keep poised.

In hockey, the most effective time for offensive plays is in the *power play*. Power, in this sense, is synonymous with offense and therefore with scoring. Automatically, in the power play (a situation in which the power team temporarily holds a one-man or two-man advantage over the team with players fouled-out) the opposing defense has all its creativity taken away from it. The "box" play is formed defensively to protect the goalie for the two-minute duration of the penalty, and the defense is unlikely to break away for an attack. Of course, when a Bobby Orr or a Rick McLeish effects this rare play, adding his precise scoring skill to obtain a successful shot on the "power" team's goal, the effect is stupendous. Most probably the attacking team, the power team, will send a man inside the defensive box as a pivot of attack for shots on goal, and it is at times like this that the power team defensemen come forward to play offensive hockey and share in the shots on goal. For a defenseman to think defense during a power play reflects a limitation on the beauty of the game. Role reversal between offensemen and defensemen in hockey can provide the element of surprise often associated with aesthetic experience.

Larry Brown, veteran running-back of the Washington Redskins, is reported to have said of his offensive strategy: "Early in a game, I'm looking for keys and trying to read defenses. Then things get tough and I stop looking and just drive people out." In this comment he highlights two strategies; when the "brains" approach does not work, try the "brawn" technique. The former deals with the skill of prediction, the application of intelligence, and is beautiful in its successful performance because finesse has been shown when the offense had to make the initiating move. The brawn approach may be interpreted as beautiful in its successful performance if the power of the effort is admired. However, it seems evident that this power technique had to take effect because of better (more beautiful) play by the defense who read his intended moves. A *Newsweek* report (December 4, 1972) cites the playing ability of Larry Brown and illustrates his use of power:

> . . . on the field, he projects a disciplined attitude, following his blockers and executing his plays with precision. Then suddenly the defense closes in and the forces within Brown are loosed. Hurling himself forward, accelerating with incredible power, switching directions, he becomes impossible for one man to tackle, difficult for even a whole gang of rivals to bring down. (p. 83)

On the other hand, where power becomes seen as violence, it loses the positive value loading that allows it to be interpreted as beauty. Violence says nothing for the beauty of strategy, either of offense or of defense.

In modern football the running-back has brought a fascinating new magic into the game (see Plate 25). Zone defenses have taken much of the glamor out of the passing game, and the explosive attacks of the running-back have replaced much of the old game. The strategy of offense, epitomized in the ground game of the runners, is making teams that confront situations normally requiring a pass respond by handing the ball to the rushers. Running-backs have not taken the game away completely from the receivers, but they have added a new dimension of beauty to the game. The arrival of Franco Harris on the Pittsburgh Steelers was said to have brought balance to the already strong passing game of Terry Bradshaw; the Steelers went on to prove what this "team balance" meant by winning the Super Bowl in 1975 and 1976.

The strategy of offense will always have an edge as long as the defense has difficulty deciding whether to "read pass" or "read run" first. The time for a split-second decision is all that a running-back needs to make his initial moves. Similarly, a lineman may charge the quarterback and expose himself to trap blocks, or, linebackers and defensive backs may drop back tentatively toward their defense zones when they should be plugging the hole in the line. The element of uncertainty that is brought in is the beauty of artistic display. The expectation of uncertainty is one of the ways of defining the aesthetic experience.

Defense

Defense is counteroffense, to put it in a more positive manner. To think positive for defense sounds almost like a contradiction in terms, yet the creative potential of the defense is no less than that of the offense, and indeed could be seen as greater. Creativity in defensive play is the artistic response or reaction to problems set by the offense. There is some argument among psychologists and artists as to whether problem solving can be equated with aesthetic production, but that is not for us to enter here. For our needs, the interpretation of creative defense rests with our understanding of creativity as a cognitive process (to which, incidentally, problem solving can be subsumed).

Reflecting for a moment on the place of the batter in baseball, in which he is presumed to be playing a primarily defensive role (the pitcher having 70 percent of the option), it seems evident that his creative attitude rests on his knowledge of the pitcher and therefore the selection of the ball that *he* wants to hit. By making the decision to select what he wants to hit, he avoids a defensive stance and takes a positive attitude to deal with what he considers his "offensive" role, i.e., to score runs. The balance of psychological as well as physical forces in the interplay between offense and defense in baseball (and their interchangeable fluctuations between teams depending on levels of play) makes it a game rich in potential for many of the finer appreciations (Angell, 1972).

The objective of the defense in football is the quarterback. Set the quarterback off balance and the ball will turn over to your own offense. The curious phenomenon attaching to players on the defense is the simple fact that the more beautifully they play, the less they play. Two objectives in defensing the quarterback are (1) to hold him in the pocket because he is more dangerous out of it, passing on the run or playing the keeper option, and (2) to force him out of the pocket because he is less effective when being chased. For containment of the quarterback in the pocket, outside pressure is applied by the defense, and inside pressure is given to squeeze him out of it. Defensive options accumulate to the benefit of the players on the defensive squad—the greater the number of options, the more beautiful their strategy.

Creative defense is a difficult notion simply because "defensiveness," as a psychological variable, usually implies the shutting down of communication between individuals and groups. As stated above, defense usually means avoiding mistakes, reducing the risks, and so forth. Creative defense in a sport should challenge the self-protective notion. Mismatching a heavier tackle against a lighter center, employing tight ends with the speed of a wide-receiver, among other options, help to establish the elements of creative defense.

Extrinsic factors affecting defense strategy vary with circumstance, from the responsive action of the home crowd yelling "Dee-fense, dee-fense, dee-fense," to the tempering of speed on the downhill run in ski-racing due to poor or changing snow conditions. The individual athlete, as much as the defensive squad, must read the limitations set by the display, whether that display is the opposite team, opposing athlete, or environmental conditions. The crowd shouting "dee-fense" is exploiting the social prerogative normally associated with victory and competitive supremacy. As these factors diminish in society the social significance will disappear; in any case, the sheer noise of 60,000 fans yelling for defense has its strategic significance in blocking the communication of audible signals. For some, this is beautiful, for others it reflects interference in the game.

There are many textbooks on "How to Play the Game"—from archery to wrestling—in which the student will find chapters on tactics and strategy. Besides being read for the technical quality of the ideas contained, they should be understood for the amount of creative thinking that goes into suggested and recommended plays, skills, and techniques. Even the nonspecialist can obtain a sense of excitement from a well-written and documented text on strategies. The non-skier can appreciate the points being made, perhaps not as precisely as the skier, but sufficient to feel that the sport contains many attractive elements, and the observer of the sport can grasp the beauty of those elements in witnessing the sport in action. The beauty of strategy is not solely in the playing, but rests as much in observing from the detached location of spectator. Spectating becomes enriched through a finer appreciation of strategy.

summary

In this chapter the definitive parameters descriptive of the beauty of sport are signified as strength, speed, precision, power, and strategy. Such terms are more definitive than flow, harmony, gracefulness, and the like, and as such, hypothetically, can lead us closer to the explanation of beauty as it applies to sport. The case is made that there are cultural antecedents for why man regards speed and strength as beautiful since such concepts are found in the folklore and mythology of many societies past and present.

In the framework of the cultural antecedents, the Olympian concepts of "Citius, Altius, Fortius" are investigated. Relational concepts, "Celeritas, Agilitas, Fortitudo, Aequitas," which are introduced in the artistic work of R. Tait McKenzie, help to move our investigations closer to definitive communication. "Fortius" and "Fortitudo" suggest strength by translation, and the mythological derivative is found embodied in the person of Hercules. Most typically, strength is found applicable to power in the athletic sense, but the impression of strength as a pure measurable quantity is inferred from a well-muscled torso, an entity which transmits its own manifest beauty. A demand for a better comprehension of this type of beauty carries over from Chapter 1.

As with the obsession for strength, so there exists a similar charismatic response to speed. "Celeritas" and "Citius" present component aspects of speed as inculcated in the heritage of man, with speed, either in performance or in artistic reproduction, found in cultural representation. The sculpture, *Brothers of the Wind,* by R. Tait McKenzie, illustrates the symbolic fascination that man has with speed both in the sport and in the art domains.

Precision represents the search for exactness, the ideal, or, in other words, the limitations that man succeeds in effecting in his aspirations toward perfection. Most typically in sport, timing and tuning speak to his best efforts for precise and accurate performance. We recognize the best efforts, the most precise results, by the most superlative athletes and accord them qualities of beauty of performance for the results they obtain. Two forms of timing are discussed, the extrinsic and the intrinsic. Extrinsic timing refers to strategy, while intrinsic timing refers to the kinesthetic impulses feeding information into the servo-mechanism of the human neuro-physiological system. Real time and perceived time are distinguishable in the precision of sport performance. Extrinsic timing is concerned more with perceived time in strategy, and this again is differentiated according to strategies of offense or of defense.

Power is seen as the product of strength and speed. Facets of power, such as ballistic or explosive power, enjoy an appeal which man finds awe-inspiring. Power is sometimes deceptive; the uncovering of real forces reveals elements of effect which can be illusory. Similarly, the gymnast creates illusion in the apparent ease with which he performs feats recognizably difficult in any other context, based on the power he exploits to deploy his body with control.

In the last analysis, the so-called definitive parameters have been instructive only to a limited degree, the final realization being that they are not explanatory. The conclusion to this exercise recommends further investigation of these terms for possible empirical analysis.

questions for discussion

1. What is the distinction between definitive and nondefinitive terms as they apply to determining the beauty of sport?
2. What are the cultural antecedents of "Citius, Altius, Fortius?"
3. Discuss at least two basic reasons why *The Olympic Shield of Athletic Sports* can be fairly called "the apotheosis of the athletic ideal."
4. Trace the mythological value of "strength" throughout history to the present and place the concept in perspective as it suggests "beauty."
5. If speed is "the new canon of beauty," is this more so for record breaking or for sports action regardless of creating a record?
6. Describe the close relationship which exists when the product of speed and risk is compared with precision. What does this close relationship tell us of finite characteristics of beauty of performance?
7. Precision can be mechanical or social. Explain the difference, and attribute the difference to the beauty of motorized and nonmotorized sports.
8. Why is threat seen as the symbolic power of danger, and how does it interfere with or embellish the aesthetic experience in sport?
9. Competition is the stimulus for strategy. Relate how strategy is interpreted as beautiful and make the case for offense or defense providing the greater aesthetic response in the athlete.

The Value Determinism
of Superlative Effects

If we did not find sport beautiful, we would not
be involved in it.

HANS KELLER

BEAUTY AND EXCELLENCE

One of the most common aspirations of man in sport is to excel,
either over others or over the level of his own previous best aptitude. From
the notion of excelling or improving, we obtain the concept *excellence,*
which means the highest level of achievement, the highest level of performance as a result of the search for improvement. As a concept, excellence
retains a sense of elasticity or relativity. In behavioral or performance
terms we may differ greatly from each other in our excellence, but there is
a closer common agreement between us for the recognition of excellence
cognitively and affectively. Excellence in a cultural context is that to which
we accord the ascription of beauty. When Hohler (1974) states that
beauty is seen as a basis for culture, he is echoing the interpretation given
by Maheu. The efforts of the elite athlete, the high-level performer, the
"superstar," demonstrate man's aspiration to the highest standards of
physical endeavor, and out of these efforts come elemental features which
we can describe as beautiful. Using Hohler's terms of "other aesthetic
categories," we can focus attention on speed, power, control, strategy
(offense and defense), and similar manifestations of physical activity
which separate the excellent from the run-of-the-mill or ordinary. Further,
we can say that *competition* is the whetstone against which the athlete

227

sharpens his abilities in his search for excellence. Hence, excellence as a concept should be viewed in athletics as a search both for greater self-realization (subjective, intrinsic) and for social recognition (objective, extrinsic). In self-realization the athlete experiences the kinesthetic excellence, the "joy of effort" and in social recognition he is perceived by others to have aesthetic qualities in the movements of his sport. (In social recognition he may achieve accolade, prestige, esteem, pecuniary reward, or he may receive nothing more than a nod of approbation. The athlete reserves the right to ignore or acknowledge social recognition, but many times he will not be aware of it.)

Extending the idea of excellence to its logical conclusion, we arrive at *perfection*. Perfection is not elastic or relative, it is absolute. As an absolute, it is beyond the reach of man. The closest that man comes to the manifestation of perfection is in his perpetration of the "ideal." The ideal is man's reification of excellence at the point most proximal to that which he adjudges to be perfection. Perfection appears to be a universal in the thinking of man; it is, at least, cross-cultural. The ideal, on the other hand, has its own cultural determinism.

The perfect game has never been played, just as the perfect race has never been run, nor the perfect throw been made. From this we might deduce that if any athletic event is regarded as an art, then there is in the minds of men some concept of what the perfect game or race might constitute. This premise might be put in pure artistic context by restating that the perfect picture of a landscape has yet to be painted, or that the perfect dance has yet to be choreographed and danced. No less so than the painter, sculptor, author, composer, dancer, or actor, the athlete seeks his own perfection in creative production. Seeking that perfection in performance need not be for the athlete the object of creating a work of art, for he reserves the right to view sport not as art but as some other cultural medium by which he tests his physical, psychological, and spiritual being. The result of his own seeking, however, *can* be regarded both by himself and by others as an art-work, something which stirs a sense of beauty. The contribution that this makes to culture is underscored by Jokl (1974):

> As the science of music derives rules of harmonization, orchestration, and thematic design from the works of great composers, so the physician who reflects upon sport and athletics starts out from observations of outstanding performances. To music as well as sport at its best is applicable the dictum that "culture is the pursuit of excellence."

The pursuit of excellence in sport is manifest in the phrase "Citius, Altius, Fortius." Record attainment in any sport is the benchmark for excellence at any given time. It is the phenomenon of the broken record, the new attainment, which demonstrates pragmatically that perfection lies at a point beyond excellence. Thus, perfection remains in the realm of the abstract for the man of sport. Placing this condition in the context of surfing, Slusher (1967) states:

> In many ways surfing speaks to the "loner." Thus, it does seek coopera-
> tive excellence as much as personal development. In surfing, man's
> existence offers an opportunity to attain true being. Being, as is, might
> well be called the personification of perfection. (p. 179)

Being, in the noun form, is the "personification of perfection," as relevant to the nonathlete as to the athlete. This is the totality of self, the sound self-concept and self-image, the fullness of absolute identity. The essential abstraction remains as fundamentally imponderable for the psychologist as for the philosopher. Perhaps the best interpretation of being as the personi-fication of perfection is a spiritual one, with the acknowledgment of abstractions such as perfection being more readily acceptable from a spiritual perspective. This acknowledgment should not interfere with a discussion of the beauty of sport, nor should the idea of perfection be restricted to the abstract when we are seeking explanation for that unique beauty.

For the purpose of rationalizing his own line of argument, Hohler (1974) claims a distinction between "beauty" and "aesthetics." This dis-tinction is not held in this book, but the train of thought that Hohler evinces from this distinction finds comparable agreement elsewhere in this text. To quote Hohler (from Whiting and Masterson, 1974):

> Our effort to outline the beauty of movement is based on knowledge of
> the actual difference between beauty and other aesthetic categories. In
> our interpretation we see beauty as the *basis* of culture in movement. It
> becomes an everpresent guide in those physical activities in which the
> performer aspires to higher standards in his performance. In its con-
> nection with vital human relationships, which man achieves by his self-
> transformation, it becomes one of the basic human needs. . . .
>
> A brief glance at the relation of beauty and aesthetics in the field of
> movement has shown that beauty is only one aspect defining a certain
> quality in aesthetic movement. Conveying beauty is the basis for higher
> forms of aesthetic and artistic communication. In this interpretation
> beauty assumes the form of the basic category of aesthetics. (pp. 55–56)

Hohler's "self-transformation" must be equated with Frayssinet's "transcendental" level of human movement in sport, but whether such "self-transformation" should be viewed as "one of the basic human needs" is a question open for discussion. Those students of sports studies who are familiar with texts on the psychologies of play and of sport will readily identify "self-transformation" as a "heightened state of arousal." Now, there is much agreement that man is an arousal-seeking being, but the classical literature of psychology does not identify arousal as one of man's basic needs. Certainly "stimulus-addiction" is not a basic need, but is a heightened state of arousal and therefore can be interpreted as the search for that step in the hierarchy of experience which goes beyond "self-actualization." It appears logical that self-transformation would be a state of being that is achieved only after the individual has determined his self-actualization. And, in context with our discussion on the relation of beauty, excellence, and perfection, the stage of self-development which reflects a hierarchical shift from self-actualization to self-transformation should be viewed as one more step toward the ideal. The ideal in sport means ideal form, and is a realizable aspiration but one rarely achieved. (See "The Most Beautiful Sport," the closing section of this chapter.)

THE FUNCTIONAL AESTHETIC IN SPORT

According to Bouet (1968) there exists a functional aesthetic in sport. From the point of view of the spectator, he says, there are qualities and canons of aesthetic value subscribing to sport, examples of beauty which are indistinguishable from technical perfection of sports action in competition. One of the major points of the functional aesthetic in sport is that it is value-relational dependent upon shades of meaning attaching to excellence of performance in competition. Whatever is beautiful in sport is not just "beauty," but "beautiful sport." This functional specificity is unique in the thinking of Bouet. The functional aesthetic is also interpreted as the aesthetic function for the purpose of emphasizing certain important dimensions of sport categorized such as beauty, harmony, sublimity, and drama. We cannot afford to make false judgment that athletes are not interested in the arts even though many may disregard this place in culture and life, for many athletes find spontaneous sources of beauty through their sport. For example, skiers and canoeists actively involving themselves in reaction to the forces of nature, employing their skills to experience an aesthetic joy of their movement, on the snow or the river, find themselves spontaneously moved by the beauty of nature around them and their own role in their sports.

Bouet stresses the importance of focusing attention on the aesthetic function in sport more so because it is so often latent, both in terms of sport and aesthetics. Often we seize the beauty of an event because we wish to live that event. From one perspective, we can claim that we have an inner wish to effect an action or a movement in such a way that we either obtain aesthetic reaction in others who see and acclaim us, or else we just wish to feel that we have done a beautiful thing from within, so to speak. To be graceful has long been an admirable faculty in men and women. To impart graceful movement to a javelin, or to imbue oneself with the graceful ascent of the soaring glider, to become a part of the graceful synergic unity of a crew stroking a shell to a rhythmic cadence—all these manifest in the athlete an impression of kinetic accomplishment. Whether the athlete performs freely or competitively, he is made sensitive to these kinesthetic experiences. It is important to note that this feeling is lost to the athlete who overplays his ability to the point of demonstrating a type of circus virtuosity. Spontaneous virtuosity is aesthetic, whereas the blatant display of virtuosity is crass. In the spontaneous sense, virtuosity reflects a notion of inner harmony, of peace with oneself in being and in accomplishment. (See Chapter 5.)

The aesthetic function in sport embraces concepts both of beauty lived kinesthetically and of beauty lived strategically. Each gives the athlete proof of the "plastic" beauty of his own body. Quoting de Coubertin: "Sport produces beauty since it makes a living sculpture of the athlete." The proportions of such athletes as Jesse Owens or Wilma Rudolph highlight what is meant by the "plastic" beauty of the human athletic form. Part of this "plasticity" is explainable by the pure health of the athlete, a factor of aesthetic note as far as the spectator is concerned.

For further clarification of the aesthetic function, Bouet borrows the concept of agonistic beauty from Souriau. Agonistic beauty has specific application to explaining the beauty of sport because agonism speaks primarily to the dynamism of human beings. This dynamism embodies a sense of time and measured variations of time, i.e., acceleration and deceleration, along with dimensions of space and variations thereof. In agonistic terms, the beauty of sport can be deduced by spatio-temporal analysis. But to articulate this by example, we need only turn to such sports as skiing, in which the design of the runs can qualify the aesthetic potential, or to gliding, in which the power and scope of a thermal set the conditions for aesthetic potential, or to ball games where the speed and trajectory of the ball is modified for strategic, and therefore aesthetic, potential. The suggestion that sport is beautiful is intended to have more meaning for the person who is interested in sport rather than one who has no interest in sport yet who might be deeply interested in the arts. In the most general sense, we draw from our knowledge of the arts to help us better appreciate the beauty of sport and so we are not dependent on advice from connoisseurs of art who may see sport only as grotesque. The concept of the aesthetic attitude is something that usually is accorded only to people with great interest in and appreciation for the arts, but there is no reason why others should not be granted the experience. Most people know what they like and beauty often has a personal relativity. Therefore we might say that just the recognition of beauty provides the condition for an aesthetic attitude. No special attitude may be necessarily involved in the perception of beauty, but some sports action becomes beautiful for us and therefore fascinates us as an aesthetic object. For some of us, this experience is regardless of identification with a winning or losing side. Indeed, there are no good reasons why a spectator at a sports event should have a detached aesthetic attitude—he has every right to witness his sport as he wishes— but there is every likelihood that his visit to the stadium will be rewarding to him in some emotional or visceral fashion, even if in the end he says it was not enjoyable. People adopt attitudes according to what they are watching. In this event, they may or may not have the aesthetic experience of beauty. "The spectator is frequently conscious of the interplay between intelligent and inanimate movement and of the contrast between them," says Elliott (1974). For example the flight of a thrown football, obeying the laws of physical flight, plays some part in the description of the beauty of the throw.

The functional aesthetic, as Bouet (1968) elaborates it, embraces both the subjective and objective domains of aesthetic experience and appreciation as we define them in this text. Bouet does not seek to separate those feelings experienced both through the personal action of a sports event and through the witnessing of others or of the natural surroundings. Thus, as a master glider pilot, Bouet could relish the subjective aesthetic of his own skill and likewise be attuned to the objective aesthetic of the sky, clouds, and landscape below. The major lesson that we learn from him is that very often the subjective and objective aesthetics are nonseparable. As Herrigel (1953) also reminds us: "In the case of the archer, the hitter and the hit are no longer two opposing objects but are one reality." In this respect, the following sections of this book must be read critically for the claim that is made for consideration of the two separably identifiable modes—the objective and the subjective.

THE OBJECTIVE AESTHETIC

The objective aesthetic is that sense of beauty which is observed in an art-work. It is the recognition that there is both beauty and artistic quality in the art-work, and as such is both an intellectual (cognitive) and an emotional (affective) response. What we refer to here as objective aesthetic, Santayana (1955) terms "expression." In his description of expression as applying to an art-work, he emphasizes that the recognition of that expression's presence is dependent on the experience or learning of the viewer. The case is made that the art student with experience and learning in the arts can apply these to his recognition of what is beautiful in sport from an objective standpoint. The student of the arts employs his observations of skilled sports performance to tell him that elements of the action have definitive artistic interpretation for him. On the other hand an athlete need have no background in art, he need not evoke any aesthetic sense of beauty from classical art-forms, yet by virtue of his athletics, he recognizes at will facets of sport which he considers beautiful. His reference points are found in the elements of athletic movement, knowledge of human action under conditions of agonistic encounter, and an instinctual kinesthetic symbiosis. His terminology is not of the arts, but *is* of aesthetic stimulation; his symbols of communication are bound up in the body, in an unspoken muscular empathy, and not effete verbalizations. The distinction between the objective aesthetics of the art student and the athlete becomes clearer in light of their respective past experiences and learning. Equally clear, each has much to offer the other for the full appreciation of the beauty of sport. There are rare instances of athletes who have been art students and who therefore have the best of both perspectives. These few people are testimony to some of the major contributions made to the study of the beauty of sport, and they understand best the difficulty of separating the objective aesthetic from the subjective aesthetic.

In his efforts to find clarification between two basic forms of aesthetic response, Aspin (1974) enters the notions of "attending" and "experience." He points out that "seeing a work as an aesthetic object involved *attending* to its surface and form" (italics added), and he says a parallel word might be "appraising." This attending and appraising is known as "aesthetic activity," which involves judging, observing, estimating, valuing, and otherwise paying attention from a detached standpoint. On the other hand, when the sense of detachment is lost, when the perceiving of a work stirs in the viewer a spontaneous and visceral (psycho-physiological) response, an aesthetic "experience" can be said to have taken place. Aspin elaborates:

> Here then is the claim: that to see something *as* an aesthetic object is to see it and attend to it *as* an object worthy of observation and *attention* in and for itself, for its own sake, in its own right, quite apart from any instrumental use or practical purpose to which it may be put, or from any consequence that it may have—whether religious, economic, or moral. Aesthetic discourse is thus fundamentally a disinterested mode of discourse, concerned only with the intrinsic features of the objects and performances upon which it is brought to bear (and in this respect it might be considered to have a point of similarity to the disinterested activity that is a "sport"). It is not conducted in accordance with the canons of, interchangeable with, nor reducible to any other mode of discourse, any other way of looking at things, such as the moral, the religious, the prudential, the scientific, and so on.

> To see something as "aesthetic," then, seems to require, in addition, that we do so adjudicate it in terms of the sorts of effects it has on us in our

contemplation of it and, further, in accordance with the extent to which it exhibits or comes up to certain standards. In other words, an "aesthetic" appraisal of something refers to the activity of adverting to and appreciating the perceived *merit* of that thing, by *attending* to it and by applying various criteria of evaluation to it. And in fact this "unpacking" of the concept of "the aesthetic" looks very like at least one lexical definition, which speaks of "the aesthetic" as "pertaining to the giving of pleasure in accordance with some canons of excellence." (pp. 129–130)

By "aesthetic discourse," Aspin means the psychic interplay between the viewer and the art object. Thus, he is saying that aesthetic attention and response are separate from moral, religious, and scientific attention and response. He is not saying that aesthetic discourse cannot or should not be subjected to scientific inquiry, and by virtue of his separation of attention and response as being two modes of aesthetic discourse, he is aiding in scientific definition. Aspin is explicit in drawing our attention to the merit of an object, to the evaluation criteria that can be applied in estimating that merit, but the most significant point he makes is that excellence and beauty are closely linked in the minds of men. Aspin's agreement with our own deductions (*viz.* "Beauty and Excellence") is encouraging but unenlightening. The scientific problem remains the same.

There is a close interplay between objective and subjective aesthetics which lends more confusion than relief to our analysis. An example of unwitting transference from the one to the other can be found in the following comments by Kovich (1971):

> The tumbler senses something of brief snatches of freedom, something of precarious balance in unsupported space, of underlying rhythm, and of forces initiated by himself acting upon himself. He becomes sensitive to the elements of space, force, and time in his world of movement. From this viewpoint, we see that it is not just the man's body performing; it is the whole man. The total performer then becomes both artist and material. Man and his movements become the art. (p. 42)

The interplay between the subjective and objective aesthetics hinges on the transference of perceptual process. The "seeing" to "feeling," or indeed, the "feeling" to "seeing" transformation alluded to by Kovich finds similar expression in the scientific writing of the nineteenth-century philosopher-psychologist, Herbert Spencer. In his book *Synthetic Philosophy,* Spencer (1885) echoes the best thought of the German school of philosophers and poets, but in his own consciousness of new developments leading toward the foundation of the science of psychology, he focuses attention on the role played by perception. Perception, in strict psychological parlance, implies the employment of the senses for cognitive understanding of reality and the environment. Spencer was well aware that the study of "perception" as a branch of inquiry in psychology was similar to what the ancient Greeks had understood as "aesthetic." However, for Spencer, the concept of aesthetics had to be recognized for its cultural impact regarding the study of beauty. His distinction between aesthetics and perception, a noteworthy clarification for us today, is put into clearer perspective in what he writes of human movement. His comments are singularly instructive for the study of the beauty of sport, for he speaks of the perception both of observed beauty and of "felt" beauty:

> Movements of the body pleasurable to self, and associated with the consciousness of gracefulness (as in skating), are movements of a kind that bring many muscles into moderate harmonious action and strain none. An awkward motion is one that implies sudden change of direction, angularity, destruction of much momentum, excess of muscular effort; whereas a motion called graceful—a motion in curved lines, flowing one into another without break, is a motion in which little momentum is destroyed, no undue exertion thrown on any muscle, no power lost. And while in the actor the aesthetic consciousness is mainly constituted by this feeling of moderate but efficient muscular action without check, without strain, without loss, the consciousness of gracefulness in the observer arises in large measure from sympathy with the feelings implied by such motions. Turning to forms, we observe that the delight in flowing outlines rather than in outlines which are angular, is partly due to that more harmonious unstrained action of the ocular muscles, implied by perception of such outlines: there is no jar from sudden stoppage of motion and change of direction, such as results on carrying the eye along a zig-zag line. Here again, then, we have a feeling accompanying an activity that is full, but contains no element of pain from excess. In the more complex combination, including many forms presented together, it is relatively difficult to trace out the principle; but I see sundry reasons for suspecting that beautiful arrangements of forms are those which effectually exercise the largest numbers of the structural elements concerned in perception, while overtaxing the fewest of them. Similarly with the complex visual wholes presented by actual objects, or by pictorial representations of objects, with all their lights and shades and colours. The requirement for harmony, for subordination, and for proportion—the demand for a variety sufficient to prevent monotony, but not a variety which too much distracts the attention, may be regarded as all implied by the principle that many elements of perceptive faculty must be called into play, while none are overexerted: there must be a great body of the feeling arising from their moderate action, without the deduction of any pain from extreme action. (p. 82)

The introduction of neuronal reference, the physiological micro-structures associated with psychological experience, is a feature of the new scientific search for identifiable criteria leading to the better understanding of human behavior. The origins of behaviorism as a separate branch of psychological inquiry are patently evident. Out of these roots sprang two major elements in the development of psychology: (1) the application of empirical procedure for the establishment of generalizable rules about the behavior of man, and (2) experimental animal psychology. Spencer was not a behaviorist, he was an associationist; behaviorism is a twentieth-century development in psychology. The role of experience is valuable for the heightening of current perceptions, and aesthetic perception is more refined the more an individual has to call upon for association with similar perceptions in the past. As a fundamental Spencerian suggestion, this point speaks directly to what is said elsewhere in this book about the sport-specificity that an athlete has in being able best to appreciate the beauty of his sport.

Perceptions can be made more acute with learning, as the psychology of selective perception tells us. Yet there is still not satisfactory explanation for optical and perceptual illusions. This is significant for discussion of observations made on the way athletes perform, appearing to do with ease what other information tells us is difficult. One of the more acknowledged manifestations of the objective aesthetic is stated in the precept "effortlessness." In those sports which ascribe aesthetic components to their best levels of achievement, the representation of the human body appearing to do actions defying tension or strained effort brings to the athlete qualities more subtle than merely superlative skill. Effortlessness in the gymnast is relatively easy to accept because incipient manifestations of strength, even with fluidity and grace, do not deceive us, i.e., we *know* that strength is involved. The case is slightly different for figure skating, however, where the contact with reality (the actual blade on the ice) is less well understood even when clearly visible. Hence, the figure skater who defies that tenuous contact, and who demonstrates with jumps and turns that there is nothing of significance from which to leap and equally little upon which to alight, confuses our sensitivities to hypnotic effect. In the words of one reporter writing in the November 28, 1974, issue of the *St. Paul Pioneer Press:*

> Before the crowd realized it, semi-classical music filled the vast arena and Miss Lynn had flowed into a measured, mesmerizing display of free-skating that appeared to defy time and space with its grace and seeming effortlessness. (p. 25)

The hypnotic effect that effortlessness has in skating is far more potent than the effortlessness of the gymnast. The spatio-temporal "reality" components of the gymnast are easier to grasp, cognitively and behaviorally, than are those of the skater. This would suggest, by extension, that the affective response to the skater should be more intense than it is to the gymnast. What is true for our comprehension of the figure skater executing leaps and turns is equally true for the way we perceive the speed of the speed skater. The effect is so much more mesmerizing since we fail to conceptualize the apparent minimal contact between blade and ice in the production of such power and speed. "As I rolled into my stride," states Barbara Lockhart, former U.S. speed skater, "it seemed as if my feet weren't even touching the ice . . . and it really felt effortless." Equally troublesome for our understanding is the angle of incidence that the skater makes with the surface of the ice on the turns—a feature which is given exaggerated inclination by professional hockey players turning quickly to change direction of play. The lack of understanding that we admit to here is identical with our lack of understanding of the illusion of "bent" parallel lines in the Miller-Lyer Illusion. This lack of understanding is not suspect but it tells us something about the limitations we face in trying to explain the objective aesthetic.

Santayana in *The Sense of Beauty* ascribes the quality of beauty to an object as a result of the pleasure deriving from its perception. This mirroring or reciprocal effect, while logically understandable as a phenomenological explanation, disregards disparate conclusions separating the object-*qua*-object from the observer as sensate connoisseur. The extension of the Santayana theory allows for anything to be seen as beautiful according to the values held by the observer. Some modern derivations of the theory recommend that "aesthetics" encompasses the ugly—not allowed by Santayana—and hence, violence is beautiful if that is where your values lie. The beauty of object-*qua*-object depends on the formalization of accepted principles, often cross-culturally significant. Intelligence and education in the service of the cultural transference of symbol and ideal usually engender common experiences to a shared agreement on what is beautiful. This is so, at least within groups, though it is not universally applicable.

The transference of learning, as it applies to the recognition of beauty in an object, is both intrapersonal and interpersonal. We build on our experiences of what is beautiful, as well as learning from others. Whether the transference of learning about beauty carries as much force cross-culturally is open for discussion. Child and Iwao (1964) reported shared agreements on the beauty of ceramic pottery between Occidental and Oriental observers. By comparison, American gymnasts and aficionados of the sport acknowledge without question the beauty of performance displayed by Japanese athletes.

It is clear that the objective aesthetic in sport can be investigated cross-culturally, and it can be speculated that such findings would contribute to explanation of the phenomenon. Great athletic events, particularly those recorded in the annals of the Olympics, suggest a sympathy of appreciation operating between peoples of differing nationalities. This sympathy may well rest on aesthetic rather than nationalistic criteria. The words of Elliot (1974), in Whiting and Masterson, become particularly pertinent in light of this speculation:

> When sport has harmful rather than beneficial consequences, excessive competitiveness is usually the cause, yet competitiveness is the basis of much of the beauty and sublimity of sport. The problem facing sport is that of realizing its own idea, for we have achieved a conception of sport as a domain of contest in which actual harm is avoided, and in which defeat can be avenged only under the same condition. Sportsmen and spectators must ensure that the contest neither degenerates into nor gives rise to conflict. If, further, sportsmen and sports administrators ensure that sport continues to exhibit beauty and sublimity, it will become apparent that individuals and even nations are capable of regulating and using competitiveness for their mutual benefit. This will not solve any particular problem outside sport, but it will constitute a ground for hope. (pp. 115–116)

Elliott may or may not be interpreted as evangelistic, depending on how you read him, but there is a close proximity between what he is saying about the future of sport and what Jack Scott says (see Chapter 5, "Self-expressive Athlete").

Great Moments in Sport

"Great moments in sport," says White (1975), "are not the sole property of those who experience these moments by instigating them. For the spectators at athletic events may participate in those factors which make a given moment great for the athlete himself." He states that the great moment in sport can be seen as an "evanescent unity of athlete and audience . . . in the mutual awareness and enjoyment of human bodily excellence," adding that this is a reciprocal experience as well as a shared experience. The great moment can be temporally restricted or diffuse, but in either case, it is dependent on the presence of others to grant it the significance of greatness. There is an implicit uniqueness reflective of great intensity, an occasion which is heightened the more so by the witnessing of it by great numbers of people either directly or through the media. By definition, the great moment is a social event.

The sixth game of the 1975 World Series ranks as a great moment in sport, not just because it clinched the Series for Cincinnati, but because the play seesawed and became tied 6–6 in the eighth, until, in the twelfth inning, Carlton Fisk hit a home run into left field. Fisk is quoted as saying, "I don't think I've ever gone through a more emotional game." Games which are said to have matched that one are the seventh game in the 1960 Series when Bill Mazeroski hit a homer; the fifth game of the 1956 Series in which Don Larsen demonstrated perfect pitching; and the fourth game of the 1947 Series, which was won on Lavagetto's last-out double play that simultaneously broke up the Floyd Bevens' no-hitter.

The discussion of the temporal nature of the "moment" is taken up by White (1975), who agrees that a great moment need not be a nonreducible time-instance. The examples he gives are taken from baseball, but the framework in which he structures his argument is applicable in many other sports:

> We then readily discover that the duration of one great moment in sport may require the passage of many moments of measured time. The great moment might be one play in a game, one game in a season, or the entire season itself. Baseball provides prominent examples of each: Willy Mays' catch (sometimes referred to as The Catch) in the 1954 World Series, Don Larsen's perfect game in the 1956 World Series, and the Mets' dramatic closing sweep to the eastern division pennant in 1969. All three are legitimate great moments, but obviously the only example corresponding to an intuitive understanding of moment is the first, the Mays catch. As a consequence, our conception of Larsen's great moment must be broadened so that that moment includes the complete objective duration of the game itself. For if Larsen had walked Dale Mitchell (the 27th man he faced) instead of striking him out, the perfect game would never have existed, the potential great moment just another "might have been." Similarly with the Mets' pennant drive, only in this case the duration includes months, the length of an entire season. For if the Mets had been leading or at least in the running for the pennant all during the season, then the drama of their closing surge would have been impossible and the greatness reduced to a successful but mere workmanlike performance. The many (objective) moments comprising the daily rhythm of winning and losing are all necessary (but not sufficient) conditions for one great moment happening as it did. But it is important to preserve the fact that although the actual duration of sports' great moments frequently contain many moments, there is still only *one* great moment. Its singularity imprints an individuating unity on the event, so that regardless how much time measured according to objective standards the event required, the various experienced aspects of that moment can and must be understood as parts of one whole. (p. 131)

Conceptually, White states that time becomes insignificant in real terms, that time experienced in the great moment of sport can be seen as drawing together the future and the present as well as encapsulating the past into the present. Unfortunately, time is not an explanatory factor. At best it is a referent, one which defies reduction to explanation beyond agreed universal principles. As a referent it is useful for identification of factors subscribing to beauty in sport, as the discussion on speed and precision in Chapter 7 shows.

In response to what L. A. Reid (1974) says concerning the aesthetic attitude toward sport, Carlisle (1974) in Whiting and Masterson's *Readings in the Aesthetics of Sports*, presents a positive account drawing on four major premises, with special emphasis on great sport. He believes that the aesthetic analysis of sport must take as its starting point what the best in sport represents. By focusing on four main features of great sport which he claims have aesthetic importance, he draws analogies with established art forms.

The first feature of great sport is that it has expressive and evocative elements. This feature has two components: (1) effects associated with the movement qualities of the players in which such things as speed, control, grace, lightness, and power are symbolized in the movements, and (2) effects associated with human life values such as courage, heroism, patience, wit, and intelligence which are symbolized in movement. Carlisle suggests that the spectators respond to this symbolism, and in particular cases are held in awe by the "power" and the "greatness" of athletes. There is some room for the case to be made that the "folkloric mystique" of sport can have aesthetic interpretation.

The second feature of great sport is defined as intellectual beauty, a beauty related to the essential problem of the task at hand and how it should be solved. For Carlisle "a beautiful play would be characterized by solutions to problems marked by such things as: lack of error, and the use of economical, difficult, spectacular, original and rich sets of maneuvers, and by logical unity in which there is subordination to a unifying play or method against an equally matched opponent." We identify this precept as another way of categorizing "strategy," and share with Carlisle his opinion that when the play in sport is stated "in the form of solutions of this sort, it can be surprisingly and excitingly beautiful."

The third feature of great sport is drama, a crucial feature of all sport deriving from challenge and conflict endemic and definitive of sport. The dramatic impulse is different in different sports but the example of baseball serves to illustrate. In baseball there is the successive duelistic interplay of the pitcher with the batter allied to dramatic tensions built up or relieved according to whether there are runners on base. A further set of dramatic possibilities arises when the ball is hit or missed, and fielded or flubbed. Carlisle states: "In the ball games which are evenly matched, there is successive tension and release as the balance of attack (offense) and defense is altered and goals (scores) result." In this respect Carlisle shares the viewpoint of Kaelin for "the well-played game." The drama of sport ultimately reveals the hero and the vanquished, further testimony to the "folkloric mystique."

The fourth and final feature of great sport is unity. Specifically, Carlisle means the "unity of drama," which can occur in team games or in great solo performances. The drama of the game must swing one way and then the other with a final resolving climax. The unity of the game is not based solely on drama but incorporates "the movement qualities, the skilled performance, and the intellectual aspects [in which] there is organic interrelatedness and wholeness." (See Chapter 6.)

The Unforgettable Game

This usually is defined as the one in which no other game in any other season, no single shot or save on goal had ever meant so much either to the player or to the spectators. When that game is a series play-off in a league or state championship, the game is especially electrifying in the playing and all the more stimulating and satisfying. Coming from an underdog position, coming into the game with a "jinx" (such as a ten-season loss record to this particular opponent), coming in with the best man injured and unable to play—these are all factors which stir up expectancies in a particular direction. But there is always that margin of hope, that sense of "if only we can . . . (whatever) . . . then we will pull it off. . . ." But what if the unexpected occurred? Take the case of the basketball semifinal in which the opposing team surges six points ahead whenever the big center, brought in for the last five minutes of the closing quarter, narrows that gap to one. Back to a six-point lead, then again down to one with less than a minute to go and the seconds ticking down. Foul. The opposing team takes the free throw with ten seconds on the clock, misses, and the rebound is snatched from near the rim, and the guard has passed off down court even before his feet have come down. The fans start screaming for a time-out, but none remains. The big forward running with the ball is forced to pass off to a guard who shoots from the side; the ball rims, bounces up and away from the basket and with 0.00 showing on the clock, one point hanging there as the difference between win and lose, the center has come round from "nowhere," is high in the air, and with the ball still in play, he pops it back into the basket.

"The unforgettable game" illustrates the aesthetic effect obtained by spectators witnessing dramatic decision in the narrowest of time spans. The nature of "the expectation of the unexpected" has become fulfilled, the basis for the aesthetic experience.

THE SUBJECTIVE AESTHETIC

Scientific inquiry recommends that a problem first be identified, that an analysis of the component parts of the question be deduced, and that a methodology be assigned as a procedure toward solving the question. The subjective aesthetic in sport is a problem which has puzzled sport theoreticians in recent years, and while many can agree that they all know what it means, none can indicate a source in the literature to attach authority to his stated belief. Underlying the question in hand there resides a particular dilemma, which is clearly defined by Thomas (1974) when she states:

> The idea that each performer brings to the experience a background, technique, self-concept, and perception which is different is consistently advanced by sport and aesthetic theoreticians. It is argued further that inherent in this uniqueness and individual aloneness, is the impossibility of drawing conclusions, generalizations, or universal truths about either the aesthetic or sport experience. It is even more difficult to empathize without some kind of personal involvement in one or both of these experiences. (p. 74)

To establish a basis of agreement on what we might identify as the subjecive aesthetic, we should draw some statements from athletes and others testifying to the presence of such a quality. Several examples will give a broad indication of how this phenomenon is viewed or communicated. Many quotations used to elaborate specific points elsewhere in this book concordantly describe the phenomenon also.

John Brockington, formerly of the Green Bay Packers football team, is reported as having said: "The long run is the biggest thing, the biggest thrill for a running-back, when you break past that last man and you're going all the way for the long one." Larry Csonka, formerly with the Miami Dolphins, held the opposite view; his feelings of real thrill was being able to gain six yards through the line: "I'd rather carry the ball for three yards than go for the long gainer; any time I run for six yards it's great, beyond that it's gravy." Robert Lipsyte, the noted reporter and commentator on sports, has written several books on the subject. In one of these, *Assignment: Sports,* he quotes Yuri Vlasov, the great Russian weightlifter, as saying:

> At the peak of tremendous and victorious effort, while the blood is pounding in your head, all suddenly becomes quiet within you. Everything seems clearer and whiter than ever before, as if great spotlights had been turned on.
>
> At that moment you have the conviction that you contain all the power in the world, that you are capable of everything, that you have wings. There is no more precious moment in life than this, and you will work very hard for years just to taste it again. (p. 82)

The sense that the expression of great power can bring a transcendental communion with another consciousness is made explicit by what Vlasov says. While Lockhart (1973) does not claim transcendental communication as a result of her speed skating, she does bring a sense of deep subjective aesthetic in her account of a 3,000-meter race. Her sense of amazement accompanying the realization that she was skating faster than ever before was superseded by a feeling of exhilaration:

> The greatest joy of all came from the total, 100 percent concentrated effort.
>
> I would like to tell you a little about my favorite race and the one in which I feel I did the best in my entire skating career. That was the 3000 meter in Innsbruck, Austria, in 1964. The gun went off, I got off to a good start. The 3000 meter race covers almost two miles so you don't want to expend all of your energy at once, you have to conserve it over the distance. As I started rolling into my stride, it seemed as if my feet weren't even touching the ice. All the training, the effort put into it, all the time and work on technique all paid off at this moment. Everything seemed to gel—and it really felt effortless for that time. It didn't seem as if my muscles were aching or straining, but instead it felt as if I were flying across the ice. I looked toward my coach; he signified two seconds under, then the next lap, four seconds under, the five and six—it seemed as if there was no end to how fast I could go. *I could gain speed and gain speed;* I was truly exhilarated! It was at this time I felt the joy that I had never felt before, even winning national titles, setting records—I had never felt this great an exhilaration from sport. (p. 45) [Italics added.]

Roger Bannister, the great British miler, is reputed to have said: "The sportsman is consciously or unconsciously seeking the deep satisfaction, the sense of personal dignity which comes when body and mind are fully coordinated and they have achieved mastery over themselves." Bannister states the overall frame of reference in which the subjective aesthetic can be perpetrated. In a similar vein, Kaelin (1968) states: "The feeling of being at one with nature, using it to fulfill our own aims with consummate ease, is a direct aesthetic response of the mover to his motion." The "back to nature" aspect and the belief in a personal sense of "power" is given further endorsement by Willis Reed, former basketball star with the New York Knickerbockers. Reed was quoted in a *Look* magazine article, April 6, 1971, as saying:

> Playing pro basketball is a job to me, but sometimes in a close, tough game, I get the same kind of excitement I get out of hunting. When I get a chance to match strength and wits with a powerful opponent, it satisfies my ego and certain urges in me. (p. 72)

Such experiences are not unique to one man or woman, and the fact that they are found in the behavioral repertoire of many suggests that they can be researched. Paul Kuntz (1974) has gone so far as to assert: "There is a psychology of aesthetics, the kinesthetic-empathetic, that explains the delight provided by athletic performance." Kuntz is a philosopher who is stating what we believe to be true, the purpose of inquiry behind this text, but we obtain little further direction from him. Carolyn Thomas, another philosopher, does provide some direction.

Thomas (1974) brings to the question of subjective interpretations of beauty in sport both (1) the recognition that the question appears insoluble, and (2) the scientific attitude necessary for a rational approach to be taken toward its better understanding. By proposing that certain criteria be critically analyzed, she sets the thinking student on the right scientific path toward resolving the question, and is fair in not promising success as a result of scientific enterprise. These criteria are intent, expertise, involvement, and whole man acting. A clue might be snatched from her comment above on empathy and personal involvement, but the proposed criteria that she suggests are explored substantively to give us direction.

By *authenticity of intent,* Thomas means that before we can judge whether a sport experience satisfies aesthetic criteria, we must be assured that the sport-intent, the integrity of our athletic action, is pure and unadulterated. Gymnasts and high-board divers will readily identify problems finely separating both criteria of "sport" and "aesthetics" in respect to this criterion, and their incisive inquiry will sharpen the perspective of it. Thomas is aware that development of intent prior to any sport action may presuppose cognitive analysis, thus setting the stage for involvement in and later reflection upon the aesthetic experience in sport, but she suggests that the athlete should not expect such a unique encounter for it may only happen once in a lifetime. Wanting to win, which may set up conditions for the subjective aesthetic in sport, should neither interfere with the spontaneity of action nor deprive involvement in the experience when it occurs. Wishing to win is part of the authentic intent, the guarantee to self that excellence is sought, but the "perfect moment" could come anytime, even experiencing a loss, so long as the struggle has been authentically joined. Kaelin (1968) reinforces this judgment in his discussion of the "well-played game," but White (1975) doubts that the experience is transferrable as communicable information. White states:

> When performing with excellence, the athlete is normally in a state of positive awareness, if not explicit knowledge, that he is so performing. Frequently such awareness is mute; i.e., it could be verbalized neither at the very moment of performing, nor after the fact, regardless how glib or perspicuous the athlete may be. Although such awareness may be largely subliminal, it is the nature of this awareness to guarantee a certain sense of self-satisfaction with his performance and with himself. (p. 129)

Excellence is separated from wishing to win, at least by implication, thus suggesting an emphasis on performance for self-expressive purpose rather than for social acclaim. The reference that Thomas makes to "perfect moment" might be an echo of what White refers to as "great moment." We might suspect that there is a slight difference between the two, even disregarding any equivocation centering on the meaning of "moment" in the time-frame. It appears there might be a more substantive dichotomy.

To take an example, in recent baseball history the perfect moment occurred when Bernie Carbo hit an improbable eighth inning pinch home run, his second in the 1975 World Series, to tie up the game 6–6. The count on him when he hit was two balls and two strikes. Fimrite (1975) reported:

> Carbo leaped in joy and wonder at his own feat and danced and clapped his hands as he rounded the bases before plunging into a hysterical mob of teammates at home plate. *Johnson contrived to prolong the moment* by sending Carbo in to play left field in the ninth, the crowd celebrating his arrival there with another standing ovation. (p. 26)   [Italics added.]

Thus, the question is raised: can the moment be prolonged? The question rightly focuses on authenticity of intent.

Secondly, Thomas states, there is the requirement that the sport performance exhibit qualities of *expertise* and consistency for the perfect moment to have the chance to occur. Expertise does not mean perfection, but rather is a relative quality. The technique of an athlete is polished to a point where he has a consistent command or mastery (Keller, 1974) over the subject matter of his sport—the ball, the oar, the javelin, the sail, the board. Sophistication comes after mastery and is more likely to set the conditions by which the perfect movement is experienced. Sophistication of technique allows the athlete to "transcend thoughts of body" and to "direct his attention away from himself and technique" toward the feeling of the sport experience. Bannister (1963) says that his running simultaneously liberated "both body and mind."

The third criterion, according to Thomas, is *involvement-relation,* in which the athlete demonstrates a complete commitment to his sport transcending cognitive considerations of technique. Transcendence contributes to the establishment of an aesthetic experience which, later, can be objectified upon reflection. "The unity or integration of man and sport is a necessary criterion for the perfect movement to occur," says Thomas. Extraneous features to the sport, such as climatic conditions or crowd reaction, are ignored in this situation of involvement-relation. After the event, the athlete has the ability to reflect upon his sense of unity with his sport. As an example, Thomas cites Roger Bannister (1963): "I was running now, and a fresh rhythm entered my body. No longer conscious of my movement, I discovered a new unity with nature. I found a new source of power and beauty."

The fourth criterion presented by Thomas for the critical analysis of the subjective aesthetic in sport is labeled *whole man acting*. Conclusively, she recommends that "the body be experienced as a subject rather than as an object." This whole man requirement for the aesthetic experience to manifest itself frees man from the culturally imposed dualism of mind and body. Thomas states:

> To maintain that human existence, or man in his experiential world, is dualistic in nature is to disparage the body or to treat it as an object incapable of experiencing the world in a subjective, personal, or affective manner. (p. 77)

Following the four criteria for critical analysis, the *reflective description* is recommended as the mode for "data" collection. If the four criteria have not been explicit enough for the athlete to grasp the process and thereby respond with a reflective description, the definition of the perfect moment should assist in resolving that omission. The student-athlete is referred to the original essay by Thomas, particularly pages 78–82, in which both the perfect moment (Sartre) and the peak-experience (Maslow) are discussed in parallel terms.

The scientific approach recommended by Thomas is found in social science where the collection of judgments, opinions, values, and feelings provide the basis for empirical substantiation of knowledge. The student is advised, therefore, to fully understand methodologies of social survey research before embarking on data-gathering. He will need to know about question writing as well as questionnaire construction. He will need to sensitize himself to possibilities of bias or "leading" statements in his question. Without sound methodology he would be gravely misled if allowed to proceed further in his search for the scientific truth governing the laws of the subjective aesthetic in sport.

To bring psychological empiricism into the inquiry of the subjective aesthetic, we should ask questions of cognitive, affective, and behavioral significance. If, as Kuntz suggested, there is a kinesthetic-empathetic paradigm which helps to explain the subjective aesthetic, is it mainly (1) the sensory perception of the limbs and body in motion, (2) the cognate recognition of motor learning capacities, (3) the emotional identification of endocrine activity, or (4) some interactive effect of each or parts of each of these three possibilities? Further, how do we identify the differences underlying the reasons for cognitive, affective, and behavioral dispositions in respect to the subjective aesthetic? Taking each in order, we can attempt some initial detection of substantive presence.

The *cognitive* process can be approached by reference to an experience reported in a sports magazine of national significance. In May 1975 the Golden State Warriors won the four-game N.B.A. championship series, outscoring an acknowledged superior team, the Baltimore Bullets. All the games were "turn-arounds." Rick Barry, captain of the Golden State Warriors basketball team, expressed his opinion of the transcendental nature of the series in an interview with Pat Putnam, staff writer for *Sports Illustrated:*

> "I'm not really sure," Barry was saying in the happy confusion after the series had ended, "but I do know this is what basketball is supposed to be all about. We made reality out of fantasy. This is the type of season you only dream about. It just doesn't happen. I guess that makes us the lotus."
>
> The lotus?
>
> "I have a friend, a priest," he said. "When things look bad, he always says that from the mud grows the lotus."
>
> "I've looked at the tapes and I've watched us win," Barry said recently. "And even now it's hard to believe. I just never thought we could do it. Funny thing, after seeing the tapes I finally understand why the fans were so excited. While we were playing it was hard to realize what was happening." (p. 37)

The salience of this quotation is found in the fact that Rick Barry had the opportunity to bring a sense of personal academic inquiry to a situation which, in its enactment, provided him with some mystery, some unanswered questions. From what he tells us, there was an intensity of concentration on the game process, changing situations dealing with on-the-spot decision making, which took total control of cognitive process to the exclusion of other factors. But he does not deny that there were coincident emotional experiences at any given time, thereby suggesting an interactive effect. Indeed, the major clue to inquiry that he has provided recommends that athletes who experience a subjective aesthetic when photographed performing should provide the best source of analysis to account for what was taking place at the given time. Often, sports commentators will "interview" an athlete immediately after the conclusion of a great athletic feat, but this is often inadequate, and certainly lacks the specificity of control that scientific inquiry demands. Obviously, the athlete cannot be brought so quickly to a cognitive appraisal of his recent performance; there needs to be a period of time to elapse between the conclusion of such an intense and total experience and the time when rational, cognitive assessment can be made with full access to recall. Maximal recall will be available at a time when the first full stresses of sport have had time to subside, and before other life experiences take place allowing the process of forgetting to begin.

Access to the *affective* process in explaining the subjective aesthetic of sport is equally as remote as access to the cognitive process. Indeed, it is probably more difficult. Recall appears to be the main avenue of approach, although there appears to be no reason why telemetric information could not be monitored. It is purely speculative at this stage to express opinion, but reference can be made to quotes about recall. Speaking of an "other-worldliness" of the subjective aesthetic, McDonnell (1967) cites the feelings of a young gymnast describing his experiences:

> The ceiling trades places with the floor; then the floor with the ceiling. And then very abruptly and seemingly miraculously, you find yourself standing on your own feet. You feel like you have transgressed into one exciting world and then back again. You feel wonderful. You cannot name what that feeling is, but it does not matter. As long as it is there, you will keep returning to that world. (p. 6)

By "feelings," we understand what the gymnast is expressing of the affective domain. He is suggesting that there is "another world," one which might be purely an affective world, but which can be visited only through the medium of intense physical effort. Clearly, if this is so, that world is unknown to those who have never tested themselves to their physical limits in sport. For some sport theorists, the affective world is the "true" world, the definitive world of sport; Slusher (1967) is one of these:

> When sport *is as it is,* it achieves the dignity and grace of ecstasy. It *says* something meaningful to the performer. Its motivation comes from inner involvement. . . . *Knowing* is simply not sufficient; sport requires *inner* authenticity. A quality of *emotion* rarely achieved. (p. 61)

Slusher appears to be saying that the affective response to sports activity is the true definition of sport. If this is so, he surely ennobles the phenomenon, but in doing so, takes it out of the reach of the masses—unless he is saying that each individual has the right to get out of sport what he wants, i.e., affective as well as physical and cognitive response. (Here we touch upon the difficulty of translating into behavioral terms that which the philosopher tells us.)

Separating the *behavioral* (physical) process from the cognitive and affective processes for analytic purposes leads us toward some assessment of physiological responses or the mechanical analysis of movement—the science of kinesiology. Basic problems arise if we approach too close to these facets of inquiry, although it is important to have some broad knowledge of them for interdisciplinary analysis. The present-day athlete and student of sport sciences is obtaining sound interdisciplinary education, valuable to him for a better understanding of himself as well as of his sport. The mere physical experience of sports action is not sufficient for a realization of the aesthetic "force" of sport. In any sports context, the knowledge of *self* in the perpetration of a given act, be it throwing the javelin or weaving a strategic pattern through a backfield to score a touchdown, will serve to initiate the appropriate physiological response. If what was perceived of self belies nothing more than the commonplace, the physiological response will not be particularly noticeable. On the other hand, a feeling of exultation or ecstasy will mark the presence of a physiological response cognizant of some exceptional self-perspective. In support of this thesis, the Organizing Committee for the Games of the XXth Olympiad in *The Scientific View of Sport* presents the opinion that

> Sport and art may be interpreted as analogous phenomena through their similar *resonance* in the person who experiences them, through the *absence of purpose* which is a feature of both, through the *"reaching out"* of sporting performance beyond the individual himself, through the "cultural value" of supreme achievement in sport, which is "produced" in "creative action." (p. 38)

"Creative action" is the key phrase, indicative of supreme physical effort employing skills dependent on spontaneous cognitive process. The concentration on the game process has been suggested before as underlying physical behavioral adjustments. Sports behavior is responsive to rapid decision making, the motor coordinates of which often *appear* to predetermine it. We speak of "reflex reaction" in this respect, often forgetting what the true nature of reflex means physiologically. Reaction time is closer to what we mean when we speak loosely of "reflex reaction," when reaction time is stated as an expression of speed of response to a stimulus—what is often called "hand-eye coordination." The *post hoc* analysis of physical performance appears to be easier than the analysis of cognitive or affective process, but even then, it is difficult to find sources in which the separation is made. There always appears to be an implication of the other processes, as hinted by Billy Kidd in an interview quoted in *Life,* March 6, 1970:

> In 1966 I had this really incredibly exciting three weeks when I was winning—Killy would win something, then I'd win something, then Killy'd win and then I'd win. It was constantly like it would be if you get into a really neat discussion with your favorite friend—your adrenalin running constantly, and you're so much more aware, things are so much more intense—very nicely intense. (p. 59)

By associating "adrenalin running" with intensity and awareness, Billy Kidd suggests a basic physiological explanation for the subjective aesthetic. Soldiers returning from Vietnam have spoken of seeking special battle and combat assignments strictly for the purpose of getting themselves into situations where the adrenalin was pumped into the body system by reaction to war conditions. Some of these soldiers were suspected of having deliberately sought "adrenalin addiction" or adrenalin "highs." The relationship of this phenomenon to the one involving risk taking discovered in sky divers and race drivers by Ogilvie (1974) in his personality investigations appears to be remarkably close. The physical-behavioral process, for the purposes of analysis, is as important from the perspective of the sky diver who employs gravitational force for his fall, as for the weight lifter who employs counter-gravitational force in his effort to lift maximum weight.

From a personal perspective, the scientific analysis of the subjective aesthetic can have only ideographic value, but we can afford some respect in our recognition of the ideographic case when presented by a scientist who indulges in sport. Bouet (1948) claims to have found an understanding of time and space through his aesthetic appreciation of gliding. The exploration of the sky provides a detached joy (*jouissance desintéressée*) which can be defined by three component elements. First, there is the balance of risk against the opportunity for a new perspective of time. Second, deriving from the successful achievement of this fine balance, there develops a sense of liberated self owing to a cosmic feeling of the grandeur of space. Finally, through observing the spatio-temporal qualities of soaring as an art-work, a richer comprehension of the world adds to the detached joy. Out of the experience of detached joy there develops an aesthetic attitude toward soaring which Bouet philosophically terms "finality without end."

Stimulus-addiction, or "adrenalin addiction," and the "detached joy" may have something in common with another subjective aesthetic phenomenon. In his autobiography *Speed with Style,* the late Peter Revson, who was a racing driver, makes reference to a condition that appears to have overtones of personal aesthetic experience. "I don't get the Triple-High that some drivers seem to need," he writes, and footnotes the meaning of the Triple-High as a condition in which psychological, emotional, and physical wavelengths coincide at their highest points. The analogy with sound wavelength is easy to accept, and there is potential here for an interpretation of several harmonious elements fusing, as is found in music, to create a fundamental aesthetic effect. Athletes who experience the Triple-High claim that they are invincible, but regardless of that claim, they often get beaten.

Stimulus-addiction, detached joy, or Triple-High, the terminology is unimportant—what is important is the apparent presence and therefore accessibility and commensurability of a life process indicative of what we are identifying as the subjective aesthetic. The underlying premise of this assertion rests on the axiom: "If it exists, it exists in quantity, and this quantity can be measured." This is not to say that the student should blindly accept this axiom, since it is one which invites argument. The axiom derives from Thorndikian psychology and is fundamental to the empirical turn of mind.

Risk Taking

The subject of risk taking can be taken as a subset of the subjective aesthetic for the purpose of our analysis. As a component element in the aesthetic, risk is identified as a measure of uncertainty due to insufficient information, the element of chance or "alea" (Caillois, 1964). Risk taking, however, is not "blind" chance, such as the gambler takes on the random occurrence of an event, although Roberts and Wicke (1972) report that self-testers (risk-takers) are "more likely to prefer games of chance."

We can believe that risk-takers in athletics are loners (Ogilvie, 1974) from what we know of the subjective aesthetic experience being an individualized encounter. Ogilvie says of the risk-taking athlete: "Their favored relationships are transitory in nature, requiring only a superficial commitment; they neither seek nor encourage deep emotional ties with others." Can we conclude that their separation from the social role of friendship or family allows them that much more time for contemplation of self? If so, is that self-contemplation one which seeks to increase the occasion of, or heighten the aesthetic experience in sport? Recalling the discussion by White (1975) on the meaning of the "great moment" in sport, we find a subjective parallel in the constitution of the risk-taking athlete. Where the "great moment" is great only on account of the social dimension in which it is framed, the great moment for the self-expressive athlete is one which he tries to relive regardless of the social significance. Whether risk-takers are closer in touch with the availability of the repeated great moment of personal merit is debatable. Is the great moment that they seek to repeat identifiable with Maslow's "peak-experience"? The "peak-experience," by definition, is a rare event and is reputed to have overtones of mystical or spiritual experience attaching to it. (The logical extension of this point becomes spurious, leading us to ponder whether risk-takers seek or come closer to a better understanding of their own mystical being, and therefore, of man.)

Psychologist Bruce Ogilvie has made the study of the personality of athletes the primary focus of his scientific investigations during the past decade. As a result of his analysis of the profiles of such athletes as sky divers and race car drivers, he has been able to define the major components of the risk-taking personality. The findings presented by Ogilvie (1974) are valuable for the student of the beauty of sport because he suggests that there is a form of "stimulus addiction" which he equates with the active seeking of psychic ecstasy. "Like most humans," says Ogilvie, "risk-takers need stimulation and excitement [but] for them there is a special form of psychic ecstasy found by living on the brink of danger." His observation that there are many athletes with a need to seek special excitement at the extreme limits of their physical and emotional endurance in high-risk sports is instructive for our acceptance of the principle of stimulus addiction.

Looking further into the overall personality profile of the typical risk-taker recommends associative thoughts underpinning deeper inquiry into the beauty of sport. Thus, it is significant to note that risk-takers are like artists in their nonconformity, their abstract reasoning powers, their creativity, and their independence. What separates them from artists is their periodic need to extend themselves to absolute physical as well as emotional and intellectual limits. The risk-taking athlete has a strong sense of reality, necessary for the phenomenological interpretations of the sport-aesthetic. He has a high degree of emotional control, making him an admirable subject for the reflective description of aesthetic experience in sport as recommended by Thomas (1974).

Again, the risk-taking athlete expresses a great will to dominate. The search for supremacy over nature (mountain-climbing) or victory over an opposing competitor or team (wrestling, football) inspires him to excel. But the risk-taking athlete does not excel in spite of risk. The risk-excellence paradigm is ripe for further exploration as an interactive factor with potential to account for some aspect of the beauty of sport.

THE MOST BEAUTIFUL SPORT

The discussion of efforts made by man to achieve perfection led to the acknowledgment that the best he could reasonably attain was the demonstration of an ideal—in sport, an ideal form. Ideal, in this sense, is the realizable, and is not synonymous with abstract perfection. The ideal in "ideal form" might be equated synonymously with the epithet "straight from the book." In the truest sense of ideal form in sport, we can think of ideal pitching, ideal batting, ideal running, ideal balance, or any other kind of ideal performance. When we speak of ideal conditions for the game or the encounter, we are ascribing to the environment those qualities which will have least interference or add greatest assistance to our own objectives of ideal form in our sports endeavors. Ideal conditions for an attack on land or water speed records are not the same as those for hang-gliding. Thus we recognize that the ideal is both attainable and realizable and at the same time differs according to our sport needs.

The ideal form in sport is an intangible, a fleeting moment, or a total game. It is recognized but cannot be pinned down. It can be described, and most probably will be replayed. If it is described, then the limitations placed on words will impose similarity on repeat performance, yet in actuality the replaying will never be identical. If we can pin down the broad components, the essential commonalities, we can learn to recognize ideal form again and again. This is axiomatic for all the arts, as well as for sport, and therefore is fundamental to our aesthetic education. In support of this contention it is worth drawing upon the discussion that Roberts (1975) presents in his analysis of *The Sense of Beauty* by George Santayana:

> Although Santayana would not deny that the general form of the aesthetic response is the same among all men, he thinks it inconsistent to state that what is beautiful to one ought to be beautiful to another when things cannot have for any two men exactly the same value. (p. 92)

Value appears to be the key word, and while we may assume for our own purposes that all who find beauty in sport share an equal value for sport, we should be prepared to go one step further. Values presuppose preference, and so we might suggest that even within sport people will have different preferences for each type of sport according to their experience or association with it. This will be especially true with respect to athletes past and present.

There are at least two basic and separate strata of values operating in the appreciation of sport. Both, depending on your perspective, can be interpreted as subscribing to the beauty of the event. The separation between the two fundamental strata typifies the dichotomy which Jonathon Baumbach (1970) senses between being an artist and a fan:

> What interests me as a novelist is the event of a basketball game, the pleasures of style and skill, the psychological pressure. What interests me as a fan is the result. I want to see my team win no matter what. The two are not mutually exclusive, though often incompatible. . . . To see a game, to appreciate it as spectacle, one has to be to some extent disinterested in the outcome. The pleasures, however, are less intense. My sense is that a fan experiences a game as he experiences the world. (p. 140)

The epigrammatic nature of this quotation might be seen as a cardinal statement for future value orientations both of society and sport. When an athlete or ex-athlete reflects on his perception of the most beautiful sport— his own, of course—he frames that reflection in ideal form. That ideal form for Jay Wright (1969), poet and playwright (and former baseball player), is both personal and cultural:

> And at that moment I could think of baseball as the realization, the summit of a masculine esthetic—an esthetic which, as in the highest art,

summarizes a man's life, sets him in a historical context where he measures himself against the highest achievement and where he feels that he is perpetuating the spirit of the best of his chosen work. (p. 39)

From the point of view of the literate self-confessed fan, Angell (1972), in *The Summer Game,* puts the "masculine esthetic" of Jay Wright into terms specific to baseball as played by men:

Good pitching in a close game is the cement that makes baseball the marvelous, complicated structure that it is. It raises players to keenness and courage; it forces managers to think about strategy rather than raw power; it nails the fan's attention, so that he remembers every pitch, every throw, every span of inches that separates hits from outs. And in the end, of course, it implacably reveals the true talents of the teams on the field. (p. 43)

Roger Angell also makes the statement elsewhere in his book, that the reading of box-score statistics provides an esthetic "joy" equivalent to what a musician might experience in reading a fine score of sheet music by a famous composer. The literary artist, the man with facility in the choice and use of words, can be as evocative as the athlete himself in expressing for others what is perceived as beautiful in a sport, but the athlete holds the edge over the literary man by virtue of having the power of self-expression in physical terms. The best the literary artist can aspire to is limited by the communication gap known as "interpretation"; he can interpret only, he cannot give us by transference, as it were, that athletic experience in physical terms. This dilemma cannot be overcome, but we can explore it further in our consideration of the most beautiful sport.

Frequent reference is made to the fact that the athlete of a given sport knows more about the beauty of that sport than nonathletes or athletes of other sports. A well-fashioned gun, a bow, and a supremely modeled golf club all serve the purpose of precision sports to place a small object in a small target at a great distance, yet what is beautiful for the marksman of riflery may not be understood for the golfer, and vice versa. Each could "educate" the other on the respective "feel" of their instruments, on the "sound" made at the time of release or impact, and on other similar (yet dissimilar) facets of their respective sports, but each still retains his own greater insight. If, other things being equal, we focus on the pose/action of the marksman and the golfer, can we isolate what is beautiful about each of these sports from an objective perspective? Once again, each athlete individually could educate us about the beauty of their particular sports action or repose.

In some respect, Hussey (1929) taps the resource of components contributing to the sport-specific aesthetic when he states:

> Those who have never rowed day in and day out in an eight are perhaps unconscious of the beauty that an oarsman sees in a crew well together, or feels if he is in such a boat. . . . The aesthetic side of football is perhaps the most obscure, but it is by no means the least pronounced. There is a sadistic gratification to be derived from the sensuous experience of the scrum; the rank stench of sweat, the rough serge of other men's shorts grazing one's cheek, the smere [sic] of mud, the pervading slight soreness. More truly aesthetic is the sensation of shoving in a well-drilled and well-opposed scrum, where every man's locked and straining, part of a larger whole. (p. 25)

The reference to "scrum" is to English rugby which is currently gaining great popularity in America, but what Hussey says is to some extent evocative of a power drive by an offense on a third down and one yard to go, or a second down and goal to go. Most certainly, *The Onslaught,* a sculpture by R. Tait McKenzie, gives this impression, being as it is a representation of American football at the turn of the century. Indeed, it is fair to say that *The Onslaught* has greater aesthetic significance for a lineman or a tackle or the ball-carrier than it has artistic significance (the power to imbue aesthetic response) for the art connoisseur. From the side, *The Onslaught* presents the effect of a cresting wave, a breaker by the seashore, where the ball-carrier in mid-dive is falling over the line. In the words of Hussey, "there is a mighty rhythm, almost a surge, in the straining, swaying, heaving bodies." What football player does not inwardly recognize this situation as a part of his inner being, his authentic athletic identity? The scene presented by *The Onslaught* is similar to what is seen in almost every football game when a drive is made for the last yard of a down or goal.

For Norman Mailer, formerly a boxer of no mean rank, the most beautiful sport is boxing. He is never so eloquent in describing the beauty of boxing as when he is writing about Muhammad Ali. Indeed, writing about Ali brings out the best that Mailer has to say about boxing. In an article for *Life,* March 10, 1971, entitled "Ego," Mailer wrote about the first classic confrontation of Muhammad Ali and Joe Frazier; as a part of setting the scene for the round-by-round description, he spoke of elements of the sport and its adherents which allow entry to the better appreciation of that special beauty. If we take his concept of the "language of nature" as a restatement of the beauty of nature, the coincidence of symbolic meaning brings us closer yet:

> There are languages other than words, languages of symbol and languages of nature. There are languages of the body. And prize-fighting is one of them. A prizefighter . . . speaks with a command of the body which is as detached, subtle and comprehensive in its intelligence as any

exercise of the mind. [He expresses] himself with wit, style, and an esthetic flair for surprise when he boxes with his body. Boxing is a dialogue between bodies, [it] is a rapid debate between two sets of intelligence. (pp. 18–19)

The value that the literary artist brings to the writing of a sport is so much improved when the writing is given the stamp of one "who has been there." We believe the same to hold true for the painter who paints sports action, and for the sculptor who molds the best of athletic performers and performance. A writer such as Norman Mailer or Jack London appears to know by instinct the right choice of words that by sound invoke and are evocative of action. Our respect is sustained for the academic commentator, also. Michel Bouet is a master glider pilot as well as being a leading sport sociologist who has made several comments on the aesthetics of sport. In one instance he quotes Geblewitz as saying: "The beauty of movement plays a greater role in tennis than in football," and later supports this opinion himself by commenting on what he perceives to be component factors in support of this judgment.

In tennis there are elements of absolute aggressiveness (*grande ardeur combative*) between opponents, balanced by courtesies of the greatest aesthetic quality; the service provides a multitude of possibilities for rich and beautiful expression, finely coordinated action (*geste*), and simultaneous dynamism and precision. Turning to Kermadec for additional support to the superlative aesthetic nature of tennis, Bouet indicates that a quality of relationship must exist between the trajectory of the ball and the stroke played which is comparable to the relationship between a dancer and the music of the dance. In the latter sense, where limits of "perfection" are attained, one loses a conceptual grasp on whether the meeting of the player and the ball is the effect either of the player or of the ball. Tennis also has its literary exponent in the name of John McPhee. Writing in *Levels of the Game,* McPhee (1970) illustrates a point that Bouet and Kermadec would agree serves to distinguish an aesthetic criterion of tennis:

> Graebner's drive is deep to Ashe's backhand corner, and Ashe intercepts it with a beautiful, fluid crosscourt stroke. In the follow-through, he is up on his toes, arms flaring. Ashe's backhand is one of the touchstones of modern tennis. (p. 36)

Putting this image into the words of Arthur Ashe, the same idea of rising up on the toes to play a shot is stated as: "I can feel my serve from my toes to my fingertips—I don't have to look, it just flows" (quoted in *Levels of the Game,* by John McPhee). These words of Arthur Ashe also echo the words of Bill Russell spoken during a Dick Cavett television show in 1970. Russell was being interviewed on his judgment of basketball as a sport and as a career. In one of his statements, Russell spoke of the beauty of the sport:

> . . . a hook shot—it's a flowing action—almost everything is. Basketball is an art-form. If you were to take some pictures of slow motion of some of the shots of these great shooters—everything goes as it flows. . . . A shot starts on your toes and ends up on your fingertips and just ripples through your body.

Jonathon Baumbach, in an article for *Esquire* entitled, "The Aesthetics of Basketball," is in agreement with Russell when he states: "Basketball is a balletic game and teams often inspire their opponents as if they were playing in concert." This suggestion that the two teams blend into one action as in a ballet, opera, or drama is an interesting new departure for the study of the '"well-played game" (Kaelin, 1968). As a study in physical counterpoint, basketball, like hockey, presents one of the fastest expressions of artistic opposition in sport. The purest counterpoint comes in boxing, fencing, wrestling, judo, and the martial arts.

In 1972 Co Rentmeester, a staff photographer for *Life,* described an assignment on rowing in the following terms:

> What excited me most when I started the sculling story was just the sight of the shell itself—its lines, its grace, its speed as it sliced through the water. Many people consider rowing a brutal and graceless sport, but I believe it's one of the purest forms of sport [because] it requires not only an ultimate physical conditioning, but great sensitivity in balance and reflexes. It is not a social sport. It's rough and it's agonizing [and] I wanted to show the guts, the persistence, the mental toughness, the mood, and the loneliness that you have to have in this sport. (p. 3)

Besides being a photographer, Rentmeester competed for Holland in the 1960 Olympics as a sculler. Hence, his judgment on the beauty of rowing relates directly to his knowledge of the sport. Applying his art to his former sport, and giving his own feelings-description, satisfies many conditions simultaneously in our own search for meaning in the beauty of rowing as a sport (see Plate 12). In the photo-journalism article entitled "The Single-sculler's Search for Pain," Jim Dietz speaks of "that tremendous feeling of moving across the water." One of the photographs accompanying the text is particularly reminiscent of R. Tait McKenzie's sculpted mask, *Effort.*

The "joy of effort" remains mystical, as does the interpretation of the sport of archery, which for Elmer (1953) is the most beautiful. In that sport he sees power and grace, line and form, most elements that comprise a taxonomy for the beauty of sport:

> The writhing of a shaft past the bow and its flight through fields or potent but unseen forces are so puzzling even while so beautiful. All that

> is artistic within us responds to the grace of a bending bow. Our strength
> of body may be taxed to exhilaration by a powerful weapon, or we may
> be charmed by the sprightly response of one contrived more delicately.
> (p. 12)

Described in the terms of the nondefinitive components of beauty, such as
grace or delicacy of line, the aura of mysticism prevails. The mysticism
loses some of its magic, however, when more definitive terms describing the
potency of force, the "strength" of the bow, and potential flight of the
arrow are given consideration. To be sure, Elmer speaks nondefinitively of
the flight of the arrow for its beauty, but there is the sense of the real
dynamics of flight, and how these could be altered by atmospheric conditions, implicit in his aesthetic observation.

"Riding the pipeline" means something special to surfers. The "pipeline" is the effect made by a particular wave as it breaks over the sub-
merged reef in Hawaii, such that while the base of the wave is still cresting
up, the crown begins to break over, making a tunnel or funnel. To ride the
pipeline, the surfer must do many things, and only "masters" ever really
accomplish the feat. It is beautiful because successful performance encompasses so many features identified as contributing uniquely to the beauty of
sport. To begin with, the correct wave must be predicted—not all waves
develop the pipeline. Having identified the wave, the surfer must judge
where to ride it, where to drop over the crest and shoot the exact point
where the rolling pipeline forms. To do this he employs balancing techniques on his board which affect both speed and direction. The pipeline
closes over and behind the surfer so that he is riding down a blue-green
funnel created by the sea. The one end is open and he can emerge at will
and ride up over the crest to complete his trip. Tom Sabaca, among a few
others, has this ability. The control he exhibits over the power of the wave,
his balance and poise in effecting that control, and the choice he makes
regarding when he will go in and come out, are as nearly an expression of
perfection in that sport as could be determined.

Former world champion skier Billy Kidd describes his sport as "just
super exciting." In an interview with *Life* reporter Richard Meryman,
March 6, 1970, Kidd gives an illustration of why his sport is so thrilling for
him:

> There's a place in the Kitzbuhel downhill where you shoot down this
> wall so steep you're almost in a free fall for about 100 feet and you
> make this long 60-degree right-hand turn that falls away from you—like
> turning on the outside of a basketball—and you're going maybe 50 or 60
> mph—and its super rutty and bumpy. And then you thread onto this
> road that's flat for 30 seconds—and that's the race right there, so you
> have to hit the road with as much speed as you can, and I hit it so
> that just my top ski catches the road. It's just incredibly thrilling to me to

hit it just perfect so one ski holds me from going over the edge where it drops off a hundred feet into big trees. (p. 56)

To be taken to the rim of danger, to take oneself to the edge where risk is measured in fine slices, appears to be for particular athletes the essence of enthrallment. At the point where the athlete, as it were, "looks over the abyss," yet returns, survives to relive the event at his own choice, must sum up for him the reality of his own power.

What the role of athletic performance means to the individual must be seen as unique. People differ in their values, their hopes and fears, and in their self-perceptions. Sport for one may mean self-actualization in social terms, for another it means solitude or an establishment of the self that one recognizes and must live with regardless of human frailty. The imposition of the values of others on your own is unacceptable, and in this regard, the comments of Elliott (1974) are interesting:

> . . . we have to understand the appeal of certain sporting activities, for example the Marathon, which are entirely devoid of beauty and in which the element of contest between man and man does not seem to be the chief thing. It is not that the athlete conquers the distance, but that he conquers everything in himself which strives to prevent him from accomplishing his end. Mountain climbing is the most sublime of all sports, unless we allow circumnavigating the world alone under sail, or rowing across the Atlantic, to be sporting activities. We can easily be led into the error or supposing, however, that in these sports man conquers the mountain or the sea. This is *hubris*. Mountains and the sea do not issue challenges, and they can neither defeat man nor be defeated by him. The nature that is conquered is the nature within the sportsman himself: fear, fatigue, dispiritedness, pain, loneliness, and so on; and his performance is understood not so much as a personal achievement but as a presentation of what a human being morally is, of what in a sense we are all capable of, and to which we are all called in our various stations and conditions of life. It is unfortunate that this inspirational aspect of sport should have been somewhat discredited by the mystique of a struggle with a more or less personified external nature, and by a tendency to focus too closely on the purely personal aspect of the achievement. The athlete's desire to obtain knowledge of his own capacities and limitations, for example, is entirely his own affair. (pp. 114–115)

This thesis of Elliott is reflective of that presented by Roland Barthes in his commentary for the film *Of Sport and Man*. The point is well taken; the anthropomorphism of the mountains and the sea is unacceptable to us so long as we are looking for a scientific purity of expression. But what is wrong with a little symbolism? The symbolic interpretation of mountains issuing challenges is less troublesome than the assertion that the Marathon is a sport devoid of beauty. Are there athletes or others who would challenge this assertion? Are there students who would recommend that the concept of "endurance" should have been included in either of the chapters of this book dealing with definitive and nondefinitive parameters of symbolic communication for the beauty of sport? This section on the most beautiful sport has been selective. Not all sports were considered, referred to, or quoted. This is as much an acknowledgment that there is not *one* most beautiful sport, except that one which we hold as such for our own purpose. The claim that any one person makes for the most beautiful sport cannot be made at the expense of the opinion of others.

s u m m a r y

Value determinants of superlative sports effects are subjectively assessed and can be product or process oriented. The discussion of excellence, the ideal, and perfection, as these are interpretable as aesthetic, centers on personal as well as observed supreme athletic performance. Perfection is not realizable in human performance terms; the ideal is the best that man can achieve and becomes the hallmark of excellence.

The functional aesthetic in sport, an idea originating in the thinking of Michel Bouet, noted French sociologist, represents an interactive function deriving from the pursuit of excellence in sport. The functional aesthetic embraces kinesthetic and strategic beauties which can be experienced simultaneously, sequentially, or uniquely. In certain sports, such as gliding or whitewater canoeing, the functonal aesthetic satisfies elements of beauty in nature as well as beauty in art (the performance).

Taking a step toward differentiating the kinesthetic and the strategic, the process and the product, an attempt is made to provide insights associated with the so-called objective and subjective aesthetics. The objective aesthetic expresses the cognitive or intellectual (learned) experience of the beauty of nature or of art, with attendant emotional or affective response, whereas the subjective aesthetic states the physical-behavioral experience of beauty with attendant viscero-affective responses. Aspects of the objective aesthetic in sports are framed in concepts like "great moments in sport" and "the unforgettable game." Great sport is both evocative and expressive; it is only great sport in social terms. Personal performance evokes the subjective aesthetic. The scientific analysis of the subjective aesthetic presents problems of data collection, no less so than research design or methodology. Stimulus addiction appears to be related to risk taking in sport, both elements appearing to be closely correlated with what is understood as the subjective aesthetic in sport.

The objective aesthetic deals mainly with how we witness ideal form in art and in sport, how we intellectually (cognitively) appraise and attend to that which is beautiful. Our reactions to great moments in sport are usually of an affective or emotional content in which we respond to the dramatic form of a game, following and understanding its climactic pitch, sharing in the expectation of the unexpected to obtain a truly visceral excitement as if we were actually participating. In the subjective aesthetic, we analyzed those factors which we believed were component parts of the personal beauty of sport. For some, that personal beauty appeared to carry a loading of risk, and it was recommended that a further study of risk-takers, after the lead taken by Ogilvie and his associates, should be conducted for our enlightenment.

Perhaps this chapter should have opened with the provocative statement on the most beautiful sport, if only to have caught the attention of the student-athlete assuming that the commentary had to be on *his* sport. *His* sport is the most beautiful, of course, just as *yours* is the most beautiful. But will you agree to disagree, or will you seek to instruct each other? Will each of you want to learn how the other fellow's sport is "most beautiful"? The question is rhetorical, but hopefully it stimulates discussion.

questions for discussion

1. What is "stimulus-addiction" and how is it interpreted in the subjective aesthetic of sport?
2. Select a sport, one that you can make the best case for as "the most beautiful sport." What are the essential characteristics of the chosen sport?
3. What are the postulated physiological and psychological (perceptual) parameters defining the objective aesthetic?
4. What is the difference between a "great moment" in sport and an "unforgettable game"? Is it legitimate to call these events "beautiful"?
5. In what respect can cognitive, affective, and behavioral processes enlighten us on the subjective aesthetic in sport?

The Basis for Inquiry and the Need for Explanation

Beauty is a form of Genius—is higher, indeed, than Genius, as it needs no explanation.

OSCAR WILDE

INTRODUCTION

The sentiment expressed by Baron Pierre de Coubertin in his "Ode to Sport": "O Sport, you are Beauty," speaks for all who hold sport to be beautiful. Men and women are excited by skilled sports performance in which speed, strength, strategy, and concomitant factors are employed to explore human limitations. They enjoy participating for the personal experience of these effects and they enjoy watching others in their endeavors. The beauty of sport is both self-expressive and laudatory. "Beautiful!" is an accolade for the superlative athlete—and it is an unspoken feeling of self-accomplishment.

The concept of "athlete" is one which man has devised in the history of his cultural development to explain visually and experientially the phenomenon of excellence. Aspiration to physical achievement brings a person close to the mystery of his own physical structure, an experience all children go through, to where the recognition of others' physical achievements become culturally recognizable and intuitively acceptable. Knowing how well others do in sport is testified to by how well we can perform ourselves. The beauty of our own athletic performance is stated in how well we achieve, whereas the beauty ascribed to others is defined by how well we might hope to achieve.

If a sense of agreement has been reached that sport can be ascribed as beautiful, the question can be raised: Should the beauty of sport be subject to scientific inquiry? Equally applicable is the question whether the beauty of sport should be subject to humanistic inquiry. Scientific inquiry usually prescribes explanation in causal terms with the objective of indicating if there are laws of nature prevailing. Humanistic inquiry, on the other hand, is satisfied if the laws of logic are sustained.

Concepts in the abstract are limiting, particularly from an explanatory standpoint. Concepts such as speed, harmony, strength, rhythm, grace, precision, power, and control, when applied to sport, allow levels of comprehension only within systems of agreed symbolic communication. Such systems of symbolic communication are suitable only for humanistic inquiry, yet they lend much valuable substance to the development of theoretical testimony. Much of the theoretical testimony to the interpretation of sport in aesthetic terms rests on the basic premise that sport is an art-form and the athlete is an artist. As a mode of self-expression, sport is undifferentiated from all other culturally recognized arts. The argument is presented that connoisseurs of sport, particularly the athletes themselves, are opposed to accepting the reduction of sport to purely "physical" criteria. Sport as a work of art is associated most closely with dance as a work of art. The human form, since the time of Classical Greece, has been considered aesthetic. Indeed, the Greeks defined aesthetics as anything to do with perception by the senses. Today this definition is still acceptable, but elements attaching to the "transcendental" have been added, not the least of which is the discussion of Maslow's "peak-experiences" occurring in sport. Tony Jacklin, the British golfer, has testified to this phenomenon.

All of us know what we mean when we exclaim "Beautiful!" Those of us involved in sport certainly know what we mean, whether we experience it inwardly or whether we witness it in the skilled performance of others. But we retain our individuality.

Two basic philosophic approaches to sport science present essentially disparate viewpoints in application. One approach is *science for sport,* while the other presents the idea of *science of sport for man.* In the former, science serves sport for the improvement of performance with production objectives. Technological innovations have typified this thrust of *science for sport,* and these have reflected advances in the physical sciences, the only limitations placed on the athlete involving ethical principle and the risk of harm to the athlete. Advances in the social sciences in the service of sport, particularly in the psychology of sport, have tended toward a dehumanization of sport through infringement of the basic civil rights of participants. The professionalization of attitudes toward play and sport, filtering down to high school athletics, is a case in point. In the *science of sport for man* approach, sport is regarded a human phenomenon geared to performance for self-improvement rather than for productivity or the satisfaction of production objectives. In the latter instance, the role of the person is valued more highly than the result he achieves. The beauty of sport is tied more closely to the science of sport for man.

Sport is viewed by many as a subset of play, but at least one sport sociologist, Edwards (1973), separates it completely from play. In either case, sport is one of those nondefinitive words, and like aesthetics, it retains a freedom of interpretation which is reflective of the global conceptualization of play. The discussion of the subjective and objective aesthetics has been entered in Chapter 8, and the literature of empirical research finds supporters in both camps. The objectivist viewpoint of the aesthetic is supported by Child (1964) and by Child and Iwao (1964), while subjectivist argument is given greater support by Eisenman and Coffee (1964). The conflicting theories indicate the necessity for better understanding of the underlying components of aesthetics, and this can come about only by the definitive thrust of empirical research. The need for inquiry is patently evident from the increasing interest and attention being paid to the aesthetics of sport. The field is broad and there are many options for the serious researcher. Some of these options are discussed in this chapter, and in Chapter 10 two avenues of approach are illustrated in "case study" format. As was observed in tracing the information for Chapters 2 and 3, the employment of the empirical technique with library research proved fruitful.

THE NEED FOR INQUIRY

The experience of the aesthetic in a sport appears to depend upon personal preference for a particular sport, and may or may not generalize across all sports at the individual level. The fact that most people are aware of what is beautiful in sport does not help to solve the problem, since individual preferences preclude any commonality of the perception of beauty. The aesthetic response to the beauty of human action may or may not be exclusive of the response to animal or machine action. At this point of speculation it becomes evident that initial inquiry benefits analysis of the problem.

Both terms, "aesthetics" and "sport," are global in their conceptualization. Thus the freedom of interpretation that they provide is a hindrance to solving the problem outlined above. The contemporary meaning of aesthetic, designating the theory of the fine arts or the science of the beautiful, derives from the interpretation that Baumgarten and the eighteenth-century philosophers and poets gave to the concept. The phenomenological interpretation of the term has changed little, as Berenson's description of the "Aesthetic Moment" reveals:

In visual art the aesthetic moment is that flitting instant so brief as to be almost timeless, when the spectator is at one with the work of art he is looking at, or with actuality of any kind that the spectator himself sees in terms of art, as form and colour. He ceases to be his ordinary self, and the picture or building, statue, landscape, or aesthetic actuality is no longer outside himself. The two become one entity; time and space are abolished and the spectator is possessed by one awareness. When he recovers workaday consciousness it is as if he had been initiated into illuminating, exalting, formative mysteries. In short, the aesthetic moment is a moment of mystic vision. (p. 93)

Philosophical inquiry into aesthetics is a soundly established area of study, and there are many treatises which testify to this observation. Empirical inquiry, on the other hand, conducted by students of psychology, seeks to explain aesthetics by methods more commonly used in the behavioral sciences, and this literature is scant and diffuse.

The "mystic" quality of the aesthetic has not deterred psychologists from attempting to explain the phenomenon. The earliest psycho-physical investigations into the nature of beauty, the aesthetics of color, were carried out by the German psychologist Fechner in the late nineteenth century. These studies predicted a trend in empirical aesthetics which found endorsement in the opinion of Langfeld (1920) that:

. . . the ideal of aesthetics should be a vigorous scientific one if it is to keep in touch with reality and serve the needs of those who are searching for a wider experience. (p. 18)

The wider experience for the beauty of sport should be couched in empirical or scientific procedure, according to our interpretation of Langfeld. This is but one avenue of inquiry, as was indicated at the outset of this chapter.

It may be possible to speak of experiencing an "aesthetic," which would describe a feeling of elation or a sophisticated intellectual appreciation in response to witnessing "the beautiful." Cassirer (1944) states:

That beauty is not an immediate property of things, that it necessarily involves a relation to the human mind, is a point which seems to be admitted by almost all aesthetic theories. . . . Beauty cannot be defined by its mere *percipi*, as "being perceived"; it must be defined in terms of an activity of the mind, of the function of perceiving and by a characteristic direction of this function. It does not consist of passive percepts; it is a mode, a process of perceptualization. But this process is not merely subjective in character; on the contrary, it is one of the conditions of our intuition of an objective world. The artistic eye is not a passive eye that receives and registers the impression of things. It is a constructive eye, and it is only by constructive acts that we can discover the beauty of natural things. The sense of beauty is the susceptibility to the dynamic life of forms, and this life cannot be apprehended except by a corresponding dynamic process in ourselves. (p. 167)

At the current level of discussion, it is not necessary to argue the side for either a predominantly emotional or intellectual basis for the "aesthetic," since the interactive effect may prove to be nearer the truth.

For example, there is a strong belief among aestheticians that while a spontaneous emotional feeling may be "fired" within a person and so be described as a beautiful or aesthetic experience, there is the added factor that previous knowledge of what caused the effect aids in priming a person for that aesthetic experience.

Moving from the aesthetic as a response to the acquisition of an aesthetic in a behavioral sense—in which the desired behavior pattern is learned for the strict purpose of providing an aesthetic—an area of endeavor in sports performance is found which is unique in its competitive demands. Thus, in such sports as diving, gymnastics, and skating, a successful performance is greatly dependent upon the aesthetic quality of execution. Occasionally the individual components of a graceful movement are isolated by the viewer and interpreted as an "aesthetic." The resulting personal response is derived either from an empathy for the action itself or from a personal interpretation of the composition, form, and technique of the movement. In this regard films of sports events often become, after the event, the same as the event itself, while sculpture, painting, graphic arts, and literature involve only selected moments of action as personally interpreted by the individual artist or author. (See Chapters 2 and 3.)

Whether there is a difference between the aesthetic experienced in response to the art-form representing sport, and the "aesthetic" experienced in response to the sport performance, raises the kind of question that directs attention to the beauty of sport. Thought and discussion deriving out of this and similar questions should direct us to closer examination of, and perhaps accounting for, the problem as identified. We may ask if a sculpture of a diver executed by R. Tait McKenzie is any more aesthetically pleasing or provocative than the witnessing of a superlative diver executing a half-gainer. Time and space dimensions intrude, as well as the background experience that we call upon. The specificity of the artist and the diver obliges each to look for differing component parts. What the artist would see in the sculpture pertains more to art, whereas what the diver would see in the sculpture pertains more to the sport and the physical characteristics of the pose. These would not be unilateral observations by each, except in extreme cases, but rather each would have a sympathy for the other's perspective. In each instance of the art-form implied, the piece of sculpture and the diving-action of the athlete, the elements of time and space obtrude differentially to provide separate dimensionalities. The extension of the time-space paradigm to relate the "art-form" of sport to other art-forms provides, at the very least, a phenomenological groundwork for subsequent inquiry. Once psychologists have established parameters for the identification and quantification of time and space differences as they apply to the experience of an aesthetic, then establishing the qualities which make sport beautiful will be relatively easy.

MODES OF INQUIRY

Thus far, two overall modes of inquiry have been discussed: (1) the humanistic-philosophic, and (2) the scientific-empirical. In one respect, an empirical turn of mind has been brought to humanistic investigation, and this is proposed in the method of critical analysis. Initial attempts to get to the heart of the beauty of sport as it has been represented in culture recommends several methods of analysis. Some of these have been employed prior to the writing of this text. For example, the overview of the representation of sports action in painting and sculpture can be found in Chapter 2 and Chapter 3, the essentials of which were researched some years ago.

Teleological inquiry stemming from studies in child development, which seek to correlate the development of color-form preferences with the evolution of play or game-form experience, may direct attention to factors contributing to the nascent aesthetic. It is not yet clear whether the aesthetic has matured in the growing child before the point when the demonstration of sports skills elicits the experience. Also, the question of minimal age when sports participation as a social process occurs needs clarification.

A further point of departure requires investigating the cultural modes of expression of nonliterate societies. Art styles and game forms are the basic units of study, and the way in which these are dependent upon the cognitive and perceptual styles of the society provides the medium for application. Thus, the finding by Barry (1957) that the correlation of complex art styles with severe socialization pressures toward independent behavior (rather than toward obedient behavior), and the finding by Roberts and Sutton-Smith (1962) correlating game forms with socialization practices both recommend a methodological approach toward correlating play with aesthetics hitherto not apparent in the literature.

Indeed, the literature has very little to show for the relationship between sport and the aesthetic. Two descriptive studies show that strong favorable attitudes toward the aesthetic quality of sport are held by secondary school students in Canada, Australia, England, and the United States

(Kenyon, February 1968) and by North American athletes of international rank (Alderman, 1970).

Other pertinent procedures suggest themselves: reviewing sports documentary movies and sports-page photography; content analyses of biographies and autobiographies of major sports figures; initiating closer investigation of sports with proclaimed aesthetic content and purpose (see Chapter 5, "Form-Sport: Gymnastics"), and others.

Summary review statements of some of these methods of analysis are given here, but more significant sections of the book present the substantive research embodying these modes of inquiry. Thus, as regards sports action in painting, the significance attaching to the life of George Bellows is couched in the fact that, although he was a football and basketball star in college, he never painted these sports. Instead, he painted boxing scenes, polo, and "genre" pictures of boys diving off the docks into the East River, among his other work. To research the life of Bellows would be a fascinating project; to find out why he never boxed and yet he is acclaimed as one of America's most renowned artists by virtue of his boxing scenes, "Dempsey and Firpo" being the most noteworthy.

Among sculptors, R. Tait McKenzie has brought a fine sense of movement to his athletic studies cast in bronze. There is no question about the aesthetic qualities of these art-works; hence they provide intrinsic clues to our grasp of the elusive nature of beauty in sport. The recent book by Kozar (1975) on McKenzie illustrates the wealth of information and the value of his subject in bringing a new perspective to this great sculptor and physical educator.

The review of sports documentary films such as *Solo, 60 Cycles, Ski the Outer Limits, Rowing: A Symphony of Motion,* among others, would provide new insight to the interpretation of the aesthetic in sport. Indeed, taking the title of *Ski the Outer Limits,* we are given in "the outer limits" a concept of new levels of excellence in physical performance, new creative potential for the future development of sport. In that movie, the narrator makes the comment that the unusual of today will be the commonplace of tomorrow, thereby suggesting that the creative process is an ongoing effect, as viable in sport as in any other art-form. This present text has used several quotations from *Rowing: A Symphony of Motion* to illustrate points being made at the theoretical or speculative level of discussion. Some of these points were initiated by reference to the movie, but the greater contention here is that a full-scale analysis of the movie, the points made by the interviewers, scenes depicting the beauty and power of the sport, the sense of artistic interplay between boat-builder and the finished shell, the transmittance of this artistic interplay to the athlete, the oarsman, all these factors would tell us so much more about what we seek in the beauty of sport. It goes without saying that we are dependent on the vision of the movie-maker and of the director to educate us in the provision of their insights. The point is made. The availability of material is widespread, and the initial interest has been triggered. The visual domain can provide great reward for the serious research student.

Reference has been made to those sports—the form-sports—claiming aesthetic components in their execution. Sports such as gymnastics and figure skating ascribe a great component of the scoring to aesthetic quality of performance. Kunzle (1956), author of many texts on gymnastics, says:

> The good gymnast must be graceful in movement, that is to say, have a sense of rhythm allied to control; he must have feeling for the plastic, decorative effect of a posture and for beauty of combination. (p. 212)

The clue is given here for the understanding of what "aesthetic" means, namely, that when the judge of competition becomes one entity with the performer, no longer feeling that the performance is outside of himself, then the aesthetic has been created. In women's free-standing exercises and beam in gymnastics, and in figure skating for both sexes, attempts are made by the athlete to approximate dance without destroying the fundamental characteristics of the sports. By analyzing dance, as one of the performing arts, with the objective of deducing the aesthetic components usually described as form, harmony, grace, and flow, a step will be taken closer to the clarification of the beauty of sport as a performing art. The sports that claim aesthetic components as part of their structure of performance are referred to as "form-sports." What comprises the beauty of form-sports may be transferable to other sports. Further, if component elements of the dance are thus transferable through the form-sports to other sports, then the theatre, or playing of musical instruments, as other performing arts may have transferable aesthetic criteria by which we might call sports beautiful. It is useful, therefore, to think of sport as one of the performing arts and to deduce the strength of argument stemming from that assumption. (See Chapters 4 and 5.)

Besides the foregoing examples of humanistic pursuit for inquiry into the beauty of sport, there are other approaches calling upon skills developed through an arts education. Reference to other writings is made rarely in this text, but there is resource material in abundance. Asking pertinent questions in the humanistic vein is no less important than looking to those couched in empirical terms intending to satisfy scientific criteria. Very often humanistic inquiry will be the initiating force to empirical research. This is the case with empirical testimony for the aesthetics of sport.

Several possible approaches for empirical testimony recommend themselves to the researcher: (1) testing groups of athletes for their aesthetic sensitivity; (2) seeking differences in aesthetic sensitivity between sports for groups of athletes; and (3) developing survey questionnaires to tap population perceptions.

THE MEASUREMENT OF AESTHETICS

As early as 1888 Sully and Robertson suggested that looking at the continuum "from crude enjoyment of sensation to the more refined and subtle delights of the cultivated mind" would help resolve the question of whether there is any form of beauty which pleases "universally and necessarily," as Kant holds. The psycho-physical experiments with colors and forms conducted by Fechner demonstrate the first attempt to put such advice to empirical test.

Whereas the earliest empirical studies into the aesthetic per se originate with the psycho-physical experimentation of Fechner in the nineteenth century, the greatest advances toward its understanding have evolved within the last forty-five years. The mathematician Birkhoff (1933) believed that aesthetics was reducible to mathematical expression, much as the Classical Greeks had believed. He could be justified in this belief, for had not the Greeks designed and built monuments of great aesthetic quality based on their knowledge of proportion? The basis for Birkhoff's mathematical formula for the measurement of *aesthetic value* rested on the three components of *aesthetic experience:*

1. Preliminary attention and extended attention dependent on complexity (C).
2. Value recognition or aesthetic measure which rewards (1), (M).
3. Order recognition, embracing a harmony or symmetry necessary for the effect (O).

Hence, aesthetic measure was a direct function of the number of order elements, and an inverse function of the number of complexity elements. Birkhoff claimed it to be "a quantitative index of comparative aesthetic effectiveness." Eysenck (1968) summarized the literature relevant to Birkhoff's formula and found it lacking in reliability. His own restatement of the formula as aesthetic measure being the product of order and complexity, has been empirically tested and found to be closer to the Birkhoff concept of aesthetic value. The development of the Polygon Test (Eysenck, 1968) stemmed directly from the mathematical reformulation.

Devised in 1952, the Barron-Welsh Figure Preference test was intended to test the possibility of artistic perception as a factor in personality style. The test was successful in differentiating artists from nonartists in preferences for complexity-simplicity and symmetry-asymmetry. The Art Acceptance Scale appears to be the first empirical approach to satisfying the counsel of Sully and Robertson. Beittel (1968) claimed that the test

> . . . helps to establish the notion of the true continuum of naive to sophisticated appreciation, further suggesting that differences of degree and not of kind are involved in aesthetic appreciation. (p. 60)

The objective nature of this test and its high internal consistency ($r=.82$) make it a suitable instrument for assessing the attitude dimension of aesthetic sensitivity.

The approach of the information theorists (Moles, 1966; Rump, 1968) has placed stronger emphasis on exploring complexity-simplicity and stimulus content parameters in perceptual choice and appreciation. The "maximum function hypothesis" postulated by Rump, which predicts that an individual's preference scores will show a monotonic increase up to his personal "optimum-complexity" and a decreasing trend for more complex stimuli, was supported with random designs but not with random polygons. Berlyne, Ogilvie, and Parham (1968) found the level of complexity of an object perceived by an individual to be closely related to the pleasingness or interestingness of that object for him.

Child (1962, 1964, 1966, 1970) has been prominent both as a theoretician and an empiricist in the exploration of the nature of aesthetics. His contributions toward definitional clarification, his developmental studies, his investigations of the personality correlates associated with aesthetic judgment and preferences, and his cross-cultural studies put him in the vanguard of aesthetic inquiry today. On definitional questions, Child has advocated the structuring of components of aesthetic sensitivity toward comprehension of the more general term. In contrast with McWhinnie (1969) and Beittel (1968), he prefers to retain the generalized concept as a focal point for the ultimate relationship of constituent parts. His cross-cultural studies have a major advantage over earlier studies which found no evidence of cross-cultural agreement on matters of aesthetic preference in that they compared transcultural preference of those interested in art.

Eysenck (1941) demonstrated for a number of stimulus classes (including colors, paintings, and polygons) the existence of a general factor of aesthetic *appreciation,* and more recently (1968) showed that when the influence of this factor is eliminated, a secondary bipolar factor emerges which appears to have positive and negative saturations in about equal numbers in the population studied. The bipolar factor separates individuals with preferences for the simple polygon against the complex, and for unified as opposed to diversified pictures. In a factor-analytic study of cognitive complexity-simplicity, Vannoy (1965) describes a factor which by interpretation appears to support the trend of thought expressed by Eysenck (1941; 1968), and which might be construed to relate to the finding by Child (1965) that tolerance for complexity and *aesthetic judgment* have a significant positive relation. This finding is in support of Barron (1952), and in a later study there is evidence that *aesthetic sensitivity* is related to cognitive independence and openness (Child and Iwao, 1968). Berlyne, Ogilvie, and Parham (1968) have sought to explain the aesthetic in terms of "complexity, interestingness, and pleasingness." Empirically, they extract judged complexity as a major determinant of judged interestingness and pleasingness. These findings can be related to the maximum-function hypothesis of Rump (1968), who bases his approach to the analysis of the aesthetic on the information theory expounded by Moles (1966). Rump's hypothesis refutes Lee (1938), who held that the more complex an object involving greater perceptual activity, the greater the degree of aesthetic value it attains. The importance of the "complexity" studies for the comprehension of the aesthetic is given added weight by Pyron (1966) and by Wober (1968). Wober introduces the notion of "aesthetic unit," a nonreducible bit of information, the perceptual succession of which is compared to the previous one on the two criteria of "difference" and "belonging." Ultimately the rules determining the phrasing of aesthetic units depend on the extent to which cognitive skills have been developed in particular sense modes. It is possible that in a given individual there is a preference, in terms of cognitive perception, for either music or the visual arts. Thus, an individual socialized in sport may acquire in the development of his perceptual cognitions a recognition of sport as an art-form, providing him with the sensitivity for a sport-aesthetic.

Largely, the history of the measurement of the aesthetic in man has been a task for psychologists. The behavioral components have been viewed as more accessible than the social components. From a social standpoint an assumption must be made that all people are sensitive to beauty, have a recognition of what is beautiful (at the very least, from their own base of reference). This assumption is held for social survey research into the beauty of sport.

Aesthetic Sensitivity of Athletes

Testing groups of athletes for their aesthetic sensitivity presents difficulties as to definition as well as to instruments for quantitative measurement. The supposition that athletes who engage in "aesthetic" sports like gymnastics should be more aesthetically sensitive than others needs to be tested. There is always the question of sport-specific sensitivity regarding what is beautiful—namely, a baseball player knows best the beauty of baseball, the motor-racing driver knows best what is beautiful in motor racing. The total question of the aesthetic sensitivity of athletes is highly provocative.

Aesthetic Sensitivity of Athletes Between Sports

Tests of art attitude and art judgment were administered to wrestlers, tennis players, swimmers, and gymnasts in an attempt to estimate differences in aesthetic sensitivity. Tennis players scored significantly higher than wrestlers in both art attitude and art judgment, with swimmers and gymnasts scoring about the same. None of the athletes scored higher than a control group of the general population, so in spite of their sport, gymnasts cannot claim a greater sense of the aesthetic than other people.

s u m m a r y

In this chapter some effort has been made to emphasize one of the major tenets of this book, namely that the best sense of inquiry is one which reflects an empirical turn of mind. Not only this chapter but the whole book is framed in one large question: How do we understand the beauty of sport? If it is your response that understanding is not necessary, but that the *appreciation* is all, then you would need to challenge or accept the fact that your knowledge (and therefore your appreciation) about the beauty of sport would be lacking. This chapter, like the book, addresses this challenge, for we all seek a greater appreciation in the long run.

Although Chapters 6 and 7 entertained some analysis of component elements of beauty freely designated definitive and nondefinitive parameters, a sense of uneasiness prevails. Such elements, categorized as parameters, were assumed to exist, were presumed to be recognized and accorded to by many of the population, yet what substantive evidence supports that contention? Perhaps a survey of some samples or representative groups, drawn from the population, and questioned for their recognition and acceptance of such parameters as descriptive of beauty in sport would be one direction to go. The results of such a survey would be both interesting and directional in turn. The survey is a potent technique when correctly designed and delivered.

The social science of sport recommends primarily that man should be served in the provision of information about sport which will serve his needs in sport in turn. A sense of questioning is endemic to science, and especially to social science. The social sciences do not claim to serve man, they provide information about man, and what he does with it afterwards (if he chooses to act on it at all) is his own affair. The phenomenon of sport is rich in a natural "mother lode" for the scientists of social and psychological behavior in man. Sport is not merely or purely beautiful, nor is it a total expression of reduced social sanction for the release of combative forces in man. But sport is beautiful to some extent. To what extent is not known, but students of the social science of sport can find out by asking and answering pertinent questions.

The need for inquiry has been stressed. There appear to be both behavioral and "mystical" qualities (the physical and the metaphysical) attaching to experiences categorized as the beauty of sport. Each appears to manifest itself both in the participant-performance and in the spectatorial domains, although little evidence has been found thus far to isolate mystical-metaphysical experience in the spectatorial frame of reference. In the wider text of this book, reference has been made to psycho-physiological reactions which it may be possible to monitor, and in this chapter the need to explore these techniques further is emphasized. In the main, however, this chapter has stressed social scientific techniques deriving from psychological and sociological methodologies, and has restated humanistic and analytic criteria for research. Research techniques as employed in analysis of the arts are of critical importance for the provision of supporting evidence to substantiate a claim that sport should be recognized as one of the performing arts.

One of the manifest empirical questions rests with the measurement of aesthetics. A brief history of this exercise, including efforts to define, qualify, and quantify, is elaborated from the nineteenth-century studies of Fechner to the present-day approach exploring possibilities for use of the computer based on information theory. Lastly, the concept of "aesthetic sensitivity" is introduced, presaging the empirical investigation of it in Chapter 10.

questions for discussion

1. Describe two basic approaches in which science can serve sport and state which approach is most applicable to the analysis of the beauty of sport.
2. The need for inquiry into the beauty of sport refutes the fact that mystical or metaphysical forces may be determined. Discuss the nature of this impasse between fact and belief, and state how social and behavioral scientists would face the problem.

3. The modes of inquiry investigating the beauty of sport are diverse and unrestricted. Take two basic approaches, one behavioral and one humanistic, and compare the areas of inquiry that each indicates.
4. Can aesthetics be subjected to commensurable analysis?
5. What is the difference between aesthetic attitude and aesthetic judgment?

The Role
of Empirical Investigation

The sources of art in human experience will be
learned by him who sees how the tense grace
of the ball-player infects the on-looking crowd.

JOHN DEWEY

INTRODUCTION

This chapter is a radical departure from the rest of the book, presenting examples of pure empiricism in application to the search for the beauty
of sport. Two techniques of empirical inquiry are presented as case studies;
these constitute (1) a social survey technique and (2) a simple one-way
analysis of variance, the technique used to test the significance of differences between groups. The case studies are complete, that is to say, they
are "papers" as might be delivered at a conference, or "articles" published
in a journal. As such, the case studies demonstrate two basic models for
the preparation of such papers or articles, as well as providing substantive
evidence in analyzing the aesthetics of sport. Hence, the case studies also
serve two purposes; providing of information, and illustrating at least two
ways of conducting empirical research.

SURVEY RESEARCH AND AESTHETIC QUALITIES

In substantiation of the claim that the social survey technique of
research is a fruitful method of arriving at an empirical level of understanding of the beauty of sport in culture, Osterhoudt (1972) states: "Since the
poetically contemplative leads itself only begrudgingly to linguistic or

rational analysis, the experiential element is likely to be more analytically instructive." By this, Osterhoudt suggests that what people as a group tell us of what they perceive to be aesthetic becomes a basis for further analytic inquiry. Social survey questionnaires, submitted to groups of people, are intended to do precisely that.

What are "aesthetic qualities"? The term is used frequently and perhaps loosely. Strictly speaking, a quality is a *value*. The value, or the quality, can be given a scale, usually of the "poor-excellent" range of judgment. According to the many individual opinions held by any group, a value or quality will be ranked differentially along the scale. In the initial stage of discussion, however, there must be *some* agreement by all members of a group that there *exists* a particular value or quality, or that what exists can be called a value or quality. The basic assumption that all people have a sense of what is beautiful, be it specific to their own culture or background, should not severely test the question of universal law, nor should there be serious argument as to whether beauty is a value. That beauty can be put on a scale of valuation is supported traditionally in proverbial form by such sayings as: "One man's meat is another man's poison." Thus the polarity of "good-bad," or of "excellent-poor" can be made applicable to the aesthetic.

On a more simplistic level, people can be asked in questionnaire format whether they find a particular subject or object "beautiful" or "ugly," thus reducing the option of a scaled response to a binomial option. It becomes clear, then, that question construction is vitally important in any questionnaire that will tap the values of a population. Ambiguity is to be avoided in the questions, and there must be some assurance that all the members of the sample to whom the questionnaire is distributed fully comprehend what is being asked of them. Appropriateness of question is as important as the correct written delivery of the question. Questions must be composed with two basic reference points in mind: (1) the subject matter and topic of interest for the study, and, (2) the population of whom the information is required. Once the questions are formed, they are asked of a *sample,* a randomly selected group of no less than 2 percent of the population being studied.

"Survey research," states Kerlinger (1964), "is that branch of social scientific investigation that studies large and small populations (or universes) by selecting and studying samples chosen from the population to discover the relative incidence, distribution and interrelations of sociological and psychological variables." As a working definition, this tells us that the researcher employs a specific technique from a set of options to establish sociological facts, opinions, or attitudes (dispositions). In most cases, the researcher is more interested in the psychological variables (what people think and do) than in the sociological facts. How he obtains this information is dependent on the technique he uses for collection, and to some extent this is determined by the size of sample he uses. For example, a door-to-door interview or telephone survey will be more time-consuming than a mailed questionnaire. However, many of the mailed questionnaires may not be returned, perhaps as much because they are impersonal as for any other reason, and so follow-up reminders are necessary. The personal or telephone interview usually gets on-the-spot results, but takes time, or a team of trained personnel to assist the researcher. These brief points are meant only to give a flavor of social survey research, and the student is referred to texts on that subject for more detail (e.g., *Introduction to Social Research* by Laboritz and Hagedorn, 1971).

How is social survey research valuable for investigation of the beauty of sport? Well, let us ask that question more directly. How many undergraduates at a typical urban state commuter university attend games for aesthetic purposes? In two surveys conducted at such institutions, one in the Midwest and one in a large Eastern city, the answers to that question provided similar results. Approximately 15 to 20 percent of undergraduates claim they attend sports events to witness "the beauty of movement." Women spectators make this claim more than men. With this knowledge, we now have a group of people that can be approached to question further for the "experiential element" of their aesthetic responses, as Osterhoudt recommends. With their grouped opinions, and with their specific commentaries, such a group would provide many insights into the beauty of sport. This can only be hypothesized at this time, and remains a question for future research. (The baseline of 15 to 20 percent of undergraduates responding to "the beauty of movement" question has not been followed up at this time.)

Survey research questionnaires can be constructed so that the respondent checks a particular option as "frequently," "occasionally," or "never" in respect to whether they do a particular thing as a part of their day-to-day behavior. Indeed, as a general point, it greatly facilitates questionnaire response (and therefore return) if the respondent is not required to spend time writing, but is only required to check an option. (Question construction, it may be emphasized, is a "fine art.") When the information is gathered from a satisfactory response percentage, tabulations and cross-tabulations can be made. Typically, a satisfactory return would be 60 percent, but a scale of percentage returns assessed against sample size should be consulted for acceptable statistical results to be meaningful.

In Case Study 1 following, questions were constructed such that respondents checked "frequently," "occasionally," or "never" against patterns of behavior postulated as representative of artistic pursuits, leisure activities, and sport involvement. Underlying assumptions recommend that those who check "frequently" for "active in creative arts and crafts," "active in dramatic performance," or "attendance at concerts" be regarded as people with aesthetic dispositions or sensitivities. And, if a graded question asking the respondent to check against how he qualifies himself on sports interest (deep–none) has been inserted into the questionnaire, this allows for the extraction of answers to questions about interrelationships between sport and the arts in any given population. Cross-tabulations of responses to questions dealing both with art and sport show that, generally in industrial society, people interested in sport are not interested in the arts, and vice versa, with rare exceptions. This information may come as no surprise to most observers of the contemporary scene, but it involves the use of social survey techniques to scientifically establish the fact as incontestable. However, on the positive side, further inquiry with those few people who are stimulated both by sport and by the arts (as identified by the survey) will help pinpoint criteria for establishing what is meant by the beauty of sport.

Case Study 1

SOCIAL AND BEHAVIORAL CORRELATES OF SPORT AND THE ARTS

Introduction

Contemporary society allows for clear distinctions to be drawn between the two realms of sport and the arts. Except in a few sporadic cases, it is difficult to draw a relationship between them, yet common root criteria can be traced to account for their existence. Classical historians [1]* assure us that when emerging civilizations attain order and wealth, leisure provides the opportunity for nongainful pursuit in play, spectacle, and development of the arts. A philosophical elaboration of this is provided by Huizinga [2], who rather flamboyantly would have us accept that there is no difference between sport and the arts, even in the present-day context of things. The pragmatic perspective tells us differently, and this is summarized succinctly by Wenberg, who states: ". . . we haven't seemed to find it possible in our culture to regard physical excellence as something as beautiful as musical excellence or artistic excellence [3]." The *rapprochement* of sports and the arts is still far away, but some indications suggest that more attention is being paid to the tentative links which will draw

* Numbers in brackets within this section refer to footnotes at the end of Case Study, page 288.

them closer together in the ideal blend that Classical Greece has demonstrated for posterity. Sport historians have typically depended upon artifacts and art objects for their knowledge of classical game forms and athletic pursuits [4], but recent history is not so abundant in illustrative art-forms representing sport. This can be said to indicate differences between the tightness of the social structure of Classical Greece and the looseness of modern industrialized society. Indeed, it would be curious if the relationship between sport and the arts did teach us this kind of a lesson.

Contemporary academic trends toward tracing and understanding the relationship of sport and the arts have followed several paths. Encyclopedic accounts of sport in painting [5] and in sculpture [6], philosophic treatises and dissertations on sport as an art-form [7], and investigations into the aesthetics of sport [8] have all provided alternative approaches. If sport is seen as a subset of play, the current work of Sutton-Smith [9] must be seriously considered for its point of departure, with a clarification of "the genetic epistemology of expressive structures" needed before any leap can be made toward relating sport and the arts. The ideographic focus of attention on personages who have been both artists and athletes, typified in the writing of Miller and Russell [10] and current trends in sport-reporting [11], represents a tenuous thread of association no stronger than the claim that sport, like art and music, has often been pursued as a form of self-expression. The idle musings of barroom habitués that football in slow motion is like ballet, serve no more instructive a purpose than the media broadcasting such scenes to the sound accompaniment of Big Band Jazz.

Somewhat more pragmatically, the present research sought to establish what relationship might exist between sport involvement and pursuit of the arts from self-reports of the lifestyle of undergraduates. Insofar as the typical undergraduate can be said to represent society, the findings of this study can be generalized—but only within those limitations.

For the purpose of this study, sport involvement embraces both disposition toward (interest in) sport, generally speaking, as well as expressed preference for sport pursuit, be it participating or spectating. Pursuit of the arts is categorized by the reading of novels, creative activity in arts and crafts, acting or dramatic production, and attending concerts.

Procedure

A survey questionnaire focusing on questions pertaining to pursuit of the arts and involvement in sport was composed and mailed to a random sample of 1,000 undergraduates (out of a total enrollment of 32,000) attending a large urban state university. Responses were returned by 782 of these.

Results

Results are given for interrelationships between sport involvement and four selected categories of the arts: plastic, literary, music, and performing arts. Activity pursuits in the plastic arts refer directly to creative work of painting, sculpture, or similar craft work; with respect to literature, reference is to the reading of novels; with respect to music, reference is to attendance at concerts of music; and in the performing arts, reference is to acting or dramatic performance.

Table 1.1 illustrates that there is an inverse relationship between activity in creative arts and crafts and interest in sport. Except for those who show no interest in sport, who appear to be little different in their activity pursuit of creative arts and crafts from those who are deeply interested in sport, the incidence of *frequent* pursuit of arts and crafts increases significantly, the less the interest in sport; and, similarly, the greater the interest in sport, the more likely is the person to avoid any form of active art production. This is more dramatically illustrated in Figure 1, which represents a graphical picture of the interrelationships. While the observed directions of the interrelationship from deeply interested to slightly interested in sport with respect to active pursuit of creative arts might be accounted for in the present climate of acceptability of each in

Table 1.1
Activity in Creative Arts and Crafts in Relation to Interest
in Sport as Expressed by Undergraduates (in percent)

Active in Creative Arts and Crafts	Sports Interest				
	Deep	Much	Casual	Slight	None
Frequently	16.1 (10)	25.1 (55)	25.5 (65)	33.6 (38)	17.8 (8)
Occasionally	33.9 (21)	41.6 (91)	46.5 (118)	44.3 (50)	40.0 (18)
Never	50.0 (31)	33.3 (73)	28.0 (71)	22.1 (25)	42.2 (19)
Total	100	100	100	100	100
N	(62)	(219)	(254)	(113)	(45)

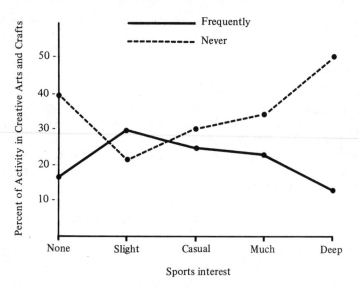

Fig. 1   Activity in Creative Arts and Crafts in Relation to
Interest in Sport

current cultural climates of society, the close similarity between those not at all interested in sport and those deeply interested in sport is both curious and challenging.

Table 1.2
Activity in Creative Arts and Crafts in Relation to Preferred Style of
Involvement in Sport as Expressed by Undergraduates (in percent)

Active in Creative Arts and Crafts	Sports Involvement		
	Participant	Both Participant and Spectator Equally	Spectator
Frequently	23.4 (48)	23.2 (65)	28.2 (50)
Occasionally	45.9 (94)	41.6 (117)	42.4 (75)
Never	30.7 (63)	35.2 (99)	29.4 (52)
Total N	100 (205)	100 (281)	100 (177)

By contrast with the clear distinction between levels of interest in sport and pursuit of creative arts and crafts, Table 1.2 shows that type of *involvement in* sport cannot be differentiated by frequency of active art pursuit. Indeed, the data suggest normal distributions of creative arts pursuit irrespective of primary expressed preference for sport involvement.

The data presented in Table 1.3 suggest that, besides the greater majority of undergraduates never indulging in acting or dramatic performance, there is no relationship between interest in sport and active pursuit of the dramatic arts. The slight trend apparent for increased frequency of dramatic performance with declining interest in sport is insignificant. Similarly, Table 1.4 shows that, regardless of preferred involvement in sport, insignificant differences appear for frequency of acting as a dramatic art among typical undergraduates. This is perhaps surprising, since a close positive relationship between acting as a performing art and active participation in sports might be postulated, whereas no such relationship would be predicted for spectatorship.

The incidence of reading novels frequently increases significantly the less interest an undergraduate has in sport (Table 1.5). The more his interest in sport, the greater is the possibility that he will never pick up a novel to read. This is dramatically illustrated in graphical form in Figure 1.2. The present data show, however, that almost 80 percent of all undergraduates interested in sport at any level read novels at least occasionally, as Figure 2 shows.

Table 1.3
Active or Dramatic Performance in Relation to Interest
in Sport as Expressed by Undergraduates (in percent)

Acting or Dramatic Performance	Sports Interest				
	Deep	Much	Casual	Slight	None
Frequently	0.0 (0)	2.0 (4)	2.6 (6)	5.0 (5)	4.8 (2)
Occasionally	21.9 (14)	19.8 (40)	15.3 (35)	10.9 (11)	14.2 (6)
Never	78.1 (50)	78.2 (158)	82.1 (188)	84.1 (85)	81.0 (34)
Total	100	100	100	100	100
N	(64)	(202)	(229)	(101)	(42)

Table 1.4

Acting or Dramatic Performance in Relation to Preferred Style of
Involvement in Sport as Expressed by Undergraduates (in percent)

| Acting or Dramatic Performance | Sports Involvement | | |
	Participant	Both Participant and Spectator Equally	Spectator
Frequently	2.1	3.2	1.8
	(4)	(8)	(3)
Occasionally	13.1	17.8	18.8
	(25)	(48)	(31)
Never	84.8	79.0	79.4
	(162)	(200)	(131)
Total	100	100	100
N	(191)	(256)	(165)

As with Table 1.2, the data observed in Table 1.6 show that, across preferred styles of involvement in sport, the significant relationships between interest in sport and indulgence in fiction disappear. Furthermore, near normal distributions for frequency of novel reading occur irrespective of preferred style of involvement in sport (as was noted for pursuit of creative arts and crafts—compare with Table 1.2).

Although it appears that with decreasing interest in sport frequent attendance at concerts increases, this trend is not significant as shown in

Table 1.5

Preference for Fiction in Relation to Interest in Sport
as Expressed by Undergraduates (in percent)

| Reading of Novels | Sports Interest | | | | |
	Deep	Much	Casual	Slight	None
Frequently	20.0	21.5	21.3	27.8	39.1
	(12)	(48)	(52)	(30)	(18)
Occasionally	58.3	59.2	69.7	58.3	50.0
	(35)	(132)	(170)	(63)	(23)
Never	21.7	19.3	9.0	13.9	10.9
	(13)	(43)	(22)	(15)	(5)
Total	100	100	100	100	100
N	(60)	(223)	(244)	(108)	(46)

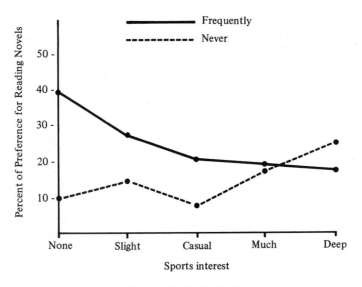

Fig. 2 Preference for Fiction in Relation to
Interest in Sport

Table 1.6
Preference for Fiction in Relation to Preferred Style of Involvement
in Sport as Expressed by Undergraduates (in percent)

Reading of Novels	*Participant*	Sports Involvement Both Participant and Spectator Equally	Spectator
Frequently	22.8 (46)	20.1 (53)	25.8 (47)
Occasionally	62.3 (126)	66.3 (175)	58.8 (107)
Never	14.9 (30)	13.6 (36)	15.4 (28)
Total	100	100	100
N	(202)	(264)	(182)

Table 1.7. It is interesting to note, however, that 70 percent or more of all undergraduates, irrespective of sports interest, attend concerts of music at least occasionally. Where it might be postulated that attendance at concerts would be most closely related to spectatorship as a preferred style of involvement in sport, Table 1.8 shows no such distinguishing relationship.

Table 1.7
Attendance at Concerts in Relation to Interest in Sports
as Expressed by Undergraduates (in percent)

Attendance at Concerts	Sports Interest				
	Deep	Much	Casual	Slight	None
Frequently	11.3	9.5	13.2	17.9	13.6
	(7)	(20)	(32)	(19)	(6)
Occasionally	58.1	64.6	64.9	59.5	61.4
	(36)	(137)	(157)	(63)	(27)
Never	30.6	25.9	21.9	22.6	25.0
	(19)	(55)	(53)	(24)	(11)
Total	100	100	100	100	100
N	(62)	(212)	(242)	(106)	(44)

Table 1.8
Attendance at Concerts in Relation to Preferred Style of
Involvement in Sport as Expressed by Undergraduates (in percent)

Attendance at Concerts	Sports Involvement		
	Participant	Both Participant and Spectator Equally	Spectator
Frequently	10.8	14.7	10.7
	(22)	(39)	(18)
Occasionally	66.3	61.1	63.1
	(136)	(162)	(106)
Never	22.9	24.2	26.2
	(47)	(64)	(44)
Total	100	100	100
N	(205)	(265)	(168)

Discussion

The inverse relationships between interest in sport and pursuit of the arts (representing activity in creative arts and the reading of novels) found in Tables 1.1 and 1.5 lend weight to the pragmatic observation that sport and the arts are, culturally speaking, worlds apart. This might constitute a blow against the "new humanists" and members of the counterculture who, pleading for the recognition of sport as purely a means of self-expression, see in the offing a blending of what present-day society commits to separate cultural enclaves. At best, as Tables 1.2, 1.3, 1.4, 1.6, 1.7, and 1.8 show, there is no relationship between interest or involvement in sport and pursuit of the arts, although the data does show that in some cases there are apparently substantial groups of undergraduates who both are very interested in sport and lead an active life in pursuit of the arts in one form or another. In respect to this latter claim, Table 1.1 shows that an average of 25 percent of undergraduates with *any* interest at all in sport practice creative artistic production frequently. This is substantial by any reckoning, and is a surprising contrast to the unexpected 20 percent or less who pursue the dramatic or performing arts at least occasionally (see Table 1.3).

People with differing preferences for style of involvement in sport (participating, as opposed to watching) might be perceived by others to constitute two very different groups or basic types. When pursuit of the arts is used as a distinguishing criterion, this image fails to hold true. Even when inverse relationships between sport and the arts occur as a result of distinguishing levels of sports interest between people, such relationships disappear when differing modes of involvement in sport comprise the criteria of distinction. What is more, there is a remarkable similarity of distribution of frequency in pursuit of the arts across all groups regardless of sport-involvement identification. Except for "acting or dramatic performance," which is skewed severely toward never indulging (see Table 1.4), these distributions of pursuit of the arts for such groups most often approach normal. Such data do little to sway argument for the rapprochement of sport and the arts. Indeed, it tends to hold up for closer scrutiny such claims that may be made on the basis of selected examples (even when grouped and presented to appear as "data").

Summary

Testing the premise that there might be some relationship between sport and the arts, 1,000 undergraduates were randomly sampled from a total enrollment of 32,000 at a large urban state university and questioned as to their interest in sport, their involvement in sport, and their pursuit of varying activities of a predominantly artistic nature. From the response of 782 of the undergraduates, it was determined that there were inverse relationships between interest in sport and activity in creative arts and crafts and the reading of novels. No relationship was found to exist between interest in sport and acting or dramatic performance or attendance at concerts of music. Similarly, there was no relationship between preferred involvement in sport and pursuit of the arts.

notes

1. Will Durant. *The Life of Greece* (New York: Simon and Schuster, 1939). George W. Botsford and C. A. Robinson, Jr. *Hellenic History,* 3rd ed. (New York: The Macmillan Company, 1948).

2. Johan Huizinga. *Homo Ludens: A Study of the Play Element in Culture* (Boston: Beacon Press, 1950).

3. Stanley J. Wenberg. "The Role of Physical Education in a Liberal Arts College." Speech given at the dedication of the Physical Education Center, University of Minnesota at Morris, October 24, 1970.

4. See E. Norman Gardiner. *Athletics of the Ancient World.* Oxford: Clarendon Press, 1930. Maxwell Howell. "Archaeological Evidence of Sports and Games in Ancient Civilizations," *Canadian Journal of History of Sports and Physical Education,* Vol. 2, Parts 1 and 2, 1971.

5. Benjamin Lowe. "The Representation of Sports in Painting in the United States; 1865–1965." Unpublished Master's thesis, University of Wisconsin, Madison, 1968.

6. Brian E. Pendleton. "Sport in Sculpture in Canada and the United States Since 1900." Unpublished Master's thesis, University of Alberta, Edmonton, 1969.

7. See Donna Mae Miller and Kathryn R. E. Russell. *Sport: A Contemporary View* (Philadelphia: Lea and Febiger, 1971). Francis Keenan. "The Athletic Contest as a Tragic Form of Art." Paper presented at the State University College at Brockport, New York, February 12, 1972. Robert G. Osterhoudt. "A Descriptive Analysis of Research Concerning the Philosophy of Physical Education and Sport." Unpublished Doctoral dissertation, University of Illinois, Champaign, 1971.

8. See E. F. Kaelin. "The Well-played Game: Notes Towards an Aesthetic of Sport," *Quest,* 10 (1968), 16–28. Benjamin Lowe. "The Aesthetics of Sport: The Statement of a Problem," *Sport Psychology Bulletin,* 4, no. 1 (February 1970), 8–15, reprinted in *Quest,* 14 (1971), 13–18. Benjamin Lowe. "A Theoretical Rationale for Investigation into the Relationship of Sport and Aesthetics," *International Review of Sport Sociology,* 8 (1971), 95–102.

9. Brian Sutton-Smith. "A Developmental Psychology of Play and the Arts," *Perspectives in Education,* 4, no. 3 (Spring 1971), 8–17.

10. Miller and Russell. *Sport,* pp. 91–94.

11. For example: "Dave Haberle, the new Big Ten golf champion from Edina, is majoring in music composition at the University of Minnesota. He will graduate this June.

. . . I'll concentrate on writing music in my spare time. . . . It's really relaxing for me to sit down with music and paper and write. . . . I've been writing some choral pieces for my church."

From Sid Hartman column, *Minneapolis Tribune,* May 18, 1971.

PSYCHOLOGICAL VARIABLES
AND QUANTITATIVE AESTHETICS

The opinions of those who view sport as aesthetic can be found in a variety of sources, representing wide agreement among individuals, but depending upon individual interpretation for the importance of their meaning. Since the aesthetic components of sport are usually described in terms which defy precise definition, agreement or disagreement warrants little more value than speculative discourse. Indeed, currently the question of whether sport is aesthetic is as fundamentally arguable as is whether it fosters aggression. Since little is understood about the aesthetic experience in man, applying the term "aesthetic" to a specific mode of expression, as in "aesthetic sensitivity," assumes that the limitations imposed upon the term are clearly understood. This is so whether or not he takes up the challenge to seek an explanation for the concept. The essential benefit obtained from applying "aesthetic" to "sport" is the provision of an avenue of inquiry into a phenomenological problem by psychologists interested in accounting for activity constituents in behavior.

The theoretical and historical statement on the quantification of aesthetics has been made in the last chapter. In this section, a few words are given about the process of measuring aesthetics, the tools and instruments developed for that purpose, and their application in the measurement of aesthetic sensitivity. But how is aesthetic sensitivity defined? To answer this question we must be aware that there are basically two forms of definition: the constitutive and the operational. *Constitutive* definitions are those which withstand the test of either natural law or logical reasoning. On the other hand, *operational* definitions are those which are postulated by a scientist for the purpose of getting on with his research. The constitutive definition is the one widely agreed on, whereas the operational definition is the one suitable for the immediate purpose and it need have no wide basis of agreement.

"Aesthetic sensitivity" is constitutively defined as the perception of simple or complex relations of color and form, and spontaneously interpreted as "naive" or "sophisticated" estimation of value. The constitutive definition is based on a computer-simulation paradigm of input-process-output. The operational definition derived for Case Study 2 states that aesthetic sensitivity is assumed to be comprised of art attitude and art judgment. Operationally, an interactive effect is believed to occur, for no claim is made for aesthetic sensitivity being the sum of the component parts.

As a psychological variable, aesthetic sensitivity would appear to be found more among artists, of any persuasion, than among other members of society. Thus, if this variable can be identified in artists, it would be possible to seek it in others with a fair expectation of finding it in some measurable quantity. On the basis of the traditional cultural separation between sport and the arts, we could expect athletes to have aesthetic sensitivity in only minute quantities, if at all. Of course, "aesthetic sensitivity" is an ill-defined variable as far as psychologists are concerned, and speculative reasoning based on such a variable is fundamentally a waste of time and effort. Hence, the necessity for an operational definition depending on "judgment" and "attitude," two psychological variables which are more substantive if not quantifiable in absolute terms.

"Personality" is widely recognized as a human variable explored by psychologists. The quantification of personality has a long history in psychology, but by virtue of its "hidden" nature, measurement instruments and techniques remain indeterminate. This disspiriting fact has not discouraged research into personality measurement, but it has sobered the opinions of those who put so much faith in the venture at the outset. Nor need we be discouraged from turning to personality theory as a possible avenue for inquiry in the aesthetics of sport. Case Study 2 employs the approach recommended by comparing the personality traits of artists with athletes. There is an underlying assumption that individuals favorably disposed toward both sports participation and the fine arts are the most appropriate for deeper investigation into the nature of the aesthetics of sport, but, more significantly, it can be assumed that the perceptual style of artists is reflected in their study and practice of aesthetics as a behavioral mode, and that if athletes appear to have personality traits in common with artists, then the basis for a clearer understanding of the aesthetics of sport might be found. This assumption is underscored by the need to know what personality traits specifically relate to aesthetic sensitivity. Furthermore, the more closely the personality profile of a sport group parallels that of artists, the more refined or sophisticated should be the aesthetic sensitivity of that sport group over others. Case Study 2 explores this hypothesis and presents results appropriately.

Case Study 2

THE AESTHETIC SENSITIVITY OF ATHLETES

On the basis of a substantial literature focusing attention on aspects of the behavior of man relative to his personality, an emergent concept of the personality profile, graphically illustrated in a delineation of traits, hinges on career choice or expressed lifestyle. This can prove useful for the exploration of qualities not normally assumed to obtain in individuals or groups except where a negative-positive polarity is attached to a variable by means of value-loading. Aesthetics, and especially aesthetic appreciation, might be said to be one such domain, and, since aesthetic sensitivity is not normally associated with athletics or athletes, the wish to investigate the aesthetics of sport must be channeled through what is understood about those whose lifestyle is aesthetics in comparison with those whose lifestyle is sport. To this end, trait theory proves to be a useful vehicle.

STATEMENT OF THE PROBLEM

Aside from the broader discussion of the generality or universality of aesthetics in man, it was believed that the aesthetics of sport might best be appreciated by those in sport who demonstrate some measure of aesthetic sensitivity. The purpose of this study, then, was to discover whether athletes differed from a control population of male undergraduates in aesthetic sensitivity, and to determine factors which might account for any differences that appeared.

Since it was also assumed that the perceptual style of artists was reflected in their study and practice of aesthetics as a behavioral mode, it was further reasoned that if athletes appeared to have personality traits in common with artists, the basis for a clearer understanding of the aesthetics of sport might have been found. This assumption was underscored by the need to know what personality traits were specifically related to aesthetic sensitivity. Thus, differences between groups of athletes identified by differences in personality profile should be reflected in differences in aesthetic sensitivity. Furthermore, the more closely the personality profile of a sport group paralleled that of artists, the more refined or sophisticated should be the aesthetic sensitivity of that sport group over others.

Since the aesthetic was viewed philosophically, as an existential, process-centered concept, and appeared to have been defined operationally in at least two distinctly different ways, questions pertaining to the problem were restated more specifically. Questions which were asked in relation to the generalized concept, and which depended solely upon the interpretation of visual forms, were:

1. Are differences between athletes and a control population of male undergraduates reflected in the *art attitudes* of each group?
2. Are differences between athletes and a control population of male undergraduates reflected in the *art judgments* of each group?

The frame of reference for the present study was based on trait theory. This derived in part from a literature of studies carried out with artists, art students, and the general population to isolate and identify personality variables related to the aesthetic experience, and in part from a literature of studies of the personality profile of athletes. For this reason, then, personality profiles of all groups were extracted from that literature and a direction of predicted relationships was hypothesized. The central hypothesis attendant to the above questions stated that the direction of differences between groups on art attitude and art judgment depended upon the similarity of the group personality profile to the personality profile of artists.

Art attitude is a subset of the set attitude, and, therefore, for this study, art attitude was operationally defined as a compound of preferential responses and evaluations which an individual makes as he views a series of art reproductions.

Art judgment is constitutively defined as the mental or intellectual process of forming an opinion or evaluation of the relative quality of art-works. Art judgment was operationally defined as the measure of agreement with the estimation of quality in an art-work as established by art experts.

For the purpose of this study, aesthetic sensitivity was interpreted as comprising art attitude and art judgment. However, these components of aesthetic sensitivity were not considered mutually exclusive nor was it believed they could be summed.

In order to make meaningful comparisons with a control group, a normal sample of male undergraduates ($N=81$) was included in the study. Besides the control group, there were four sport groups: gymnasts ($N=52$), swimmers ($N=60$), tennis players ($N=47$), and wrestlers ($N=47$).

Review of Literature

THE PERSONALITY OF THE ARTIST

The comment by Child that "into the judgment of any of us must enter a good deal of the time-bound, the culture-bound, the personality-bound" [1:6]* underscores his own approach to the study of aesthetics. However, the first doubts that the personality of an individual in some way affected his aesthetic choice has a longer history.

The earliest empirical studies which might be construed to focus attention on a relationship between aesthetic sensitivity and personality are those which investigated differences in personality between artists and nonartists [2; 3; 4]. The Rorschach studies [2; 3] described professional artists, as opposed to nonartists, N-20 and N-26 respectively, as sensitive,

---

* Numbers in brackets within this section refer to footnotes at the end of Case Study, pp. 300–301.

nonaggressive, emotionally passive, self-disciplined, of superior intelligence, and more "feminine" in social adjustments. Spiaggia [4], using an early version of the M.M.P.I., and controlling age and intelligence, found art students typically more introverted, and possessing tendencies toward depression, toward overproductivity in thought and action, and toward compulsive behavior. Support for the early empirical studies comes from Munsterberg and Mussen [5], who find that "more artists than nonartists have quiet, introverted personalities . . . and are less likely to have overt aggressive tendencies" [5:464], and who conclude that "there are important interrelationships between the choice of art as a vocation and the artist's emotional needs, conflicts, and activations" [5:464].

Credit for the initiation of the trend toward a more definitive exploration of the personality profile of art-oriented individuals is given to Barron. Employing the Barron-Welsh Art Scale in a study of personality style and perceptual choice, with forty graduate students of unspecified disciplines, Barron [6] reported characteristic differences between "artists" and "nonartists," which were supported by the subjects' own self-description. He suggested that perceptual choice depends on perceptual *attitude,* which has roots in personal relevance and therefore in experience rather than perceptual capacity.

In his succeeding study [7] Barron identified independence of judgment as a correlate central to the artist's personality. Child's major contribution in analyzing the relationship between aesthetic judgment and personality variables was to find positive correlations with such variables as tolerance of ambiguity, ambivalence, and, in support of Barron, independence of judgment.

According to Child [8], aesthetic judgment and tolerance for complexity are significantly positively related. The factor-analytic study of cognitive complexity-simplicity by Vannoy [9] extracted an unnamed factor which appears to be somewhat similar or related to the Child observation. Pyron, in a study of attitudinal rigidity and acceptance or rejection of avant-garde art, states that "subjects who are perceptually complex and accept change may have experienced, in the past, a broader range of social, intellectual or artistic stimuli" [10:161].

Two studies have employed the Cattell 16PF Personality Inventory to draw up profiles of artists and art students [11; 12]. Warburton's study of art students $(N=32)$ showed them to be anxious $(C-, O+, Q3-)$, as well as introverted $(H-, E-)$, unaffected $(N-)$, radical $(Q1+)$, nonconforming $(M+)$, and lacking in moral concern $(G-)$. The study by Cross, Cattell, and Butcher [11] comparing artists $(N-63)$ with controls, showed the artists to be

> more withdrawn, or schizothyme, of higher dominance or assertiveness, of lower emotional stability or ego strength, of higher suspiciousness or

self-projection (called protension), of greater apprehensiveness or guilt proneness, of greater casualness or lower self-integration, of higher ergic tension, of higher autistic tendency, of "hysterical" unconcern, and finally of lower superego strength. (pp. 293–294)

In terms of second order factors, the artists showed slight overall introversion ($A-$, $M-$, and $Q2+$) but this was contradicted by clear evidence of $E+$ and no direction of F. General anxiety or neuroticism was very strong ($C-$, $L+$, $O+$, $Q3-$, and $Q4+$), as was experimentation ($M+$, $Q1+$), and moral disregard ($G-$). These last studies provide definitive evidence in support of the general frame of reference employed in the present study.

THE PERSONALITY OF ATHLETES

Similar in pattern to the above outline, the literature pertaining to the personality of the athletes illustrates the trend in methodological development to the point where, within recent years, reliable evidence provides the groundwork for a safe point of departure.

The football players that Derian [13] studied were described as more "self-confident" and "self-assured" than controls. Weight-lifters were described by Thune [14] as being less "self-confident" than a control group. The imprecise terminology mitigates against commonality of definition, particularly when, say, "self-confident" applies to implied personality variables derived differentially from tests employing projective, questionnaire, and attitude assessment techniques. Compounding the weakness in these early studies are controversial selection techniques for the samples, lack of control for contaminating factors (social or psychological), and method of the data collection.

In a recent review of the literature by Cooper [15], the athlete is described as more outgoing, self-confident, and socially confident; he is more socially aggressive, dominant, and leading; he is less anxious and more emotionally stable, less compulsive, and lower in "feminine" and higher in "masculine" interests than the normal population. In endorsement of this generalized picture, Ogilvie [16] provides evidence that athletes who retain their motivation for competition have most of the following personality traits: ambition, organization, deference, dominance, endurance, and aggression. There are fewer introverted types by adult-level competition. Emotional maturity ranges from average to high average and is complemented by self-control, self-confidence, tough-mindedness, trustfulness, intelligence, high conscience development, and low levels of tension.

Heusner's [17] unpublished study of the personality traits of champion and former champion Olympic athletes may be regarded as a classic in its early use of the Cattell 16PF Personality Inventory. His description

of the athletes having greater ego strength or freedom from general neu-
rotic tendencies $(C+)$, being more dominant or assertive $(H+)$, being
more outgoing or less inhibited $(E+)$, and showing less guilt proneness or
liability to worry $(C-)$ provides a unique opportunity for present-day
comparison using the 16PF.

The respect granted the Cattell 16PF Personality Inventory is demonstrated by the nine studies which investigate the personality profiles of
groups of athletes. Out of this literature a new trend in inquiry developed,
epitomized in the opinion that the sports participant may select his competitive sport on the basis of his personality.

This opinion is validated in part by the expressed view that, although
athletes may be differentiated according to sport, there is little evidence
that better athletes have a certain personality trait differentiating them
from poorer performers [16; 18].

Since the Heusner study, the 16PF has been used with athletes both
in Great Britain and in the United States. Sports represented in this
literature are: football [19; 20; 21]; gymnastics, wrestling, and karate
[19]; track and field, tennis, and swimming [16; 22; 23]; amateur soccer
[22; 23]. All groups studied except tennis players show tough-mindedness
$(I-)$, but thereafter major differences appear. These differences are sufficient to shatter time-honored concepts of the meaning of "team" and
"individual" sports. For example, football players in the United States
show high emotional stability $(C+)$, whereas soccer players in Great
Britain show either the opposite [24] or no trend from the normal [22].
Paralleling the personality profile of football players is that of wrestlers,
whose only departure from similarity on the profile is in relative strengths
of factors; hence wrestlers are categorized as group-dependent $(Q2-)$.
Gymnasts, swimmers, and tennis players are similar individuals in their
shyness $(H-)$ and in their lack of group dependence $(Q2+)$. As a group,
gymnasts differ from most other athletes in their lack of surgency $(F-)$.
Regarding within-sport differences, amateur soccer players differ from
professionals on such traits as emotional stability (C), dominance (E),
radicalism $(Q1)$, and self-discipline $(Q3)$. It becomes evident, then, that
there is no clearly defined "athlete" profile, but that different sport activities attract people with different psychological structures.

COMPARING THE ATHLETE AND THE ARTIST

The restrictions imposed by attenuation for comparison are evident in
the extent to which the profiles relate. The four sport groups were selected
for the weight of evidence that the literature provided for each. Gaps in the
profiles must be interpreted in two ways. Nonreference to a factor can
imply either no deviance from the normal population or lack of specific

detail in the literature. In the latter case, the author may have been satisfied with giving a general account by quoting first- or second-order factor descriptions in place of the symbols or graphical presentation.

Noting the similarities between the tennis player and the artist, and again the differences between the wrestler and both the tennis player and artist, recommends a specific point of departure. But this in turn depends on the assumption that the cognitive and perceptual functioning, and the personality style of the artist are strongly related to definitive conceptualizations of aesthetics. The latter being the case, it was hypothesized that tennis players would be more likely than wrestlers to approximate artists in aesthetic choice. This assumption rested on the presumption that the traits on which artists and athletes compare have relevance to aesthetic choice by contributing to a common perceptual style.

Whether differences in aesthetic choice between athletes by sport would distinguish them from the normal population to the extent that differences in personality profile might suggest, was open to question. Exploring the extent to which athletes by sport do differ from the norm on measures of aesthetic choice, and drawing personality profiles by group, were intended to solve much of the question. On the basis of personality, athletes would differ from the norm in aesthetic choice, and in relation to the similarity of their group profile with that of artists.

Procedure

The two tests of aesthetic sensitivity used were the Beittel Art Acceptance Scale [25] and Child Art Judgment Test [8].

Beittel Art Acceptance Scale.   In this test, the subject responds to a series of slides depicting art-works. The subject checks his agreement or disagreement with attitudinal statements printed in the answer booklet. Several statements accompany each slide presented, and the subject has 60 seconds in which to make his choice. The internal reliability for the scale is given by Beittel, based on a group $N=112$, as $r=.94$, and the split-half correlation on a "naive" group, $N=22$, $r=.87$. The scale discriminates between levels of training in art. As a check against the reliabilities presented by Beittel, internal consistencies calculated from the data pertaining to the present study were $r=.87$ for the random group ($N=50$), and $r=.92$ for athletes ($N=50$).

Child Art Judgment Test.   This test is a paired comparison test of the relative quality of art-works. In each presentation a pair of slides displays art-works of similar subject matter and treatment. Choice of either left or right slide by preference for quality tests the agreement of a subject with the qualification of experts in terms of the aesthetic judgment of the art-works. Child gave percentage differences for "agreement with experts" for naive subjects as 6 to 59 percent, and for sophisticated subjects as 57 to 99 percent, in a male population, $N=138$. Split-half correlations on the data for the subjects of this study are $r=.67$ for the random group ($N=50$), and $r=62$ for athletes ($N=50$).

TREATMENT OF THE DATA

The treatment of the data fell into two categories. To test whether athletes differ from the normal population on selected components of aesthetic sensitivity, the data for all groups were treated with a one-way analysis of variance. The emergence of significant differences was tested by the Scheffé procedure, a method for *post hoc* comparisons when an overall significant difference appears between groups.

All data were treated on the assumption that each sample of respondents typically represented the population from which they were drawn, which further assumed that in any distribution of scores for a sample, the random error associated with a particular observation was normal. It was believed that sample size was sufficient to satisfy this requirement for the analysis of variance.

The assumption that the distribution of the random error had a common variance for each population was partially satisfied. Table 2.1 gives the group means and variances for art attitude and art judgment for the control and sport groups.

Results

The art attitude of athletes. Table 2.2 presents data for the one-way analysis of variance testing the sub-hypothesis that athletes differ from the general population in attitude toward art. The null hypothesis was rejected beyond the .01 level of significance. A *post hoc* comparison of the means for all groups, employing the Scheffé method, was conducted. Table 2.3

Table 2.1

Means and Standard Deviations for the Control and Athlete Samples
for Art Attitude and Art Judgment

Samples	Art Attitude		Art Judgment	
	$\bar{X}$	S.D.	$\bar{X}$	S.D.
Control	48.53	12.15	11.42	4.42
Tennis	44.46	10.15	8.78	3.78
Swimming	43.21	8.60	9.57	3.44
Gymnastics	43.72	10.38	8.74	3.33
Wrestling	39.80	7.17	7.02	2.59

Table 2.2
Analysis of Variance for the Art Attitude of Control and Sport Groups

Source	Mean Square	Sum of Squares	df	f	p
Between Groups	458.35	1833.41	4	4.711	.001
Within Groups	97.30	22379.96	230		
Total		24213.37	234		

shows that the wrestlers differ significantly from all other groups beyond the .01 level of significance. The significant difference of wrestlers from the control population is in the direction predicted. Wrestlers were shown to be less positive in their attitudes toward art than were tennis players.

The art judgment of athletes. The one-way analysis of variance testing the sub-hypothesis that athletes differ from the general population in art judgment is presented in Table 2.4. The null hypothesis was rejected beyond the .01 level of significance. The Scheffé method for *post hoc* comparisons of the means for all groups was employed to identify groups contributing to the significance of the *F*-ratio. Table 2.5 shows that wrestlers and gymnasts differ significantly from the control group beyond the .01 level of significance. The significant difference of wrestlers and gymnasts from the control population is in the direction predicted.

Table 2.3
Difference between Means and Scheffé *Post Hoc* Comparison
of the Means for Control and Sport Groups for Art Attitude

	Tennis $\bar{X}=44.46$	Swimming $\bar{X}=43.21$	Gymnastics $\bar{X}=43.72$	Wrestling $\bar{X}=39.80$
Control $\bar{X}=48.53$	4.07	5.32	4.81	8.73*
Tennis $\bar{X}=44.46$		1.25	0.74	4.66
Swimming $\bar{X}=43.21$			0.51	3.41
Gymnastics $\bar{X}=43.72$				3.92

*$P<.01$

Table 2.4
Analysis of Variance for the Art Judgment of Control and Sport Groups

Source	Mean Square	Sum of Squares	df	F	P
Between Groups	119.58	478.35	4	9.392	.000
Within Groups	12.73	2928.76	230		
Total		3407.11	234		

Table 2.5
Differences Between Means and Scheffé *Post Hoc* Comparison of the
Means for Control and Sport Groups for Art Judgment

	Tennis $\overline{X}=8.78$	Swimming $\overline{X}=9.57$	Gymnastics $\overline{X}=8.74$	Wrestling $\overline{X}=7.02$
Control $\overline{X}=11.42$	2.64*	1.85	2.68†	4.40†
Tennis $\overline{X}=8.78$		0.79	0.04	1.76
Swimming $\overline{X}=9.57$			0.83	2.55*
Gymnastics $\overline{X}=8.74$				1.72

*$P<.05$
†$P<.01$

Discussion

It would be unduly bold to assert that the results offer a conclusive support for the strength and power of trait theory. The evidence, as presented, could have greater substantiation attributed to it than actually exists, and this would be a gross error in judgment. At best, the results indicate that there may be some merit to the approach utilized, that the predicted directions were verified on *fairly* safe grounds, and that the differences, although significant, were marginal.

Since social class differences were not controlled for, and it is well-known that tennis players come from a predominantly upper-middle and upper-class background whereas wrestlers' parentage is fundamentally lower-middle (blue collar) class, the results may in fact reflect a contamination from this variable. Nonetheless, a positivist may argue that personality factors encompass social class attributes to some extent in accounting for environmental effect in the developmental process.

More significantly, it might be pointed out that the interrelationship of certain personality traits with proclivities for aesthetic sensitivity and appreciation deserves deeper inquiry. Under the correct controlled conditions, with "local" personality profiles being drawn in each case (as Cattell recommends), positive steps could be taken toward isolating specific factors and, more importantly, their relative loadings or weighings in the identification of the aesthetic personality. The present study does little more than substantiate the need for this line of inquiry, based on an apparently reasonable hypothesis.

notes

1. Irvin L. Child. "The Problem of Objectivity in Esthetic Value." Paper prepared for presentation at the Department of Art Education, Pennsylvania State University, October 26, 1966.

2. M. Prades. "Rorschach Studies on Artists-Painter," *Rorschach Research Exchange,* 8 (1944), 178–183.

3. A. Roe. "The Personality of Artists," *Education and Psychological Measurements,* 4 (1946), 401–408.

4. M. Spiaggia. "An Investigation of the Personality Traits of Art Students," *Educationality and Psychological Measurements,* 18 (1944), 36–51.

5. E. Munsterberg and Paul H. Mussen. "The Personality Structures of Art Students," *Journal of Personality,* 21 (1953), 457–466.

6. Frank Barron. "Personality Style and Perceptual Choice," *Journal of Personality,* 20 (1952), 385–401.

7. ———. "Some Personality Correlates of Independence of Judgment," *Journal of Personality,* 21 (1953), 287–297.

8. Child. "Personality Correlates of Aesthetic Judgment in College Students," *Journal of Personality,* 33, no. 3 (1965), 476–571.

9. Joseph S. Vannoy. "Generality of Cognitive Complexity-Simplicity as a Personality Construct," *Journal of Personality and Social Psychology,* 2, no. 3 (1965), 385–396.

10. Bernard Pyron. "Rejection of Avant-garde Art and the Need for Simple Order," *Journal of Psychology,* 63 (1966), 159–178.

11. Peter C. Cross, R. B. Cattell, and H. J. Butcher. "The Personality Pattern of Creative Artists," *British Journal of Educational Psychology,* 37, no. 1 (1967), 292–299.

12. F. W. Warburton. "The 16PF Profile Group of Students on a Course of Training for Teachers of Art." (Mimeographed, 1966.) Cited in Cross, Cattell, Butcher, "The Personality Pattern of Creative Artists."

13. A. S. Derian. "Some Personality Characteristics of Athletes Studied by the Projective Method." Unpublished Master's thesis, University of California at Berkeley, 1947.

14. J. R. Thune. "Personality of Weightlifters," *Research Quarterly,* 20 (1949), 296–306.

15. Lowell Cooper. "Athletics, Activity and Personality," *Research Quarterly,* 40 (1969), 17–22.

16. Bruce Ogilvie. "Psychological Consistencies within the Personality of High-Level Competitors," *Journal of American Medical Association,* 205, no. 11 (1968), 780–786.

17. W. Heusner. "Personality Traits of Champion and Former Champion Athletes," *Handbook for the 16PF Questionnaire* (Champaign, Ill.: Institute for Personality and Ability Testing, 1962).

18. R. M. Behrman. "Personality Differences Between Non-swimmers and Swimmers," *Research Quarterly,* 38, no. 2 (1967), 163–171.

19. W. Kroll and W. Crenshaw. "Multivariate Personality Profile Analysis of Four Athletic Groups," in G. S. Kenyon, ed., *Contemporary Psychology of Sport* (Chicago: Athletic Institute, 1970).

20. W. Kroll, W. Crenshaw, and K. H. Peterson. "Personality Factor Profiles of Collegiate Football Teams," *Research Quarterly,* 33 (1962), 566–573.

21. Phillip Langer. "Varsity Football Performance," *Perceptual and Motor Skills,* 23 (1966), 1191–1199.

22. J. E. Kane. "Personality Profiles of Physical Education Students Compared with Others," in F. Antonelli, ed., *Psicologia Dello Sport* (Rome: Federazione Medico-Sportiva Italiana, 1966).

23. J. E. Kane and J. L. Colloghan. "Personality Traits in Tennis Players," *British Lawn Tennis,* 35 (July 1965), 18–19.

24. A. G. Dimsdale. "Two Personality Dimensions of a Small Sample of British Athletes," *Bulletin of the British Psychological Society,* 21, no. 72 (1958), 171–172.

25. K. R. Beittel. "Experimental Studies of the Aesthetics Attitudes of College Students," *Research in Art Education* (Kutztown, Penn.: National Art Education Association, 1956).

summary

The social sciences seek to explain a wide spectrum of psychological and sociological behaviors in man; among these can be considered both aesthetics and sport. The fact that progress in explaining each of these is limited at present, and that there appears to be a generalized conceptual bond between the two, suggests that any research into the combined field of inquiry might bring into focus new ways of looking at each.

The ostensible gap between sport and art seen in mature society mitigates against explanation of sport as aesthetic. Yet popular opinion seems to subscribe to this concept on a far wider basis than is suggested by the literature.

Between childhood experience and social maturity there remains to be discovered valuable evidence needed to solve the wider problem presented in seeking to account for sport in terms of comprehensible aesthetics. Since the research cited in Case Studies 1 and 2 depended on the assistance of university athletes and others, who are seen as socially mature, any contribution made by these studies toward understanding the problem posed by the aesthetics of sport must be seen for their limitations.

Thus, this summary of Chapter 10 culminates a specific discussion on two methods of analysis. In overall terms, the chapter represents both the best intentions of empirical inquiry and the beginnings of research in the field. As a point of departure for the further analysis of the beauty of sport, this book has attempted several things. It has attempted to demonstrate a variety of ways of looking at the problem and of singling out questions pertinent to the problem. A number of hypotheses, some inferred and others explicitly stated, have been presented. In as many cases as possible, the evidence to test the hypotheses has been presented. Sometimes the evidence has been weak (in the number of paintings and sculptures of sports action) and sometimes incomplete, serving only to indicate the next important step to be taken (as in the two case studies). But in all cases, the testing of the hypotheses was conducted with sound scientific rigor.

On other levels, analytic inquiry and speculative discussion recommended that variables be assigned the power of symbolic communication for the transference of shared ideas on what constituted the beauty of sport. Such variables were found to be similar to those pertinent to dance and other performing arts, and lent a sense of affinity between those arts and sport. Sport was found, or assumed, to have overriding dynamics of movement not typically found in the other arts, and these were explored for their internal consistency if not for construct validity. Indeed, construct validity would be a sound technique to recommend to the serious student seeking to test some of the assertions found in Chapters 6 and 7.

Two major domains for discussion were presented in Chapter 8, where focus was placed on dichotomous domains of human behavior subsumed to embrace all aspects of aesthetic experience. By drawing the attention of the student to the so-called "subjective" and "objective" categories of aesthetic experience, support was found in a psychological distinction separating the cognitive, affective, and behavioral domains. Dependency on this frame of reference was no more than tentative and directional. Indeed, as with many of the avenues of thought pertaining to the beauty of sport, such dependency led to the formulation of questions (and more questions) rather than providing answers or offering insights.

If, as a result of reading *The Beauty of Sport,* the student of sport studies can be stimulated to ask more questions as he seeks the answers to some of those contained herein, one of the major purposes of this book will have been accomplished. The asking of questions, self-imposed, guarantees the life of a creative mind, and the creative enterprise, either in problem solving or in the production of art, guarantees in turn a lively and flourishing existence.

Lastly, this book has presented some ideas from a variety of disciplines—from the arts, from the social sciences, and from philosophy. The cross-disciplinary nature of the text satisfies the best requirements for the study of sport in society. That sport is beautiful speaks to the value that society places on sport; that society does not fully understand just how beautiful sport is justifies the expression of the thesis presented here.

questions for discussion

1. Discuss what is meant by social survey research, and state how it can aid the researcher in uncovering factors contributory to the analysis of the beauty of sport.
2. Critically analyze Case Study 1, placing emphasis on how the original investigation could have been improved.
3. What is aesthetic sensitivity? What are the difficulties presented by constitutive and operational definitions?
4. Critically analyze Case Study 2, placing emphasis on ways in which the original study could have been improved.
5. Make recommendations for further empirical analysis, or present a case refuting the need for explanation of the beauty of sport.

Bibliographical References

ABELL, W. *The Collective Dream in Art: A Psycho-Historical Theory of Culture Based on Relations between the Arts, Psychology, and the Social Sciences.* Cambridge: Harvard University Press, 1957.

ADLER, W. "McKenzie—a Moulder of Clay and Men," *Outing,* 64 (February 1915), 586–596.

ALDERMAN, RICHARD B. "A Sociopsychological Assessment of Attitude Toward Physical Activity in Champion Athletes," *Research Quarterly,* 41, no. 1 (March 1970), 1–9.

ALDRICH, VIRGIL C. *Philosophy of Art.* Englewood Cliffs, N.J.: Prentice-Hall, 1963.

ALLPORT, GORDON W. *Becoming: Basic Considerations for a Psychology of Personality.* New Haven: Yale University Press, 1955.

ALLSOP, BRUCE. *The Future of the Arts: A Study.* London: Pitman, 1959.

AMERICAN FEDERATION OF ARTS. *American Painting Today.* New York: Oxford University Press, 1939.

ANGELL, ROGER. *The Summer Game.* New York: The Viking Press, 1972.

ANTHONY, D. W. J. "Sport and Physical Education as a Means of Aesthetic Education," *Physical Education,* 60 (1968), 1–7.

APPIA, ADOLPHE. *The Work of Living Art.* Coral Gables, Fla.: University of Miami, 1960.

ARCHINEL, JOHN. "List of Works by R. Tait McKenzie." *Journal of Health, Physical Education and Recreation,* 15 (February 1944), 61–66.

304

ARENS, WILLIAM. "The Great American Football Ritual," *Natural History,* LXXXIV, 8 (1975), 72–81.

BADY, RENE. *Le Problème de la Joie.* Fribourg en Suisse. Librarie de l'Université, 1943.

BANNISTER, ROGER. *The Four Minute Mile.* New York: Dodd, Mead, 1963.

BARKER, VIRGIL. *American Painting: History and Interpretation.* New York: The Macmillan Company, 1950.

BARNETT, J. H. "Research Areas in the Sociology of Art," *Sociology and Social Research,* LXII, July 1958.

BARR, A. H., JR. *Painting and Sculpture in the Museum of Modern Art.* New York: Simon and Schuster, 1948.

BARRON, F. "Complexity-simplicity as a Personality Dimension," *Journal of Abnormal and Social Psychology,* 48 (1953), 163–172.

———. "Personality Style and Perceptual Choice," *Journal of Personality,* 20 (1952), 385–401.

———. "Some Personality Correlates of Independence of Judgment," *Journal of Personality,* 21 (1953), 287–297.

BARRON, F., and GEORGE S. WELSH. "Artistic Perception as a Possible Factor in Personality Style: Its Measurement by a Figure Preference Test," *Journal of Psychology,* 33 (1952), 199–203.

BARRY, HERBERT, III. "Relationship Between Child Training and the Pictorial Arts," *Journal of Abnormal and Social Psychology,* 54 (1957), 380–383.

BARRY, JACKSON G. *Dramatic Structure: The Shaping of Experience,* Berkeley: University of California Press, 1970.

BARRYMORE, ETHEL. "Why No Degas in Baseball?" *Look,* 17 (1961), 104–107.

BAUMBACH, JONATHON. "The Aesthetics of Basketball," *Esquire,* LXXIII, no. 1 (January 1970), 140–146.

BAUR, J. I. H. *Philip Evergood.* New York: Whitney Museum of American Art, 1960.

BAXTER, RICHARD. *High Rejoicing, or The Nature and the Order of Rational and Warrantable Joy.* London: Printed for Francis Tyton and Jane Underhil, 1660.

BEAN, DAVID. "Personality and Attitude to Sport (Communication Four)," in J. D. Brooke, "Pilot Studies from the Evaluation Course," *Physical Education,* 60, no. 180 (1968), 59.

BEHRMAN, ROBERT M. "Personality Differences Between Non-swimmers and Swimmers," *Research Quarterly,* 38, no. 2 (1967), 163–171.

BEITTEL, KENNETH R. "Experimental Studies of the Aesthetic Attitudes of College Students," *Research in Art Education,* Seventh Yearbook. Kutztown, Pa.: National Art Education Association, 1968.

BELL, CLIVE. *Art.* New York: Capricorn Books, 1958.

BELLOWS, EMMA S. *The Paintings of George Bellows.* New York: Alfred A. Knopf, 1929.

BENNETT, ARNOLD. "The Prize Fight," *New Statesman and Nation,* XIV (December 1919), 349.

BENTLEY, ERIC. *The Life of the Drama.* New York: Atheneum, 1964.

BERENSON, BERNARD. *Aesthetics and History*. New York: Pantheon Books, 1948.

BERLYNE, D. E. *Conflict and Arousal and Curiosity*. New York: McGraw-Hill, 1960.

BERLYNE, D. E., J. C. OGILVIE, and L. C. C. PARHAM. "The Dimensionality of Visual Complexity, Interestingness and Pleasingness," *Canadian Journal of Psychology*, 22, no. 5 (1968), 376–387.

BEST, DAVID. *Expression in Movement and the Arts*. London: Lepus Books, 1974.

BIRKHOFF, GEORGE D. *Aesthetic Measure*. Cambridge, Mass.: Harvard University Press, 1933.

BLAI, BORIS. "R. Tait McKenzie the Artist," *Journal of Health, Physical Education and Recreation*, 15 (February 1944), 61.

BLANCHARD, WILLIAM H. "Ecstasy Without Agony Is Baloney," *Psychology Today*, 3, no. 8 (January 1970), 8–10.

BLAND, ERNEST A., ed. *Olympic Story*. London: Rockliff, 1948.

BLOCK, H. A. "Toward the Development of a Sociology of Literature and Art-Forms," *American Sociological Review*, VIII, June 1943.

BLUMER, H. "Collective Behavior," in *Review of Sociology: Analysis of a Decade*, ed. J. B. Gittlet. New York: John Wiley and Sons, 1957.

BOOTH, E. G., JR."Personality Traits of Athletes as Measured by the MMPI," *Research Quarterly*, 29 (1958), 127–139.

BOUET, M. "Contribution à l'Esthetique du Sport," *Revue d'Esthetique*, 1 (1948), 180–194.

————. *Signification de Sport*. Paris: Encyclopedie Universitaire, 1968.

BOWERMAN, BILL. "The Secrets of Speed," *Sports Illustrated*, August 2, 1971.

BRASCH, R. *How Did Sports Begin?* New York: David McKay, 1970.

BREUNING, M. "Bellows in the National Gallery," *Art Digest*, 19 (January 1, 1945), 22.

BRODBECK, A. J. "Placing Aesthetic Developments in Social Contexts: A Program of Value Analysis," *The Journal of Social Issues*, XX, no. 1 (January 1964).

BROGAN, D. W. "The Problem of High Structure and Mass Culture," *Diogenes*, no. 5 (1954).

BROWN, CAMILLE, and ROSALIND CASSIDY. *Theory in Physical Education*. Philadelphia: Lea and Febiger, 1963.

BROWN, GEORGE S., and DONALD GAYNER. "Athletic Action as Creativity," *Journal of Creative Behavior*, 1, no. 2 (Spring 1967), 155–162.

BROWN, JOSEPH. *Joe Brown: Retrospective Catalogue*. Published by the artist, 1968.

BROWNELL, BAKER. *Art Is Action*. New York: Harper, 1939.

BRUCE, VIOLET ROSE. *Dance and Dance Drama in Education*. Oxford, N.Y.: Pergamon Press, 1965.

BRUNETIÈRE, FERDINAND. *Art and Morality*. New York: Crowell & Company, 1889.

BULLEY, MARGARET HATTERSLEY. *Art and Everyman:* A basis for appreciation; forming a general introduction to the study of all types, ages and countries. London: B. T. Botsford Company, 1951–1952.

BULLOUGH, EDWARD. "The Perceptive Problem in the Aesthetic Appreciation of Single Colours," *British Journal of Psychology,* 2 (1908), 406–463.

BURLAND, COTTIE ARTHUR. *Man and Art.* London and New York: Studio Publications, 1959.

BURT, CYRIL. "The Factorial Analysis of Emotional Traits," *Character and Personality,* 7 (1939), 238–299.

CAFFIN, CHARLES HENRY. *Art for Life's Sake.* New York: The Prang Company, 1913.

CAILLOIS, ROGER. *Man, Play and Games.* New York: The Free Press of Glencoe, 1964.

CASSIRER, ERNST. *An Essay on Man.* New Haven: Yale University Press, 1944.

CASTENADA, CARLOS. "Further Conversations with Don Juan," *Esquire,* March 1971.

Catalogue of the National Museum of Racing. Saratoga Springs, N.Y.: 1963.

CATTELL, RAYMOND B. *The Scientific Analysis of Personality.* Baltimore: Penguin Books, 1965.

CATTELL, RAYMOND B., and HERBERT W. EBER. *Handbook for the Sixteen Personality Factor Questionnaire.* Champaign, Ill.: Institute for Personality and Ability Testing, 1957.

———. *Handbook Supplement for Form C of the Sixteen Personality Factor Questionnaire.* Champaign, Ill.: Institute for Personality and Ability Testing, 1970.

———. *Manual for Forms C and D of the Sixteen Personality Factor Questionnaire.* Champaign, Ill.: Institute for Personality and Ability Testing, 1962.

CHARTERIS, J. *This Is Gymnastics.* Champaign, Ill.: Stipes, 1969.

CHILD, IRVIN L. "Aesthetic Judgment in Children," *Transaction,* 7, no. 7 (May 1970), 47–51.

———. "Observations on the Meanings of Some Measures of Aesthetic Sensitivity," *Journal of Psychology,* 57 (1964), 47–64.

———. "Personal Preference for Simple Forms," *Psychological Monographs,* 51, no. 5 (1962), 68–74.

———. "Personality Correlates of Aesthetic Judgment in College Students," *Journal of Personality,* 33, no. 3 (1965), 476–571.

———. "The Problem of Objectivity in Esthetic Value," paper prepared for presentation at the Department of Art Education, Pennsylvania State University, October 26, 1966.

CHILD, IRVIN L., and SUMIKO IWAO. "Personality and Esthetic Sensitivity," *Journal of Personality and Social Psychology,* 8, no. 3 (1964), 308–312.

CLARK, KENNETH. *The Nude.* New York: Doubleday and Company, 1959.

COBB, JOHN R. "Toward Clarity in Aesthetics," *Philosophy and Phenomenological Research,* 10 (1950), 169–189.

COCHRAN, ALASTAIR, and JOHN STOBBS. *The Search for the Perfect Swing.* Philadelphia: J. B. Lippincott Company, 1968.

COLLINGWOOD, ROBIN GEORGE. *Essays in the Philosophy of Art.* Bloomington: Indiana University Press, 1964.

Contemporary American Painting. Urbana: University of Illinios Press, 1948.

Contemporary Art in the United States. New York: I.B.M. Corporation, 1940.

CONWAY, CARE. *The Joy of Soaring.* Los Angeles: The Soaring Society of America, 1969.

COOLEY, WILLIAM W., and PAUL R. LOHNES. *Multivariate Procedures for the Behavioral Sciences.* New York: John Wiley and Sons, 1962.

COOPER, CHARLES WILLIAM. *The Arts and Humanity: A Psychological Introduction to the Fine Arts.* New York: Philosophical Library, 1952.

COOPER, LOWELL. "Athletics, Activity and Personality," *Research Quarterly,* 40, no. 1 (1969), 17–22.

CORTISSOZ, R. *American Artists.* New York: Charles Scribner's Sons, 1922.

COX, W. D., ed. *Boxing in Art and Literature.* New York: Raynal and Hitchcock, 1935.

CROSS, PETER G., R. B. CATTELL, and H. J. BUTCHER. "The Personality Pattern of Creative Artists," *British Journal of Educational Psychology,* 37, no. 1 (1967), 292–299.

CURTI, M. *Growth of American Thought.* New York: Harper and Brothers, 1951.

DANIELS, ARTHUR S. "Sport and Human Relations," in *International Research in Sport and Physical Education,* ed. E. Jokl and E. Simon. Springfield, Ill.: C. C Thomas, 1964.

DAVIDS, A. "Psychodynamic and Sociocultural Factors Related to Intolerance of Ambiguity," in *The Study of Lives,* ed. R. W. White. New York: Atherton Press, 1963.

DEMILLE, AGNES. *The Book of the Dance.* New York: Golden Press, 1963.

DERIAN, A. S. "Some Personality Characteristics of Athletes Studied by the Projective Method." Unpublished Master's thesis, University of California at Berkeley, 1947.

DEWEY, JOHN. *Art and Education.* Barnes Foundation Press, 1954.

———. *Art as Expression.* New York: Capricorn Books, 1934.

DIMSDALE, ALAN G. "An Investigation into the Personality Profiles of a Group of Physical Education Students," *British Journal of Physical Education,* 1, no. 3 (May 1970), xviii–xx.

———. "Two Personality Dimensions of a Small Sample of British Athletes," *Bulletin of the British Psychological Society,* 21, no. 72 (1968), 171–172.

DOBZHANSKY, THEODOSIUS G. *Mankind Evolving: The Evolution of the Human Species.* New Haven: Yale University Press, 1965.

DOWNES, W. H. *The Life and Works of Winslow Homer.* Boston: Houghton Mifflin Company, 1911.

DOWSING, GRETCHEN S. "Coaching for Amplitude in Free Exercise," *Woman Coach,* 2, no. 1 (1975), 26–30.

DUBOIS, P. E. "The Aesthetics of Sport and the Athlete," *The Physical Educator,* 31, no. 4 (1974), 198–201.

DULLES, R. F. *America Learns to Play*. New York: Appleton-Century-Crofts, 1940.

DUMAS, G. *La Tristessee et la Joie*. Paris: F. Alcan, 1900.

DUMAZEDIER, JOFFRE. "Some Remarks on Sociological Problems in Relation to Physical Education and Sports," *International Review of Sport Sociology*, 3 (1968), 5–16.

EBERLEIN, H. D. "R. Tait McKenzie: Physician and Sculptor," *Century*, 97 (December 1918), 249–257.

EBERSOLE, B. *Fletcher Martin*. Gainsville: University of Florida Press, 1954.

EBY, FREDERICK, and C. F. ARROWOOD. *The History and Philosophy of Education, Ancient and Medieval*. New York: Prentice-Hall, 1947.

ECKER, D. W., R. JOHNSON and E. F. KAELIN. "Aesthetic Inquiry," *Review of Educational Research*, Vol. 39, No. 5, December 1969.

EDGELL, C. H. *Sport in American Art*. Boston: Museum of Fine Arts, 1944.

EDWARDS, HARRY. *The Sociology of Sport*. Homewood, Ill.: The Dorsey Press, 1973.

EISENMAN, RUSSELL, and SANDRA COFFEE. "Aesthetic Preferences of Art Students and Mathematics Students," *Journal of Psychology*, 58, no. 2 (1964), 375–378.

ELIOT, A. *Three Hundred Years of American Painting*. New York: Time, Inc., 1957.

ELMER, ROBERT P. *Archery*. Philadelphia: Penn Publishing Company, 1953.

EMERSON, RICHARD M. "Games: Rules, Outcomes and Motivations" (mimeographed, 1968).

Encyclopaedia Britannica: A New Survey of Universal Knowledge. Chicago: Encyclopaedia Britannica, 1968.

ENZER, H. "Gambits and Paradigms: Sociology and the Beaux Arts," *Arts in Society*, 3, no. 3, 412–424.

EVANS, JOAN. *Taste and Temperament*. New York: The Macmillan Company, 1939.

EYSENCK, HANS J. "An Experimental Study of Aesthetic Preference for Polygonal Figures," *Journal of General Psychology*, 79, no. 1 (1968), 3–17.

————. " 'Type' Factors in Aesthetic Judgments," *British Journal of Psychology*, 31 (1941), 262–270.

EYSENCK, HANS J., and MAUREEN CASTLE. "Training in Art as a Factor in the Determination of Preference Judgments for Polygons," *British Journal of Psychology*, 61, no. 1 (1970), 65–81.

FAIRE, SISTO. *Civilita, Arte, Sport*, 2nd ed. Rome: Societa Editrice Dante Alighieri, 1970.

FAIRS, J. R. "When Was the Golden Age of the Body?" *Journal of the Canadian Association of Health, Physical Education and Recreation*, 37, no. 1 (1970), 11–24.

FECHNER, G. T. *Vorschule der Aesthetik*. Leipzig: Breitkopf and Hartel, 1949.

FEIBLEMAN, J. K. *Aesthetics*. New York: Duell, Sloan, and Pearce, 1949.

FIMRITE, DON. "Everything Came Up Reds," *Sports Illustrated*, 43, no. 18 (1975), 20–27.

FISCHER, ERNST. *The Necessity of Art, A Marxist Approach*. Baltimore: Penguin Books, 1963.

FISCHER, J. L. "Art Styles as Cultural Cognitive Maps," *American Anthropologist*, 63 (1961), 79–93.

FORD, C. S., E. T. PROTHRO, and I. L. CHILD. "Some Transcultural Comparison of Esthetic Judgment," *Journal of Social Psychology*, 68 (1966), 19–26.

FRAYSSINET, PAUL. *Le Sport Parmi les Beaux Arts*. Paris: Dargaud, 1968.

FREUD, SIGMUND. *A General Introduction to Psychoanalysis*. New York: Simon and Schuster, 1952.

FRIEDLANDER, M. J. *On Art and Connoisseurship*. London: B. Cassirer, 1942.

GALINSKY, G. KARL. *The Herakles Theme*. Oxford: Basil Blackwell, 1972.

GALLICO, PAUL. *Farewell to Sport*. New York: Books for Libraries, 1938.

GANDER, A. "Harmony in Artistic Gymnastics," *F.I.G. Code of Points*. Zurich: Neue Zurcher Zeitung, 1968.

GARDINER, E. NORMAN. *Athletics of the Ancient World*. Oxford: Clarendon Press, 1930.

GARDNER, HELEN. *Art through the Ages*. New York: Harcourt, 1959.

GEBLEWITZ, E. "Aesthetic Problems in Physical Education and Sport," *Bulletin of the Federation International d'Education Physique*, No. 3, 1965.

GENASCI, JAMES E., and VASILLIS KLISSOURAS. "The Delphic Spirit in Sports," *Journal of Health, Physical Education and Recreation*, 37, no. 2 (February 1966), 43–44.

GERBER, ELLEN. *Sport and the Body*. Philadelphia: Lea and Febiger, 1972.

GITTLER, JOSEPH B., *Review of Sociology*. New York: Wiley, 1957.

GOLDSTEIN, HARRIET and VETTA. *Art in Everyday Life*. New York: Macmillan, 1954.

GOODRICH, L. *Thomas Eakins: His Life and Work*. New York: Whitney Museum of American Art, 1933.

GOODRICH, L., and J. I. H. BAUR. *American Art of Our Century*. New York: F. A. Praeger, 1961.

GOTSHALK, DILMAN WALTER. *Art and the Social Order*. New York: Dover Publications, 1962.

GRAHAM, DAVID. *Common Sense and the Muses*. London: William Blackwood and Sons, 1925.

GREEN, GEOFFREY. *Soccer: The World Game*. London: The Phoenix House Ltd., 1953.

GREENBERG, CLEMENT. *Art and Culture*. Boston: Beacon Press, 1961.

GROSS, KARL. *The Play of Men*. New York: Appleton and Company, 1901.

GROSS, EDWARD, and G. P. STONE. "Embarrassment and the Analysis of Role Requirements," *American Journal of Sociology*, LXX (1964), 1–15.

HAMILTON, E. *Mythology, Timeless Tales of Gods and Heroes*. Boston: Little, Brown & Company, 1942.

HAUSER, A. *The Social History of Art*. New York: Vintage Books, 1958.

HAYS, WILLIAM L. *Statistics*. New York: Holt, Rinehart and Winston, 1953.

HEIN, HILDA. "Performance as an Aesthetic Category," *Journal of Aesthetics and Art Criticism*, XXVI (1970), 381–386.

————. Play as an Aesthetic Concept, *Journal of Aesthetics and Art Criticism,* 22 (1968), 67–72.

HENRY, BILL. *An Approved History of the Olympic Games.* New York: G. P. Putnam's Sons, 1948.

HENTOFF, NAT. "Tennis Power," *Evergreen Review,* 12 (December 1968), 57–59.

HERBERT, MARTIN. "Joy: The Agony and the Ecstasy," *Story of Life,* Part 25, 1969–1970.

HERRIGEL, EUGEN. *Zen in the Art of Archery.* New York: Pantheon Books, 1953.

HEUSNER, WILLIAM. "Personality Traits of Champion and Former Champion Athletes," *Handbook for the Sixteen Personality Factor Questionnaire.* Champaign, Ill.: Institute for Personality and Ability Testing, 1962.

HÖHNE, E. "Coubertin on the Place of Art in Modern Olympism," *Bulletin of the National Olympic Committee of the German Democratic Republic,* 14, no. 4 (1969), 31–40.

HOLBROOK, LEONA. "A Man of Our Professions," *Journal of Health, Physical Education and Recreation,* 38, no. 4 (May 1967), 30–33.

HOLMBERG, O. *Per Henrik Ling: His Life and Gymnastic Principles.* London: Ling Association, 1939.

HOLME, B. "Sport as a Challenge to Artists," *Design,* 61 (January 1960), 125–127.

HUIZINGA, JOHAN. *Homo Ludens: A Study of the Play Element in Culture.* Boston: The Beacon Press, 1950.

HUME, DAVID. *A Treatise on Human Nature,* ed. L. A. Selby-Bigge. Oxford: Clarendon Press, 1964.

HUNTER, ADELAIDE. "Contributions of R. Tait McKenzie to Modern Concepts of Physical Education," *Research Quarterly,* 30 (May 1959), 160–66.

HUSMAN, G. F. "Aggression in Boxers and Wrestlers as Measured by Projective Techniques," *Research Quarterly,* 26 (1955), 421–425.

HUSSEY, CHRISTOPHER. *R. Tait McKenzie: A Sculptor of Youth.* London: Country Life Ltd., 1929.

IBRAHIM, HILMI. "Comparison of Temperament Traits among Intercollegiate Athletes and Physical Education Majors," *Research Quarterly,* 38, no. 4 (1967), 515–522.

International Encyclopedia of the Social Sciences, ed. David L. Sills. New York: The Macmillan Company, 1968.

ISHAM, S. *The History of American Painting.* New York: The Macmillan Company, 1927.

IWAO, S., and I. L. CHILD, "Comparisons of Esthetic Judgments by American Experts and by Japanese Potters," *Journal of Social Psychology,* 68 (1966), 27–33.

KAELIN, E. F. "The Well-Played Game: Notes Toward an Aesthetics of Sport, *Quest,* 10 (1968), 16–28.

KAHN, ROGER. *The Boys of Summer.* New York: Harper and Row, 1971.

KANE, JOHN. *Sky Hooks.* Philadelphia: J. B. Lippincott Co., 1938.

KANE, J. E. "Personality and Physical Abilities," in *Contemporary Psychology of Sport*, ed. G. S. Kenyon. Chicago: Athletic Institute, 1970.

————. "Personality and Physical Ability." Tokyo, Japan: International Conference of Social Science, October 1964 (mimeographed).

————. "Personality Profiles of Physical Education Students Compared with Others," in *Psicologia Dello Sport*, ed. F. Antonelli. Rome: Federazione Medico-Sportiva Italiana, 1966.

KANE, J. E., and J. L. COLLOGHAN. "Personality Traits in Tennis Players," *British Lawn Tennis*, 35 (July 1965), 18–19.

KAPLAN, M. *Art in a Changing America*. Urbana: University of Illinois Press, 1956.

KAVOLIS, V. *Artistic Expression: A Sociological Analysis*. Ithaca: Cornell University Press, 1968.

KEENAN, FRANCIS W. "The Athletic Contest as a Tragic Form of Art," *International Review of Sport Sociology*, 10, no. 1 (1975), 38–54.

KEIRAN, JOHN. "A Philadelphia Physician Who Turned Men to Stone, *Journal of Health, Physical Education and Recreation*, 15 (February 1944), 71.

KENYON, GERALD S. "A Conceptual Model for Characterizing Physical Activity," *Research Quarterly*, 39 (March 1968), 96–105.

————. "Six Scales for Assessing Attitudes Toward Physical Activity," *Research Quarterly*, 39 (October 1968), 566–574.

————. Values held for physical activity by selected urban secondary school students in Canada, Australia, England, and the United States. United States Office of Education Contract S–376. University of Wisconsin, February 1968.

KEPES, G. *The Nature of Art and Motion*. London: Studio Vista, 1965.

KERLINGER, F. N. *Foundations of Behavioral Research*. New York: Holt, Rinehart and Winston, 1964.

KNAPP, ROBERT H. "An Experimental Study of a Triadic Hypothesis Concerning the Sources of Aesthetic Imagery," *Journal of Projective Techniques and Personality Assessment*, 28 (1964), 49–54.

KNAPP, ROBERT H., JANET BRINNER, and MARTHA WHITE. "Educational Level, Class Status, and Aesthetic Preference," *Journal of Social Psychology*, 50 (1959), 281.

KNAPP, ROBERT H., JANET BRINNER, and MARTHA WHITE. "Educational Level, Art and Their Personality Correlates," *Journal of Projective Techniques*, 24 (1960), 396–402.

KOPPETT, LEONARD. *All about Baseball*. New York: Quadrangle, 1967.

KOVICH, MAUREEN. "Sport as an Art Form," *Journal of Health, Physical Education and Recreation*, October 1971.

KOZAR, ANDREW J. *R. Tait McKenzie: The Sculptor of Athletes*. Knoxville: The University of Tennessee Press, 1975.

KRAMER, JUDITH. "The Sociology of Art and the Art of Sociology," *Arts in Society*, 3, no. 4, 630–635.

KROEBER, A. L. *Configurations of Culture Growth*. Berkeley: University of California Press, 1944.

KROLL, WALTER. "Sixteen Personality Factor Profiles of Collegiate Wrestlers," *Research Quarterly*, 38 no. 1 (1967), 49–57.

KROLL, WALTER, and WILLIAM CRENSHAW. "Multivariate Personality Profile Analysis of Four Athletic Groups," in *Contemporary Psychology of Sport,* ed. G. S. Kenyon. Chicago: Athletic Institute, 1970.

KROLL, WALTER, and KAY H. PETERSON. "Personality Factor Profiles of Collegiate Football Teams," *Research Quarterly,* 36, no. 4 (December 1965), 433–439.

KROUT, J. A. *Annals of American Sport.* New Haven: Yale University Press, 1929.

KUH, KATHERINE. *Art Has Many Faces.* New York: Harper, 1951.

KUNTZ, PAUL G. "Aesthetics Applies to Sports as Well as to the Arts," *Journal of the Philosophy of Sport,* 1 (1974), 6–35.

KUNZLE, G. C. *Olympic Gymnastics.* London: James Barries, 1956.

KUPFER, JOSEPH. "Purpose and Beauty in Sport," *Journal of the Philosophy of Sport,* 2 (1975), 83–90.

LABAN, RUDOLPH. *The Language of Movement.* Boston: Plays Inc., 1974.

LABAN, RUDOLPH, and F. C. LAWRENCE. *Effort.* London: Macdonald and Evans, 1947.

LABOVITZ, SANFORD, and ROBERT HAGEDORN. *Introduction to Social Research.* New York: McGraw-Hill, 1971.

LAHR, JOHN. "The Theatre of Sports," *Evergreen Review,* October 1969.

LAKIE, WILLIAM L. "Personality Characteristics of Certain Groups of Intercollegiate Athletes," *Research Quarterly,* 33 (1962), 566–573.

LANG, KURT, and GLADYS ENGEL LANG. *Collective Dynamics.* New York: Thomas Y. Crowell Company, 1961.

LANGER, PHILIP. "Varsity Football Performance," *Perceptual and Motor Skills,* 23 (1966), 1191–1199.

LANGER, SUSANNE K. *Problems of Art.* New York: Charles Scribner's Sons, 1957.

LANGFELD, HERBERT S. *The Aesthetic Attitude.* New York: Harcourt, Brace and Company, 1920.

LAPLACE, JOHN P. "Personality and Its Relation to Success in Professional Baseball," *Research Quarterly,* 25 (1954), 313–320.

LARKIN, O. W. *Art and Life in America.* New York: Holt, Rinehart and Winston, 1964.

LASCARI, ARNO. "Esthetics and Mechanics in Artistic Gymnastics" (mimeographed, University of British Columbia, 1973).

LAWTHER, JOHN D. *The Psychology of Coaching.* Englewood Cliffs, N.J.: Prentice-Hall, 1951.

LEE, HAROLD N. *Perception and Aesthetic Value.* New York: Prentice-Hall, 1938.

LEONARD, F. E., and G. B. AFFLECK. *A Guide to the History of Physical Education.* London: Henry Klimpton, 1947.

LETHABY, WILLIAM RICHARD. *Form in Civilization.* New York: Oxford Press, 1957.

LIPSYTE, ROBERT. *Assignment: Sports.* New York: Harper and Row, 1970.

LOCKHART, BARBARA. "The Joy of Effort," *The Foil,* Spring 1973.

LOWE, B. "The Aesthetic Sensitivity of Athletes." Unpublished Doctoral dissertation, University of Wisconsin, 1970.

———. "The Aesthetics of Sport: The Statement of a Problem," *Sport Psychology Bulletin,* 4, no. 1 (1970), 8–13.

———. *The Representation of Sports in Painting in the United States: 1865–1964.* Master's thesis, University of Wisconsin, 1968.

———. "Social Origins of Sport Predating the First Recording of the Olympic Games, 776 B.C." Paper presented at the Fourth International HISPA Seminar on the History of Sport, University of Leuven, Belgium, April 1975.

———. "A Theoretical Rationale for Investigation into the Relationship of Sport and Aesthetics," *International Review of Sport Sociology,* 8 (1971), 95–102.

LOWE, B., and R. BORKOWSKI. "Reflections on Sport as Mythology in Industrial Society." Paper delivered to the Third Canadian Conference on the History of Sport, Halifax, Nova Scotia, August 1974.

McDONNELL, PATRICK. "The Bar and the Body," *Modern Gymnast,* IX, March 1967.

McHENRY, M. *Thomas Eakins Who Painted.* Privately printed for the author, 1945.

McKINNEY, R. *Thomas Eakins.* New York: Crown Publishers, 1942.

McPHEE, JOHN. *Levels of the Game.* New York: Bantam Books, 1970.

McWHINNIE, HAROLD J. "The Effect of a Learning Experience on Preference for Complexity and Asymmetry," *Perceptual and Motor Skills,* 28 (1965), 119–122.

———. "A Review of Research on Aesthetic Measure." Columbus: Ohio State University, 1969 (mimeographed).

MACKENZIE, MARTIN M. *Toward a New Curriculum in Physical Education.* New York: McGraw-Hill, 1969.

MAHEU, RENE. "Sport and Culture," *International Journal of Adult and Youth Education,* 15, no. 4 (1962), 6–12.

MAO TSE-TUNG, *On Art and Literature.* Peking: Peking Foreign Languages Press, 1960.

MARGOLIS, JOSEPH. "Aesthetic Perceptions," *Journal of Aesthetics and Art Criticism,* 19, no. 2 (1960), 209–214.

MARVIN, FRANCIS S. *Art and Civilization.* London: Books for Libraries, 1928.

MARX, K., and F. ENGELS. *Literature and Art.* New York: International Publishers, 1947.

MASLOW, ABRAHAM. *Towards a Psychology of Being.* Toronto: Van Nostrand, 1965.

MASTERSON, D. "Le Sport et l'Art," *Education Physique et Sport,* 94 (1968), 13–16.

MAURON, CHARLES. *Aesthetics and Psychology.* London: Hogarth Press, 1935.

MEAD, H. *An Introduction to Aesthetics.* New York: Ronald Press, 1952.

MEAGER, R. "Aesthetic Concepts," *British Journal of Aesthetics,* 10 (1970), 303–322.

MECHLIN, L. "The Olympic Art Exhibition," *American Magazine of Art,* 25 (September 1932), 136–150.

METHENY, ELEANOR. *Connotations of Movement in Sport and Dance.* Dubuque, Iowa: William C. Brown, 1965.

METZI, E. "Art in Sports," *American Artist,* 26 (November 1962), 30–37.

MEYERS, BERNARD SAMUEL. *Understanding the Arts.* New York: Holt, 1958.

MILLER, DONNA MAE, and KATHRYN R. E. RUSSELL. *Sport: A Contemporary View.* Philadelphia: Lea and Febiger, 1971.

MILLER, SUSANNA. *The Psychology of Play.* Baltimore: Penguin Books, 1968.

MILLMAN, D. J. "The Art of Gymnastics," *Modern Gymnast,* 11 (1969), 18–20.

MOLES, ABRAHAM. *Information Theory and Esthetic Perception.* Urbana: University of Illinois Press, 1966.

MUELLER, J. H. "The Folkways of Art: An Analysis of the Social Theories of Art," *American Journal of Sociology,* XLIV (September 1938), 222–238.

MUKERJEE, RADHAKERNAL. *The Social Function of Art.* New York: Greenwood, 1954 (1971, Reprint).

MUMFORD, LEWIS. *The Myth of the Machine.* New York: Harcourt, Brace & World, 1966.

MUNRO, THOMAS. *The Arts and Their Interrelations.* New York: Liberal Arts Press, 1949.

———. *Toward Science in Aesthetics.* New York: Liberal Arts Press, 1956.

MUNSTERBERG, ELIZABETH, and PAUL H. MUSSEN. "The Personality Structures of Art Students," *Journal of Personality,* 21 (1953), 457–466.

MURRAY, D. N. "Psychology and Art Today: A Summary and Critique," in *The Problems of Aesthetics,* eds. Elisco Vivas and M. Krieger. New York: Holt, Rinehart and Winston, 1953.

NANDI, SUDHIRKUMAR. *An Enquiry into the Nature and Function of Art.* Calcutta, India: University of Calcutta, 1962.

NASMARK, H. "Aesthetics and Sport," *Bulletin of the International Federation d'Education Physique,* no. 1, 1963.

NATIONAL ART MUSEUM OF SPORT. *The Artist and the Sportsman.* New York: NAMOS, 1968.

———. *The Ball in Sport.* New York: NAMOS, 1968.

———. *Sport and Western Sculpture.* New York: NAMOS, 1968.

NEWMAN, EARL N. "Personality Traits of Faster and Slower Competitive Swimmers," *Research Quarterly,* 39, no. 4 (1968), 1049–1953.

NICKLAUS, JACK. *Golf My Way.* New York: Simon and Schuster, 1974.

NISBET, R. A. "Sociology as an Art Form," in *Sociology on Trial,* ed. M. Stein and A. Vidich. Englewood Cliffs, N.J.: Prentice-Hall, A Spectrum Book, 1963.

OGILVIE, BRUCE. "The Personality of the Male Athlete." AAHPER Convention, Las Vegas, March 1967 (mimeographed).

———. "Psychological Consistencies with the Personality of High-Level Competitors," *Journal of American Medical Association,* 205, no. 11 (1968), 780–786.

————. "The Sweet Psychic Jolt of Danger," *Psychology Today,* October 1974.

OGILVIE, BRUCE, THOMAS A. TUTKO, and IRVING YOUNG. "The Psychological Profile of Olympic Champions: A Brief Look at Olympic Medallists," in *Psicologia Dello Sport,* ed. F. Antonelli. Rome: Federazione Medico-Sportiva Italiana, 1966.

Organizing Committee for the Games of the XXth Olympiad, Munich, 1972. *The Scientific View of Sport.* New York: Springer Verlag, 1972.

OSTERHOUDT, ROBERT. "An Enquiry Concerning Sport and the Fine Arts" (unpublished paper, mimeographed, 1972).

————. *The Philosophy of Sport.* Springfield, Ill.: C. C Thomas, Publishers, 1974.

PAGANO, R., ed. *Contemporary American Painting.* New York: Duell, Sloan and Pearce, 1945.

PARIS, W. F. *The Hall of American Artists,* vol. VII. New York: Tabord Press, 1932.

PAXTON, HARRY T. *Sport, U.S.A.* New York: Thomas Nelson and Sons, 1961.

PENDLETON, BRIAN B. "Sport in Sculpture in Canada and the United States since 1900." Unpublished Master's thesis, University of Alberta at Edmonton, 1970.

PERRY, R. HINTON. "The Relation of Athletics to Art," *Outing,* 49 (1902), 456–63.

PITTMAN, D. J. "The Sociology of Art," *Review of Sociology,* ed. J. B. Gittler. New York: John Wiley and Sons, 1957.

PLATT, JOHN R. "Beauty: Pattern and Change," in *Functions of Varied Experience,* eds. D. W. Fishe and S. R. Maddi. Homewood, Ill.: Dorsey Press, 1961.

PLEKANON, G. *Unaddressed letters; Art and Social Life.* Moscow: Foreign Languages Publishing House, 1957.

PORTER, FAIRFIELD. *Thomas Eakins.* New York: George Braziller, 1969.

POURET, H. "Is Sport an Art?" *Report of the Tenth Session of the International Olympic Academy,* pp. 129–133, Athens, 1970.

PRADOS, M. "Rorschach Studies on Artists-Painters," *Rorschach Research Exchange,* 8 (1944), 178–183.

PSZCZOLA, LORRAINE. *Archery.* Philadelphia: W. B. Saunders, 1971.

PUTNAM, PAT. "Even Now Its Still Hard to Believe," *Sports Illustrated,* 43, no. 17 (1975), 34–37.

PYRON, BERNARD. "Rejection of Avant-garde Art and the Need for Simple Order," *Journal of Psychology,* 63 (1966), 159–178.

RACY, R. F. "The Aesthetic Experience," *British Journal of Aesthetics,* 9, no. 4 (1969), 345–352.

RAYNAL, MAURICE. *Modern Painting.* Geneva, Switzerland: Albert Skira S.A., 1953.

READ, HERBERT. *The Meaning of Art.* Harmondworth: Penguin Books, 1963.

REID, L. A. "Aesthetics and Education," in *Readings in the Aesthetics of Sport,* eds. H. T. A. Whiting and D. W. Masterson. London: Lepus Books, 1974.

REUNING, KARL. *Joy und Freude.* Swarthmore, Pa.: Swarthmore College Bookstore, 1941.

RICHARDSON, E. P. *Painting in America.* New York: Thomas Y. Crowell Co., 1956.

ROBERTS, J. M., and B. SUTTON-SMITH. "Child Training and Game Involvement," *Ethnology,* 1, no. 2 (1962), 166–185.

ROBERTS, TERENCE J. "Sport and the Sense of Beauty," *Journal of the Philosophy of Sport,* 2 (1975), 91–101.

ROBINSON, C. E. *Hellas: A Short History of Ancient Greece.* New York: Pantheon Books, 1948.

ROBINSON, E. P. *American Romantic Painting.* New York: E. Weyhe, 1944.

ROBINSON, RAY (with DAVE ANDERSON). *Sugar Ray.* New York: Viking Press, 1969.

ROE, A. "The Personality of Artists," *Educational and Psychological Measurements,* 4 (1946), 401–408.

ROSEN, J. C. "The Barron-Welsh Art Scale as a Predictor of Originality and Level of Ability in Art," *Journal of Applied Psychology,* 40 (1955), 335–360.

ROSENBERG, B. G., and C. N. ZIMET, "Authoritarianism and Aesthetic Choice," *Journal of Social Psychology,* 46 (1957), 296.

RUDNER, RICHARD. "The Ontological Status of the Aesthetic Object," *Philosophy and Phenomenological Research,* 10 (1950), 380–388.

RUMP, E. E. "Relative Preference as a Function of the Number of Elements in Abstract Designs," *Australian Journal of Psychology,* 20, no. 1 (1968), 39–47.

RUSSELL, WILLIAM F. "I'm Not Involved Anymore," *Sports Illustrated,* August 4, 1969.

RYLE, GILBERT. *The Concept of Mind.* London: Hutchinson, 1963.

SANTAYANA, GEORGE. *The Birth of Reason and Other Essays,* ed. Daniel Cory. New York: Columbia University Press, 1968.

———. "Philosophy on the Bleachers," *Harvard Monthly,* 18 (1894), 181–190.

———. *The Sense of Beauty.* New York: Dover Publications, 1955.

DE SAUSMAREZ, MAURICE. *Basic Design: The Dynamics of Visual Form.* London: Studio Vista, 1964.

SCHACK, W. *And He Sat among the Ashes.* New York: American Artists Groups, 1939.

SCHAIE, K. WARNER. "On the Relation of Color and Personality," *Journal of Projective and Personality Assessment,* 30, no. 6 (1966), 512–524.

SCHILLER, FRIEDRICH. *On the Aesthetic Education of Man,* ed. E. M. Wikinson and L. A. Willoughby. Oxford: Clarendon Press, 1968.

SCHUTZ, WILLIAM C. *Joy: Expanding Human Awareness.* New York: Grove Press, 1969.

SCOTT, JACK. *Athletics for Athletes.* Oakland, Calif.: An Other Ways Book, 1969.

SEWALL, JOHN IVES. *A History of Western Art.* New York: Holt, 1953.

SEWTER, A. G. "The Possibilities of a Sociology of Art," *The Sociological Review*, XXVIII (October 1935), 441–453.

SHEEDY, ARTHUR. "Une grande oubliée: La Dimension esthétique en education physique." Paper presented at the Congress of the International Association of Colleges of Physical Education, Prague, September 15–19, 1974.

SLOTS, MICHAEL A. "The Rationality of Aesthetic Value Judgments," *Journal of Philosophy*, 68 (1971), 821–839.

SLUSHER, H. S. *Man, Sport and Existence*. Philadelphia: Lea and Febiger, 1967.

SMITH, GEORGE. *All Out for the Mile*. London: Forbes Robertson, 1955.

SMITH, LEVERETT T., JR. *The American Dream and the National Game*. Bowling Green, Ohio: Bowling Green University Popular Press, 1975.

SOURIAU, ETIENNE. *Aesthetic Categories*. Paris: C.D.U., 1963.

SPARSHOTT, F. S. *The Structure of Aesthetics*. London: Routledge and Kegan Paul, 1963.

SPENCER, HERBERT. *The Principles of Psychology*, 2nd ed. New York: Appleton and Company, 1885.

————. *Synthetic Philosophy*. New York: Appleton and Company, 1885.

SPIAGGIA, M. "An Investigation of the Personality Traits of Art Students," *Educational and Psychological Measurement*, 10 (1950), 285–291.

Sport in American Art. Boston: Museum of Fine Arts, 1944.

STEBBINS, CLAY B. "Achievement in Sport as a Function of Personality and Social Situations." Unpublished Master's thesis, University of Wisconsin at Madison, 1969.

STERLING, C. *Still Life Painting*. New York: Universe Books, 1959.

STEWART, JACKIE, and PETER MANSO. *Faster: A Racer's Diary*. New York: Farrar, Strauss and Giroux, 1972.

SULLY, JAMES, and GEORGE G. ROBERTSON. *Aesthetics, Dreams, and Association of Ideas*. New York: J. Fitzgerald, 1888.

SUTTON-SMITH, BRIAN. "The Sporting Balance." Paper presented at the International Workshop of the Sociology of Sport, Macolin, Switzerland, 1969.

SWANSON, GUY E. *The Birth of the Gods*. Ann Arbor: University of Michigan Press, 1966.

SWEET, F. A. *George Bellows*. Chicago: The Art Institute of Chicago, 1946.

TALAMINI, JOHN, and C. PAGE. *Sport and Society*. Boston: Little, Brown and Company, 1972.

TALMOR, SASCHA. "The Aesthetic Judgment and Its Criteria of Value," *Mind*, 78 (1969), 102–115.

THEILHARD DE CHARDIN, PIERRE. *Activation of Energy*, trans. René Hogue. New York: Harcourt Brace Jovanovich, 1971.

THOMAS, CAROLYN. "Toward an Experiential Sport Aesthetic," *Journal of the Philosophy of Sport*, 1 (1974), 67–87.

THUMA, ROBERT F. *The Grace of Man*. Pittsburgh, Pa.: The Myers and Shinkle Company, Printers, 1897.

THUNE, J. B. "Personality of Weightlifters," *Research Quarterly*, 20 (1949), 296–306.

TOLSTOI, LEV NIKOLAEVICH. *What Is Art?* New York: Oxford University Press, 1942.

TOYNBEE, L. "Some Notes on the Paintings of Contemporary Games," *The London Magazine,* 1 (1961), 57–60.

TUNIS, J. R. *The American Way of Sport.* New York: Duell, Sloan and Pearce, 1958.

TURNER, RALPH H., and LEWIS M. KILIAN. *Collective Behavior.* Englewood Cliffs, N.J.: Prentice-Hall, 1957.

UMMINGER, W. "Encounters with Sport and Art," *Sport 69,* pp. 2–3, Munich, 1969.

VALENTINE, C. W. *The Experimental Psychology of Beauty.* London: T. C. and E. C. Jack, 1919.

VALERY, P. *Aesthetics.* London: Routledge and Kegan Paul, 1964.

VAN DALEN, D. B. *A World History of Physical Education: Cultural, Philosophical, Comparative.* Englewood Cliffs, N.J.: Prentice-Hall, 1953.

VANEK, MIROSLAW, and BRYANT J. CRATTY. *Psychology and the Superior Athlete.* London: Macmillan-Collier Co., 1970.

VANNOY, JOSEPH C. "Generality of Cognitive Complexity-Simplicity as a Personality Construct," *Journal of Personality and Social Psychology,* 2, no. 3 (1965), 385–396.

WALKER, J., and M. JAMES. *Great American Paintings from Smibert to Bellows, 1729–1924.* London: Oxford University Press, 1943.

WEISS, PAUL. *Nine Basic Arts.* Carbondale: Southern Illinois University Press, 1964.

————. *Sport: A Philosophic Inquiry.* Carbondale: Southern Illinois University Press, 1969.

WEITZ, MORRIS. "The Role of Theory in Aesthetics," *Journal of Aesthetics and Art Criticism,* 15, no. 1 (1956), 27–35.

WHITE, DAVID A. "Great Moments in Sport: The One and the Many," *Journal of the Philosophy of Sport,* 2 (1975), 124–132.

WHITING, H. T. A., and D. W. MASTERSON. eds. *Readings in the Aesthetics of Sport.* London: Lepus Books, 1974.

WHORF, BENJAMIN LEE. *Language, Thought and Reality.* Cambridge: M.I.T. Press, 1956.

WILSON, R. N., ed. *The Arts in Society.* Englewood Cliffs, N.J.: Prentice-Hall, 1964.

WITHERALL, WARREN. *How the Racers Ski.* New York: W. W. Norton and Co., 1972.

WITT, GUNTER. *Sport in der Kunst.* Leipzig: Seemann, 1969.

WOBER, M. "Towards an Ecological and Informational Theory of Aesthetics," *Bulletin of British Psychological Society,* 21 (1968), 235–239.

WOHL, ANDRZIE. "Conception and Range of Sport Sociology," *International Review of Sport Sociology,* 1 (1966), 5–18.

WOOD, NORTON. *The Spectacle of Sport.* Englewood Cliffs, N.J.: Prentice-Hall, 1957.

WRIGHT, JAY, "A Diamond-bright Art Form," *Sports Illustrated,* June 3, 1961, pp. 32–39.

ZOELLER, K. W. "The Art of Sportsmen," *Country Life,* 69 (February 1936), 10–17.

ZORACH, W. *Art Is My Life.* New York: World Publishing Co., 1967.

Index